# Motivate! Inspire! Lead!

# Motivate! Inspire! Lead!

## 10 Strategies for Building Collegial Learning Communites

**RoseAnne O'Brien Vojtek**

**Robert J. Vojtek**

CORWIN
A SAGE Company

*For information:*

Corwin
A SAGE Company
2455 Teller Road
Thousand Oaks, California 91320
(800) 233-9936
Fax: (800) 417-2466
www.corwinpress.com

SAGE India Pvt. Ltd.
B 1/I 1 Mohan Cooperative
   Industrial Area
Mathura Road, New Delhi 110 044
India

SAGE Ltd.
1 Oliver's Yard
55 City Road
London EC1Y 1SP
United Kingdom

SAGE Asia-Pacific Pte. Ltd.
33 Pekin Street #02-01
Far East Square
Singapore 048763

Printed in the United States of America.

*Library of Congress Cataloging-in-Publication Data*

Vojtek, Roseanne O'Brien.
Motivate! inspire! lead!: 10 strategies for building collegial learning communities/RoseAnne O'Brien Vojtek, Robert J. Vojtek.
    p. cm.
Includes bibliographical references and index.
ISBN 978-1-4129-2806-9 (pbk.)
    1. School management and organization. 2. Teacher-principal relationships. 3. School improvement programs. 4. Motivation in education. I. Vojtek, Robert J. II. Title.

LB2805.V65 2009
371.2'07—dc22                                    2008056028

This book is printed on acid-free paper.

09   10   11   12   13     10  9  8  7  6  5  4  3  2  1

| | |
|---|---|
| *Acquisitions Editor:* | Debra Stollenwerk |
| *Associate Editor:* | Julie McNall |
| *Production Editor:* | Eric Garner |
| *Copy Editor:* | Gretchen Treadwell |
| *Typesetter:* | C&M Digitals (P) Ltd. |
| *Proofreader:* | Susan Schon |
| *Indexer:* | Jean Casalegno |
| *Cover Designer:* | Scott Van Atta |

# Contents

# Preface

## ■ MOTIVATING OTHERS

Let's face it, like most school leaders, there comes a time when you are standing face-to-face with at least one teacher who isn't interested in learning during professional development, refuses to use the newly adopted program the way it was intended, has "been there, done that" when you suggest implementing the latest research-based instructional practice, or seems to be "marching to the beat of his or her own drum" rather than collaborating with the team to achieve the school's mission, vision, and goals. As the school leader, what do you do? How can you motivate, inspire, and lead when some people aren't willing to follow?

The walls of isolation are crumbling. Administrators are expected to establish Professional Learning Communities (PLCs). Yet not all PLCs are created equal. Just because you put people together in a room doesn't mean they are productive, able to accomplish the task, or achieve their goals. As a school leader, how do you motivate people so they will cooperate, collaborate, and work together? And, if, by chance, your faculty is already there, how do you inspire and lead them to the next level by building a collegial learning community?

You may be asking, what is the difference between a PLC and a collegial learning community (CLC)? We define a collegial learning community as *a group of professional educators within a department, school, or district that hold themselves and each other accountable for working together to achieve their shared goals, purpose, or school's mission through positive interdependence, reciprocal relationships, shared decision making, professional learning, and mutual responsibility.* In other words, a collegial community is much more than simply "defining the mission, vision, values, and goals; and structuring time for educators to work together." As you will learn from this book, there are ten motivational strategies that must be firmly embedded within a school culture if educators are to learn together, share in the decision-making process, build mutual relationships, work interdependently, and hold each other responsible for achieving optimal performance and the school's desired results.

As a school leader, you may be wondering, how can I motivate, inspire, and lead the faculty and staff members I work with to become a collegial learning community?

To do so, the first question that needs to be answered is, "What do you mean by motivation?" Is it that you really want to "control" the teachers and expect them to "do what you want them to do"? For example, do you want to motivate them so they will use cooperative learning in each of their lessons? And when they do, what happens? Do you write them a glowing evaluation, praise them for being excellent teachers, and perhaps even reward them by giving them fewer duties than "those teachers" who choose not to be as compliant? And for those saboteurs who choose to close their doors and teach using more traditional methods, do you give them a bad evaluation for being "defiant"?

As you may have guessed, this book takes a different approach to motivation. This book will demonstrate that over the course of time, motivation from external rewards, coercion, and sanctions will not bring the passion and joy back into the teaching and learning profession. Nor will it produce or sustain effective, high-performing collegial learning communities.

This book is not about how to *make* people do what you want them to do because, as we will explain, no one can make someone do something they don't want to do. No one can change someone if that person doesn't want to be changed. School leaders will discover that if they truly want to stimulate interest and commitment, the question should not be "How can I motivate my staff?" Instead we should be asking ourselves, *"How can I create the conditions within which the members of my school community will motivate themselves to achieve our collective and morally compelling mission, vision, and goals?"*

Motivating and sustaining high-performing collegial learning communities is everyone's responsibility. It requires systemic effort, lateral and vertical capacity building, and collective action from all factions of the educational system to build and sustain quality innovations that achieve short-term and long-term goals and accomplishments. It requires bold leadership and a strong commitment to change the culture of the school. Therefore, this book targets and challenges any and all school administrators, school leaders, or school teams that want to improve the quality of life within their own school setting, district, or system, to build a community of highly motivated, dedicated, and engaged certified and noncertified staff members.

Although we may, at times, sound as if we are talking about certified teachers, the discussion also applies to administrators and noncertified staff members. All staff members are knowledge workers, support workers, and leaders. For purposes of this book, therefore, when we talk about *teachers, staff, faculty,* and *educators,* unless specifically stated, we are talking about all employees (certified and noncertified) who work within the school community. Likewise, the word *school* may also be substituted for *district,* and vice versa, depending upon if the reader is a superintendent, central office administrator, building level administrator, or school staff member.

## ■ MOTIVATION BEGINS WITHIN

This book is designed to help school leaders motivate and inspire others to achieve the compelling mission (work) of the school. Ideally, to achieve the greatest value and benefit (bang for your buck) from this book, the ideas can—and should be—applied simultaneously at both the district and school levels. In the real world, however, this is not always possible. Therefore, we advocate for school leaders to look first within, at yourself and your school. Take care of yourself first by changing those things you have the power and control to change. Meaningful, long-term, and deep changes begin from the inside out. Change begins with you because, as any recovered addict will tell you, the only person who has the power to change you is yourself. The cliché, "Attitude is everything," is more than just a cliché. Sometimes the hardest, yet the most critical, change is simply your own attitude.

Central office administrators, teachers, staff developers, and others may find this book helpful. But our primary focus and goal is to provide school leaders and administrators with the tools and resources they need to help motivate, inspire, create, lead, and sustain high-performing collegial learning communities. The situations and examples used for discussion purposes will be specific to school leaders. Although we will describe a specific incident, the concepts can be extrapolated or transferred to other levels and specific content areas beyond those described in the case studies. For example, the case study may focus on a professional development learning experience for primary math teachers, but as part of the discussion we will help readers understand the essential conditions necessary to increase motivation and transfer key points, strategies, and tools into their own context and current situation.

## ■ PURPOSE OF THE BOOK

Instead of motivation through fear, intimidation, and control, this book will equip school leaders with a clear understanding of the ten strategies needed to motivate, inspire, and lead a high-performing collegial learning community. It will provide readers with authentic situations that help identify the essential conditions that must be in place to empower staff members to motivate themselves, achieve their greatest potential, and perform at optimal levels.

Specifically, this book is designed to help school administrators and leaders discover the essential conditions that (1) allow certified and non-certified staff to become competent and confident in what they are doing; (2) build strong relationships with others along with a desire to work together to achieve the sought-after results; (3) improve the quality of life with the school system and community to stimulate and nurture internal motivators (e.g., interest, efficacy, fun, purpose, meaning, belonging, choice, empathy, hope, and enjoyment); and (4) most important, help school leaders identify and build the competence (i.e., knowledge, skills, experience, dispositions) that teachers need to become empowered, autonomous, collaborative, and interdependent. Ultimately teachers are happier facing the challenges that each new day brings when they are able to balance their competence and skill level with what they see as being meaningful and purposeful. The trickle-down effect is that their students are going to enjoy learning more and thus make greater student gains.

## ■ ORGANIZATION OF THE BOOK

In Chapter 1 we begin with a brief discussion of motivational theory and introduce our *optimal performance model*. We present a brief insight into the theories, research, and assumptions about motivation to provide a deeper understanding about motivation and reveal why inspiring, empowering, recognizing, and appreciating staff members for good work is more effective than using threats, coercion, and punitive measures for poor work.

Chapter 2 will help you understand that motivation begins within— within yourself as a leader and within your school. The change must first begin within if school leaders are to create the conditions that motivate, inspire, and lead others to achieve optimal performance.

Chapters 3–12 explore each of the ten motivational strategies in depth to equip school leaders with the knowledge, skills, and techniques necessary to create the essential conditions that directly apply to a specific motivational strategy. We will define the motivational strategy and explain why it is important. Each chapter presents an authentic case study that helps the reader define that motivational strategy and understand the essential conditions that increase the likelihood for school communities to motivate themselves in ways that lead to optimal performance and results. After each case study, readers are presented with a set of discussion/reflection questions; a brief explanation of the critical issues and/or essential conditions found in the authentic situation; and ideas, suggestions, and strategies to consider and/or implement in similar situations. A summary of key points and next-step reflection questions is found at the end of each chapter. Appendix A collectively charts the basic needs touched upon in each chapter. For readers wanting more resources, we provide a list of our favorite references for each motivational strategy in Appendix B.

In Chapter 13 we challenge all school leaders to accept our *call for action*.

## ■ USING THIS BOOK

This book is designed so that it can be read from cover to cover, or readers can skip right to the part of the book that interests them the most. Even though there is no hierarchy for introducing the ten motivational strategies, we believe strongly that to build and sustain high-performing collegial learning communities, school leaders must first create the conditions that provide the quality of life that supports a collegial learning community and is conducive to optimal performance. This is why we encourage readers to progress linearly through the book the first time they read it to gain an understanding of all ten motivational strategies.

Readers do not need to fully implement or master any single strategy before moving on to the next. In reality, however, from our research on motivational theory and experiences working with a number of educators across the country, the more all ten motivational strategies are embedded into the school culture, the greater the likelihood that staff members are internally motivated to carry out the compelling mission of the school with a sense of urgency and purpose. It is when the ten motivational strategies are firmly institutionalized, their essential conditions have become strongly embedded within the context of the school setting, and the behaviors and practices associated with each strategy are institutionalized within the school culture (including the climate, procedures, policies, processes, structures, and norms) that all members of the school will be more likely to find themselves working together as a collegial learning community in a state of optimal performance, thus accomplishing their mission.

Although appropriate and effective policies are critical to the successful efforts of a school community, this book will not address policy issues. Nor will this book focus on student motivation. These two issues are beyond the scope of this book. Likewise, this book assumes readers have a basic understanding of the various motivational theories.

Additional information, resources, and a study guide can be found at www.optimalperformancemodel.com.

## ■ ABOUT THE CASE STUDIES

The case studies in this book were extracted from authentic situations that occurred in schools and districts. To ensure anonymity, the names and places have been changed and some details have been modified.

Each motivation chapter begins with an authentic situation to highlight the motivational strategy. Later in each chapter, you will read about each leader's actions in response to his or her situation. Even though we provide one ending to the story, the ending is not a recipe. In life, as with each case, there could be any number of "solutions." We describe only one solution as a guide for discussion so that there is closure to each case. We urge you to consider alternative solutions that will work for you within your unique situation and context. "If this happened to me, I would. . . ."

In many administrative courses, you may be given a case or scenario and be asked to solve it. We lead you down that path with our "What would you do?" questions. Remember, too, that one size fits a maximum of one. As much as situations may look similar, attempting to replicate a solution without taking into account the context with its unique variables may not give you the anticipated result you desire. The suggestions and ideas at the end of the chapters are practical strategies that *may* be replicated and cost very little (both time and money) to implement *when* they are congruent with your school's culture.

Again, there is no recipe. In cooking, a recipe is a quantitative description of a qualitative process. A friend that is a chef in the San Francisco Bay Area once told us that he doesn't mind divulging his recipes because with only the recipe and not the technique people will not achieve his exact result.

## ■ BEFORE YOU BEGIN

We have several considerations and cautions. First, *context is important.* What works in one setting may very well fail in another setting. What motivates one person may turn another person off completely. You will read throughout this book that you must understand and perhaps even challenge the current context and the explicit and hidden assumptions, beliefs, values, and norms within your school before you can create, implement, and sustain the motivational strategies and essential conditions to achieve optimal performance.

Second, every person is unique. *Know the people* with whom you work—their interests, values, assumptions, and passions. What gets them excited? What makes them want to do something? What are their individual and collective strengths, and what do they avoid at all cost? When you recognize people to show them how much they are appreciated, make sure to personalize it. By understanding the context and the people within the school community, you will be able to select from a number of techniques and tools to help you work more effectively. Most important, if one technique doesn't work, choose another. Often, something will work for a while, and then it loses its "punch." It is imperative that you understand your culture, your context, and that you spend time really getting to know the people you work with.

Third, *change takes time*, and *it isn't always easy.* Be patient, persevere, and stay the course. We hope that because you are reading this book you are ready to take the plunge. But even if you aren't ready to jump right in, we urge you to get your feet wet.

Fourth, *motivation begins with you.* Discover who you are—your beliefs, your assumptions, your values, and your actions. Then simply choose one thing, either about yourself or something that you do, and make a change. You can't change other people if they don't want to change. But you can change yourself! By changing even one thing about yourself, you may have a greater impact on others than you could ever imagine. We invite you to try.

Finally, *levels of motivation fluctuate.* Even when all the motivational strategies and essential conditions are in place to achieve a state of optimal performance, people move in and out of that state for a variety of reasons. No one exists in the zone, at their peak, in a state of flow, or at a level of optimal performance every minute of every day. In fact, like Stella, from *How Stella Got Her Groove Back* by Terry McMillan (1997), people may not find their "groove" for quite some time, based on personal issues and overwhelming circumstances. But even during those times when people find themselves not quite "with it" or performing at optimal levels (we've all had days like that), merely having the motivational factors and conditions in place will increase the likelihood that your school community will continue to persevere, stay on course, and progress toward your target goals.

As a school leader, you will make a difference in the lives of those working within your school community when you improve the quality of life within the organization, build relationships and interdependence among your staff members, provide the skills that lead to competence, and empower others to achieve a shared vision and a morally compelling mission.

We encourage you to use this book as a guide for understanding, implementing, and embedding the ten motivational strategies and essential conditions that will enable you to motivate, inspire, and lead collegial learning communities that sustain and achieve optimal levels of performance to accomplish your desired results.

# Acknowledgments

Where to begin? There are so many great educators and leaders who have touched our lives and inspired our work that it is difficult to name each and every person. Like actors at the Academy Awards, we want to make sure that we recognize all of our many colleagues and friends who have learned with us, mentored us, supported us, and shared our dreams for the quality of life that must exist within every school if we are to build and sustain collegial learning communities that can accomplish the shared vision and mission and achieve optimal levels of performance. A special thanks to each of you; we are forever grateful—you know who you are.

We began this project with Rachel Livsey who helped us frame our thoughts for this book. When Rachel left Corwin, Debbie Stollenwerk took over the project and helped us bring it to completion. We greatly appreciate your encouragement and support for our work.

While at the University of Oregon, we had the opportunity to work with many outstanding educational leaders—both faculty and students. We wish to express our sincere appreciation to Dr. Richard Schmuck, the late Dr. Philip Runkel, and the members of the Organization Development (OD) Cadre. The many hours we spent learning with and from you as we planned, implemented, and evaluated OD interventions have grounded us firmly in the principles of OD.

We have had the great fortune of working with and learning from staff developers across the United States through our work with the National Staff Development Council (NSDC). We would especially like to recognize Dennis Sparks, Stephanie Hirsh, and the past and present members of the NSDC Board of Trustees. We greatly appreciate the dialogue and conversations that led us to challenge ourselves to improve the quality of professional learning for every teacher, in every school, every day, to ensure all students achieve high levels of learning.

In addition, we would like to thank all of the many administrators, faculty, and staff with whom we currently work in Bristol Public Schools and Avon Public Schools in Connecticut. We especially wish to acknowledge members of the Ivy Drive Elementary School and Avon High School learning communities. We would also like to acknowledge our friends and colleagues at the Connecticut Association of Schools and the Tri-State Consortium for the opportunities to engage in new learning and deeper understandings about how to motivate, inspire, and lead.

We would like to thank our families, especially our parents and two daughters, Caroline and Holly, for their patience, encouragement, and support.

Finally, we consider ourselves to be the luckiest two people alive. Not many couples are able to understand and share their work, their passion, their joy, and their personal lives. We are blessed with the ability to motivate, encourage, inspire, and support each other while we work and while we play. It doesn't get much better than this!

*—Rosie and Bob Vojtek*
August 30, 2008

# ■ PUBLISHER'S ACKNOWLEDGMENTS

Corwin greatly acknowledges the following reviewers:

Amie Brown
Gifted ELA Teacher
Floyd County Schools
Rome, GA

Mary B. Herrmann
Superintendent of Schools
Winnetka School District 36
Winnetka, IL

Beth Madison
Principal
George Middle School
Portland, OR

Dana Salles Trevethan
Principal
Turlock High School
Turlock, CA

Teresa Tulipana
Principal
Park Hill School District
Kansas City, MO

Shelley Joan Weiss
Mentor Trainer for the Association of Wisconsin School Administrators
Principal, Waunakee Community Middle School
Waunakee, WI

# About the Authors

**RoseAnne (Rosie) O'Brien Vojtek,** PhD, has served as an elementary principal at Ivy Drive Elementary School in Bristol, Connecticut, for the past ten years. Previously, she was the Director of Instruction for Oregon City School District in Oregon and an elementary principal at Joseph Gale Elementary School in Forest Grove, Oregon. Rosie also taught for eleven years in the Winston-Dillard School District in Oregon at both the elementary and middle school levels.

Rosie earned her bachelor's degree in Elementary Education from Oregon State University and her master's and doctorate in Curriculum and Instruction from the University of Oregon. Her doctoral dissertation, "Integrating Staff Development and Organization Development" won the 1994 Outstanding Dissertation Award from the National Staff Development Council.

Throughout her career, Rosie has emerged as a leader in many professional organizations. Currently, she is Connecticut's State Representative to the National Elementary School Principal's Association (NAESP) and serves on a number of committees for the Connecticut Association of Schools (CAS). Rosie has served as: the Area I-A Coordinator for Phi Delta Kappa (1991–1994); a member of the International Society for Technology in Education (ISTE), serving on several task forces for the National Education Technology Standards (NETS) projects; and past president (2000) and member (1995–2001) for the National Staff Development Council (NSDC) Board of Trustees. In addition to these affiliations, Rosie has worked as an adjunct faculty member at the University of Oregon, Portland State University, and Lewis & Clark College. She has presented and consulted at numerous local, state, and national conferences on topics related to staff development, organization development, leadership, change, and technology. Rosie is also an Exemplary Educator for SMART Technologies.

Together with her husband, Bob, the Vojteks coauthored the "Technology Column" for the *Journal of Staff Development* (JSD 1995–2000). She coauthored an ERIC Monograph, *Effective Staff Development for Teachers: A Research-Based Model* in 1994 with Dr. Meredith Gall. Rosie also was a member of the NSDC Standards Revision Task Force and NSDC Standards Revision Technology Subcommittee that produced *E-Learning for Educators.*

Currently Rosie lives with her husband, Bob, in Bristol, Connecticut. She can be reached at rvojtek@edovation.com or through their Web site at www.optimalperformancemodel.com.

 **Robert J. Vojtek,** PhD, is an engaging speaker whose teaching experience spans middle school to graduate school. His administrative experience includes Chief Information Officer (CIO) at two universities (Concordia University in Portland, Oregon, and the University of Hartford in Connecticut), Dean of Graduate Studies (The University of Hartford), and Manager of Instructional Technology Services (Harvard University) where he provided professional development in the utilization and integration of technology for the Harvard Law School. He is currently employed by Avon Public Schools in Connecticut, where he designed a pre-engineering program for Avon High School and is the Unified Arts Coordinator.

Bob began his career as a junior high school teacher in the Los Angeles Unified School District. He worked at the College of The Redwoods where he served as the Vocational Technical Division Chair and Department Chair for Drafting and Technology. He established the AutoCAD Authorized Training Center and was voted the 1987 Top AutoCAD Instructor for the United States and Canada. In 1995, Bob completed his doctorate from the University of Oregon. His dissertation was titled, "The Role of Computer Coordinators in the Implementation of the Internet as a Tool for School Improvement and School Reform."

Bob has been active in numerous professional organizations and received recognition as an Exemplary Educator by SMART Technologies. He currently serves as a member of the Tri-State Consortium, a learning organization devoted to assisting school districts in New York, Connecticut, and New Jersey in using student performance data to develop a rigorous framework for continuous school improvement.

Bob was Associate Professor of Education at Concordia University as well as an adjunct faculty member at three other colleges and universities. He has presented and consulted at numerous local, state, and national conferences on topics on technology, staff development, organization development, leadership, and change. Bob has served as a lobbyist for the Oregon Community College Association (OCCA) and he received a scholarship from the MIT Hartford Alumni Association to attend the Science and Engineering Program for Teachers (SEPT).

Currently Bob lives with his wife, Rosie, in Bristol, Connecticut. He can be reached at vojtek@edovation.com or through their Web site at www.optimalperformancemodel.com.

# Introduction

## ■ PICTURE THIS

*Juggling my school lunch tray and half-empty can of soda, I (Rosie) cautiously twisted the door knob and gently pushed open the door to the staff room so as not to spill the soda or drop the chicken nuggets, fries, and Jell-O sliding around on my plate. As the door slowly opened, and I made my way into the room, I heard Allison's emphatic voice saying, "I can't imagine myself still being a teacher five years from now! It just won't happen. I can't keep up this pace! I just can't! Teaching isn't what I thought it would be. It isn't fun anymore. There has to be something else I can do."*

*As the words poured out from her, a hush fell over the staff room as the other seven teachers realized that the principal had just entered the room.*

*Allison, a second-year teacher, looked up. She blushed. The panicked look that engulfed her face said it all.*

*Eight pairs of eyes were now fixed on me, the principal, as I set my tray down on the table, pulled out a chair, and joined the teachers. All of a sudden, I didn't feel like eating anymore. I glanced at each of them, looking into their tired and weary eyes, searching for the right words to say.*

*But there were none.*

*I sat at the table and felt their eyes pleading with me to find a way to make life better, emancipate them from all the mandates that were weighing them down, set them free, and help them soar. How I longed to give them wings to help students in their classrooms learn and achieve to their highest potential based on their own diagnosis of the situation, student learning, teaching styles, and professional judgment. I dreamed of watching every teacher smile from the sheer enjoyment of helping students learn while instinctively knowing that they are making a significant difference in the lives of the students they teach.*

*Allison's statement became the catalyst for dialogue among the veteran teachers and the neophytes on my staff. As I listened to them talk, I heard their frustrations. I felt their defeat and lack of hope. How they longed for a better life.*

*During the next ten minutes as we talked over lunch, the teachers spoke candidly about how tired they were of being told how to fill out the new form, only to find out a few weeks later that central office had once again changed their minds, and teachers would need to record the data in a different format on a new form all over again. They were tired of practicing for statewide testing and teaching to the test. They were tired of the cycle for collecting assessment data that left them frustrated because there wasn't time to analyze the data and implement new strategies before the next round of assessments began. They were overwhelmed by all of the trainings for new innovations that were coming and going even before they felt competent in using what they learned from the*

*(Continued)*

(Continued)

*last inservice. They were frustrated because everything seemed disjointed and didn't always align with the new report card and how the teachers "thought things should be done." Most of all, they yearned to make learning fun for students and to be able to use student curiosity and interest to drive instruction rather than being worried that they wouldn't be on the same page as the teacher next door.*

*Just as the bell rang to send them back to class after their twenty-minute lunch, Allison stood up, pushed in her chair, grabbed her tray and summed up the entire conversation by saying, "If I knew this was what teaching was going to be like, I would have done something else." The room was pierced by the sharpness of the words. A deafening hush clouded the room as one by one the teachers stood up, dumped their lunch trays, put leftovers back into the staff refrigerator, and filed out of the staff room leaving me there, in silence, to finish my lunch.*

*I left lunch that day frustrated and angrier than I have ever felt in my entire career at a world that has spent decades searching for ways to recruit the best and the brightest young people into the field of education, yet does little to make sure they want to stay. Allison is a prime example of one of the best and brightest new recruits into the field of education. She is an excellent second-year teacher, highly competent and qualified, who cares deeply about her students. Allison is one of the first to arrive at our school each day, and one of the last to leave each night. But, in less than two years, her passion for teaching and her joy for helping students learn were gone. Her light was rapidly burning out.*

*That night, when I got home, all of my pent up thoughts and frustrations came pouring out over dinner. Once again, Bob listened as I vented about what I could do to "fix" everything and make it better. As we talked, and I reflected upon the lunch conversation, I knew it was time to do something.*

*I finally acknowledged the one question that has kept haunting me and tearing at my soul. Throughout my career, I have heard the words, "those who can, do. Those who can't, teach!" Yet, did we ever stop to ask ourselves, "why?" Why is it that we can't retain the Allisons of the world? Why do we continue to lose the best and the brightest teachers to other professions? What can we do to support them? What can we do to motivate them? What can we do to inspire them? What can we do to keep them? How do we help them make a difference?*

Thus began our quest to help educators find ways to put the passion back into teaching, rediscover the joy of helping all students learn, and realize that they can and do make a difference in the lives of the students they work with.

This book is written for, and dedicated to, all of the educational leaders and stakeholders who, like us, want to improve the quality of life for all educators, especially the Allisons, by helping them achieve optimal levels of performance during the processes of teaching and learning so that we can all live, learn, work, and teach in collegial learning communities.

## ■ WHAT IF?

*What if . . . the classroom, school, or district where you work was the one place you couldn't wait to get to each morning and the hardest place to leave at the end of each day? What would it look like? Sound like? Feel like?*

The reality of life in the schools for many teachers today is reminiscent of life in the sweatshops for factory workers during the Industrial Revolution. Morale is low. The quality of life within the schools for adults is shabby and in a state of disrepair. School administrators and teachers are treated like second-class citizens rather than respected for the professionals they are.

Innovations are bombarding teachers at an overwhelming rate as well-meaning central office administrators, who react from outside pressure, heap innovation upon innovation onto teachers. Administrators, fearful of being "on the list," are frantically searching for that golden fleece, that panacea, that certain something, that somehow and in some way will magically transform student learning, raise student test scores, and "leave no child behind."

In far too many schools, teachers are handed scripts and pacing guides that dictate what, when, and how to do their jobs. Outside "experts" prescribing districtwide one-size-fits-all workshops declare that by following their *recipes* all will be well. Seldom, however, have these outside "experts," busy hurling edicts at teachers, set foot into the schools, let alone the classrooms, and taken into account the unique needs of each individual student, classroom, school, or district. Teachers are overwhelmed and overburdened with report after report. In many instances, teachers are reassessing students so frequently there is no time to analyze the assessment data, design learning goals and interventions from the data to meet individual student needs, or implement strategies to see results. It is a vicious cycle with little time for self-reflection and a lot of time for self-doubt and questions about what difference any of this makes in the lives of their students anyway.

Many teachers will tell you that they no longer find meaning and purpose in the work they do. It is easier to find ways to externalize and blame the system rather than to take ownership and responsibility through an inherent sense of locus of control and efficacy. Worst of all, they question if what they are doing is making a difference in the lives of the students with whom they work. Often teachers feel helpless, defeated, and that their work has little value or useful purpose. Yet even when they should be elated because their student test scores go up, and their students make adequate yearly progress as defined "from above," far too often, their answer to whether or not they feel they are making a difference remains an emphatic "no." As a teacher from a New York City school recently described, "You work so hard to help students achieve, and as soon as they [central office] see that you have made progress, they change the rules and move the target."

After a decade of standards-based educational reform and accountability, the field of education is a very different place. National curriculum organizations (e.g., National Council For Teachers of Mathematics), state departments of education, and local school districts have developed comprehensive standards, clearly defined learning goals, and simplified curriculum guides. Finally, teachers have explicit knowledge and a clear understanding of what students need to master by the end of their course or the end of the year. For all of the bad publicity and fallout from the standards and accountability movement, especially the No Child Left Behind (NCLB) legislation, there are still some important and positive gains. First, and most important, educators today know and understand what the students they are working with need to know and be able to do to achieve academic success. At the same time, most of our teachers are highly skilled and trained in content and pedagogy. They are able to make informed professional decisions from a "menu of options" that would help them meet the personalized needs and individual learning styles of each child. But instead of being allowed the freedom to work autonomously as professionals within clearly defined boundaries to reach explicit target goals and achieve high standards, teachers are handed a single program, often with a script and schedule, and told "this is what you must do." More and more, teachers and administrators are feeling defeated, helpless, devalued, and worthless. Confidence and self-esteem are at an all-time low.

It is no wonder that educators have lost the passion and joy for teaching and learning that brought them into the educational profession in the first place. The expectations and challenges, especially those that are beyond their control, are increasing. Teachers and administrators are burning out and leaving the profession faster than ever before. Unfortunately, we have not spent nearly enough time improving the quality of life within our school communities to ensure educator retention.

There is a famous quote that can be attributed to Roland Barth from several decades ago still floating around in staff development circles. Using a transportation analogy, he reminded educators that when you get on a plane, the flight attendants instruct passengers that in case of an emergency they need to put the oxygen mask on themselves first, before they take care of other people.

The field of education has not heeded this very important message. If we are to improve student achievement today, in order to prepare productive and successful citizens of the world tomorrow, we must stop what we are doing and take care of the adults in the school communities first, so that they can better meet the needs of the children we serve.

On January 30, 2004, Dr. Dean Ornish was talking with Oprah Winfrey about heart disease, eating right, and the power of meditation. During the conversation, Dr. Ornish said that what really motivates people to make long-term changes in their behavior and the way they live is not the fear of dying, but the joy of living. He claimed that when people focus on being happy to be alive, they manage stress better, they increase their stamina and energy, they exercise more, and ultimately their hearts and brains get more blood. He said that because of this change in perspective, "you can actually reverse disease" (as cited in Hudson, 2004). We believe the same holds true for teaching and learning.

## ■ THE FEAR FACTOR

The accountability movement, especially the top-down mandates and sanctions under No Child Left Behind, have left educators anxious, "stressed to the max," in other words, "fearful of *dying*." More and more educators are feeling emotionally and physically overpowered by the threat and/or reality of their students not achieving adequate yearly progress as defined by states; their schools being placed on "the lists"; and "well-meaning" state departments of education, central office administrators, and/or outside consultants targeting their schools and classrooms offering help, support, and the "right way" to proceed. And, always looming in the back of educators' minds is the threat that their students will use vouchers to go elsewhere, their school will be reconstituted or closed, and/or they will lose their jobs. The perception of many certified and non-certified school-based staff members is that there are too many "sticks" being used to motivate them to do their jobs. But, as Dr. Ornish explained, this type of "fear-driven motivation will work for only so long before the person goes back into denial" (as cited in Hudson, 2004) and the teacher closes the classroom door.

Likewise, Fullan (2005) states that for sustainability of innovations that lead to high levels of performance becoming institutionalized and embedded within the culture, there must be "continuous improvement, adaptation, and collective problem solving in the face of complex challenges that keep arising" (p. 22). Deep learning is one of eight factors that lead to sustainability. Fullan, based on W. E. Demming's suggestion that the prescription for success is to "drive out fear," states that to achieve deep learning and thus sustainability, we must "reduce the fear factor." To do this, we must shift the paradigm from *fear of failure* to one of *failing intelligently.* This means being able to learn and grow from your mistakes. What if we, as Farson and Keyes (2002) in their book by the same name, all believed that *whoever makes the most mistakes wins?*

Pfeffer and Sutton, in *The Knowing-Doing Gap* (2000), demonstrate how, in many workplaces, there is still a great deal of fear and distrust of management. They state that there is still "far more talk than action about using enlightened and humane management techniques" and this fear and distrust of management, they contend, "undermines organizational performance and, more specifically, the ability to turn knowledge into action" (p. 109). Pfeffer and Sutton continue by saying that:

> Fear helps create knowing-doing gaps because acting on one's knowledge requires that a person believe he or she will not be punished for doing so—that taking risks based on new information and insight will be rewarded, not punished. When people fear for their jobs, their futures, or even for their self-esteem, it is unlikely that they will feel secure enough to do anything but what they have done in the past. Fear will cause them to repeat past mistakes and re-create past problems, even when they know better ways of doing the work. (p. 109–110)

Fear and distrust within the school system, especially vertical fear from the top (i.e., teachers fear principals and principals fear superintendents), impede educators from turning what they know (their knowledge) into what they do (their actions). When managers (or administrators) demand results, "no matter what," learning, as well as the application of any new knowledge and skills, is inhibited. People are more likely to falsify or hide information. Andrew Grove of Intel (as cited in Pfeffer and Sutton, 2002) summed it up this way:

> The fear that might keep you from voicing your real thoughts is poison. Almost nothing could be more detrimental to the well-being of the company. . . . Once an environment of fear takes over, it will lead to paralysis throughout the organization and cut off the flow of bad news from the periphery. (p. 123)

Fear has two other disastrous effects on any organization according to Pfeffer and Sutton (2000). First, instead of looking at the long-term benefits of an innovation, people become paralyzed by the short-term fears and consequences from the implementation of the new plan or program. Secondly, fear creates a focus on individuals rather than on the collective "we." People tend to kick into survival mode, focusing on self-preservation at the expense of the collective good. Pfeffer and Sutton summarize management by fear this way:

> In organizations such as these the management philosophy is that people will work hardest if they're trying to avoid punishment. Avoiding punishment for yourself means finding ways to blame and punish others. In such a setting, there's no reason for people to work together for collective benefit, and lots of reasons for them to undermine each other's work and reputation. (p. 127)

Because of a winter storm in February 2007, JetBlue, an airline that prides itself on its passenger friendly image, suddenly found its customer service record spiraling downward. The airline was forced to cancel more than 1,100 flights, leaving passengers stranded. Many passengers sat on the tarmac for as long as ten hours waiting to take off. Even five days after the storm had passed, one quarter of all JetBlue flights were still being cancelled (JetBlue, 2007b).

Most companies facing similar circumstances would see heads flying and people fired. Yet, on NBC's *Today Show* on February 20, 2007, JetBlue Chairman David Neeleman told coanchor Matt Lauer that no one would lose his or her job because of this incident. Instead he said his company found a weakness in their system and would be 100 percent better because they "know what failed, what can be fixed, and what will be fixed" (as cited in Bell, 2007). Neeleman said it was a "horrifying experience" to watch the passenger-friendly image they had worked so hard to create being destroyed by the ice storm. But even while holding himself and the company accountable for what happened, he saw this as a learning opportunity. It gave JetBlue a determination to be even better than they were before. "It's not so much what happened to you, but how you react to it," he said, and continued:

> I don't run the airline for one quarter's results. We are going to go overboard to make sure that we give the credit back to the customer, that we apologize and explain what happened. More importantly, we will explain why this will never happen again, and then when we do that, we will offer something no other airline will offer customers and we will be held accountable with a laser beam focus to a *Bill of Rights* that we will have with us every day. (as cited in Bell, 2007)

JetBlue's retroactive *Bill of Rights* (see JetBlue, 2007a) came before Congress could impose such requirements, because as Neeleman told Lauer:

> I know what is right for our customers. We don't set out not to take care of our customers. Why should Congress tell us how to treat our people? We should be able to do that. We want to do it because it is the right thing to do and it keeps us focused on the future. (as cited in Bell, 2007)

It cost the company approximately $20–$30 million, yet no one lost their job. Instead, JetBlue learned from its mistakes, built a stronger infrastructure, and discovered a higher level of accountability, determination, and focus.

What if school districts could operate like JetBlue, taking responsibility for helping all students learn, not because Congress tells them what to do, but because educators know what is right and what their students need? What if the current educational accountability system was no longer grounded in fear of failure and punishment, including the fear of losing one's job or having your school reconstituted because of a single high-stakes yearly assessment? What if school districts could become learning organizations, able to fix their mistakes, build a stronger infrastructure, and—in the process—discover a higher level of accountability, determination, and focus? What if schools created their own "Bill of Rights" for students that became the mission and accountability system that all educators hold in front of themselves every day with a laser-like focus? What if schools were founded on the promise of bringing humanity back to teaching and learning?

What if we create the essential conditions so all educators focus on the joys of teaching and learning rather than on the fears of dying and failure?

## ■ THE CONTROL FACTOR

Often motivation is confused with control. According to Edward Deci (1995) there are two types of controlled behavior: *compliance* and *defiance*. Deci says, "compliance means doing something because you are told to do it," while defiance "means to do the opposite of what you are expected to do just because you are expected to do it" (p. 3). Instead of motivating people by getting them to comply with what the leader wants them to do, Deci argues for motivating people by stimulating, inspiring, nurturing, and creating the conditions that allow them to be "self-governing" or autonomous.

## ■ INTERNAL MOTIVATION

Most educators enter the field of education because they are internally motivated to do so. They have a deep desire to help others learn. Their greatest reward comes from the smallest of things, such as a student who understands a concept and can successfully complete a learning goal or task. When, however, the internal motivation is lost, the meaning, purpose, competence, self-confidence, efficacy, and the knowledge that you are making a difference is gone. Educators then lose their reason and desire to work. Morale becomes low. Consequently, many teachers simply collect their paychecks and wait for retirement or leave the profession and find ways to reinvent themselves in a different line of work.

Mihaly Csikszentmihalyi (2003) says that people who are happy, who understand clearly defined goals, who find the match between their skills and the challenges they face, who feel they belong and spend time with others, and who are immersed in complex activities that serve a greater purpose will be much more productive because they enjoy the work that they do. Csikszentmihalyi defines this motivational state as *flow*. We define this state as *optimal performance*.

Instead of motivation through fear, intimidation, and control, we must create the conditions that allow us to inspire, energize, and nurture educators to become internally motivated, discover flow, and rekindle the passion and joy of teaching and learning. Using Dr. Ornish's approach of helping people to make long-term behavioral changes, we must decrease or eliminate the use of "sticks" and "carrots" (extrinsic motivators) and increase the use of motivational strategies that lead to helping educators discover the joy in teaching and learning. We can do this by improving the quality of life within the school setting, fostering the conditions that enable and empower teachers to do their work and perform at optimal levels to achieve desired results, and helping both certified and noncertified staff members build relationships and find the pleasure of collaborating together within their school community. We must help educators rediscover the meaning and purpose in the work they do, gain self-respect, and recognize that they can and do make a significant difference in the lives of the students and families whom they serve. Most important, to achieve optimal performance, we must provide the leadership and structures that build relationships, autonomy, competence, and interdependence among educators. Ultimately the goal is to ensure that all members of the school community are internally motivated and achieve levels of optimal performance by letting their passion for teaching and joy of learning flow.

## ■ ISOLATION TO COLLEGIALITY

We have all experienced it—the school that makes you feel warm, welcome, and happy to be there, and the school that makes you feel cold, indifferent, and like an intruder who doesn't belong. It is hard to put your finger on what it is, but you know the difference the moment you step inside. Amazingly, one school can be that friendly, caring place, and another school, ten blocks away, still in the same district, can be the complete opposite. So what is it that makes the difference?

**Figure 0.1**   House Is to Home

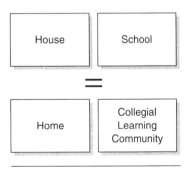

We define that difference as the *quality of life for all individuals within the school setting.* The best way for us to describe what we mean by quality of life is through the analogy: *House* is to *home* as *school* is to *collegial learning community* (see Figure 0.1). That is to say, when we think of a house we think of a building. When we think of a home, we think of a warm, cozy, inviting, family environment. The same is true for a school. When we think of school, we think of an institution. When we think of a collegial learning community, we think of an interdependent, caring team of people who are learning and working together to achieve a morally compelling mission, be the best they can be, and make a difference.

Throughout this book, we discuss interdependence. Unless stated otherwise, when we refer to interdependence, we are talking about positive interdependence. In the Preface, and later in Chapter 11, when we discuss positive interdependence, we define a collegial learning community as *one in which a group of professional educators within a department, school, or district hold themselves and each other accountable for working together to achieve their shared goal, purpose, or school's mission through positive interdependence, reciprocal relationships, shared decision making, professional learning, and mutual responsibility.* We also explain in Chapter 11 that just because faculty are put into groups to collaborate and learn from each other doesn't make them a team or help them work together interdependently or even more efficiently. In order for schools to become collegial learning communities, the ten motivational strategies and essential conditions must be strongly embedded within the school culture.

Most important, as you will learn in Chapter 3, the quality of life must exist as a solid foundation if administrators are to create the conditions for achieving optimal levels of performance. When quality of life supports the collegial learning community, schools become the place that teachers, administrators, and students can't wait to get to in the morning and hate to leave at night!

## ■ IMAGINE . . . WHAT IF?

*What if . . . the classroom, school, or district where you work was the one place you couldn't wait to get to each morning and the hardest place to leave at the end of each day? What would it look like? Sound like? Feel like?*

This is one of the most powerful exercises we have used with educators to help build a high-performing collegial learning community. We encourage you to use it now by yourself or with your study group before you continue reading this book. It will give you baseline information about yourself and your school environment as well as provide you with insight into your own school culture. As you read the book, you can refer back to your notes to compare your current situation with your vision of a quality school culture. When you are ready to take the plunge, we encourage you to use this activity with your school staff (both certified and noncertified) and/or your school improvement teams, including students and parents as appropriate, to identify the mental models that will help you design the school of your dreams.

To begin, fill in Figure 0.2 on the next page. Spend quality time *dreaming* about what it would take to make your school the one place you couldn't wait to be each morning and the hardest place to leave each night.

Often when I, Rosie, do this exercise, I picture myself standing in the middle of the *Cat In The Hat* ride in Seuss Landing at Universal Studios in Orlando. I use that setting as a starting point, a mental model, for what I want our elementary school to be. Of course, there is a lot more to it than just the *Cat In The Hat* ride. We can't begin to tell you how many times I have made Bob stand in line so I can try to figure out how to transform my school and emulate the *Cat In The Hat* ride. I have dreamed of being able to capture that kind of excitement, the vivid colors, the storybook (learning) coming alive, the feeling of being enthralled, and the joyous sounds of happy children of all ages (obviously I am thinking of the beginning of the day rather than the end of the day when the kids are tired).

Think of a place that you enjoy. Somewhere that you can't wait to get to and hate to leave (e.g., a vacation spot, a favorite place in your house) and begin there. What is it about that place that makes it so enjoyable? What would your school be like, if it were like your favorite spot?

**Figure 0.2**    Looks Like, Sounds Like, Feels Like

| What Would It Look Like? | What Would It Sound Like? | What Would It Feel Like? |
| --- | --- | --- |
|  |  |  |

After you have completed the chart, put a check by those items that you already find in your school.

Put a star by those items that you want to make sure become a priority for you and your school.

Use Figure 0.2 as a guide while you read the rest of the book. After you finish each chapter, go back and look to see if the ten motivational factors and/or the essential conditions you just read about are included in your chart. Are they already present in your school? Or did you list them because you wish they were? If you didn't list them, but you think they are important and something you want to see at your school, add them into the chart.

Now, before you continue, write a paragraph that describes your school, the way you would most like it to be, so it is the one place you and others cannot wait to get to each day.

_____

_____

_____

_____

_____

We encourage you to use this same activity with your staff. It is listed again with further details and suggestions on our Web site at www.opti malperformancemodel.com. In addition, you may also download a study guide with tools to record your thoughts as you continue reading this book.

## ■ SO, WHAT?

We began our quest to help educators find ways to put the passion back into teaching, rediscover the joy of helping all students learn, achieve high levels of performance, realize that they can and do make a difference in the lives of the students they work with, and know there is hope for a better tomorrow. Like us, as you begin embedding the ten motivational strategies and essential conditions into your unique situation, you will find the educators you work with more likely to achieve and sustain levels of optimal performance. Our hope is that someday all educators will live, learn, work, and teach in a high-performing collegial learning community to achieve levels of optimal performance and successfully accomplish their school's morally compelling mission.

# 1

# Understanding Motivation

■ **PICTURE THIS**

*This morning, like so many mornings, I (Rosie) found myself, once again, running late for work. In a panic, I remembered that I had to let our five-year-old golden retriever, Hercules, outside one last time or he wouldn't make it until Bob or I got home from work. Without thinking, I opened the door to let him out. As soon as I did, Hercules whizzed right by me.*

*Hercules was gone in a flash! He had found freedom! I had forgotten to put the leash on him. Since the battery on his collar was dead, our electric fence would not keep him in our yard. Bummer!*

*As I ran out the door, calling him back, I realized it was no use. Hercules was already halfway to the end of our yard. I yelled to him, "Hercules! Come home, Hercules!" He stopped, turned around, gave me that look that says, "That's what you think," and then quickly turned his attention past the edge of our yard. With a burst of speed, he raced toward the street.*

*My heart sank. "There is no way I am going to get to school on time now," I thought, as my mind instantly began to race. I tried to think about how I was going to catch Hercules and get him back inside the house. A task easier said than done.*

*First, I grabbed his favorite treats. By the time I tried to show them to him, he was too far away. I ran back inside to grab his favorite ball. I raced back outside, squeezing it and yelling to get his attention. Hercules was, by now, on the sidewalk, racing down the street. He heard the squeak of the ball, a sound that will usually bring him running right back to play—but not today. He just looked back, giving the ball a quick flash, and without missing a beat, kept right on running down the street to the end of the cul-de-sac.*

*The only other thing I could think of that might entice him to come home was the car. Hercules loves riding in the car. I raced back inside, got my car keys and his leash. I unlocked and opened the car door, yelling his name, once again. "Hercules, let's go for a ride."*

*(Continued)*

(Continued)

*Hercules, who by now was clear down at the end of our street sniffing the grass, just looked up and flashed me a look that said, "No, thank you. Not today." He wasn't interested in the car. He found freedom.*

*To make a long story short, I had to get into my car, drive down to the end of the street, open the car door, pat the seat and call his name. Hercules could see that he was going to get a real ride and enthusiastically jumped into the front seat. Little did he know how short the ride home was going to be!*

## ■ WE ALL HAVE OUR PRICE

All of us are a bit like Hercules. We love our freedom, but ultimately other people can find ways to motivate and entice us to do what they want or need us to do. By probing, they soon discover what it takes. All of us have our price.

For some of us, we will do something for someone else because we like that person and want to "make their day" or show them how much we care. Other times, we hold out for money, chocolate, dinner and a movie, or something else that we want or need. We bargain. We barter. We find ways to bribe.

Sometimes we can find the right motivator to get someone to do what we want them to do. Other times, we can't. A motivator that works once or twice may not work a third time.

Ever since Eve searched for ways to get Adam to take a bite of the apple, people have searched for ways to get others to do what they want them to do. I can open a car door, as I discovered with Hercules, but I can't make him run and get inside. People, like Hercules, can't be forced to do what someone else wants them to do, unless they choose to do it.

Madeline Hunter (1982), an educational professor at UCLA who was most known for her work on mastery teaching, once said, "You can lead a horse to water, but you can't make him drink. But, you can salt his oats!" She was talking about finding ways that would get students and/or teachers motivated enough to want to do something. Opening the door of an idling car in front of the neighbor's yard for Hercules was enough to "salt his oats."

We all look for ways to "salt the oats" and get people to do what we want them to do. As a wife, I look for ways to get Bob to take out the trash and take me out to dinner so I don't have to cook. As a husband, Bob tries to get me to cook at home so we have time to watch a movie after dinner before we go to bed. Often we compromise, and order in a pizza and watch a movie!

As administrators and staff developers, we want teachers to use what they have learned during inservice training in their classroom with their students. Or we want them to administer the required student assessments, complete the forms, and submit them to the central office before the due date. So, how do we *make them* do it? Better yet, how do we *make them* enjoy it and want to do it? What are the motivators, "the oats," and how do we "salt" them to get people to do what we want them to do?

Oh, if only it were that simple.

# ■ WHAT IS MOTIVATION?

As we said in the introduction, when people talk about motivation, most often they are talking about "how to get someone to do what they want them to do." Or, "How can I make myself do ____?" For me, it is often finding a way *to make myself* get out of bed and run three miles before going to work. Trust me, I would much rather lie in bed and sleep that extra forty-five minutes!

Motivation is often defined as giving yourself or someone else a reason or an incentive to do something. To get myself out of bed to run in the morning, for example, I promise myself all kinds of things, such as, I will look thinner, I will feel better, or I can eat chips for lunch and drink wine with dinner.

Motivation can also be a feeling, an interest in, or an enthusiasm for behaving in a particular way. It has to do with how committed a person is to completing a task and how good he or she feels about doing it. I always feel good after I have finished my run. It is probably the "runner's high" after those endorphins kick in or the songs I listen to with my iPod that help me lose track of time and get into the groove of running. I have often wondered how I can capture that same feeling and enthusiasm when I have to go outside and pull weeds. Since I grew up on a nursery and spent most of my Saturdays and summers hoeing and weeding, I have to really "psych" myself up and promise myself all kinds of rewards to be able to put on my gloves and grab my hoe. Yet other people find this type of work relaxing and fulfilling.

So why is it that some people find some activities rewarding, and some people loathe the same activity? Why is it that sometimes people can successfully complete a task or achieve their goals, and other times they don't?

There are many individual characteristics that influence motivation. For example, years of experience, age, level of knowledge and skill, efficacy, and locus of control all have an affect on a teacher's motivation. Likewise, characteristics related to the context and current situation, such as alignment, values, beliefs, trust, interest, enjoyment, curiosity, fun, challenge, etc., also help to determine how much effort a teacher is willing to put forth on a particular project, goal, or activity.

Although many administrators and school leaders describe their colleagues and subordinates as being "lazy," "unsupportive," "unwilling," "uncooperative," or "unmotivated," there is really no such thing as an "unmotivated" person. What those leaders really mean is that their colleagues will not do what they want, need, or expect them to do. Even if a person does not get out of bed in the morning, he or she is still acting on his or her own personal goal (not getting out of bed), whether or not others approve of their behavior. We may not always agree with what the other person is doing, but individuals are the keepers of their own motivation. Try as we might, *we can't change people if they don't want to be changed, and we can't make people do what we want them to do if they don't want to do it!*

Thus, the question is not how can we make people do what we want them to do? We can't. The real question is, how can we create the conditions that will inspire and intrinsically motivate others to accomplish the school's vision and mission and achieve optimal performance and results?

## ■ THEORIES ABOUT MOTIVATION

There are many different theories about how to motivate people. One need only visit a library or bookstore to see the numerous volumes that have been written on the topic of motivation. Like diet books, the different theories about how to motivate others are ubiquitous, diverse, and often incompatible with one another. Psychologists have never reached agreement about how best to motivate others. Likewise, educators find themselves debating this very same topic.

Most teachers hope that their students find the unit of study and assignments so enthralling that they naturally and intrinsically gravitate toward learning and doing the work. The reality is that there are many topics that students find boring, uninteresting, unstimulating, unchallenging, and simply "not worth putting forth the effort." So teachers find themselves looking for those "positive reinforcers" they can use to entice, coerce, and reward students (the carrot) and when that fails, they fall back on sanctions such as keeping students in at recess or threatening a failing grade (the stick).

Administrators use the same tactics with staff members. They pay teachers to serve on committees, attend workshops, or attend training sessions outside of school hours. Those teachers who work hard to achieve school or district goals may find that the principal is willing to send them to a conference, approve additional items for their classrooms, write personal thank you notes, praise them in their newsletters, or write positive evaluations and put them in the employee's personnel files. For those teachers who appear to be "unresponsive" and "unmotivated" toward accomplishing the school's goals and mission, the administrator applies sanctions, such as withholding resources or placing a negative evaluation in his or her personnel file.

All too often, educators, looking for that "quick fix," find themselves in the age-old battle of which to use, the carrot or the stick. In reality, however, neither works well for long, nor are extrinsic rewards and sanctions going to help create the conditions that encourage and inspire others to motivate themselves and achieve optimal performance.

## ■ THE CARROTS

As soon as behavioral psychology is mentioned, most educators can immediately visualize a clear picture of the experiments Pavlov conducted with his dog to better understand natural responses, reflexes, and classical conditioning. Likewise, B. F. Skinner's initial operant conditioning experiments with rats and his later work with behaviorism provided the foundation for reinforcement theory. Even today, with all of the current research being conducted in the area of cognitive psychology, educators as well as those in corporate America still use positive and negative consequences and rewards. Behavior modification and reinforcement theory are still the basis for many classroom management and discipline programs being used by educators and parents. In spite of the fact experience has taught us that rewards and sanctions are not effective motivators over time, we still search for that "quick fix" and the one carrot that we can dangle that might make the difference.

Stickers for students, raffle tickets for participants, pay for teachers, and other extrinsic rewards will work for a while. But they soon lose their power to motivate and control behavior. What once was interesting and fun is no longer intrinsically rewarding. Like Hercules, people soon want more, and their price goes up. When the resources are gone, or the reward is withheld, people find something else to do with their time and energy.

Alfie Kohn (1993) presents his case against what he calls "pop behaviorism," a prevalent culture in our society of "Do this, and you will get that." He provides research-based arguments and evidence to demonstrate that rewards are not effective in changing behavior over time or for improving and enhancing performance. Kohn explains that in a token economy program "when the goodies stop, people go right back to acting the way they did before the program began" (p. 38). In fact, Kohn goes further by stating that:

> The troubling truth is that rewards and punishments are not opposites at all; they are two sides of the same coin. And it is a coin that does not buy very much. . . . Moreover, the long-term use of either tactic describes the very same pattern; eventually we will need to raise the stakes and offer more and more treats or threaten more and more sanctions to get people to continue acting the way we want. (p. 50)

Kohn describes, in detail, five reasons why rewards (or carrots) do not work, and why we should use intrinsic interest and motivation for a task or activity rather than using behaviorism. His five reasons for not using rewards are: (1) rewards punish, (2) rewards rupture relationships, (3) rewards ignore reasons, (4) rewards discourage risk taking, and (5) rewards undermine interest.

There is no direct relationship between extrinsic motivation and the desired behavior except the sought-after reward. Most people are eager to volunteer and complete a task when the work is challenging, meaningful, and purposeful. When, however, these same people perceive the work to be boring, routine, difficult, or distasteful, they are less likely to jump right in and work unless there is some form of compensation or reward.

We have become a token economy and a culture of people who tune into station WIFM—"What's In It For Me." If we do not see a personal benefit, purpose, challenge, or desire for an activity, most of us will not engage in the activity unless the reward (or sanction) becomes greater and more meaningful to us than the task itself. Once we have entered into this phase, forget it. We are no longer doing it for joy and pleasure. We are doing it "for the money" and/or because we "feel we must"!

We agree with Kohn when he writes:

> Behaviorism has made a substantial impact on the way we think about our work and the way we do it. But the specific programs it has wrought, such as incentive plans, do not and cannot bring about the results we want. . . . [W]e ought to face the troubling fact that manipulating behavior by offering reinforcements may be a sound approach for training the family pet but not for bringing quality to the workplace. (p. 141)

Even with Hercules, we have found that even his favorite rewards don't always work!

## ■ THE STICKS

It hasn't been that long since teachers and principals hung paddles on their walls. In fact, many adults who attended school in the 50s, 60s, and 70s still tell stories of either being whacked with a 3-inch wide paddle with holes in it or watching others being swatted in front of their classmates. Some people remember being slapped with a ruler across their hands when they held a pencil in the wrong position or used their left hand instead of their right hand. Most of us, at one time or another, can remember having to stay in at recess because our work wasn't finished on time, or we had to redo a paper because it was "sloppy" and not our best work.

Even though we swore as children, "We would never be like them," when we can't get others to do what we want them to do, we catch ourselves behaving just like our parents and teachers did. We revert back to those models we saw others using, even when most of us know in our hearts that those punishment strategies were not effective. We remember hiding school papers so our parents wouldn't find out about a bad grade, sneaking cookies and candy even though we would ruin our dinner, or lying about whom we were seeing or where we had been. It made us feel guilty, and we swore that when we were grown up and in charge, things would be different.

Yet, when seduction with rewards no longer works, we resort to coercion and sanctions. For example, a father grounds his son because he did not come home before his curfew, or a teacher keeps a student in from recess to complete her work. An administrator may write negative comments on a teacher's evaluation when she still, after attending several trainings, has not posted the essential questions on her classroom walls.

We know sanctions and coercion will work, but only for short periods of time, and only as long as we know that "big brother is watching." For example, what driver hasn't had pangs of fear when she is cruising down the highway at breakneck speeds and spies a police officer on his motorcycle pointing his radar gun at all the cars whizzing past? The tense driver slams on her brakes as she speeds by. Once past the motorcycle cop, euphoria replaces her fear and her tense body relaxes as she realizes that the police officer was pointing his radar gun at the cars traveling in the opposite direction. She may continue to drive slowly for the next few minutes, but soon she is back to her breakneck speeds, having forgotten all about the speed trap.

If the driver sees a police officer tracking speed with radar in this same spot several times, she may begin to slow down upon her approach "just in case." Of course, if by chance, this same driver had been ticketed in this area, she will be especially cautious upon her approach to this same spot. When she gets to the spot and sees an officer, she may smile to herself and say, "Thank goodness I was paying attention and slowed down today." But, seeing no one, the same driver is likely to speed up and continue on her merry way, thankful that no one was there. Whether or not the driver gets caught and ticketed, along with how many consecutive days the driver sees an officer in the same spot with his radar gun pointed at cars, will ultimately determine how soon the driver will forget all about this radar spot and simply cruise right past without regard to the speed limit.

Staff developers, like teachers, understand that proximity works. If participants or students are not paying attention, they have only to continue the conversation while moving close to that student to get his attention or walk over to a group of off-task participants to stop the conversation about where they are going to have lunch. Often proximity is all it takes to get people back on task and to coerce them into doing what you want them to do.

Like highway speeders vigilant of radar traps, teachers have learned to close their doors to hide the use of strategies they feel comfortable with or teach topics that they enjoy or feel will benefit their students, even when it is not part of the curriculum. Administrators, who have been frustrated for years by teachers who close their doors and "do their own thing," use proximity to control teacher behavior and counter the "closed-door syndrome." Administrators caught in this vicious cycle find themselves trusting teachers less. They show this by frequent walk-throughs and observations, as well as closer supervision strategies such as collecting teachers' lesson plans, reading every notice a teacher sends home, and interviewing students about what happens in the classroom. They tighten "the ropes" by providing pacing guides, scripted programs, and other forms of control.

Ultimately the school administrator is "the boss." Administrators can—through reprimands, coercion, threats, and sanctions—make staff members "do what they want them to do." But, like the highway speeder, this only suppresses the staff members' behavior and may, in fact, initiate other behaviors such as withholding, concealing, sabotaging, hostile aggression, and/or passive-aggressive actions. Coercion and sanctions only work for so long. In the end, someone wins and someone loses. Someone stays and someone leaves. Either the teacher chooses to change, or the teacher chooses or is forced to find another teaching position.

The critical point we want to make about the use of carrots and sticks is that extrinsic motivators, both sanctions and rewards, do not work! They may suppress or encourage behavior temporarily. But once the fear from the threat of punishment or the promise of the reward is withheld, people revert back to their original behavior. No matter what you try to do, in the end *you can't make a person do what they are not willing to do!*

As Kohn (1993) explains:

> Reinforcements do not generally alter the attitudes and emotional commitments that underlie our behaviors. They do not make deep, lasting changes because they are aimed at affecting only what we do. . . . What rewards and punishments do is induce compliance, and this they do very well indeed. If your objective is to get people to obey an order, to show up on time, and do what they're told, then bribing or threatening them may be sensible strategies. But if your objective is to get long-term quality in the workplace, to help students become careful thinkers and self-directed learners, or to support children in developing good values, then rewards, like punishments, are absolutely useless. (p. 41–42)

So, if not the carrot or the stick, how do you create the conditions that inspire and intrinsically motivate others to accomplish our morally compelling mission and achieve optimal performance and results?

# ■ COGNITIVE PSYCHOLOGY

Cognitive psychologists look at how people perceive the world and believe that this has an influence on how they behave. For example, Peter Senge (1990) uses this concept to explain how our mental models and our perceptions shape the world we live in and affect our assumptions and the choices we make. The differences between mental models explain how two people can observe the same event and yet describe it in very different ways. One need only ask a Yankee fan and a Red Sox fan to describe the final game in the 2004 American League Championship to hear the difference in the details and perceptions. Senge, McCabe, Lucas, and Kleiner (2000) state that, "In any new experience, most people are drawn to take in and remember only the information that reinforces their existing mental models" (p. 67). Mental models, they continue, "limit people's ability to change" (p. 67).

In her book, *The Winner's Way* (2004), Dr. Pam Brill, the founder and president of In The Zone, Inc., explains how the chemical reactions in our brain affect the "3 A's": *activation* (the physiological and physical part of your experience); *attention* (choices you make from your internal and external world that become part of your personal reality); and *attitude* (your guiding beliefs, values, and assumptions). Brill writes:

> Existing between the things that happen to you and how you respond, these three elements are the result of the unique way your brain is formed and the distinctive chemical balance resulting from the "things that happen" to you. The 3 A's are what you feel when your brain and body collaborate to produce thousands of natural chemical reactions in response to the multitude of things you encounter, including the thoughts you generate. The 3 A's collaborate to determine what you perceive and how you view it—good, bad, neutral, or marvelous. (p. ix)

Brill goes on to explain that even though people may be coping with situations that are sad, frightening, and even dangerous, when the 3 A's are aligned and in good personal fit with the situation, people can achieve their desired goals and feel at their best. Likewise, when there is a mismatch between the 3 A's and the situation, people are likely to become depressed, show apathy, irritability, and are less likely to achieve their desired goals and outcomes.

Brill writes:

> The brain is the control center for receiving and interpreting information from the external and internal world. It starts with attention. From the vast array of information swirling outside and in, you select, either consciously or as a passive passenger, items that become the objects of your attention. . . . Because each of us is hardwired differently and operating with a different set of software

(attitudes), each individual will be attracted to particular types of information, find others distracting or trivial, and be overwhelmed or underwhelmed at a different personal set point. (p. 91)

In order to live in the area that top athletes call *the zone,* (or Csikszentmihalyi (1997) calls *flow,* Maslow (1998) calls *self-actualization,* and we call *optimal performance*), Brill claims that each person must use their "power of will" to adjust and align their 3 A's with each new situation. In other words, people must learn to reframe and adjust their thinking, mental models, and assumptions. They must also take responsibility and be accountable for their own actions and choices. Instead of blaming others for doing things to them (external locus of control), people living *in the zone* realize that they have the *free will* to make the choices that will put them in control of their 3 A's.

Often, when cognitive psychologists describe motivation, they usually refer to what is called "cognitive attribution theory" or "expectancy theory." Expectancy theory says that for an incentive to be meaningful and motivational, people must make a connection between what they do and what they get. The performance must be connected to the payoff. If teachers do not believe that a particular program or educational strategy will improve their students' learning, they are going to be reluctant to use that program or strategy. Most teachers are going to want to see proof that the extra work required to learn to use the program is going to make a difference. When they see the results and buy into the program, watch out! Most educators will take it and run. But, all too often, teachers become saboteurs when the innovation is perceived to be either more of the same or extra work with no benefit. Teachers need to see the connection between what they do and the benefits and/or reward gained from their efforts.

In addition, educators must feel competent about their work. Often they are reluctant to try something if they are afraid that they will not be able to perform at the required or expected level. Teachers, who are usually willing to attend conferences and learning activities, may be unwilling to participate when they find out that they are expected to bring back what they have learned and train the rest of the teachers in their school. This is especially true if these teachers who love to learn are uncomfortable getting up and speaking in front of their peers. Or it could be that these teachers are afraid that if they go off and learn something, they may not be able to be an expert in the short amount of time before they need to teach the skill to others. This happens more than we would like to think, when schools and districts send teachers or administrators to conferences and workshops with the expectation that they will teach others. Literacy teachers, for example, are often sent to a training on how to retell stories, how to help students with written responses to text questions, or how to measure student progress using a particular assessment tool. The expectation after the training is that they provide instruction or model the strategy or tool for teachers with follow-up coaching, even if, as is often the case, the literacy teacher has not had ample opportunity to practice the strategy or use the assessment tool herself.

Expectancy theory is also based on an educator's self-esteem or the degree to which the educator takes pride in his job and achievement. It is also dependent upon the educator's self-efficacy or the ability in which he perceives the work he is doing is making a difference. Teachers with a high sense of self-efficacy believe that they can help all students, including the difficult and challenging students. Teachers with a low sense of self-efficacy believe that there are any number of external factors that get in the way of helping all students learn. These external factors include but are not limited to poverty, parents who are uncooperative or unsupportive, and students who are unmotivated. Teachers with high self-efficacy are more likely to hold high expectations for all students and also hold students accountable for accomplishing their work. Teachers with low self-efficacy are more likely to criticize their students, make excuses for their students, expect less, and even give up on them.

To find an effective incentive to motivate educators, leaders who apply expectancy theory must identify the degree to which the teacher values the incentive, the degree to which they perceive their performance will lead to the desired outcome, and the degree to which they can successfully perform and achieve the required outcome. The incentive is therefore equal to the educator's self-efficacy, self-esteem, ability, and belief that his/her performance is worth the effort and that he/she can successfully achieve the intended outcome.

Cognitive attribution theory states that for people to achieve success they must: (1) be willing to put forth effort (motivation), (2) have the knowledge and skills to do the job (competence), and (3) have a supportive environment that provides the resources necessary to do the work (quality of life within the organization). In other words:

WILL + SKILL + SUPPORT = SUCCESS

If teachers, for example: (1) are willing to implement and use an intervention strategy or program because they believe that it will help their students learn, (2) have been adequately trained in "how to" implement the innovation, and (3) are given sufficient resources and ample time to practice in a risk-free environment to support the program—then there is a strong probability that they will be able to make the program work and help their students achieve.

Figure 1.1 shows how the ten motivational strategies to create high-performing collegial learning communities and lead to optimal performance are aligned with the cognitive attribution theory.

**Figure 1.1**    Will Plus Skill

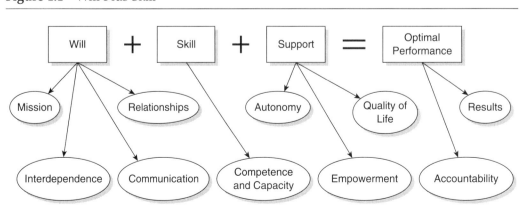

# ■ WHAT IS OPTIMAL PERFORMANCE?

*Suppose, for a moment, that you are picnicking at your favorite lake with several of your best friends. The lake is smooth as glass, and there is not a cloud in the sky. The sun is already hot, even though it is only 9:00 A.M. in the morning. Anticipation swells inside you as you struggle to put on your water skis and untangle the ski rope as the boat pulls away. You are oblivious to the chilling temperature of the water as you grip the rope and feel the gentle pull of tension.*

*"Hit it!" you scream. Your best friend gives the boat the full throttle, and in a flash, you are up on your feet, kicking off one ski and jumping the wake on either side of the boat. You laugh with pleasure as you glide from side to side, pulling back and racing forward, completely engaged in the activity. Your concentration is at its peak. Somewhere in your unconscious mind, you are aware of the boat, your skis, and the changing scenery. But all of your focus, your total being, is on your performance and achieving your goal of a perfect ride.*

*As the boat pulls you around the corner, the shore looms into view. As you ski close to the edge, immersed in the joy of the activity, you let out one last thunderous scream, wishing that you could hold on to this moment forever. Instead, you let go of the rope, gliding to shore, knowing that you nailed it!*

If water skiing is not your thing, select your favorite activity and replace it with the water skiing scenario. It can be reading a good book, a game of chess, sharing a cup of coffee with a good friend, gardening, jogging, walking your dog, playing the guitar, or anything that you love to do.

At times like these, when you are totally immersed within an activity, when all of the elements of the experience are in harmony with each other, and when the activity or task you are engaged in becomes its own reward, Mihaly Csikszentmihalyi (1997) says you are in a state of *flow*. Csikszentmihalyi writes:

> These exceptional moments are what I have called *flow experiences*. The metaphor of *flow* is one that many people have used to describe the sense of effortless action they feel in moments that stand out as the best in their lives. Athletes refer to it as being *in the zone*, religious mystics as being in *ecstasy*, artists and musicians as *aesthetic rapture*. (p. 29)

We call it optimal performance.

Csikszentmihalyi goes on to define the flow experience in the following way:

> When goals are clear, feedback relevant, and challenges and skills are in balance, attention becomes ordered and fully invested. Because of the total demand on psychic energy, a person in flow is completely focused. There is no space in consciousness for distracting thoughts, irrelevant feelings. Self-consciousness disappears, yet one feels stronger than usual. The sense of time is distorted; hours seem to pass by in minutes. When a person's entire being is stretched in the full functioning of body and mind, whatever one does becomes worth doing for its own sake; living becomes its own justification. In the harmonious focusing of physical and psychic energy, life finally comes into its own.

It is the full involvement of flow, rather than happiness that makes for excellence in life. When we are in flow, we are not happy, because to experience happiness we must focus on our inner states, and that would take away attention from the task at hand. . . . Only after the task is completed do we have the leisure to look back on what has happened, and then we are flooded with gratitude for the excellence of that experience—then, in retrospect, we are happy. . . . The happiness that follows flow is of our own making, and it leads to increasing complexity and growth in consciousness. (p. 31–32).

If a person is to continue to achieve the state of *flow,* he or she must continue to learn and develop his knowledge and skills and to face ever-increasing complexity and demanding challenges. It takes a great deal of energy to continue to build capacity. When we are bored and apathetic, we are unable or unwilling to put forth the effort to complete the challenge. Likewise, if we are too worried or anxious to face the task, we find ways to cope and avoid the challenge. For teachers, this may mean closing their doors and doing what they have always done, the same way they have always done it.

Csikszentmihalyi says that the more work takes on flow-like characteristics, the more people will get involved and enjoy what they are doing. When workers understand the goals and expectations, possess the knowledge and skills to complete the task, receive specific and explicit feedback, and are met with few distractions and a sense of autonomy, the "feelings it provides are not that different from what one experiences in a sport or an artistic performance" (p. 38). The more people tend to be in the state of flow, the happier, more motivated, and productive they become.

Educators are likely to experience a sense of flow when they are immersed in complex activities that serve a greater purpose, such as helping students learn, and when they can see the results of their work (their students' achievement). At times like these, they experience some of their happiest and most productive moments. If you ask teachers why they teach, most of them will tell you it is from the joy of watching their students learn. Teachers often talk excitedly about the "ah ha" experience, when the light bulb suddenly goes on inside a student's head, after days of struggling to help a student achieve the learning goals. Or they may find themselves engaged in flow-like activities while being so immersed in their lab experiment or art lesson that they are suddenly and unexpectedly jolted back into reality by the sound of the bell marking the end of the period.

The amount of time a person experiences flow depends on what counts as a flow experience. If we count only those moments of the "most intense and exalted flow experiences, then their frequency would be rare" (Csikszentmihalyi, 1997, p. 33). If we are willing to count "even mild approximations of the ideal condition as instances of flow" (p. 33), it will occur much more frequently.

Like Csikszentmihalyi has done with *flow,* numerous experts and writers have given definition to a euphoric state or condition in which an individual is engaged in an action, work, or activity in which he or she is able to complete the task and achieve the goal to his or her highest level and potential. The activity or task itself, based on an innate sense and/or morally compelling purpose, is its own reward.

For example, in the psychological realm, one of the most familiar terms, *self-actualization,* was coined by Abraham Maslow. According to Maslow (1998), a person achieves self-actualization when he or she finds that the activity or work they are engaged in provides its own satisfaction. It brings self-fulfillment and its own sense of self-achievement. The work is its own reward. People at this state recognize their individual strengths and potential and do all they can to become everything that they are capable of being. For example, a musician plays the piano for his own enjoyment or to share his passion of music with others.

Stephen Covey's *The 8th Habit* (2004), "Find your voice and inspire others to find theirs" describes how leaders can help others to achieve this state by *first finding your own voice* and then inspiring others *to find their voices.* To do this, he asks readers to think about life in this simple way:

> A whole person (body, mind, heart, and spirit) with four basic needs (to live, to learn, to love, to leave a legacy), and four intelligences or capacities (physical, mental, emotional, and spiritual) and their highest manifestations (discipline, vision, passion, conscience), all of which represent the four dimensions of voice (need, talent, passion, and conscience). . . . As we respect, develop, integrate, and balance these intelligences and their highest manifestations, the synergy between them lights *the fire within*[1] us and we find our voice. (p. 84)

Csikszentmihalyi's (1997) metaphor for flow, that "sense of effortless action" a person feels "in moments that stand out as the best in their lives" (p. 29) is the concept behind the terms *self-actualization, peak performance, flow experiences, getting your groove, living in the zone, aesthetic rapture,* and *finding your voice.* In other words, these terms represent *individuals* enthralled in an activity in which they effortlessly actualize and perform to their highest potential to achieve desired results.

## ■ OPTIMAL PERFORMANCE DEFINED

The way in which we define optimal performance uses that same metaphor, but pushes the concept into yet another dimension. We define *optimal performance* as *the state in which individuals within the school community are enthralled in complex, job-embedded educational work and learning experiences that serve a greater purpose, have a clear and specific focus, provide knowledge and feedback about the results of educator effort, intrinsically captivate educator attention, are balanced between the challenge of the activity and the knowledge and skill of the individual, and clearly make a difference in helping all students achieve personalized and collective learning goals.* Optimal performance consists of a stream of flow-like experiences within a school setting that empower interdependent, high-performing collegial learning communities to collaboratively and successfully accomplish their shared, morally compelling mission (work).

It just isn't enough for educators to engage themselves in teaching and learning activities that are interesting, fun, exciting, and at the correct level of difficulty. It isn't just about water skiing, playing chess, or reading a good book. There are several critical attributes within our definition of optimal performance, which push it into the next dimension.

First, educators are *enthralled* (completely focused and captivated) in *complex, job-embedded educational work and learning experiences.* The flow-like experiences arise from the day-to-day work and the learning from the work that teachers are doing in much the same way as a surgeon might find in an emergency operating room when he is able to use his knowledge, skills, previous experiences, and learning in-the-moment to save a patient's life.

Secondly, these work experiences or activities must be helping to *serve a greater purpose* and *clearly make a difference* in the lives of student(s) and help to forward the *shared, morally compelling mission* (important work) of the school. For example, it isn't about teaching what a single teacher feels is important, but making sure that students learn and achieve the benchmarks, standards, and outcomes that have been defined by either the school, the district, the state, or the country. It is about "the big picture" and working toward a common good.

Last, and most important, it is about empowering an interdependent school community to collaborate and work together collegially on successfully accomplishing the shared, morally compelling mission. That is not to say that teachers do not still plan their own individual lessons, although they can collaborate on units, lessons, and common assessments. It doesn't mean that everyone has to team teach or teach the same lesson on the same day or in the same way. It does, however, mean that if educators are to achieve optimal performance, that they are empowered to do the work that will help the school community achieve its mission, given the latitude to make precise choices about how they go about the work to best meet the personalized needs of the students in their classrooms (Fullan, Hill, & Crévola, 2006), and are held accountable and responsible for successfully achieving the desired results. The critical attribute that makes this different is positive interdependence—not one of us, or a few of us but all of us have the shared responsibility for achieving our compelling school's mission.

As leaders, if we want the educators within our schools to achieve *optimal performance,* it makes sense that we discover ways to create the conditions that afford our teachers the ability to perform at their highest levels as frequently as possible. To do this, we, as leaders, must be explicit and direct about creating and implementing the conditions to energize, motivate, inspire, and lead others in this age of the knowledge worker.

The time has come to recognize, respect, and utilize the knowledge and skills of all educators. We must retire the carrot-and-stick management strategies used to control the work of our teachers and students. As school leaders, we must inspire and empower educators as we tap into their creativity, talent, and expertise. Most important, we must create the conditions that allow us to recognize and release the potential of all educators and create high-performing collegial learning communities. The optimal performance model that we describe throughout the remainder of this book will help administrators and school leaders do just that.

# ■ OPTIMAL PERFORMANCE MODEL

The ten motivational strategies that we describe later in this book, in detail, are based upon our extensive knowledge, experiences, and research on motivation. These motivational strategies provide the framework for our *optimal performance model.* They are the critical components that will help school administrators and leaders create the conditions to meet the individual and collective needs of all individuals within their school community, release the human potential, and attain a level of *optimal performance* to successfully achieve the school community's morally compelling mission.

Unlike many models, the optimal performance model is not hierarchical. That being said, however, we do suggest that school leaders begin by creating a quality of life, as we describe in Chapter 3. Just as Maslow (1998), Glasser (1998a, 1998b), and others recognize that the basic survival needs must be in place before people can move to other levels of motivation, we believe that the quality of life must be in place before staff members will be able to move to other levels of our optimal performance model. You will see as you read each chapter, the motivational strategies are interdependent and often become an essential condition for other motivational strategies. Because of this, school leaders must weave together the various motivational strategies. The more the essential conditions are embedded within the school culture, the more likely staff members will be motivated to perform at optimal levels interdependently, as a collegial learning community.

We observe the first view of the optimal performance model from a typical perspective in Figure 1.2.

From this perspective, we see one possible order of introduction from quality of life beginning at three o'clock and progressing counterclockwise.

**Figure 1.2**   Optimal Performance Model

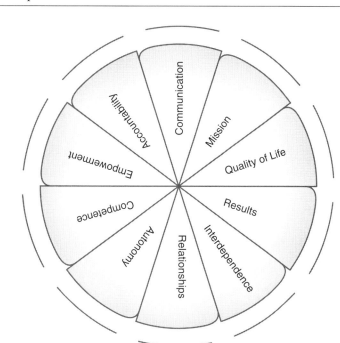

In your context and culture the order you choose to progress through the strategies may differ from the model above.

The key to the model is perspective. Observing the model from a different vantage point may reveal new and powerful insights, as illustrated in Figure 1.3.

**Figure 1.3**   Optimal Performance Model Shifts in Perspective

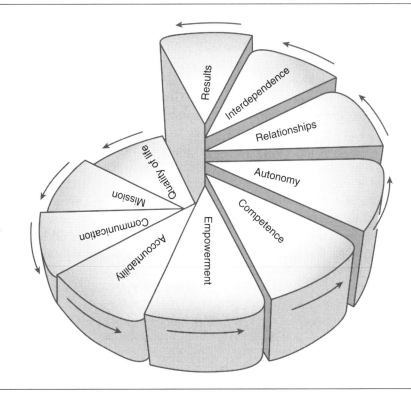

Like a spiral staircase, motivation does gain momentum and synergy as you continue to integrate and embed the use of each of the motivational strategies within the culture, structures, processes, and procedures of the school community. The stronger and more developed each of the essential conditions becomes within the school culture, the more likely educators will be to perform at optimal levels. Although it appears that the model climbs in an ordered progression, the reality is that it doesn't matter in what order the motivational strategies are used.

For example, instead of using an accountability activity, then an empowerment activity, followed by a competence activity, the school leader could just as effectively use a relationship-building activity, followed by an autonomy activity, and then a quality of life activity. In fact, to be effective, school administrators need to assess the current situation, determine what seems to be weak or missing and what seems to be strong and embedded within the current culture. Then, they use this information to determine the best course of action. In addition, once school leaders have established relationships with their staff members and know what motivates each individual, they can personalize their use of motivational strategies. For example, if a person is motivated because he is allowed the freedom to make decisions, school leaders would select a strategy that utilizes freedom of choice (such as autonomy and empowerment) to inspire and motivate him. Just as teachers differentiate instruction for students, school leaders must individualize motivational strategies to inspire the members of their school community to perform at optimal levels.

As we have demonstrated earlier in this chapter, the behaviorist approach to motivation is only a temporary fix. You can use it to "salt the oats" for a limited amount of time before the carrots or the sticks lose their potency and effectiveness. Instead, the ten motivational strategies of our optimal performance model are grounded in cognitive psychology and the basic need fulfillment theories of a number of psychologists and experts such as Maslow, Glasser, Herzberg, Covey, and others. (See Appendix A, "Satisfying Basic Needs," for a brief summary of each theory, a list of specific needs, and how the needs align with our ten motivational strategies.)

## ■ TEN MOTIVATIONAL STRATEGIES

After an extensive review of the literature on motivation, we have identified ten motivational factors that will help educational leaders create the conditions that lead to high-performing collegial learning communities. These ten strategies provide the conceptual framework for our optimal performance model.

The optimal performance model provides a comprehensive guide to help school leaders motivate all of the adults working within a school community to collectively achieve, to their greatest potential, and make a difference in the lives of their students and their families. The more these strategies are utilized by leaders and embedded within the school culture, the more likely a school community will be to work collaboratively to achieve optimal performance.

The remainder of this book will help you, the reader, gain an in-depth understanding of each of the ten motivational strategies, the essential conditions that help administrators and school leaders motivate, inspire, create, lead, and sustain high-performing collegial learning communities and achieve optimal performance. Throughout the following chapters, we will explore a number of techniques and ideas to help you motivate, inspire, create, lead, and achieve optimal performance levels from your school community. We will use case studies to help you better understand and recognize the essential conditions that need to be in place for each of the ten motivational strategies. We hope that after you read each chapter, you will take time to reflect upon your current situation, your desired situation, and what you can do to create the conditions within your school setting and your leadership style to build a high-performing collegial learning community that achieves optimal levels of performance.

The next chapter of this book will focus on you, the school leader, and the ability to deal with the pressures of the job. To make any lasting or deep changes in how people feel when they work, we believe that motivation begins within—within ourselves and within our school setting. As we have said before, we have to help ourselves before we can effectively help others.

## CHAPTER SUMMARY

Numerous volumes have been written on the topic of motivation. Different theories about how to motivate others are ubiquitous, diverse, and often incompatible with one another. Far too many schools and districts still base their use of motivation on the work of behavioral psychologists. As we have demonstrated in this chapter, the behaviorist approach to motivation is only a temporary fix. You can use it to "salt the oats" for a limited time before the carrots or the sticks lose their potency and effectiveness.

The time has come to retire the carrot-and-stick management strategies used to control the work of our teachers and students. As school leaders, we must recognize and respect educators as the professionals they are by utilizing their knowledge and skills. In this age of the knowledge worker, to build the human infrastructure we must inspire and empower educators by capitalizing upon their creativity, talent, and expertise. Most important, we must create the conditions that allow us to recognize and release the potential of all educators and create high-performing collegial learning communities.

The optimal performance model, with its ten motivational strategies, is grounded in cognitive psychology and the basic need fulfillment theories of a number of psychologists and experts that we describe throughout the remainder of this book to help administrators and school leaders do just that.

We define *optimal performance* as *the state in which individuals within the school community are enthralled in complex, job-embedded educational work and learning experiences that serve a greater purpose, have a clear and specific focus, provide knowledge and feedback about the results of educator effort, intrinsically captivate educator attention, are balanced between the challenge of the activity and the knowledge and skill of the individual, and clearly make a difference in helping all students achieve personalized and collective learning goals.* Optimal performance consists of a stream of flow-like experiences within a school setting that empower interdependent, high-performing collegial learning communities to collaboratively and successfully accomplish their shared, morally compelling mission (work).

## NEXT STEPS

As a result of reading this chapter, take a few minutes to reflect upon the following questions:

1. What motivational theories are at work within your school or current situation's context?

2. What motivates you?

3. Think about those people with whom you work. Who are they and what is it that motivates them?

4. How can you use what you know about others to personalize how you will motivate, inspire, and lead them?

5. What would your school or current situation look like, sound like, or feel like if the attributes of the optimal performance model were strongly embedded within your school or current situation's culture?

## NOTE

1. Interestingly, Covey, and coauthors Roger and Rebecca Merrill, coined the phrase "the fire within" in the book, *First Things First* (1996), that later became the theme for the 2002 Winter Olympics in Salt Lake City, "Light the Fire Within." This identifying theme was actualized by athletes, volunteers, and viewers around the world.

# 2

# Leadership Within

## ■ LEADERSHIP MATTERS

Leadership really does make a difference. As a school leader, everything you say and do, or don't say or do, makes a difference. It isn't just the "big" things that have a huge impact on the effectiveness of your school community. Often, it is the little things that mean the most to people. The little things you say and do can have a tremendous impact on the morale, on how teachers view themselves and others, and how effectively they are able to work together to achieve their goals.

As we said in Chapter 1, you can't always change the way others behave, and you definitely can't make people do something they don't want to do. But you do have the power to change yourself!

Understanding yourself, what you believe, how you feel, how you perceive your school and those you work with, and how you view and interpret a given situation or action, is critical to understanding yourself as a leader. Whether you realize it or not, every decision you make is based on how you perceive the information and/or interpret the situation or action at any given moment.

We all know that there are things in our work and personal lives that are beyond our control. Whether it is a mandate from central office, limited resources, or high-stakes testing, we are bombarded with numerous issues and decisions that need to be made every day. Some of these issues are merely annoying while others are highly stressful. But, even though we don't have the power to change many of the directives that affect our lives, we do have the power to change ourselves and the way we perceive and confront each issue. Simply changing just one thing about yourself, or doing one thing differently, can make a profound difference on how you perceive the world and how others perceive you.

That is why, before we describe each of the ten motivational strategies in detail and help you discover how you can implement them into your own school setting, we have dedicated this chapter to building "Leadership Within."

## ■ PICTURE THIS

*Even though Gary Burnham gently hung up the phone, he felt like throwing it across the room. After talking with the curriculum director, he now had one more item to add to the staff meeting agenda that was already way too long and sure to send his staff over the edge. How he dreaded welcoming them back from their summer vacation with a long list of district mandates for the coming year. The beginning of each new school year used to be a joyous occasion, filled with anticipation and excitement. The sights and smells of fresh paint, polished furniture, brightly decorated bulletin boards, and up-to-date curriculum materials always put smiles on the faces of revitalized teachers as they anticipated the arrival of students, toting their backpacks overflowing with new school supplies, eager to learn. September used to be fun! But, no more.*

*Gary had two hours to meet with the teachers after they returned from lunch to discuss his six-page agenda. On his list, of course, were the usual issues: safety (e.g., blood-borne pathogens, fire drills, lock-down procedures); housekeeping (e.g., attendance, bus, budget, supplies, duty schedules, class schedules); discipline (e.g., rules, detention); teacher evaluation (e.g., teacher goals, lesson plans, classroom observations); and building committees.*

*In addition, this summer, the district adopted a new accountability plan, which would require a significant time commitment from all staff members. In the back of his mind, Gary was worried about how the superintendent was going to use the results of this accountability plan to evaluate him and his effectiveness as an instructional school leader. He realized he needed to be enthusiastic about the accountability plan in order to get teachers to buy into it and work to achieve the board's stretch goals. Likewise, he was scared that the amount of effort it would take from all staff members would push them over the edge.*

*Gary thought about how he was going to explain the new student database system changes. These changes would dramatically affect the report card and assessment data entries that teachers were required to maintain. He wondered how the teachers would receive the news of the new procedures for entering and accessing data that would help the district collect and analyze information for the accountability plan. Ultimately, this information would help teachers in preparing their students for the statewide assessments in the spring. But could he help them to see the benefits of the additional work so they would embrace these changes in a positive way? He was especially worried about telling them that they were each required to sign up for three training sessions after school to make sure they understood how to use the system.*

*During the summer, Gary and a couple of teachers had worked closely with the district technology support staff to redesign the school Web site. Gary's personal goal was to have all teachers posting current homework assignments, displaying student work, and other relevant class information in a timely manner. In addition, the PTA was adamant about all teachers utilizing e-mail to maintain contact with parents.*

*The message from the curriculum director that Gary needed to deliver to his teachers was that the revised trace maps and pacing guides for all subject areas would be posted on the district Intranet site as soon as she finished making changes to the documents. The curriculum office hoped to have them posted before the end of the day. "Of course," as she explained, "teachers must understand that they need to check them periodically for any updates and changes. These are," in her words, "working documents." Teachers were expected to download these curriculum documents and follow them during the year. She was also looking for volunteers to serve on several district committees to realign the various curriculums with the state standards and then make sure that each content area is aligned with and between all grade levels and courses.*

*As Gary picked up his materials, and mentally put on his armor before leaving his office to face his staff, he wondered when he and his staff would have the time or the energy to work on the character education and differentiated instructional strategies projects they had prioritized as important building initiatives last spring.*

## ◼ RECOGNIZING STRESS AND ANXIETIES

Grab a post-it note tablet and take five minutes to reread the scenario about Gary Burnham above. Write down all the issues (one issue per post-it) causing him stress before he meets with his staff at his "Welcome Back To School" meeting. Then, we encourage you to take an additional five minutes to do this for *your* current situation. Write as many issues as you can think of that are causing you stress, anxiety, keeping you from getting a good night's sleep, and/or keeping you from enjoying the teaching and learning process. We know there are many, so don't be shy. Put them all down. Ready, set, write!

Once you have finished, take your post-its about Gary and arrange them into the four quadrants that appear in Figure 2.1. Do the same, but on a different chart, for your stress items. As you place them in the quadrants, you will need to think about how much stress/anxiety they cause you (high stress or low stress) and whether or not it is something you have the control or power to change (can change or can't change).

**Figure 2.1**   Recognizing Stress and Anxiety

|                            | Can Change | Can't Change |
| -------------------------- | ---------- | ------------ |
| **Low Stress and Anxiety** |            |              |
| **High Stress and Anxiety** |           |              |

## High Stress, Can Change

When you have all of the issues placed in a quadrant, take a look first at those things that you can change. If you have high-stress items that you have the power to change, these issues should be your top priority! You have the power to take these items off your plate. So, don't waste time, as the Nike slogan says, "Just do it!" These issues are the "no brainers."

## Low Stress, Can Change

Likewise, you may have issues that you have the power to change, but they are low stress items. In this case, you may choose to make the changes, or not, based on whether making changes is even worth it. If the time and effort it takes to change these items is greater than the stress they are causing you, you may simply choose to preserve the status quo. It is up to you. Don't spend too much time fretting about items in this quadrant, since you said they are not causing you much stress or anxiety anyway.

## Low Stress, Can't Change

Take a look at those items that are low stress items you can't change. These items are bothersome, but you probably are not losing sleep over them. You may not like them, but, hey, there are a lot of things we have to do that we do not like. So, just deal with it. If you can change your attitude about any of these issues, do it. If there are things you can do and get off your list, don't procrastinate, just get them done. In other words, make the best of it, and move on. Most likely, since you put the items into the low stress quadrant, they probably don't bother you much anyway.

## High Stress, Can't Change

That leaves those high stressors that you have no ability or power to change. These are issues far beyond your control. We all have them. Several come to my mind quickly, such as administering one-shot, high-stakes tests for accountability, reading about our school scores in the newspaper, testing special education students at levels that are not at their current level of instruction, following pacing guides and or a scripted program to teach your content that do not allow for individual differences in learning, etc.

Sometimes it is difficult to face the next day, or the next school year, knowing that you have all of these high-stress issues that you have no control over staring you in the face. You may not have the power to change them, but there is hope. There are some things you can do. Let's begin with Gary in Figure 2.2.

Look at the grid that we have completed for Gary Burnham. You may not have put the issues in the same quadrants as we did, but that is okay, because what might be a high-stress item for us, may not be a high-stress item for you or Gary. For example, Gary may think that the new accountability data system is the best thing since sliced bread. Or, because his computer skills are weak, he may be petrified of using or helping his teachers to use the data system.

**Figure 2.2**    Gary Burnham's Stress and Anxiety Chart

|  | Can Change | Can't Change |
|---|---|---|
| **Low Stress and Anxiety** | • two hours to cover a six-page agenda with teachers<br>• school Web site and e-mail<br>• building initiatives | • trace maps and curriculum materials placed on the Intranet and changed periodically<br>• volunteers for curriculum committee |
| **High Stress and Anxiety** | • how new accountability plan would affect effectiveness as an administrator<br>• attaining teacher buy-in for accountability plan | • mandates from central office<br>• new accountability plan<br>• teachers mandatory training for data system |

## Low Stress, Can Change

Gary placed three items in this quadrant. These are the "Nikes" (Just do it). Gary can:

1. Postpone talking about some of the things on his agenda until a future meeting or he can create a memo with the information items his staff can read and refer to at a later time. This will give him more time at his staff meeting for the big-ticket items.

2. As much as Gary wants "a current and useful Web site," there are ways to create a Web site so changes don't need to be made daily. He and his staff can start to slowly build the resources and information on the Web. He can also talk with the parents and staff about treating e-mail as they would a phone call. Parents need to understand that teachers will do all they can to return the e-mail, but they must give teachers time to respond. A teacher's first job is to help students learn. Parents need to understand that teachers can't stop working with students in the middle of the day to answer e-mail messages the instant they arrive. Teachers, however, must still respond in a timely way to parent questions and concerns.

3. Finally, if character education and differentiated learning are shared building goals, Gary needs to capitalize on the enthusiasm and energy already generated for the topics. He can begin with a survey to find out how and when teachers want to work on the initiatives. He (and perhaps a committee) can then structure their work based on teacher availability. For example, he may want to plan "dine and discuss" dinners, brown bag lunches, or breakfast club events. He may not get everyone, but those he gets will create the energy to continue to move the school forward.

## High Stress, Can Change

Gary placed two items in this high-stress quadrant—all the more reason for him to make changes quickly!

1. Gary may *wonder* about how the new accountability plan would affect his evaluation and effectiveness as an administrator, or he may *worry* about this, based on his previous work record and/or relationship with the superintendent. If there is a union, Gary could find out from his union officers what discussion has taken place with district officials about using the new accountability plan for evaluation purposes. Or he could ask that it be a topic that is placed on the next administrative meeting (because we are sure he isn't the only person thinking about this issue). Gary could find a time to talk with the superintendent about his concerns. Or he could learn more about the accountability plan process through district training, reading books, talking with colleagues within or outside his district, or taking courses in data analysis, strategic planning, etc.

2. Although it may seem difficult to get teacher buy-in and support for the new accountability plan, it can easily be done. It is all in how Gary presents it to his staff, from his tone of voice, his body language, and the words he uses at the first meeting, as well as during numerous follow-up conversations throughout the year. Gary needs to help teachers find the meaning and purpose in using the accountability plan, help teachers through the management and use of the system, and help teachers see how it is helping them to make a difference when working with students. Most of all, he needs to find ways to recognize teacher and school accomplishments and find ways to help teachers celebrate their successes. This is not a one-day selling job—this is going to take a full-time commitment. But, as you will see later in the book, accountability is a very effective and valuable motivational strategy!

## Low Stress, Can't Change

These are items that are "itches" but aren't worth spending a lot of time worrying about. In Gary's case, he can't change these things, but there are some things he could do to make the situation better. For example:

1. Gary may be able to find a teacher, library clerk, or building aide willing to check the Intranet once a month to see if there have been changes made to any of the district trace maps and/or curriculum materials. Or he could suggest to the curriculum department that when they make changes, they notify building administrators so they in turn can notify teachers. When changes are made, Gary can then notify teachers, or even better, use a building aide or parent volunteer to make the copies for teachers.

2. Everyone has way too much to do, and Gary can begin with this comment. In addition, he can recognize the teachers who serve in this capacity and thank them for their time and help. He can stress the importance of having representatives from the school on the various committees and explain how important it is for their school to have a voice in the decisions that are being made. Gary should try to "spread the wealth," so the same people aren't serving on all the committees. At the same time, using Glasser's (1998a) choice theory, there will be people who are motivated by power and want to have a voice, or who are motivated by freedom and want to have a choice in what and how they teach. He should seek out these people to help fill their personal need of power or freedom, while at the same time, allowing them to represent the school and serve on committees. Most of all, he needs to continue to recognize and

appreciate those teachers taking the time to serve. We will talk more about recognizing and appreciating teachers later in the book.

### High Stress, Can't Change

These are the most difficult issues of all to deal with. But recognizing that every job has issues like this can help Gary. Choosing his attitude, and making the most of any situation, will go a long way in helping him and, ultimately through him, help his teachers to cope and deal with any issues in this quadrant. There are three issues in this quadrant that Gary listed: (1) new mandates and initiative from central office, (2) new accountability plan, and (3) mandatory training for the district data system.

The best technique we have found for helping ourselves and others deal with those high-stress issues that we can't change is through an activity we call "relax, release, let go." Read on, and we will show you what we mean.

## ■ RELAX, RELEASE, LET GO

Several years ago I (Rosie) had a second-grade student that we will call Trevor, who had an acute writing phobia. I am not talking about a little depression. I am talking about a psychologically paralyzing condition that caused him to stay home from school. When Trevor did come to school, he often sat at his desk crying for days at a time, afraid to pick up his pencil and write.

Through the course of the next three years, his parents, his doctors, and our staff tried many different strategies and techniques to help him get over his phobia. One effective technique for helping him get past his anxiety was to use a set of index cards we laminated and put on a key ring. He kept them in his desk, and he used them first thing in the morning before he got started with his work and at other times during the day when he felt the stress and tension mounting. These cards were simply a tool to help him *relax*, *release*, and *let go* of the feelings that were causing him stress. It also put him in control over the situation. It wasn't that he could change his writing assignment, but that he could decide how he would approach it. Let us give you an example (see Figures 2.3 and 2.4 on pages 38 and 39).

*Trevor's fifth-grade teacher asked the class to write an expository essay on "who discovered America and why." As soon as Trevor heard the assignment, he shut down. The tears welled up in his eyes, his hands trembled, and he started to hyperventilate.*

*Trevor's teacher quickly reminded him to take out his cards. The first thing he did was "relax." He took deep breaths until his breathing became calm and he regained his natural rhythm. At the same time, Trevor went through several other relaxation exercises to relax his feet, his legs, his thighs, all the way up to his shoulders, neck, and head.*

*Once Trevor was calm, he could "release" his tension by identifying what was causing him stress, fear, and anxiety. Once Trevor realized that his stress was from being overwhelmed by the five-paragraph essay he had to write, he could release his feelings and begin to deal with them. By understanding the cause, Trevor was able to find a solution to his problem.*

*(Continued)*

(Continued)

*Trevor took control of his situation by recognizing the issues causing his anxiety. This did not mean that he would not have to write the essay. But, in his case, Trevor could select a solution that would work for him from a menu of options, so that he could "let go" of the problem and get on with the task. Over time, as Trevor became more skilled at relaxing and releasing his feelings, he also began to choose more complex solutions. At first, he and his teacher agreed that he could only write a quarter of the page. She drew a line marking the spot. If Trevor wanted to write more, he had to get permission. This solution helped to scaffold the task and make it less overwhelming for him. It wasn't long before Trevor was begging to write more, and his teacher moved the mark a little further on the page. They did this until Trevor completed the assignment.*

*While Trevor was at our school, he used these cards for various reasons almost every day. By the time he moved on to middle school, his control over his feelings became greater and the use of the cards decreased.*

The question you may be asking yourself is what does this example have to do with you and/or your staff?

Look at the three issues Gary put in the *high stress, can't change* quadrant, or the issues you put into that same quadrant. You (and Gary) probably feel a lot like Trevor did at the thought of writing a five-paragraph essay. Even though those issues can't be changed, there is a way for you (and Gary) to take control and find an acceptable solution to help you deal with them.

First, you need to stop, *relax*, and breathe deeply! Use whatever stress relaxation techniques work for you, such as breathing, listening to music,

**Figure 2.3** Relax, Release, Let Go Strategy Cards

| | |
|---|---|
| R—relax.<br>Take deep breaths.<br>R—release.<br>Release the tension.<br>L—let go.<br>Get rid of everything that is stressful or causing anxiety. | 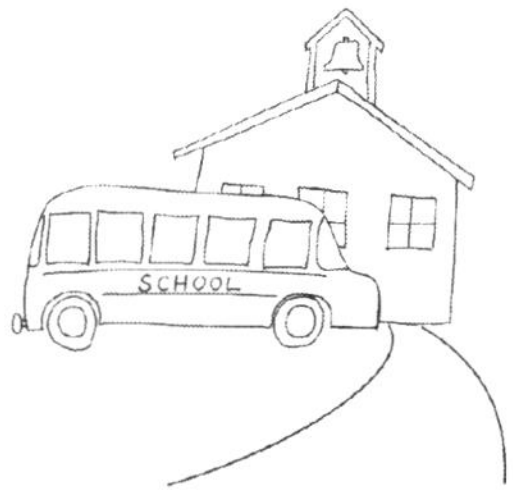  |
| R—relax.<br>Take deep breaths.<br>R—release.<br>Release the tension (identify what is causing stress and anxiety and release it).<br>L—let go.<br>Find acceptable solution(s) and get on with it. | 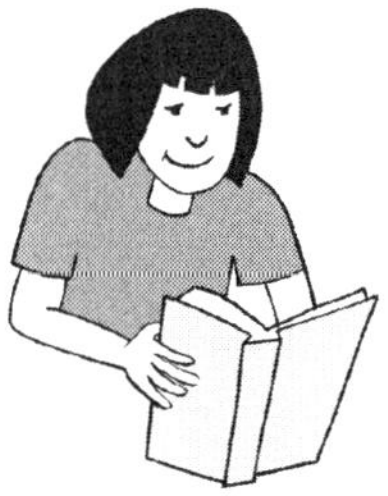 |

**Figure 2.4**    Trevor's Specific Issue: Relax, Release, Let Go Cards

| Leave mom in the morning.<br>R. R. L.<br>Call mom after school.<br>Get right to work. |  |
|---|---|
| Write.<br>Do my breathing.<br>R.R.L.<br>Stop writing where the teacher tells me.<br>Ask teacher if I want to write more. |  |

running, or in the case of my administrative certification cohort group, eat chocolate! Often when I (Rosie) feel stressed or overwhelmed with paperwork, I visit classrooms and find ways to get involved helping students and teachers. It isn't long before I remember why I became a principal in the first place and begin to relax. Whatever it is, find a way to relax, so you can *release* your anxiety and stress.

Second, as you *release* the tension, you need to look deep inside yourself to identify those high-stress issues. Recognize them for what they are—the part of your job that has to get done that you either do not like or do not agree with. Every job has this kind of stress. Some jobs have more stress than others. Once you recognize the stress-related issues and accept them for what they are, you can take a deep breath, release them, and move on by finding an acceptable solution.

It sounds easy when you read these words. But, take a look at the sample cards, in Figure 2.5, describing two potentially stress-creating situations for a teacher, "test taking skills" and "sharing my trip to Japan," and you may not be so sure.

The more you and or your staff can change your attitude and put your own signature or way of doing something on a high-stress issue, the more control you will feel over that issue that you can't change. This is why "Choose your attitude," one of the four principles from the *Fish! Philosophy* (Lundin, Christensen, & Paul, 2000) can be such a powerful morale booster.

One of the biggest frustrations for veteran teachers is no longer being able to teach whatever they or their students find interesting. Since the standards movement began a decade ago, the curriculum is much more

**Figure 2.5**   A Teacher's Specific Issues: Relax, Release, Let Go Cards

| | |
|---|---|
| *Teaching Test-Taking Skills* <br><br> 1. Take deep breaths. <br> 2. R.R.L. <br> 3. Realize that not everything is fun. <br> 4. Practice often, but in short bursts as much as possible. <br> 5. Do it first, so that I can reward myself with something fun. |  |
| *Sharing My Trip To Japan* <br><br> 1. Take deep breaths. <br> 2. R.R.L. <br> 3. Check my mapped curriculum so I know what students need to know and be able to do (what concepts to teach). <br> 4. Find learning standards/ objectives/goals that can align with what I want to share about Japan (through literature, economics, money, etc.). <br> 5. Share my information and artifacts to provide transfer, meaning, connections, and understanding. | |

defined for each grade and content area. From the curriculum mapping that most districts have completed, educators learned that there are topics that were taught every year and others that were never taught. For example, while working in one district with science teachers, K–12, we found that almost every grade taught nutrition, built bridges, did the egg drop, and a host of other common topics. Yet, not one science teacher in that district was teaching the concepts of light or sound.

As an administrator, what do you do when you discover one of your teachers, who spent three weeks during the summer visiting Japan, is teaching Japan instead of the defined curriculum? In an age of high-stakes accountability how can we afford to have a teacher share what she has learned, as well as all the artifacts she brought back, if it is not part of the curriculum? Yet we know, when a teacher is able to share Japanese candy with students, show them how to fold origami shapes, compare and contrast the Japanese kanji characters with the English language and writing styles, students will become as excited as their teacher. Some of our fondest memories from childhood were probably those times when we had a teacher who shared her passions and interests with us. Yet, if all of our students are going to achieve the rigorous standards, teachers no longer have the luxury to teach what they want to teach.

Or is there a way to accomplish both?

As a school leader, when a teacher comes to you upset because the pacing guide no longer affords them time to teach their favorite topics, you need to help them *relax* (take deep breaths or use other relaxation techniques) and *release* their feelings by identifying what it is that is causing them the stress (in this case, wanting to teach a topic that is not in the curriculum). You can help your teacher *let go* and take control of the issue by finding an acceptable solution. In the case of sharing the Japanese culture with students, have the teacher focus on the processes (performance standards and skills), rather than subject matter content. For example, no matter what grade or topic, teachers can find a process (i.e., writing, computation, speaking, reading, reasoning skills, and problem solving) that students need to practice and develop, while at the same time doing so through the context of the Japanese culture. For example, an English teacher may have students reading Japanese folk tales or writing haiku's to practice communication skills. A math teacher may have students converting the dollar to the yen and figuring out how much an item would cost using Japanese currency.

When teachers begin to plan their lessons or units based on the process skills and performance standards, rather than the content standards, they can use any content to help students develop and hone their skills. One very important word of caution, however, is that if there is more content within a course than time allowed to teach (which is far too often the case), teachers need to think *carefully* about how much time they can afford to deviate from the required content. Instead of taking class time to share topics of interest, a teacher could teach a mini-course in an after-school program, form a club, do a family fun night on the topic, or plan a special assembly during lunch recess. One of my best memories from fourth grade, for example, is that my teacher and his wife took every student in our class, in groups of four, on a special field trip after school. Where there is a will, there is still a way, even in the age of high-stakes accountability.

Unfortunately, the high stress and anxiety from issues over which we have little or no power to change, may, for some people, become so intense that they need to find another line of work, for themselves, and the students they teach. This is one reason why so many educators leave within the first five years of their educational careers. It is definitely what Allison was describing to her colleagues and the principal during the scenario at the beginning of this book.

While working with student teachers, I had the difficult task on several occasions of helping them to choose another profession. It was a very difficult time for them and for me. One man, for example, who was in the middle of student teaching, came to the realization that he was not meant to be a teacher. It was difficult for him to tell his family; after all, they had sacrificed to put him through school. Although he was devastated and felt like a failure, I could also feel his relief. Six months later, when I met him on the street delivering mail, he was a totally different, successful person.

As difficult as it is sometimes to let them go, helping teachers, those who are not committed to the morally compelling mission of teaching and learning, make the decision to leave the profession may be the best thing we can do.

## ■ KNOW YOURSELF

I (Rosie) have often wondered what it would be like if I didn't like myself. After all, we can all find ways to avoid others, but we can't avoid ourselves. Yet, how many of us really know ourselves; that is, what we believe, how we feel, what we like, or how we would react in any given situation? Have you ever, for example, said or done something and then wondered, where did that come from?

After practicing lockdown procedures at the beginning of the school year, for example, a fifth-grade student asked me if I would be scared if someone really was in our school causing me to activate our "interior security plan." I wanted to answer him honestly, but I didn't want to scare him by appearing not to be in control of the situation. I thought for a moment before I answered. I remember two situations: one several years ago when, as principal, our school had gone through a series of bomb threats; and two when, as a teacher, I had an eighth-grade student in my classroom who had brought a gun to school. Fortunately, as it turned out, the gun was unloaded. The student just wanted to show his friends. Remembering how I dealt with both situations, I said, "I don't think I'd be scared while it's happening. I probably wouldn't even think about being scared until after I knew everyone was safe." That seemed to satisfy him, but it left me wondering, how would I feel if I really had to put our school into lockdown mode?

*Intrapersonal intelligence,* or knowing who you are and what you are about, is one of four intelligences (i.e., language, interpersonal, intrapersonal, and existential) that Gardner (2000, p. 8) says is "crucial for all leaders" to develop. Gardner's revised conceptualization of an intelligence is a "biopsychological potential to process information that can be activated in a cultural setting to solve problems or create products that are of value in a culture" (p. 33–34). He says that this revised definition:

> suggests that intelligences are not things that can be seen or counted. Instead, they are potentials—presumably neural ones—that will or will not be activated, depending upon the values of a particular culture, the opportunities available in a culture, and the personal decisions made by individuals and/or their families, schoolteachers, and others. (p. 34)

Leaders who are skillful at interpersonal intelligence have a keen awareness of their strengths, weaknesses, and goals—and they are prepared to reflect regularly on their personal course. Gardner (2000) says intrapersonal intelligence "involves the capacity to understand oneself, to have an effective working model of oneself—including one's own desires, fears, and capacities—and to use such information effectively in regulating one's own life" (p. 43).

Effective school leaders make time for self-reflection and self-evaluation on a regular basis. They get to know themselves by reviewing what happened during an event, a conversation, or a single day; evaluating the effectiveness of their actions; and focusing on what they could do to be even more effective should a similar situation arise in the future. Some leaders do this at the end of the day while they are shutting down their computers and securing the school office. Some leaders may do this over dinner with a colleague or significant other. Others may choose to keep a journal, writing either before they go to bed or first thing in the morning. Still others may review the course of the day as part of their routine while getting ready for bed or waiting to fall asleep. When reflecting, it is important to focus on more than simply your behavior or the outcome. Dig deeper and think about how you felt, what you believed, and how others viewed your actions.

If you have the luxury of working with other administrators in your school, schedule time, if not at the end of each day, at least once or twice a week, to debrief as a group on recent past events—specifically, how effectively you worked together as a team, and what you could do to improve on your effectiveness in the future. Use your colleagues as a mirror to help you reflect upon your own performance and to view your own performance from an additional set of eyes. Applying what you learn from such reflections will challenge your thinking and lead to continual personal and professional growth.

According to Gardner, Csikszentmihalyi, and Damon (2001):

> The optimal development of a person requires first satisfying the most basic needs (food, shelter, sex), then addressing higher-order needs (companionship, competence), and finally attempting to cultivate more sophisticated capacities (generosity, forgiveness, self-discipline). The most developed individuals exhibit a sense of autonomy and maturity, while at the same time maintaining a connection to the wider community, to vital traditions of earlier times, and to people and institutions yet to come. (p. 242–243)

The authors go on to define two "lines of development," that of *competence,* or the knowledge and skills that are necessary for their work, and *character,* a set of values and morals that an individual uses in a given situation. Even though a person of good character may not always make the best or right decision, if they have strong character, they will "have the discipline to judge whether a course of action was, in retrospect, well motivated and judicious" (p. 243). Gardner et al. continue by saying that for optimal development to occur, a person must also fulfill two potentials: *differentiation* (becoming a person who has strong character, competence, and "autonomous individuality"); and *integration* (a person who has strong network connections and relationships; a person whose values, actions, goals, and thoughts are aligned and in harmony; and a person who works toward and accepts mutual responsibilities and shared meanings) (p. 243).

Performing at an optimal level requires you to develop your intrapersonal skills and truly understand yourself. The more time you spend getting to know yourself, your goals, your beliefs, your values, your attitudes, and how you have acted in previous situations, the less you (and others) will be surprised by your words and actions and the more effective you will be in leading others to develop their own optimal levels of performance.

# ■ KNOW OTHERS

It is important to spend time getting to know the people that work with you. Like effective classroom teachers who know their students well, school leaders must know and understand all staff members: what they like, what they believe, what they value, what they think, what they need, and how they might act in any given situation. School leaders must recognize the individual strengths and weaknesses of each person to successfully: define, clarify, and establish the school vision, purpose, and goals; scaffold the challenges; provide training of essential learning; support the desired behavioral changes; and continue and sustain the momentum to achieve optimal performance and results. Effective school leaders understand the relationship structure, how individuals are connected and interconnected with others at their school. The more administrators know about each staff member, from the custodian to the secretary to the teachers, the more likely they will be to find ways to motivate, inspire, and lead them to accomplish the school's mission.

As you will learn in the chapters on relationships and interdependence, spending time on group maintenance issues (e.g., checking-in, team-building, communication, collaboration skills, working together for a common good, and debriefing group effectiveness) is as important as the time devoted to the task itself. Just as it is important for school leaders to know each staff member, staff members must also have time to get to know and understand everyone who works at their school. If your goal is for each committee and group to become a successful collegial learning community, you must begin each meeting with time for members to "check-in," get to know, and catch-up with each other. Likewise, there must be time to debrief the meeting before it is adjourned.

It sounds easy, but it takes energy to create the structures that allow you to know and understand each staff member and for them to know and understand each other, and you, too. Depending on the size of your staff, connecting with each person will take more or less time. The best way to find out about individual staff members is to ask questions. You can get to know your staff during lunch, before and after school, and during outside events (e.g., at parties, at games, at professional development workshops or conferences, dinners, during the summer). Likewise, during goal-setting sessions and formative and summative evaluation meetings, ask questions about their professional strengths and weaknesses, interests, passions, and talents. Structure your staff meetings and/or committee meetings to include brief team-building and check-in activities. Along with building relationships and connections among staff members, you will also discover new information about the people you work with at your school.

At my (Rosie's) school, for example, several times each year we *play* different games, such as guessing which baby picture belongs to which staff member, guessing which one of four statements about a person is true and which three are fabricated, guessing which staff members lists which book or movie as their all-time favorite, and guessing which unknown fact belongs to which staff member, just to name of few. We all have fun and, at the same time, get to know more about each other.

According to Gardner (2000), the most effective leaders have strong interpersonal skills that allow them to understand the aspirations and fears of others (p. 8). Gardner defines interpersonal intelligence as a "person's capacity to understand the intentions, motivations, and desires of other people and, consequently, to work effectively with others" (p. 43). In addition, Gardner says that effective leaders must ask existential questions to help "audiences understand their own life situation, clarify their goals, and feel engaged in a meaningful quest" (p. 8).

Daniel Goleman (1998) argues that the single most important factor of a successful worker (star performer) is emotional intelligence. To be effective, school leaders must develop and utilize the five elements of the emotional intelligence framework. That is, the skills of *personal competence*: (1) *self-awareness* of your emotions, (2) *self-regulation* and managing your emotions, (3) *motivation* of yourself and *social competence*, (4) *empathy* and the ability to recognize emotions in others, and (5) *social skills* and having the ability to handle relationships (p. 24–28). Goleman believes that no matter where we work or what we do, developing the elements of emotional intelligence and utilizing them at work "can help us not just compete, but also nurture the capacity for pleasure, even joy, in our work" (p. 316).

*Empathy*, the ability to walk in someone else's shoes and feel what he or she is feeling, is probably one of the most important emotional intelligence skills a school administrator can develop and use. It doesn't take long after administrators leave the classroom to forget what teachers go through each day. Yet, we need to take an active interest in how our staff members are feeling, listen to their concerns, and anticipate and meet their needs to the best of our abilities. We may not always agree with a staff member, and that is okay, but they need to understand that we are aware of their feelings, needs, and concerns. Sometimes, after I (Rosie) have listened to a staff member go on and on about an issue, I am at a loss of what he expects me to do. So, I ask, "What can I do to help you?"

More often than not, what I get is, "You already have. I just needed someone to listen to me." They need to know you are there, you understand, even if you can't do anything to help them. Most of all, they just need to know that you care about them enough to take the time to listen.

To successfully motivate, lead, and inspire others, school leaders must know and understand each individual who works with them. There are no rules for motivating others because, as we said before, what motivates one person may not motivate another. What works in one situation doesn't always work the next time. This makes the role of being a motivational leader all the more difficult and challenging.

Jim Loehr and Tony Schwartz (2003), in their book *The Power of Full Engagement*, remind us that:

> Leaders are the stewards of organizational energy—in companies, organizations, and even families. They inspire or demoralize others first by how effectively they manage their own energy and next by how well they mobilize, focus, invest, and renew the collective energy of those they lead. The skillful management of energy, individually and organizationally, makes possible something that we call full engagement. (p. 5)

How then do school leaders skillfully manage the energy that helps others to achieve levels of optimal performance? Once you begin to know and understand each individual, what can you, as a leader, do to challenge your staff to achieve your high expectations and your school's morally compelling mission without overwhelming staff members and burning them out?

## ■ CREATE ENERGY, BUILD RESILIENCE, SUSTAIN MOMENTUM

Why is it that some people are able to bounce back after a trauma or setback, while it seems to take its toll on others? Why do some members of your staff adapt to changes easily, even welcoming a new initiative, while other staff members experience anxiety, stress, sadness, and even anger over the very same initiative?

Loehr and Schwartz (2003) write, "Energy, not time, is the fundamental currency of high performance" (p. 4). In addition, they write, "performance, health, and happiness are grounded in the skillful management of energy" (p. 5). When asked, most administrators will tell you there is not enough time in a day to get the job done. In fact, by the end of most days their to-do lists are longer than they were at the beginning of the day. Loehr and Schwartz contend that even though "the number of hours in a day is fixed, the quantity and quality of energy available to us is not" (p. 5). They continue:

> It is our most precious resource. The more we take responsibility for the energy we bring to the world, the more empowered and productive we become. The more we blame others or external circumstances, the more negative and compromised our energy is likely to be. (p. 5)

Loehr and Schwartz list four principles for becoming fully engaged. These are:

> *Principle 1.* Full engagement requires drawing on four separate but related sources of energy: physical, emotional, mental, and spiritual energy (p. 9).

> *Principle 2.* Because energy capacity diminishes both with overuse and underuse, we must balance energy expenditure with intermittent energy renewal (p. 11).

> *Principle 3.* To build capacity, we must push beyond our normal limits, training in the same systematic way that elite athletes do (p. 13).

> *Principle 4.* Positive energy rituals—highly specific routines for managing energy—are the key to full engagement and sustained high performance (p. 14).

## ■ FIND EQUILIBRIUM

As school leaders, it is up to us to keep the organizational energy flowing. To do this, we must remember to take care of ourselves first, so that we can help others sustain their energy levels. One of the most important things we can do for ourselves is to find the balance between our schoolwork and our personal lives.

If you are currently a school leader, you know that your job is 24/7 and that it could, if time allowed, be even more. One of the things I (Rosie) have learned over time, however, is that no matter how long and hard I work, I can still only do what I can do. There is only one of me, even though on many occasions I find myself double-booked in classrooms, meetings, and events. If only I had a clone!

For whatever reason, when I talk to other school administrators, they consistently tell me that they never have time for lunch and yet wonder why, at the end of the day, their head hurts and they feel so tired. And, it is true. I wouldn't have time for lunch either, except that I have learned to balance my personal need (to eat and take a break) by using lunch as a time to build relationships and connect with staff members and students.

On several days each month, I have lunch with students—with an entire class in their classroom; with an entire class in the cafeteria (while as I am eating and talking with students, I am also watching the flow of the cafeteria); or with a winner from our character education monthly drawing, who has won lunch with the principal for him/her and two of their friends, and the ice cream of their choice. On other days, I rotate my lunchtime, so that I am in the staff room for lunch during different lunch periods. In this way, I can sit and talk with teachers on a personal or professional level. By being accessible in the staff room with teachers, they have the opportunity to ask me questions, tell me what they need, discuss student or parent issues, and anything else that is on their minds. When the teachers see me enjoying my lunch with them, for whatever reason, they relax and sense that everything is under control versus the times they see me in my office completing paperwork or making phone calls. Then, whether or not their perceptions are accurate, they sense that I am overwhelmed. From their comments, I can feel their anxiety level increase. By taking time to eat my lunch with teachers or students, I am able to reenergize myself, while at the same time reassuring teachers that everything is under control, as well as taking the time to connect and build relationships.

This is just one example of how school leaders can reenergize themselves and continue to work at the same time. I wish I could say that I was as good at making sure I lifted weights and ran at least three–five days each week, got to bed before 10:00 P.M., and had time to go to church on Sunday and then brunch with family or friends, instead of frantically trying to get caught up on the work I didn't finish during the week. But, as hard as I try, I can't always say that.

The first step in becoming fully engaged is to understand the importance of balancing your life and sustaining your energy level. Each of us must define our purpose by answering the question, "How should I spend my energy in a way that is consistent with my deepest values?" (Loehr & Schwartz, 2003, p. 15). It is important to reflect upon those things that are most important and keep focused on our priorities. Next, we must face reality by gathering the evidence of how to manage our energy through the choices we make. Once we know what we are doing, we can take action to close the gap between the person we are now and the person we want to become.

As a school leader, it is also important to help the adults you work with effectively manage their own energy and find ways to balance periods of high stress with sufficient time to recover. This is critical if you are going to help them achieve high performance, both individually and as a school community, and sustain their high performance during those high-stress, stormy seasons. To be fully engaged, staff members must be physically energized, emotionally connected, mentally focused, and spiritually aligned. School leaders should help teachers focus their energy and purpose on the positive things they can do, rather than the negatives; the internal things they can control, rather than the external things they can't; and on others, rather than on themselves. As you will learn in the chapter on mission, you need to create a shared vision, grounded in values and purpose that is morally compelling and meaningful. In addition, you need a plan that defines a mission that all staff members are willing to invest their energy into accomplishing. Ultimately, school leaders must create the rituals, "precise, consciously acquired behaviors that become automatic in our lives, fueled by a deep sense of purpose" (Loehr & Schwartz, 2003, p. 166). These rituals will serve as the tools for managing the energy that is necessary for achieving the school's mission.

Resilience is the ability to persevere and adapt to change, especially when times get difficult and things don't go as planned (Reivich & Shatte, 2002). Our ability to be resilient is what helps us to cope with change and manage stress, anxiety, and frustration. Our resilience has an impact on our perceived happiness, the quality of our health, our ability to sustain and enjoy friendships, and our success at work.

The strategy of "relax, release, let go" described in this chapter is a technique you can use to help build resilience. It will help you to recognize and understand the feelings that are causing you or your staff to feel stressful, anxious, angry, or depressed. By understanding your feelings, you can release them and concentrate on the problem or issue that is causing you to feel the way you do. Once you understand the problem, even though you may not be able to change, you can find a way to take control of the issue by adapting to the change and/or finding a way to motivate yourself that meets your needs. Using Glasser's (1998a) choice theory as a framework, for example, you might: collaborate with others to complete the task (belonging), influence others through your work on a task force or committee (power), make choices as to when or how you complete the task (freedom), or change your attitude and find ways to make the task more enjoyable (fun).

Self-efficacious people tend to be more resilient because they know that what they do makes a difference. As a school leader, you can help your staff develop a sense of efficacy by recognizing and labeling for them those things they do that are making a difference. Instead of letting them place the blame on outside forces (e.g., poverty, lack of parent support), empower your staff to take responsibility for their actions and develop their internal locus of control. Encourage them to take ownership and develop a sense of pride for their accomplishments. Make sure that teachers have the knowledge and skills necessary to feel competent. When they lack the competence for meeting the challenges of a new initiative, they will become overwhelmed, anxious, stressed, or worried. Help them build their competence and, in turn, build their confidence.

As leaders, we must remain realistically optimistic—"seeing the world as it is, but always working positively toward a desired outcome or solution" (Loehr & Schwartz, 2003, p. 108). We must convey hope and optimism, without being a Pollyanna. We, as leaders, must believe that we can accomplish our mission, or teachers will see right through us. If we do not believe, neither will they. Cognitive theory suggests, "thoughts form the basis of our beliefs, which give rise to our emotions, which ultimately drive our behavior" (Leyden-Rubenstein, 1998, p. 74). As we said in the introduction, we must help our teachers to focus on the joy in teaching, rather than the fear of failure. The best way to help them find hope is to establish those challenging, yet achievable, realistic, measurable goals; monitor their progress; and recognize and celebrate each success along the way. We will discuss this more in the accountability and results chapters.

## CHAPTER SUMMARY

When dealing with people and issues, based on our competence, prior experiences, and dispositions, all of us will approach changes and issues differently. What may restore energy and build resilience for one person may place additional stress on another. This is part of what makes motivating others challenging. The more you get to know individual staff member's likes, dislikes, knowledge, skills, dispositions, and prior experiences, the more successful you will be at helping them to find ways to identify and release those high-stress items, so they can "relax, release, and let go."

For school leaders to effectively motivate, lead, and inspire others, they must get to know themselves first by using their intrapersonal intelligence and skills by structuring time daily for reflection and self-evaluation. They must create rituals that will help them to build and sustain optimal energy levels and resilience. School leaders must also use their interpersonal and emotional intelligence skills, especially empathy, to get to know each member of their school staff and build relationships. Rituals must become an integral part of the school culture to help all staff members build resilience and sustain optimal energy levels.

## NEXT STEPS

As a result of reading this chapter what ideas, techniques, or changes are you willing to make in your personal or professional life? Take a few minutes to reflect upon the following questions:

1. What techniques are you willing to make or what changes are you willing to try to help yourself cope and deal with stress?

2. What techniques are you willing to try or changes are you willing to make to help staff members cope and deal with stress?

3. How will you build resilience and effectively channel the energy of yourself and your staff members?

4. Generate a prioritized list of things that are important to you personally or professionally. What three things will you do, as a result of reading this chapter, to take care of yourself first, so that you can take care of others?

# 3

# Quality of Life

*Creating the Essential Conditions to*
*Support the School Environment*

## ■ PICTURE THIS

*It was 5:20 P.M. when Pete Grivalsky, principal of Monroe Middle School, looked up at the clock and realized that he had not left his office since the first incident happened at 7:20 A.M. His day began as students were just arriving to school. One student came running into the office yelling that Justin Banks had pulled a knife on another student. A rather typical day at Monroe, he thought, as he opened a drawer filled with a variety of pocketknives and handmade weapons and slid this latest confiscated knife into the drawer. He had accumulated quite a collection after only half a year of being principal at a rural community school that was more "inner-city" than most inner-city schools. Pete would never have believed that conditions like this would exist in the quiet bedroom community of Happy Valley, best known for its private college and wineries. If he had, he would never have accepted a job as principal, with no assistant, in a school with 400+ students (over a third speaking Spanish and 73 percent on free or reduced lunch). But here he was, sitting in an office that had one "revolving door" that kept hurling student after student at him to "fix" and no time for coffee, lunch, or even a quick trip to the restroom. No wonder his head hurt and he felt drained.*

*The teachers were constantly complaining that he didn't understand their needs because he was never there to support and help them in their classrooms. Their perception was accurate. He still had not completed any classroom observations. How could he? Pete couldn't get out of his office. It wasn't just the gang-related bullying and fighting problems that kept him busy. It was also the little things that teachers sent students to the office for, such as being tardy to class or not having a pencil.*

*(Continued)*

(Continued)

Students didn't mind. They just took a number outside Pete's door, waiting for a turn. More often than not, by the time Pete got to the student, the bell had rung and they were into another period. It wasn't unusual for Pete to give a student a pencil, only to discover three periods later that the student was back in his office because he didn't take his book to class. It was a losing battle.

Walking through the hallways at the end of the day was disgusting. It was not uncommon to see graffiti on the walls and locker doors smashed or dangling as he wadded through trash up to his ankles to escape. On this particular evening, Ed, the night custodian, looked up as Pete tried to sneak past. He hoped Ed wouldn't notice him, but, of course, he did. Ed was waiting. He let Pete have it again tonight.

"I am sick and tired of cleaning up this filth," Ed yelled. "There aren't enough hours in a night to get this place clean. And for what? So they can trash it again tomorrow? And the next day? And the next? The teachers don't care. The kids don't care. Nobody cares. Not even me." He stopped. "And why should we? This place is falling apart. The roof is leaking again in three places, but maintenance says they will get to it when they can. That was a month ago. The desks and chairs are falling apart. The whiteboards are so messed up, I can't get them clean. And the bathrooms—I won't even go there. You don't want to know."

Pete knew he was right. Nobody cared. The place was crumbling around them. Although Ed tried to cover up the scratches and graffiti the best he could with paint, it seemed useless. The furniture was old and hadn't been replaced since the school was built in the 1960s. In fact, the bright orange and gold staff room chairs were so old, they were now considered retro and would be worth money if the chairs weren't so worn and tattered.

"Look at this classroom," Ed said, as he grabbed Pete by the arm and pulled him into where he was beginning to work. "Just look at this mess."

The classroom looked like a war zone. The desks were in disarray, and there was trash everywhere. No one had bothered to clean up all the salt and flour that was everywhere from the 3-D world relief maps students were making. Even the teacher, Frank Thornton, had left spilled coffee on his desk, along with a half-eaten sandwich and an old banana peel.

"Just look at this," Ed said, in disgust. "If I don't clean this room, I will never hear the end of it. If I say anything to Mr. Thornton, I will get my head chewed off! My job. What gives him the right?"

Pete didn't know what to say. He just shook his head. "I know," he mumbled under his breath as he slowly turned and walked away leaving Ed to deal with the mess. Frank Thornton had been at the school longer than anyone else. Although on the surface he seemed supportive, underneath he was controlling, manipulative, and passive-aggressive in his actions. His demeanor set the climate for the school, and everyone learned quickly that you don't cross him. If anyone had a differing view in a staff meeting, for example, they were afraid to speak up. Frank wouldn't say anything in the meeting. He didn't have to. He had "the look." Every new teacher learned quickly, you don't cross Frank.

Frank's philosophy, which many staff members had learned to emulate over the years, was, "I am here to teach and you are here to learn. If you don't want to learn, then get out." Frank didn't hesitate to send students out. In fact, Pete knew that if he looked at the daily record of students who had been to his office in any given day, most of the repeat offenders were from Frank's class—day after day after day. Everyone knew that if Frank didn't like you, you were out. Using his three-strike check system, he could have a student out of his class in thirty seconds if he wanted to get rid of them.

The teachers didn't do anything they didn't have to do. Most people arrived just barely before the bell rang in the morning and often left before the last bus pulled away from the school. Monroe was filled with negative energy that was expended in parking lot conversations by various cliques that didn't get along with each other. The backstabbing, rumors, and gossip that flowed through the undercurrent of the school was vicious. No one was sacred; everyone was held hostage at some point or another. The tattling to Pete about one staff member from another was so unbearable at times, that Pete felt like he was dealing with fourth graders rather than adults.

> *Worst of all, Pete didn't know what to do. The superintendent had decided that every school was to implement action research teams. The goal of the teams was to look at student data and collaboratively design, implement, and evaluate interventions to demonstrate improved student learning. In the last all-administrator meeting, the superintendent said that even though he was giving them a "top down order" to create these action research teams, Pete and the other administrators were suppose to help teachers think that "it was their own idea." "Make them want to do it," he said.*
>
> *"Right," Pete thought, as he got behind the wheel of his car and started the engine. "I can't even get these teachers to talk with each other. How am I ever going to get them to work as a team to improve student learning?" As he pulled out of the parking lot, he was tempted, really tempted, to keep on driving and never look back.*

# ■ WHAT IS QUALITY OF LIFE?

Quality of life represents all of the essential conditions that must be in place for a school, district, and/or system to support effective and efficient learning opportunities for all individuals within the school community. These conditions include meeting the basic needs of all individuals; a positive climate; adequate and appropriate resources; and a culture of collaboration, respect, and learning. Quality of life also addresses flexible structures and a supportive work environment.

## Basic Needs

Before adults and students are able to concentrate on learning, their basic survival needs must be met (i.e., water, air, food, clothing, shelter, money). In a school environment, this includes adequate and appropriate heat, light, electrical outlets, and resources (including materials, supplies, and time) for teaching and learning. For adult workers, basic needs also include salary and benefits, working conditions, and district policy.

Teachers and students must feel safe and secure in their environment. This includes physical safety (e.g., absence of violence, weapons, and bullying) as well as emotional safety (e.g., absence of harassment and fear of failure) and security (e.g., mutual trust and respect). For adult workers, basic security needs also include job security, supervision, status, and interpersonal relationships.

## Support for the Individual

Teachers in a supportive school environment feel appreciated, recognized, and rewarded for the work they do. They are encouraged to think creatively and feel supported when they take risks and try new instructional strategies. The levels of anxiety, complexity, and challenges are appropriate for their level of competence. Teachers are provided with ongoing, job-embedded professional learning opportunities that are aligned with the school's mission and support their personal goals for helping to achieve that mission. Professional learning opportunities are individualized to meet the "just-in-time" needs of the teacher and include multiple models and modalities for learning including coaching, mentoring, networking, and online learning communities.

## Supportive Environment

The climate of the school is conducive to learning. It is a positive, warm, fun, happy, enjoyable work environment, even while serious learning is taking place. There is a sense of optimism, hope, and enjoyment in knowing that the learning is the work (Fullan, 2008), and the work that is being done is making a difference. Teachers and students are willing to try new things and are not afraid to learn from their mistakes. They are curious, interested, and enthusiastic about learning. There is a shared sense of responsibility (interdependence) among the staff, which fosters creativity and innovation. Teachers have a voice in making decisions that directly affect their classroom instruction. Most important, teachers are shielded from external pressures and interruptions so that they can accomplish their mission.

## Adequate and Appropriate Resources

Classrooms, media centers, workspaces, and other physical spaces in the school are comfortable, warm, colorful, and inviting places to be. They are filled with adequate supplies and materials for teachers to effortlessly prepare and teach their lessons. Technology is available, up-to-date, and adequate for teacher use throughout their day. Teachers have time to prepare, collaborate with others, and to continue to learn and grow professionally while they are on the job. Communication is honest, open, and timely with teachers having access to the information necessary to do their work and make appropriate professional decisions.

## Supportive Structures

The physical, emotional, social, and procedural structures that are in place in the school are flexible, adaptable, and support teaching and learning. Physical structures, such as the schedule, provide opportunities for teachers to work collaboratively within the school day. The social and emotional structures support and encourage risk taking and innovation, yet provide for what Fullan (2005) calls *cyclical energizing* (p. 27), which includes positive energizing forces as well as energy recovery rituals. Professional learning opportunities are embedded in the teaching and learning process. Communication is open and two-way, with everyone feeling their voices are heard and their ideas respected, whether or not others agree. The decisions that impact daily procedures and affect teaching and learning, including school policy issues, are based upon what is best for all individuals within the school setting and whether or not the decision will serve to further the school's morally compelling mission. Procedures can be formal or informal and are simply the "way things are done."

## Supportive Culture

The school culture is based upon shared beliefs and core values that define the norms and group agreements that teachers and administrators follow. There is a norm of collaboration, interdependence, shared decision making, mutual respect, and trust. Teachers and administrators work together to achieve the high standards of performance they have set for themselves and constantly strive to increase their own competence. They take ownership and responsibility for helping all students (not just those in their own classrooms) to achieve the high expectations and student goals that are an integral part of the school's mission. The school community takes ownership and feels proud of the work they do to help students learn.

Educators look forward to the conversations they have during regularly scheduled team meetings about student data. There is a vested interest in the results, both successes and failures, they see in student performance. Administrators and teachers respect confidentiality and make sure all voices are heard and opinions respected, thus diffusing parking lot conversations and gossip. At times, the staff may agree to disagree, but always agree to support each other to further the goals of the school. Most important, there is a sense of integrity. Staff members "walk the talk, and talk the walk."

## Respect for Educators as Professionals

In recent years, teacher bashing has become rampant in the media. Politicians carelessly fling comments to get elected, taxpayers make impulsive and disrespectful comments out of frustration from tax increases, and even well-meaning school officials are their own worst enemies. It is not uncommon, for example, for administrators to tell school boards in public meetings that they need more funding for staff development because, "These teachers just don't know how to _____. They just don't get it." You fill in the blank. It all means the same—the teachers need remediation because they can't do their job. An office receptionist or dental hygienist, on the other hand, would never think of saying that the dentist was away taking a class because "he didn't know how to do a tooth extraction." Instead, we hear comments such as, "The dentist is away learning a new surgical technique for implanting a tooth" or "to learn about the latest developments in making crowns." Like all professionals, educators must continue to learn and keep abreast of current research, trends, innovations, and best practices.

All school employees, from custodians to teachers to administrators, need to think and choose their words carefully before speaking. If we, as educators, want to be respected as professionals by the public, we need to respect and treat ourselves as the professionals we are. Being an advocate for educational professionalism begins with school leaders.

## Mutual Adaptation and Support

The word *mutual* means "directed and received by each toward the other; reciprocal" (American Heritage Dictionary of the English Language, 2006, p. 1161, Mutual). The word *adaptation* is the "change in behavior of a person or group in response to new or modified surroundings" (American Heritage Dictionary of the English Language, 2006, p. 19, Adaptation).

The word *support* means, "to provide for or maintain, by supplying with money or necessities" (American Heritage Dictionary of the English Language, 2006, p. 1739, Support). In a school environment, we define mutual adaptation and support as:

> The integration of curriculum, instruction, and the quality of work life for all individuals within the school system. School districts will simultaneously work to improve what students learn, the pedagogical methods used by teachers, and the quality of the work life in which instruction occurs for both the adults and students. The outcome of integrating staff development and organization development [that is the curriculum, instruction, assessment, and quality of life] will be one unified, systemic organization, which meets the needs of individuals of all ages, the school, and the district. (Vojtek, 1993, p. 215)

Until recently, education has been an isolated and lonely profession. Teachers closed their doors and decided what and how to teach their students. Schools closed their doors and did the best job they knew how with limited resources. Districts, ranging from one school to many, worked within their own town or city to generate funds and provide maintenance and support to keep schools operating. But the world has now entered a culture of high-stakes accountability. Schools and districts can no longer afford to work in isolation. To become a community of learners, educators must create a system for collaboration and networking that extends both vertically and horizontally, locally and globally. Fullan (2005) argues that schools can't develop these systems directly. They must use the system to develop itself. In fact, he says, "school leaders have a special responsibility to foster and support cross-system work, where people across a region, state, or country learn from each other" (p. 93). Mutual adaptation and support are essential elements for quality of life that lead to a community of learners that strive for optimal performance and results. Quality of life is the foundation for creating collaboration and interdependence among educators, two of the motivational strategies we will discuss later in this book.

## ■ NEEDS MET BY QUALITY OF LIFE

This motivational factor is grounded in organizational development (OD) theories (Schmuck & Runkel, 1994) and our research (Vojtek, 1993). It addresses the basic physiological and security needs in Maslow's (1998) hierarchy, the hygiene factors in Herzberg's (as cited in Heller, 1998) motivational theory model, the survival and fun needs from Glasser's (1998a) choice theory, and the survival need from Covey (2004). (See Appendix A.)

## ■ WHAT QUALITY OF LIFE IS AND ISN'T

Figures 3.1 and 3.2 will help to clarify what we mean by "quality of life." Figure 3.1 defines quality of life for the school environment. Figure 3.2 on page 58 defines quality of life for an individual.

**Figure 3.1**  Quality of Life in the School Environment

| Quality of Life: Supportive Environment | Quality of Life: Deficient Environment |
|---|---|
| Positive climate (feeling, tone) and school environment. | Negative or neutral climate (feeling, tone) and school environment. |
| The school feels warm and inviting. | The school feels cold and indifferent. |
| Parents, senior citizens, and others feel welcome in the school and are happy to volunteer. | It is difficult to get people to volunteer on a regular basis at the school. |
| The classrooms, library, and hallways are filled with student work and artifacts that demonstrate high expectations of learning. | The classrooms, library, and hallways are void except for purchased posters and charts on bulletin boards. |
| Laughter when appropriate and a steady hum of happy, engaged learners. | Silence, except for the voices of teachers giving directions or explaining how to do the work. |
| Hope and optimism. | Hopelessness, pessimism, and frustration. |
| Available and adequate resources to do the job in multiple ways. | Limited resources—a make-do attitude. |
| Shared responsibility, collaboration, and mutual respect. | Cliques and individual responsibility (backstabbing and parking lot issues). |
| Integrity. | Lack of trust. |
| Flexibility and adaptability. | One right way to do things. |
| Collaborative culture. | Competitive culture. |
| Recognition, encouragement, appreciation, rewards. | "I expect you to act this way. Why should I reward you for doing your job?" |
| Opportunities for collaboration. | Forced collaboration. |
| Mutual respect and trust. | Lack of respect and trust. |
| Safe and secure environment. | Dangerous, afraid to come to work for fear of what will happen next. |
| Comfortable, clean, and orderly physical environment. | Leftover, outdated, hand-me-down furniture. Rooms are dirty, in need of small repairs, lack of attention to detail. |
| Mutual adaptation and support. | Lacking mutual adaptation and support. Separation and isolation from others. |
| Noncontrolling atmosphere. | Controlling atmosphere. |
| Access to information for all stakeholders. | Information shared on a need-to-know basis. |
| Balance between home and school. | Work comes first. |
| Teachers and administrators are shielded from external pressure and interference. | Teachers and administrators are bombarded with information and requests from the outside. |
| School has adequate budget and teachers are involved in spending decisions. | District controls the funds and gives schools and teachers what they need. |

**Figure 3.2**   Quality of Life in the Individual/Group Environment

| Quality of Life: Support for Individual/Group | Quality of Life: Nonsupport for Individual/Group |
| --- | --- |
| A welcoming, warm, "happy place to be" feeling when you enter the school. | A cold, indifferent, institutional feeling when you enter the school. |
| "We are glad you are here and part of our school." | "If not you, there would be someone else to take your place." |
| Respected as a professional. | "We know what you need." |
| The school is cheerful, light, and colorful. | The school is colorless, dark, and sterile. |
| Willing to take risks, innovate, and think creatively. | Afraid or unable to deviate from the norm. |
| Mistakes and/or failures are an opportunity to learn and grow. | Fear to show weakness and admit failures. |
| "Teaching is my life." | "Teaching is my job." |
| Voice in making decisions that directly impact individual teaching. | Told what and how to do the job. |
| Willing to help others. | Willing to help self get ahead. |
| Empathy. | Lack of understanding and support. |
| Encouraged to volunteer. | Forced to volunteer. |
| Competence of individual is sufficient for the challenge. | People are either overwhelmed by the challenge or bored by the job. |
| Balance between home and work. | Not enough time in the day to get the job done. |
| Asked for opinions. | Afraid to speak up. |
| Confident, self-assured. | Unsure, afraid of making mistakes. |
| Adequate and appropriate materials and supplies provided by school. | Need to purchase materials and supplies for students and self out of own pocket. |
| A sense of belonging and support from others. | Feeling lonely, isolated, and disconnected. |
| Teachers and students flow from one learning space to another as the need arrives. | The movement throughout the school is routine and structured. |
| Smiles on teachers' and students' faces as they move through the day. People are happy. | Somber faces that show teachers and students are here because they have to be. |
| Teachers help plan their own professional growth and learning that is "just-in-time" to help them achieve personal and school/district goals. | Professional development is something done to teachers, for their own good, usually "one-size, sit-and-get events" to satisfy district needs. |
| Interdependence—"we are in this together." | Independent—"find your own way." |
| Teachers take responsibility for the work they do and the choices they make. | "Just tell me what to do and I will do it." |
| "Can't wait to get to school." | "Can't wait to get home." |

## ■ WHY IS QUALITY OF LIFE IMPORTANT?

Attitude is everything! Well, almost. It begins with the perception of whether or not your glass is half-full or half-empty. But attitude and perception are only part of what it takes to build a collegial learning community that performs at optimal levels.

Based on the Hay Group study, Fullan (2005) states:

> Successful schools had a more demanding culture . . . hunger for improvement, promoting excellence, holding hope for every child—while the less successful schools had less of a press on improvement and were more forgiving if results were not forthcoming—recognizing personal circumstances (it's the effort that counts), warmth/humor, and pleasant and collegial working environments. (p. 58)

Fullan continues saying that "working together and learning from each other" is also important in high-performing schools, but it is only powerful "when other high-demand elements are in place. There has to be some driving focus to what people are interacting about" (p. 58). In other words, there needs to be a morally compelling purpose.

Fullan (2008) has defined six secrets of change that help organizations survive and thrive. These six secrets are very much aligned with the ten motivational strategies of our optimal performance model. They include: (1) love your employees; (2) connect peers with purpose; (3) capacity building prevails; (4) learning is the work; (5) transparency rules; and (6) systems learn.

We concur with Fullan. The only way that teachers are going to be willing to work together and learn from each other is by building a culture of mutual adaptation that supports collaboration, professional relationships, structures of interdependence, and ownership for a shared, morally compelling mission. As you will see later, in Chapter 11 on interdependence, putting a group of teachers together in the same room and asking them to share information and learn from each other doesn't, by itself, transform a group of teachers into a team. Until school leaders meet the basic needs of all individuals within the school setting, we contend that teachers and students will work and exist in survival mode, the bottom rung of Maslow's hierarchy, instead of at the top, with the ability to perform at optimal levels.

Although the other nine motivational strategies that we discuss in this book are critical for motivating, inspiring, and leading others, we believe that until school leaders meet the basic needs of all individuals in the school and create a mutually adaptive, supportive structure, environment, and culture, they will only have built a school, not a "collegial learning community."

## ■ STRUCTURING QUALITY OF LIFE

It doesn't happen overnight. Strange as it may seem, you can destroy relationships with teachers, losing their complete trust for example, with one quick, stupid mistake. But to build and sustain a positive school climate, and create the quality life you strive to achieve, takes strategic thought, carefully orchestrated actions, and attention to detail to put into motion. Once the ball is rolling, it isn't something you can forget. You must be purposeful in your actions and put forth effort, even when the going gets tough, to build and sustain momentum. Even though it begins with the school leader, you are only the catalyst that inspires others to get involved.

There is a saying that you can put a bad administrator into a high-performing school, and he or she will motor along and survive because the staff energy and commitment will carry the school forward. But in reality, this only works for so long before teachers leave, burn out, or give up. On the other hand, you can put a great administrator into a negative culture, and it will kill them every time. In reality, most administrators will leave out of frustration and to save their own integrity before they whither and die at the school.

But it doesn't have to be that way!

## QUESTIONS FOR DISCUSSION

Think back to the case study at the beginning of the chapter to answer the following questions.

1. It is obvious that the above situation is not meeting the basic needs of the individuals within the school setting. Before you read the rest of this chapter, decide:
    a. Which needs are not being met?
    b. Which of the essential elements for quality of life are missing?
    c. Which, if any, of the needs of essential elements for quality of life that you have identified does Pete Grivalsky, principal, have the ability to change?

2. If you were Pete, what would you do to improve the quality of life within the school to motivate teachers? How would you prioritize your list and why?

## ESSENTIAL CONDITIONS

There are several essential conditions that were not being met in the authentic situation at the beginning of this chapter. Perhaps you were able to identify some of them. In order for Pete to improve the conditions within his school, he must address several of these essential conditions and implement strategies to improve the quality of life within his school. The essential conditions missing from the case study at the beginning of this chapter include:

1. **Basic needs.** First and foremost, the basic needs for all individuals are obviously not being met. The school is in need of repair and renovation. The fact that the roof has been leaking for over a month, the whiteboards can't be cleaned, and the chairs are from the 1960s illustrates that there is definitely a problem with working conditions. The school does not appear to have adequate and appropriate resources for teaching and learning. It must

be difficult, if not impossible, for teachers and students to feel safe and secure at school, if the knife incident is part of "a rather typical day." The adults are disrespectful to each other. It is hard to imagine that they would treat their students and their families any differently. The school is in survival mode. As long as teachers and students are on the bottom of Maslow's (1998) hierarchy, nothing else matters but "looking out for number one!"

2. **Support for the individual.** The teachers perceive that Pete doesn't care about them. In reality, Pete is so overwhelmed with discipline and school management issues that he hasn't had time to think about teacher supervision, evaluation, or simply visiting classrooms to share in the excitement of learning. Pete has not taken the time to recognize and appreciate teachers, or students for that matter. There doesn't appear to be much creativity, innovation, or professional learning taking place in the school, most likely because teachers are afraid to take risks out of fear of repercussions from other teachers. Because the teachers are in survival mode and perceive that no one cares, they aren't going to do anything more than they have to do to get by. They are, in fact, waiting to retire.

3. **Supportive environment.** There is obviously a negative school climate, as each new teacher becomes indoctrinated by Frank's controlling, manipulative, passive-aggressive power that he can simply convey with just "the look." The fact that no one crosses Frank and that he has been at the school longer than anyone else (including other administrators) means that the teachers are still betting that the newest principal, "Pete, too, shall pass."

4. **Adequate and appropriate resources.** The school is in shambles, the rooms are in disarray, and even though Ed, the custodian, works hard to remove graffiti and etched markings with new paint, it doesn't appear that Monroe Middle School is a very inviting place to be. No one seems to care; they simply exist. Because the teachers have formed cliques and have vicious parking lot conversations about one another, it is highly likely that very little, if any, collaboration, sharing, or professional learning is taking place on the job. The only forms of communication that appear to be timely are the parking lot conversations, rumors, and gossip that runs rampant.

5. **Supportive structures.** At the moment, the teachers may have the luxury of booting students out of their classrooms, for whatever reason, on a daily basis. But the school, with or without Pete's help, has not created the structures that support teaching and learning. The physical, social, emotional, and procedural structures for keeping students safe, secure, and in class are either nonexistent or not being enforced. Likewise, those structures that support well-being, collaboration, sharing, and professional learning and growth among staff members are also missing. We do not know what the staff turnover rate is for Monroe, but we estimate that it is high due to loneliness, frustration, burnout, and stress.

6. **Supportive culture.** It is difficult to have a supportive culture when no one cares about anyone or anything except his or her own survival and safety. There is no mutual respect or trust. The norms of the school are set by Frank, whether anyone admits it or not. His demeanor has set the climate and defined "how business is done" at Monroe Middle School. The vicious parking lot conversations vividly portray the "talk that gets walked."

7. **Respect for educators as professionals.** It is difficult to command respect, when there is no self-respect or respect amongst colleagues. People at the school clearly do not care for each other, either personally or professionally. In fact, mutual respect between any group (e.g., students and staff, certified and noncertified, parents and faculty, staff and administration) is null and void.

8. **Mutual adaptation and support.** It appears that this school is isolated and left to fend for itself. It is all too familiar that a school with so many problems doesn't get the help and support it needs from central office (if only at a minimum level, such as giving Pete an assistant principal to help with the discipline). The teacher and student behavior at Monroe has obviously been going on for some time, most likely having caused more than one principal or teacher to leave the school and perhaps even the profession. Where has the central office been in all of this?

Although the school is in survival mode, Pete must begin to put all of the essential conditions into place if he is going to be able to move his staff and students to higher levels of performance. Pete is going to have to give his staff support, help them build relationships and make connections, while at the same time giving them the skills and strength they need to adapt to new conditions and change. The best way to begin this process will be to foster and support cross-system collaboration, in which he and his teachers can ask questions, seek answers, and learn from others. It is by reaching out, through observations, networking, and conversations with others both in his school and across the system that Pete can help his teachers see, "It doesn't have to be this way."

## WHAT WOULD YOU DO?

1. After reading about the missing needs and essential conditions, do you agree?

2. Before you read the rest of the story, look back at what you said you would do if you were Pete. Is there anything else you would add to your list?

Read on to compare your list with what Pete chose to do.

## AND NOW FOR THE REST OF THE STORY

*Even though Pete was extremely tired and hungry, he devoured a power bar and bottle of water while driving and went straight to the gym. He quickly changed, ran several miles on the indoor track, lifted weights, and finished his workout with a short game of basketball. He was exhausted, but felt relaxed.*

*As he changed, Pete wondered why he had decided to become an administrator. He had been an effective classroom teacher. In fact, he had been named Teacher of the Year by his previous district. After Pete had been promoted to assistant principal in the same middle school where he taught, he discovered he loved working with Julie Reynolds as part of her administrative team. He admired her leadership ability and wanted to be an administrator just like her. She had made it look so easy.*

*When Pete applied for the job at Monroe, they both felt he was ready to be the principal of a middle school. Pete was a compassionate, yet competent, educator, who held high expectations for himself and others. Perhaps that was what frustrated him the most. Since he had taken this job, he no longer felt as if he was meeting his own expectations, let alone making a difference in the work he was doing. His confidence as an administrator was diminishing rapidly. He questioned his ability and just couldn't figure out why everything seemed so wrong.*

*The next day, Pete got a reprieve. He attended a workshop on action research with other administrators from his district. Over lunch, however, he found himself sharing his frustrations with Julie, still a mentor and friend, who just happened to be at the same workshop. Julie revealed that in the beginning it hadn't been easy for her either. She disclosed some of the frustrations she felt and some of the lessons she had learned along the way. "But," Julie said, summing up all she had learned from past experience, "if you remain true to yourself, stay the course, think about what is best for kids, and are willing to walk a mile in the other person's shoes, you will find your way to lead, and inspire others to do the same."*

*After the workshop, Julie and Pete grabbed a quick latte. Julie helped Pete map out a strategy that would take him through the next several weeks, when they had agreed to meet again. She explained to him that if he was going to help his school get out of "survival mode" he was going to have to "change the game plan. There isn't much time left," she said, "because if you don't gain control soon, like the Survivor TV reality show, they will boot you off the island."*

*For the first time in months, as Pete drove to the gym, he actually looked forward to going to work the next day.*

*Early the next morning, Pete hustled off to work, stopping first at the grocery store. He took the coffee, juice, cake, and supplies into the kitchen. He paged the day custodian, Tom, and asked him to make coffee and help him set up the cart so it would be ready later in the morning.*

*By then, Jackie, his secretary, had arrived. Pete asked her to keep the phone on night-mode for a few more minutes, while he quickly went over his new discipline strategy. He told her that from now on, students who came to the office because they were tardy or without a pencil, pen, paper, book, etc. would be given those materials along with a warning. The second time, from the same teacher, they were in detention. That teacher was then required to make a phone call home to let parents know what was happening. The third time from the same class, Pete would give parents the choice: they either had to escort their child to class for a day, or have their child serve a Saturday morning detention. He planned to call the superintendent to get funds to pay teachers to serve as the Saturday detention monitor. If he couldn't get the funds, he planned to do it himself. After all, he could get some work done while he watched students sit. He knew it was worth it, and once teachers, parents, and students knew the principal was serious, very few students would find themselves with a parent escort or serving detention. Each time students were sent to the office, unless it was for a serious infraction (e.g, physical fight, extortion, drugs), Jackie would give students a detention slip, a presigned pass, and send them back to class as quickly as possible. Starting tomorrow, he planned on adding a new detention duty to the schedule. He felt avenged as he planned on assigning detention duty to Frank and some of the other teachers who sent the most students to his office.*

*Pete asked Jackie to keep track of which teacher sent the student to the office and to type up a form that the teacher would fill out after the phone call was made. At the end of the month, Pete would require teachers to turn in their phone logs. He planned on recognizing and celebrating the success of teachers who did not have to send any students to Saturday detention. Of course, Jackie was ecstatic with this new game plan. After all, she was tired of being "the babysitter" for all of the students who were piled up in her office. Pete had asked Tom, while they were making coffee, if he and Ed would collect all the pencils and pens they found on the floor each day and put them in a can on Jackie's desk. That way she would always have something to give to students when they were sent to the office. Tom was glad to help.*

*(Continued)*

(Continued)

*With that done, Pete sat down with several school catalogs. He quickly picked out new furniture for the staff room that looked comfortable and inviting. He had told Tom that he was going to redo the faculty room and asked him what color he thought it should be painted. For the first time, Pete saw Tom get really excited. They decided it should be off-white to brighten up the drab green paint. Tom volunteered to get everything they would need and help Pete paint during spring break, so staff would be surprised when they came back to school. When Pete asked Jackie to place the order for new furniture, a microwave, refrigerator, a quality coffee pot, and some motivational posters, she too got excited and volunteered to make valances for the windows and matching tablecloths.*

*When it was time for announcements, Pete was standing in the office while the students read through the usual list. At the end, Pete got on the intercom, something he rarely did, and said with enthusiasm, "Good morning. It's a wonderful day to be at Monroe Middle School. The weather isn't great outside. In fact, they are predicting more rain today. But, since you are inside where it is warm and dry, make the most of your day and learn as much as you can. Make every minute count. Students, be sure to get as much of your work done at school as you can so you have time after school to do those fun things with your family and friends. Have a great day at Monroe Middle School, and always remember to do your very best!" It was a short, simple message for his first day greeting. But Julie was right. As the school leader, he needed to set the tone for the day. Pete wished he could be a fly on the wall in some of the classrooms to see the expressions on his staff members' faces. Not just with announcements, but with how quickly students would be returned to class.*

*As students were sent to the office, Pete stood by Jackie's desk and handed out pencils, a signed pass, and warned students of his new procedures. He knew that some of them would test the system, but that was to be expected. For most, once they saw he meant business, that would be the end.*

*The time was flying by. For the first time since he had been at Monroe, Pete was having fun. It was soon time to deliver the goods and show teachers he appreciated them. Pete strolled down to the kitchen, grabbed the cart, and one by one began calling teachers out into the hall. The expressions on their faces were priceless. "Ms. Bryant, could you come here, please?" Pete said as he motioned her to his door. All the students stared as she slowly and cautiously made her way to the door, worried about what she had done wrong. When she got into the hallway, Pete pointed to the cart and said, "I have regular, decaf, French vanilla, and hazelnut coffee; tea; and juice. What would you like?"*

*Ms. Bryant, like everyone before and after her, was shocked. She didn't know what to say. Finally, she said, "Well, for Pete's sake, what is this?"*

*"Not Pete's sake," he smiled and said, "Pete's cake." "Would you like a piece?" And with that he handed her a piece of carrot cake. "My way of saying, 'Thanks for all you do.'"*

*The school was abuzz. Staff members didn't know what to think. At lunchtime, the conversation, for once cheerful and lighthearted, was all about what was up with Pete? Without knowing what to call it, the cart was forever dubbed, "Pete's cake."*

*During lunch, the usual fights broke out, but Pete didn't mind. He knew that even though he was busy today, it wouldn't happen tomorrow. He had the new schedule. All students would have their lunch break first, and eat second. No middle school student would risk getting into trouble if they knew they would be last in line to get their lunch or, even worse, not able to eat with their friends. At the faculty meeting after school, he would give teachers the new schedule he would implement tomorrow. He knew it would free up his day so he could get into classrooms. Heck, he might even get to eat lunch like everyone else!*

*He knew the teachers would be anxious for the staff meeting at the end of the day. So was he! Pete had lemonade and cookies waiting for the teachers as they strolled into the library. He knew the cliques, and they all seemed to find each other after grabbing a snack. But it was different today. Although teachers were cautious, for the first time, there were actually smiles on their faces.*

*Pete began by sharing with them how he had been feeling. He described his frustration, especially the part about never being able to get out of the office. He then described his new discipline plan.*

*The teachers sat motionless, saying nothing. But he could sense the relief coming from most of his staff, knowing that Pete was finally taking control. And for Pete that felt good.*

*The next thing Pete told the teachers was that he knew that the roof had leaked for over a month and by the end of the day the school was trashed. He told them that he had been reading, The Tipping Point by Malcolm Gladwell (2000) and began to describe "the broken window theory" as part of the "power of context." Pete explained how Gladwell says that a broken window that doesn't get fixed means that no one cares and no one is in charge. As time goes on, more windows are broken, the place becomes trashed, and looting and other crimes become everyday occurrences. "In our case," Pete continued, "it is a leaky roof, old broken furniture, trash on the floors, lockers that are destroyed, and graffiti on the walls. Even though a broken window appears minor, Gladwell says, 'It is an invitation for more serious crimes' (p. 140–151)."*

*Frank couldn't stand it any longer. This was his chance to "get" Pete. "What are you going to do about it?" he asked defiantly.*

*"In the book, Gladwell says that minor, seemingly insignificant quality-of-life crimes can be the tipping point for more violent crimes. The good news for us," Pete smiled and said, "is that people can reverse the crimes by 'tinkering with the smallest details' in the environment." He saw the puzzled looks on his teacher's faces as he continued to speak. "For example, in the book, Gladwell tells the story of how New York City Mayor Giuliani and Police Chief, William Bratton, stopped the major crimes in the subway system by cleaning the graffiti off the walls, controlling the turnstiles, and arresting people who didn't pay the subway fare. According to Gladwell, 'The Power of Context says you don't have to solve the big problems to solve the crime' (p. 151)."*

*Pete looked his teachers in the eye. In a calm, assertive voice, he said, "We are going to find that 'tipping point' at Monroe. I will make sure the roof is fixed by the end of the week. Even though our school doesn't have a lot of money, I will do what I can to fix and replace the broken furniture. I am also going to do everything I can to keep students in class so you can teach and they can learn. But I need your help. We all need to take responsibility for making sure that at the end of the day the trash in your rooms has been cleaned up off the floors, desks, and tables so Ed only has to sweep and dust. Be visible in the hallways during passing times and breaks to stop the students from writing on the walls, kicking in their lockers, and throwing trash on the floor. If you see a student throw something on the ground, make that student pick it up and put it in the trash. It is going to take all of us. I promise I will do my part to turn this school around. I need your help, too." The teachers looked surprised, but liked what they heard.*

*Pete continued, telling teachers that he hadn't had time yet, but he planned on talking with the superintendent about funding for the Saturday detention. He also told them that he was going to get the local youth officers involved and provide parenting classes to explain gang behavior, bullying, and how to stop the local violence. Pete said that he was frustrated because more than a third of the parents spoke only Spanish and it was hard to get them to want to come to the school. But Becky Johnson, one of the ELL aides, said she would interpret for Pete and others whenever there was a school activity or parents needed to be contacted. Becky also agreed to translate all written messages home into Spanish so parents could read and understand them. "Like my mother said, where there's a will, there's a way. We have to get all of our families involved with their children's education." Pete sounded commanding. He didn't know where this voice was coming from, but he liked it.*

*Pete said that in the next week he would be asking for a team of teachers who would be willing to work with him on finding a violence/bullying prevention program the school could use to create a more peaceful school climate. At the same time, he wanted to find ways to help students take responsibility for their actions and pride in their school, so that, "Even if the building is crumbling around us, our students aren't vandalizing the school and speeding up the process." Pete said that he planned on visiting other middle schools to find out what they were doing. He wanted teachers who were interested to join him in the search. From their faces, it appeared as if he would get a number of volunteers.*

*(Continued)*

(Continued)

"Lastly," Pete said, "I know I have hit you with a lot, but I have several requests. The first," he said, passing out pink requisition forms, "is that I know that for a long time you have 'made do' with less than adequate materials and supplies. I also know that our school drastically needs to be renovated. I don't have the funds to do everything right now. But to get you started, I am giving each of you $300 to purchase those things you needed yesterday. I also want a prioritized list of other things you need and why." He saw the puzzled looks on their faces, so he explained, "The why will help me garner resources from central office and the school board. From the prioritized list, I will know what is first on your list." The teachers were speechless. "Give me your list no later than next Friday. I will do what I can to get what you need."

"Next," Pete continued, "I want to give you our agenda for next week's faculty meeting. I have a graphic organizer for you. You can use it or something else to help you formulate your ideas for our discussion. At our next meeting, we will discuss two items. The first item is to create a set of group agreements. I know I am going to have a few, such as we start and end all meetings on time. During the meeting, everyone is present and gives his or her full attention and respect to everyone else. What gets said in the meeting stays in the meeting and if you don't speak up in the meeting, your opinion doesn't count. I want to end all of the parking lot conversations, once and for all. That's my list, off the top of my head. I may have more by next week. Between now and then you each need to think about what 'bugs you.' Let's get the issues out on the table and create a set of group agreements that we all agree to follow."

"The second half of the meeting will be to discuss the question, if Monroe Middle School could be the one place you couldn't wait to get to each morning and the last place you wanted to leave each night, what would it look like, sound like, and feel like?" He paused, took a breath, and continued, "I know our time isn't up yet, but you have worked hard. I know I haven't said it enough, but I really do appreciate all you do to help our students learn. I am ready to help this school get back on the right track. It's time to put our heads together and make this a great place, where we all want to be, because we know that we can and will make a difference. Even though you are supposed to stay until 3:45 P.M. by contract, today you may leave early," Pete smiled and said, "that is, unless you decide to continue this meeting in the parking lot."

At that, everyone laughed. As they picked up their papers to leave, Pete caught a sneer on Frank's face. He knew that it would soon be "high noon" and he would have to do what he could to help Frank see that retirement and a new life away from school was just what he needed. Perhaps the new detention duty would push him over the edge? Pete wasn't sure, but he was pleased with the smiles and laughter as teachers filed out of the library. Several teachers gave him a high-five or thumbs-up for his performance.

Pete knew he still had a long way to go to gain their trust, respect, and build the structures that would create a quality life and lead to optimal performance. But he had taken the first step, and it felt good. Really good!

## CHAPTER SUMMARY

As you have learned from this chapter, improving the quality of life by scaffolding all the essential conditions into a school's foundation is the most critical component in building a collegial learning community that performs at optimal levels. Until a school leader is able to meet and provide for the basic of all human needs (i.e., survival; security; resources; a supportive environment, structures, culture; respect; and mutual adaptation) teachers and students will only be able to think about how they are going to take care of themselves to survive, day to day, within the school building. They will perform at minimal levels, feeling powerless, hopeless, and uncommitted, wanting only to make it until the end of the year or until they retire, whichever comes first.

A school, as an entity, cannot move up Maslow's (1998) hierarchy until the basic needs of all individuals are met. It will not matter how much data a school leader gives to teachers to examine, how morally compelling the school mission sounds, or how often teachers are made to sit together to design and implement learning interventions. At best, school leaders will discover they have created contrived collaboration, with lip service to a mission, and results that remain flatlined and static. Close examination, however, will uncover that in reality, without a quality work life within the school environment, the heart of the organization has stopped beating.

Like Pete, creating a quality work life within the school is only the first step. It takes a great deal of effort, and for school leaders the job is never done. Without quality of life, the rest of the chapters in this book are meaningless. Embedding it and the other nine motivational strategies from this book into your school, you will be well on the way to being transformed into a collegial learning community that performs at optimal levels.

## NEXT STEPS

1. Now that you have had a chance to read about how to create a quality of life within your school setting, take a few minutes to define what quality of life looks like, sounds like, and feels like within your own school setting.

2. Put a star by those things that are already in place in your school or system. Put a check by those things that you would like to implement or explore further.

3. If possible, discuss with others what you found interesting about this case study on quality of life and what you found challenging.

4. Select one or two ideas that you checked above. List the essential conditions you will need to implement them along with several techniques or changes that you can make to incorporate these ideas into your current situation.

5. Think about any barriers that may get in your way, and list ideas that can help you alleviate or decrease those barriers.

6. How will you know that these choices are working effectively? How will you define their success?

# 4

# Mission

*Defining the Important Work We Do*

*Jane Nolet looked at the clock for the umpteenth time during the elementary principal's meeting and felt as if she was going nowhere fast. This was the end of her third year in the district, and she still didn't feel as if she knew what was going on, what they were supposed to do, and most important, why they were doing it—whatever "it" was! As she looked around the room, she saw apathy, confusion, frustration, and blank stares from each of her colleagues. The meeting had already gone on for over three hours, and no one, except for central office administrators, had said a word. The superintendent had been in and out of the meeting with phone calls and assorted interruptions, any one of which would have been more exciting than what was happening at the meeting.*

*Each of the content area supervisors had their own agenda items, priorities, and turns to talk. Each supervisor presented an edict about what they expected would happen during the final assessments in May (either in the assessment, results, or record keeping). Jane took notes as they spoke, knowing that she would pass only half of it on to her staff. If she gave them everything she heard in this meeting, she knew that she would push them over the edge. She also knew that several of the supervisors would change something at least one or more times before the deadline, so waiting until the last minute to tell her teachers what to do usually worked to their advantage. It frustrated teachers because the information came late, but, as Jane explained to them, waiting until the end when all the bugs had been worked out saved the teachers hours of work redoing what had already been done.*

*(Continued)*

(Continued)

*The central office administrators bantered back and forth with the superintendent, arguing over whom they should bring in for the "Back to School" motivational speaker in August. Each of them had attended a conference and had found "the latest, greatest, perfect" presenter with "just the right message." They argued over how many substitutes they could afford at a time so they could release teachers for the second year of math training before the end of the school year. But for today, the straw that broke the camel's back was the latest revision of the literacy portfolios that promised to be even more beneficial to middle school teachers than the previous version teachers had used to record the March assessments.*

*The elementary principals and teachers were frustrated with the portfolios. For the past two years, teachers worked hard to document progress and maintain the literacy portfolios that were passed on to the middle schools. But, from all reports, the portfolios were dumped into the dark hole of the middle school basements, never to be seen again. Of course, elementary teachers were livid over this, whenever they thought of the hours they had, invested in recording student progress. Central office decided that the problem was with the format and had once again, for the third time this school year, made changes to how information would be recorded. The director of instruction said it was because they wanted to get middle school teachers to use the portfolios, and this is what middle school teachers said would be useful for them. That meant it was up to the elementary teachers to change what they were doing, again!*

*Back at her school, Jane had, ten new student referrals from frustrated teachers. Her e-mail box was full of messages from central office supervisors with further explanations of the directions and edicts from the morning meeting. Not only did she have to "sit and get" at the meeting, she had to read it again in their messages. Even more frustrating was the usual, "oops" message, with the words, "Disregard the first message, what I meant to say was . . ." or "Oops, sorry, forgot the last attachment."*

*Jane pictured herself and her teachers sitting on a catamaran, locked in irons in the middle of the bay, trying desperately to catch the wind, if only they could figure out which way it was blowing. They wanted to get to shore and get off the boat, somehow, somewhere, anywhere—it didn't matter. But as hard and as fast as they tried to move the sail from side to side, they couldn't catch the wind. They were dead in the water. No wind, just a lot of hot air! Each time their sail caught a puff of wind they were reenergized and excited. Even the short bursts that came from tacking back and forth felt exhilarating. But, just when they were getting into the rhythm, finding momentum, the wind changed directions and the boat stopped moving. Jane saw the frustration on everyone's face as the sail flapped listlessly in the breeze. They waited impatiently for the wind to kick up and lead them to shore. Jane knew time was running out before they all gave up, letting their boat drift aimlessly out to sea.*

*From numerous conversations with her teachers, Jane knew they felt exactly the same way. If only she knew which direction to point the sail, catch the wind, and help them travel safely to shore. That's assuming they knew which side of the bay they were trying to reach. They were worn out and frustrated, moving from one side to the other, pulling the lines, and adjusting the sail.*

*Jane put her head down on her desk. "Why can't they get it right the first time?" she wondered. "More important, what can I do to help us find the wind, get our boat sailing, and keep it moving until we reach the shore?"*

## ■  WHAT IS MISSION?

Take a few minutes before you read this chapter to draw a picture of your fifth-grade classroom (either in your mind or on a piece of scratch paper). What did your classroom look like? Where were the objects placed? What details do you remember? If possible, share your picture with others to explore similarities and differences.

When we have asked participants in workshops and university courses to draw a picture of their fifth-grade classrooms, no matter what their age, what country they grew up in, and where they went to school, the similarities of the drawings are revealing. The following is a list of some of the more common objects.

- Student desks
- Teacher desk
- Table
- Trash can (often two, one by the teacher's desk, one by the door)
- Pull-down map
- Pencil sharpener (usually in the back of the room or by the door)
- Counter with sink
- Windows
- Flag over the chalkboard (corner or center) in the front of the room

All too often, even the placements of these objects are exactly the same, even though the artists were years or worlds apart. There will be subtle differences, based on whether people attended public or private school, and the technologies available at the time the person was in fifth grade (e.g., record player vs. CD; film projector vs. VHS/DVD; slide rule vs. calculators vs. computers; blackboards vs. whiteboards vs. interactive SMART Boards). But, for over fifty years, the way the schools are set up to operate looks very similar.

It is difficult, if not impossible, to distinguish between a high-performing and low-performing school simply by looking at the exterior design and interior school configuration. There are far too many similarities. Likewise, walking into a school to check the climate (i.e., negative, neutral, or positive) will still not give sufficient information to determine high- or low-performing schools.

It is not until you look deep inside the school that you discover the differences in the quality of the work life for all individuals within the school setting. Quality of life is the foundation on which to build all other motivational strategies. Once, however, the quality of life supports all individuals and transforms the school into a community of learners, there must be an urgent sense of purpose, a strong driving force, that compels all adults within the school to work together to make a difference and create a better world. That strong, urgent sense of moral purpose (Fullan, 2005) is what we refer to as *the school's mission*.

To lesser or greater degrees, all schools have a mission, vision, or slogan. Most school leaders and teachers can probably even tell you they have a purpose—to teach and help all students learn (whether or not they believe in "all" students' learning). In fact, numerous schools and districts have developed carefully crafted, colorful strategic accountability plans filled with the worthiest of goals. But even the schools with the beautiful binders will not be high-performing schools if the mission remains on the shelf and never permeates teachers' hearts to radiate through the soul of the organization. To make a difference, educators have to share, own, live, and breath the school's mission—Fullan's third secret, "Connect peers with purpose" (2008). The mission, however, isn't about the document. It is all about the work!

We define mission as *the urgent, morally compelling, important work of the school or district*.

Although many schools and districts try to distill their mission into a single statement or a few paragraphs, we urge you to step back from that approach and begin to look at your mission, your purpose, that is, *the urgent, morally compelling, important work you do,* from a holistic, big-picture perspective. The mission is not just a statement that everyone memorizes or that appears on letterheads or in teacher handbooks. It is not just a set of goals and plans in a notebook that people refer to occasionally. It is not just an analysis of the data, the refinements, or celebrations of the results. It is all of this, yes, but it is so much more.

The mission is what the adult employees of the school work to accomplish every single day with a sense of urgency, pride, shared responsibility, and a driving force that is self-actualizing and fulfilling in its own right. It is not an event measured by one high-stakes assessment, nor is it a plaque on the wall or a document on a shelf. It isn't about those things that are written, although don't get us wrong, plans that get written have the ability to clarify meaning, strengthen the purpose, and hold people accountable for achieving results when all stakeholders understand, agree, contribute, share, and own the mission.

The mission of a school is all about what and how a community of learners chooses to live, speak, and perform every single minute of every single day. This important, purposeful, and meaningful work is the catalyst that drives the school community to set high standards and expectations and propels everyone forward toward reaching the target and accomplishing clearly defined and articulated goals. Every decision made by people working in the school is based on accomplishing the mission and moving the school forward. Therefore, *the mission is the work, and the work is the mission.*

In this chapter, we will discuss the essential conditions that must be in place for a school community to find meaning and purpose in the work they do. For all members of the organization to be actively engaged and intrinsically motivated, the vision, goals, and plans must be aligned with the context, culture, and structures of the school system. There must also be a strong commitment, buy-in, ownership, and support from all members of the school community.

## ■ NEEDS MET BY MISSION

Basic needs that are met with this motivational strategy include Covey's (2004) "to leave a legacy—meaning and contribution," Maslow's (1998) social need and self-actualization, Glasser's (1998a) choice theory, Deci's (1995) competence, and Sagor's (2003) usefulness, potency, and optimism. We also refer to moral purpose as defined by Fullan (2005, 2008) and professional learning communities by DuFour and Eaker (1998) and Hord and Sommers (2008). (See Appendix A.)

## ■ WHAT MISSION IS AND ISN'T

Figures 4.1 and 4.2 will help to clarify what we mean by mission. Figure 4.1 explains the difference between a school with or without a morally compelling mission. Figure 4.2 on page 74 defines a mission-supportive school environment.

**Figure 4.1**   Schools With or Without a Morally Compelling Mission

| A School With a Morally Compelling Mission | A School Without a Morally Compelling Mission |
|---|---|
| "Important and compelling work we do." | "The job we do." |
| "A cause worthy of commitment and effort." | "We do the job we are told to do." |
| Teachers feel empowered, are given autonomy, and are self-directed. | Teachers follow directions and orders. |
| There is clarity of meaning and purpose for the shared mission. | No one understands "why" they do what they do. |
| No matter the storm, the school stays the course. | Administrators decide what to do based on the way the wind blows or the latest bandwagon. |
| High standards and expectations for all—no excuses. | We will do our best, but it is okay if students don't reach our goals—we understand their circumstances. |
| School leaders are visible, accessible, and work with others to achieve goals. | School leaders hide behind closed doors, buried in bureaucratic paperwork. |
| Teachers challenge their own and each others' assumptions and beliefs. | Teachers believe their assumptions and beliefs are right and others are wrong. |
| Teachers evaluate and assess (both formative and summative) regularly and use the data to engage in analysis, reflection, refinements, and celebrations. | Teachers evaluate and assess as needed or on a districtwide or state schedule. Although nice to know, analysis of test scores is not a priority. Rarely do teachers reflect or make changes. |
| Students and teachers look forward to demonstrating what they know and can do, even on high-stakes tests. | Teachers feel it is a waste of time to teach to the test and nervously await student test results. |
| Teachers internalize the results of the tests and actualize their own efficacy knowing they can and do make a difference in how their students score. | Teachers externalize test results and either feel lucky or unlucky based on how their students score. |
| Teachers know and understand the vision and target—the SMART goals are clearly defined and articulated. | Teachers feel the bar is constantly being raised, and just when they think they have reached the target, it moves. |
| Boundaries, frameworks, standards, and expectations have been clearly defined and articulated. | Boundaries, frameworks, standards, and expectations have not been clearly defined and articulated. |
| Teachers are confident and sure of the expectations. | Teachers are confused and unsure of the expectations. |
| The school's mission is aligned and congruent with the district's mission. There is alignment between the curriculum and instruction at the school and district level. | There is no alignment between curriculum and instruction between the school and district level. Often programs and services are disjointed and at odds with each other. |
| Decisions are based on what will help the school best accomplish the mission. | Decisions are based on whatever sounds good at the time. |
| There is alignment between teacher behavior, student learning, and the goals of the district. | Teachers independently make their own decisions based on what they think/feel is best. |

**Figure 4.2**   Structuring a Mission-Supportive School Environment

| A Mission-Supportive School Environment | A Mission-Deficient School Environment |
|---|---|
| Quality of life permeates the school. | Basic needs are not met for all individuals. |
| Shared meaning and purpose are clearly articulated. | No one understands why they do the things they are told to do. |
| Everyone understands, agrees, and can articulate the components of the mission (i.e., purpose, beliefs, vision, goals, actions, expectations) even without looking at documents. | There is confusion as to what the school's vision and mission really are. The school plan was developed by the administrator and a small group of people. It is in the teacher's handbook, given out each fall and collected each spring. |
| Time to dialogue and reach consensus toward shared assumptions, beliefs, and values. | Fear of discussing individual assumptions, beliefs, and values. |
| Mutual trust and respect for others. | Lack of trust and respect for others. |
| Interdependence with shared responsibility for all students. | Isolation, working alone and responsibility for only "my" students. |
| Open, honest, two-way communication, with frequent conversations and dialogue. | Fear of speaking up and sharing information. |
| Information is current and shared with all stakeholders with a vested interest. | Information is shared on a "need to know" only basis. |
| Teachers are involved in the decision-making process as appropriate. | Decisions are made at the top and teachers are told what to do and how to do it. |
| Collaborative environment. | Competitive and/or isolated environment. |
| All staff members are given support and resources to accomplish the mission. | Teachers "make do" with resources, including time, materials, and supplies. |
| Teachers have time for collaboration, which includes looking at data, planning and implementing interventions, and evaluating the effectiveness and results. | There is little time for teachers to individually or collaboratively examine student data, plan and implement interventions, or evaluate their own effectiveness and results. |
| Teachers are provided with "just-in-time" professional learning opportunities so that their competence is equal to the challenge. | Staff development is done to teachers for their own good—they don't know what they need. Most often teachers "sit and get" whether it meets their needs or not. |
| Teachers are held accountable for successfully achieving the school's mission. | Teachers are evaluated on showing up and doing their job. |
| Teachers share in the recognition and celebrations of their successes. | Individuals are recognized and single efforts/results are rewarded/appreciated. |
| There is an innate sense of duty to put forth effort to achieve the mission. | "No reason to work longer or harder than I already do." |
| The mission is meaningful and purposeful for the work that needs to be done. | Teachers don't understand "why we do the things we do." |
| There is top-down and bottom-up buy-in, ownership, responsibility, and support for the work that needs to be accomplished. | Top-down and/or bottom-up buy-in, ownership, responsibility, and support are nonexistent. |
| Moral purpose to make a positive difference. | Lack of commitment and purpose. |
| Everyone feels a strong sense of duty for accomplishing the shared mission in order to make a difference (build a better world). | "I am here to teach, and you are here to learn—what difference does it make, anyway?" |

# ■ WHY IS MISSION IMPORTANT?

According to DuFour and Eaker (1998):

> The *sine qua non* of a learning community is shared understandings and common values. What separates a learning community from an ordinary school is its collective commitment to guiding principles that articulate what the people in the school believe and what they seek to create. (p. 25)

Shared understandings, assumptions, values, and guiding principles are the basis on which a school defines its mission.

Defining a mission by making each component explicit helps all members of the school community answer questions such as: "What is our purpose?" "Why do we exist?" "What do we hope to accomplish?" "What difference do we want to make?" and "What do we wish to become?" In addition to providing answers to questions such as these, it helps to create understandings and build consensus around a set of core beliefs, values, and assumptions from which all members of the school community will base their work and make decisions. Mission brings clarity of meaning and purpose to the work. It creates a structure for a shared vision (what can be achieved) and delineates the methods that will be used to actualize the school's high expectations, standards, and goals.

Most teachers become teachers because "something ignites their passion and creates in them an individual vision or purpose" that is aligned with helping others learn. "The most powerful relationship between an organization and an individual is when the individual's purpose and the organization's purpose work together" (McGehee, 2001, p. 136). In other words, a school leader says, "Our mission is to make sure all students can . . ." and the teacher says, "Yes, and I am confident, willing, and able to help all of our students reach our target goals." There is nothing more powerful than when the purpose of the individual and the passion for his or her work is aligned with the mission of the organization. When that happens, Tom McGehee (2001) says, watch out. That is when "whoosh" happens.

"No one can bulldoze change" (Fullan, 2004, p. 7), although like us, you have probably known many who have tried. "The litmus test of all leadership is whether it mobilizes people's commitment to putting energy into actions designed to achieve improvements" (p. 7). Fullan makes the case that leaders must have a moral purpose if they are going to be effective leaders. If school leaders, however, are going to mobilize, energize, and inspire others to jump "onboard," they must do more than just tell people this is what they want them to accomplish. The mission process we describe next is essential in creating the momentum and synergy that leads to what Ouchi and Segal (2003) call "poetry in motion" (p. 157) or a sense that all of the members of a collegial learning community are in sync and are all moving in harmony with the goals they are trying to achieve.

Mission is a motivational strategy that allows school leaders to create the conditions that captivate a collegial learning community, fill them with a sense of urgency, inspire them to work diligently to accomplish their shared moral purpose, in sync and harmony with others to achieve "poetry in motion" or what we have defined as optimal performance.

## ■ STRUCTURING MISSION

Moral purpose is the driving force that invites teachers to jump "onboard" because, after all, everyone wants to make a difference and leave a legacy. But moral purpose only gives the work educators do definition, meaning, and a cause worthy of becoming involved. By itself, moral purpose, or a cause, can provide the inspiration for the work, but it is not the mission (Secretan, 2004, p. 64–65). The cause is only a piece of the mission albeit an important component. Mission requires the consensus of the group, team, or school and is defined by the vision, measurable (SMART) goals, and a process to accomplish the work.

As we said above, the mission is the work, and the work is the mission. That being said, when we talk about mission, there are a number of components that comprise every school's mission, whether these components are tacit or explicit. But, as you look at the list, don't let the complexity overwhelm you. In the early 1990s, many schools embarked on a strategic planning process that took so long to complete that, by the time the schools/districts finished the work, many educators were too exhausted to do what they set out to accomplish (Vojtek, 1993). Because of this, Fullan (1993) coined the phrase, "ready, fire, aim" (p. 31), which gave people permission to get started doing something, even if all the details had not yet been worked out.

We urge you to look at the following components for what they are— part of a process that is clarified through actions of those who share the vision, live the work, and learn together each small step of the way. Warren Bennis (2003) summarizes what we mean when he writes:

> Especially today, in the current volatile climate, it is vital that leaders steer a clear and consistent course. They must acknowledge uncertainties and deal effectively with the present, while simultaneously anticipating and responding to the future. This means endlessly expressing, explaining, extending, expanding, and when necessary revising the organization's mission. The goals are not ends, but ideal processes by which the future can be created. (p. 153)

The components of a school's mission include

- Articulated, shared, and agreed upon beliefs, values, and assumptions
- Established and agreed-upon group agreements (norms) for the way members treat each other and work together
- Clarity of purpose and shared meaning (i.e., what is important; what the school is about)
- Clearly defined set of high expectations, boundaries, frameworks, standards, curriculum, and assessments
- Alignment and congruence of the school's mission within the system (i.e., district mission, teacher competence, teacher behavior,

student learning goals, resources, structures, policies, budget, and support)

- Clearly articulated vision (target)
- SMART goals (i.e., strategic and specific, measurable, attainable, results-oriented, and time-bound) that are meaningful to the work
- Action plans (i.e., implementation strategies, personal and shared responsibilities, resources needed, cost; timeline, indicators of success)
- Formative and summative evaluation process and cycle that includes time for reflection, refinement, and celebrations

Many of these components are found in various strategic planning, school accountability, school improvement, or school reform models. It doesn't matter which planning method you use to help you and your staff define your school's mission. No one model or method is the best. Use whatever fits your style and best helps you to define your morally compelling purpose.

What gets written is important. But it is the process in which your mission gets created, shared, implemented, evaluated, and refined over time that is critical to achieving the work you set out to accomplish. Pay attention to the details, especially alignment of the components, communication and clarity of the purpose, agreement and understanding of the goals, and a shared responsibility and accountability for achieving the vision. The success of the mission is dependent upon the level of commitment with which everyone understands, accepts, owns, and shares responsibility for the work they do. This level of commitment is demonstrated by the degree to which members of the school community *live the mission* each day with interdependence, urgency, and integrity for the work that matters most.

## QUESTIONS FOR DISCUSSION

1. It is obvious from the authentic situation at the beginning of this chapter that the district and school do not have a clear picture of where they are going, what they are doing, or why. Before you read the rest of the story, decide what essential conditions are missing, and what, if anything, Jane Nolet, as the principal, has the ability to change.

2. If you were Jane, what would you do to find the wind, get the catamaran sailing, and keep it moving steadily toward the shore? In other words, how does Jane help her staff collaboratively define, align, and achieve their mission?

## ESSENTIAL CONDITIONS

There are several essential conditions that are not being met in the case study at the beginning of this chapter. Read on and see if you agree with us.

1. **Quality of life, especially mutual respect and trust.** From the description so far, it is difficult to know if all the components of quality of

life are in place at Jane's school. There is not, however, a lot of trust and mutual respect taking place between central office administrators and elementary principals, as demonstrated by the looks on their faces and the lack of participation by elementary principals during the meeting.

2. **Communication that is open, honest, current, and two-way.** Again, during the meeting, the central office administrators told elementary principals what to do and how to do it. There was no open, two-way dialogue. Likewise, Jane said that she would only share half of what the supervisors said, mostly to protect the teachers from being "pushed over the edge."

3. **Shared and aligned meaning, purpose, assumptions, beliefs, and values.** It is clear from the meeting that there is not a clearly articulated, aligned, and shared meaning and purpose in the work being done by the district. In the case study, what doesn't get said is as important as what does. The fact that the central office administrators and supervisors are arguing over how many substitutes they can use, who to bring in for the motivational speaker, and what the priorities for the district are, speaks volumes about the lack of shared meaning, purpose, goals, assumptions, beliefs, and values.

4. **Established SMART goals and a definition for successful achievement.** Everyone has their own agenda. This is demonstrated by the conversations about choosing the speaker, not the message; the number of substitutes instead of what teachers will learn; and individual agendas by supervisors who can't give explicit directions the first time. The district has not established SMART goals or if they have, they are not using them to make decisions. Jane feels like she and her teachers are stuck "in irons" on a catamaran in the middle of the bay, drifting aimlessly. This description attests to the school's lack of SMART goals to define their work and successful accomplishment.

5. **Clearly defined boundaries, frameworks, standards, goals, and expectations for educators' work known and understood.** Why would anyone in this district need to understand boundaries, frameworks, standards, goals, and expectations? The teachers are clearly in the mode of "just tell me what you want me to do, and I will do it," while being frustrated because "they [central office] can't ever get it right the first time." There is no ownership or buy-in for what is being done. Jane and her teachers have externalized their locus of control and feel only the responsibility for completing the tasks they are told to do.

6. **Compatibility and alignment between the district and school's mission.** What is the district and/or school's mission? What is *the urgent, morally compelling, important work* [they] *do?* Jane and her teachers do not feel a sense of urgency or the importance of the work they are doing (thus the feeling of drifting aimlessly). How can teachers find the moral purpose in the work they do when they are in the mindset of having others tell them what to do and how to do it? Or how can they feel compelled to do the important work if the emphasis is the record keeping (the format in which

the data are recorded on the literacy portfolio forms) rather than on the analysis of student assessment results and how these results inform instruction? Obviously, it is difficult for teachers to feel compelled to record the same data on portfolio forms three times!

7. **Alignment between the mission, teacher behavior, and student learning.** Because there appears to be no clear mission, it is difficult to say if there is alignment between the teacher behavior and student learning. What is clear, however, is that there is no connection or alignment between the different content areas, as demonstrated by the supervisors' behaviors.

8. **Adult competence matched to the challenges of the mission.** Again, what is not said is probably more telling than what is said. The focus for professional learning at the beginning of the school year is on the motivational speaker, not the message. Don't get us wrong. Motivational speeches can be powerful when the message is clearly aligned with the mission and goals of the school or district. Motivational speeches that happen at just the right time with the right message (aligned, purposeful, and meaningful) can be the catalyst that propels the district or school forward to carry out the mission. The competence to achieve the mission, however, is clearly not the focus when the speaker is more important than the message or the number of substitutes becomes more important than what teachers will know and be able to do. The fact that central office is worried about how many substitutes they can have at one time leads us to believe that the district is conducting a "sit and get, one-size-fits-all" training session, rather than just-in-time learning based on the individual perceived needs of teachers. To be effective, job-embedded, just-in-time learning experiences should occur within the context of the school or classroom, during the school day, in the form of collaboration, coaching, modeling, or peer observations.

9. **Time, support, and resources for professional learning and growth.** From the limited discussion in the scenario about professional learning (i.e., substitutes for mathematics, motivational speaker) it appears that staff development is not continuous, ongoing, or job-embedded. Rather, the district seems to use a pull-out training model based on fads or available speakers.

10. **Top-down and bottom-up buy-in, ownership, effort, and support.** Leadership is top-down—telling principals and teachers what to do. Jane and her teachers are putting in effort (doing what they are told to do), but have not "bought in" to the work they are doing. They have not internalized the mission. Their locus of control is externalized. They do not grasp whether or not the work they are doing is making a difference. Without knowing which shore to sail your boat to, it is difficult to know when you have achieved your goal or how the work you are doing is making a difference.

11. **Clarity of the mission, with a sense of urgency to accomplish it.** As we said above, there is no clear mission, including vision, goals, or expectations. Nor is there a sense of urgency to accomplish the work.

12. **Meaningful and purposeful mission for everyone doing the work.** When everyone is arguing over the speaker and presenting their own agendas, there is no vision. It is difficult for followers to follow when leaders don't know where they are going. It is even more difficult to find meaning and purpose to the work one is doing when stuck in irons and drifting aimlessly out to sea.

13. **Collaborative relationships and interdependence.** The tone of the meeting for administrators was anything but collaborative and interdependent. Central office leaders, each with their own agendas, were clearly on their own page. Throughout the meeting, nothing was aligned. There was no single voice, just many supervisors talking "at" elementary principals rather than "with" elementary principals. Although Jane and the teachers were all on the same catamaran, it is unclear whether teachers have established collaborative relationships or feel a shared responsibility for working together to help students learn. Since there is no clear mission, however, the district and the school have not created collaborative relationships or built interdependent structures to achieve *the urgent, morally compelling, important work* [they] *do*.

## WHAT WOULD YOU DO?

1. After reading the above discussion about the essential conditions that need to be in place, do you agree or disagree? Would you add or change anything?

2. Before you read the rest of the story, look back at what you said you would do if you were Jane Nolet. Is there anything else you would add to your list?

Read on to compare your list with what Jane chose to do.

## AND NOW FOR THE REST OF THE STORY

*Each Saturday, Jane and her husband made it a ritual to walk to the local Starbucks, which just happened to be in a bookstore several blocks from their house. As her husband read the paper and drank his coffee, Jane browsed the books in the business section, looking for some "miracle" that could help her get "out of irons." Of course, there wasn't a fairy godmother to wave her magic wand. There never is when you need her most. But Jane did find a book that caught her eye; INSPIRE! What Great Leaders Do (Secretan, 2004). She picked it up off the shelf, found a comfortable chair to nestle down in, and began turning the pages as she sipped the coffee that was already beginning to get cold.*

As Jane turned the pages in the introduction, a paragraph caught her attention. It said:

Motivation is something we "do" to someone; inspiration is something that is the result of a soulful relationship. Anyone who has had the privilege of working with a great mentor in their lives knows and appreciates the difference. The mentor is not in it for themselves; they are offering a gift to you, an act of love and service. Their generosity of spirit and their gift of learning is what inspires—them and you. Motivation comes from a place of self-concern—"I want to change your behavior with a reward or incentive, so that, if you meet the targets or goals I set for you, I will meet my own needs and goals." Inspiration, on the other hand, comes from a place of love and service, with no strings attached—"I love you and wish to serve and teach you and help you grow." When we motivate, we serve ourselves first; when we inspire, we serve others first. (p. xxxi)

As Jane read the words, it became clear to her that she and her teachers had lost the reason they had gone into education in the first place—teaching students and helping them learn. Not that they weren't doing "it," but that they were simply going through the motions. Being so caught up in the day-to-day edicts and succumbing to "what they were told to do" had knocked the heart and soul right out of teaching and learning.

Jane read on:

When we are motivated, our emotions and behavior are determined by external powers. When we are inspired, our emotions and behaviors are determined from within. (Secretan, 2004, p. xxxi)

This was exactly what had happened to Jane and her teachers. Somehow, as their leader, she needed to find a way to inspire herself and her staff. Secretan was right. Great leaders didn't purposefully set out to get others to "do things. They were trying to practice a way of being and thus inspire—not motivate—people to change and enhance themselves and the world" (p. xxx).

Jane realized that to get the catamaran out of irons and move to shore, it would be up to her to change the current situation. She realized that what she and her teachers were missing was a reason, a passion, and a cause that compelled them to do their work. Jane spent the rest of the weekend getting connected with her own feelings and those of her teachers. Why had they lost the passion that brought them into teaching? She looked deep inside herself to find her "voice" so she could use it to inspire her teachers. Being a middle manager, Jane knew there were things about her school and job that she couldn't change. But maybe there was something she could "tweak" ever so slightly to breathe new life into a school that was going nowhere fast. Jane spent the rest of the weekend planning how she could inspire her teachers and help them "live their work," not simply put in the hours to "do their job."

At her staff meeting after school on Tuesday afternoon, Jane looked at the tired, late-in-the-school-year faces of her teachers as she handed one of four different chocolate bars to each of them. She gave kindergarten and first-grade teachers a Hershey Chocolate, second- and third-grade teachers a Hershey Special, fourth- and fifth-grade teachers a Krackle, and other teachers, such as special education, music, etc., a Mr. Goodbar. Jane told them they could eat the candy, but needed to use the wrapper to find three other people with different candy bars to form a group. Once the groups were formed, Jane asked the teachers to use chart paper and different colored markers to make a four-circle Venn-Diagram (one circle for each group member) to show what the teachers did each day in their classrooms that was the same and what they did that was different. She gave each group ten minutes to do the task and then had each group report out. It was interesting to hear how many more similarities there were than differences. Several teachers commented on this.

*(Continued)*

(Continued)

Jane could see how a year of teaching had taken its toll on her teachers. She sat on the table in the library and began talking with them, first by acknowledging how they felt and then describing how she felt. To describe herself, she used her catamaran example, and as she did, she saw heads nodding and heard sighs of relief that came from the teachers as they realized that someone finally understood. "But," she said, "it doesn't have to be that way."

Rather than present teachers all of the edicts Jane heard last week at the administrator's meeting, she decided she would put them in a memo and give them to her staff later. Instead, she passed out a copy of the "group agreements" that her staff had put together during the first months she was principal at the school. During her first year, she had posted them in the staff room and, each following year, had put a copy of them in the teacher's handbook. But, beyond that, the staff had done little to review or use the group agreements. Jane reminded teachers that "norms" were "behaviors that are either approved of by the collective group of teachers, disapproved by the group, or neutral. This approval or disapproval could be explicit or tacit, verbalized or simply 'known' that this is how it is. Norms are the way in which we go about doing our day-to-day tasks—working together, interacting, and relating to each other. They simply exist because of what and how we do things at our school," Jane explained. "To understand and make things we like better or to change the things we don't like, we need to begin with a set of group agreements—which we hope will become the established norms for how we work together."

Jane asked teachers to look at the list they had formed three years ago to see if they were doing what was written, if there were things they no longer agreed to do, or if there were norms they wished to add into the culture of the school. She had teachers rate each agreement statement on a scale of 1–4, with 4 being "we live it" and 1 being "not here." There were ten items on the list, which included statements such as: we will start and end each meeting on time; we will be prepared for each meeting; we may not always agree, but we will listen and respect each other's opinions; we will examine all points of view before making a decision; and we will work together as a community of learners.

She asked teachers to add up the points. The average was somewhere around 32 out of 40. Jane asked which of the agreements the teachers felt the best about and which needed to either be changed or improved. She asked if anything was missing? No one thought of anything, but Jane knew that was okay. The foundation was there, and by the end of the discussion, the teachers had agreed the statements were valuable and agreed to work harder to make the agreements the school norms. In her mind, Jane knew there were a couple of agreements that she wanted to add (i.e., one on interdependence, one on working together to achieve the school mission). But these would come later, once she built the structures that created interdependence and the staff defined, articulated, shared, and owned their school mission. Jane was, however, pleased with how well the staff accepted the agreements they had created several years ago. She knew that once the mission was established, they would revisit the norms, and at the beginning of the next school year, she would have them sign a pact that said, "I agree with this list as our norms, I can explain them, and I will live them."

Jane spent the rest of the meeting working with her teachers to help her school find their cause, their morally compelling purpose. Jane asked her teachers, "What if your own child was a fifth-grade student who had attended our school for the past six years and was now moving on to the middle school in two months? Would he or she have gained the knowledge, skills, and dispositions to have accomplished everything you would want your own child to know and be able to do? Would he or she enjoy learning? Would they like school? Would they have had all of the experiences in school that you would have liked them to have? Would they have the strong foundation that would help them to be ready for middle school, high school, college, and beyond? No matter which of you were their teachers, would they have acquired the same level of proficiency?"

*Jane stopped and let the room sit in silence for a minute, giving her teachers time to think. Then she said, "What if your own child was starting kindergarten at our school next year? What if you had the chance to mold our school, and make it the best place in the world for your child to get that foundation—to help him or her to have a successful life and career? How would what you want for your own child change the work that we do?" As she spoke, she saw an "ah, ha" realization sweep over their faces. She continued, "Knowing that your child can't be in your classroom but will be in the classrooms of your colleagues—look around, at them, at us—how would you want them, all of us, to work with your child and help him or her learn? What kind of experiences would you want our school to give to your child? What would you like your child to be able to do by the time he or she leaves us at the end of fifth grade?"*

*"As you know," Jane said, "there are some things we can't change, such as statewide testing and literacy portfolios (at which everyone nodded their heads and smiled). But, keeping that in mind, what work is important for us to do, to help your child . . . all children . . . learn? How will we accomplish that very important work?" With that, Jane had her teachers write down their thoughts for ten minutes. Jane wrote, too.*

*At the end of the ten minutes, Jane said, "All of the children who come through our doors should be as important to us as if they were our own children. Our calling as teachers, our moral purpose, our urgent responsibility, our work, our mission, is to help each and every child learn and achieve as if they were our own children—from the first day of kindergarten until the last day of fifth grade." Jane asked her teachers to share with their candy bar group what they had written on their paper. By the end of the hour, they were to combine everyone's ideas into one bulleted list. She had them begin their list with, "If every child in our school was as important as our own children, we would want . . ." Jane joined a group, shared her ideas, and participated as an equal member.*

*When they were finished, she asked one person in each group to read what the teachers had written. It was powerful. Jane said she would collect the papers, type them up, give all the teachers copies and post them in the faculty room. She said that next week after school, they would continue to work on creating a description of the morally compelling, important work they do at their school. This shared statement would begin to define the mission for the school by explaining their purpose, their calling—the important work they do together each day.*

*Then, she looked at the clock. It was thirty-five minutes past the time the meeting was suppose to end. Jane couldn't believe it! All of her teachers had stayed late, without a word that the meeting had run over. When Jane realized this, she quickly apologized, but said that she was pleased that everyone had been so engaged in the work that they, like her, had forgotten the time. Then, before they left, she gave them one last assignment. "If you had to summarize the morally compelling, important work we do into one sentence, what would it be? Some kind of slogan, motto, brand name, something that will, when we see it, not say everything, but remind us of our moral purpose and our mission in life. Think about it. As you come up with ideas, write them on the whiteboard in our faculty room. Thank you all for the hard work you did today at our meeting and for everything you do to help our kids learn."*

*As the teachers left the meeting, she could see by their faces that this had been a very productive meeting. Several teachers made comments to her as they left the meeting about how different it was to think about their work in terms of what they wanted for their own children or about the messages written within the paragraphs shared by the different groups. One fifth-grade teacher, Todd Dawson, who was often one of the last to get onboard with any new initiative, stayed back after most of the people had left. As Jane was taking down the Venn Diagrams to hang in the staff room, he came up to her and began helping. Todd didn't say anything for a while. He just helped. Then, as if the dam burst, he said, "Jane, I am a sailor, and at first, I thought your analogy*

*(Continued)*

(Continued)

*about the catamaran wouldn't float. But I began to think about it and how it relates to us as a school. It not only works, but the fact that you used a catamaran makes it even more impressive. Do you realize that a catamaran has two pontoons? I thought of it as one pontoon for you and one for us. In order to take better advantage of the wind, we need to know when to shift to your side, and you need to know when to shift to our side. Looks like we've already begun to shift. I'm ready to help us sail our cat. With you at the tiller, we can do it. Thanks."*

*Jane smiled. She knew she had a long way to go. She planned to ask her district for money to get the teachers together during the summer for at least one day to continue to do the work. If she couldn't get money, she decided she would do it anyway, with whoever would volunteer to meet with her over pizza, salad, or even sitting at her house by her pool. Jane knew there was still a lot of work to do to help teachers share their own beliefs and values, challenge their own and each others assumptions about learning, create a vision (target) and a set of goals they wanted to achieve. In the meantime, Jane would continue to work with her teachers during faculty meetings.*

*The wind was beginning to change direction. For the first time, Jane could feel the way the wind was blowing. She felt the wind loudly clap the sail with the breeze, trimming the sail (pulling the sail in), adjusting the tiller, and feeling that the power of the wind was propelling them. They were close-hauled (sailing as close to the wind as possible). Jane knew she would need to stay the course. It wouldn't be easy to make it to shore. She and her staff would probably get pretty good at tacking back and forth to keep up the momentum. But, finally, their catamaran was moving, and the warm, crisp sea breeze felt good as it moved them forward.*

## CHAPTER SUMMARY

We define mission as *the urgent, morally compelling, important work of a school or district.* Although many schools and districts try to distill their mission into a statement or a few paragraphs, we urged you to step back from that approach and begin to look at your mission, your purpose, the work you do, from a holistic and detailed perspective. The mission isn't about the document. It is about the work. As we said, "The mission is the work, and the work is the mission."

We discussed the essential conditions that must be in place for a school community to find meaning and purpose in the work they do. For all members of the organization to be actively engaged and intrinsically motivated to share the work, the vision, goals, and action plan must be aligned with the context, culture, and structures of the school system. There must also be strong commitment, buy-in, and support from all members of the school community. It is up to the leader to find his or her own voice and moral purpose, and in doing so, to inspire others to share in the important, compelling work that is the mission of the school.

This is not an easy process, nor is it a one-time event. It means that leaders must engage in a process that is endless in their effort to explain, define, revise, and expand on the school's mission. As Warren Bennis (2003) says, "the goals are not the ends, but ideal processes by which the future can be created" (p. 153).

## NEXT STEPS

1. Think about your own school's mission, your purpose, that is, *the urgent, morally compelling, important work you and your teachers do.* Is it something that you can put into words? Write or describe your mission to someone else.

2. Is your mission something that is shared and lived by everyone on your staff?

3. If you could take a picture, a hologram (a three-dimensional image of your school that records all of the patterns and interactions of the people doing the work, no matter what angle or perspective you look at), what would your school look like, sound like, or feel like, as you and your staff carry out the mission of your school? Make a list of what you see, hear, and feel. Put a star by those things that are already in place in your school or system. Put a check by those things that you would like to implement or explore further.

4. Select one or two ideas and list several techniques or changes that you can make to build a stronger mission. Think about the barriers that may get in your way, and list ideas that will help you alleviate or decrease those barriers.

5. How will you know that your staff members are sharing the vision, working diligently toward the goals, and accomplishing the mission?

6. How will you, as the leader, continue to keep your own boat sailing toward the distant shore (your vision) as you work to achieve your mission?

# 5

# Communication

*Using Shared Vocabulary
and Definitions to Clarify
Purpose Through Dialogue*

■ **PICTURE THIS**

*Joseph Smyth, principal, had just finished the faculty meeting from hell. It hadn't helped that he had arrived at the faculty meeting late because of an unexpected visit from the assistant superintendent who was scheduling the use of his high school cafeteria and gymnasium for the upcoming district "data fair." The assistant superintendent's timing couldn't have been worse, and Joe did everything he could to get through her agenda, until finally he simply handed her over to his secretary to order refreshments for the event from the food service program.*

*As he arrived in the library, the faculty meeting was well underway. Jerry Brown, the vice principal, was facilitating—big mistake! Although Joe liked Jerry and respected his consistency with discipline issues, Jerry had no people skills. He made a good "hatchet man" because of it, but he had a way of turning people off and shutting them down.*

*With Jerry taking the lead, the group had zipped through the first three agenda items and had landed on the topic of technology. As Joe entered the room, the boisterous sounds coming from several teachers filled the normally quiet space. Although he couldn't see who was shouting beyond the shelves of books, he figured it was the usuals—Carl Burnhart, David Johnson, and Maria Burrell, three of his most vocal and opinionated staff members. The teachers were engaged in a heated debate over how to spend the $45,000 the booster club had raised over the past year to purchase technology for*

*(Continued)*

87

(Continued)

*the high school. The rest of the faculty looked on, some with disgust, some with frustration, and several who really could care less about the entire conversation, since they didn't plan to use technology in their classrooms no matter how accessible it became.*

*Most of the teachers didn't even notice as Joe sat down at the table between his building technology coordinator, Dennis Hunter, and Mary Roberts, the English department chair. "We're in trouble," Joe thought, as he glanced first at his teachers' faces and then turned his attention to what had become a shouting match between several teachers.*

*"The $45,000 will go a long way to purchase the refurbished computers," David Johnson shouted. "We could put at least two or three computers into every classroom and still have enough left over for at least two labs."*

*Mary leaned over to Joe and whispered, "He wants to spend the money on the computers that Waldon Electronics Corporation is replacing. He thinks if we have them refurbished they will support the work that our students are doing."*

*Joe knew that Waldon Electronics was one of the biggest businesses in the state. He shivered as he remembered a similar horror story from a colleague in another district who had accepted refurbished computers from another corporation, only to spend more money paying to dispose of the computers than they spent originally to purchase them. This is not what Joe planned to discuss.*

*"No doubt, they will give us a good deal. What do they have to lose?" Dennis Hunter, the technology coordinator shouted back. "They could give those old dinosaurs away without charging a penny and still make money not having to dispose of them. What makes you think these computers will be any good? If they were, Waldon would keep them!"*

*Joe decided to slow the meeting down by interrupting, "I'm sorry I was late, but have you discussed other funding priorities? Jerry, did you share with them a copy of the minutes from our last building technology meeting?"*

*Jerry shook his head, "No."*

*Seeing this, Joe turned to Dennis and said, "Why don't you share with them the recommendation from the technology committee."*

*Dennis hesitated, because he knew that speaking out against three of the most vocal staff members could be the kiss of death. They were dead set on purchasing the refurbished computers. Carl wanted his own lab, no doubt about it. He knew that if they put in another lab, he would be able to claim it. Maria, who taught history by having students do one report after another, knew that having several computers in her classroom would make it even easier to continue to instruct without teaching. Before Joe had walked in, all three of the teachers had put their stakes in the ground on this issue, making it difficult for anyone else to speak up.*

*Dennis cleared his throat and thought, "Here goes nothing." Then he said, "At our last technology committee meeting, with a couple of our booster club parents, several students, and some of you . . ." and he looked around at the department chairs who sank further down into their seats . . . "We decided to use the $45,000 to purchase projectors, interactive SMART Boards, and DVD players." A silence that you could have cut with a knife fell over the room. Dennis continued, "Now that every teacher has at least one computer in their classroom, it only makes sense that we add interactive technology so we can take advantage of the computers we have."*

*"Oh brother," came a loud sigh from the back of the room as Frank Crowther, math teacher, turned the page of his newspaper as loud as he could.*

*"Yes, but we think the money can go a lot further by purchasing more computers for each of the classrooms," explained Carl Burnhart. "This is an incredible deal. Did your committee talk about that?"*

*"Yes," Mary Roberts, who wasn't afraid of anyone, spoke out. "But we want our students to use technology to enhance their presentation skills, especially on their senior projects. On the nights students present their projects, we borrow all of the projectors from the district and still need to rent some. We need the technology to support this work," she stated emphatically.*

*"Yeah, but who needs all those bells and whistles? SMART Board, indeed! What happened to good old poster board, markers, and glue? We have a chance to get more bang for our buck if we buy the computers," David Johnson added.*

*"Maybe, but who is going to support all those computers?" Dennis asked. "We will spend all of our time fixing those old dinosaurs and keeping them running. I, for one, don't have the time to keep fixing old junk. Neither does Waldon. Why do you think they're getting rid of them?" he asked.*

*"Why would you have to keep fixing them? They will be refurbished and upgraded," Maria added.*

*"We don't want yesterday's technology. Do you realize, we could buy new computers for a little more than what it will cost us to upgrade the hard drives and memory on the pieces of junk you're talking about?" Dennis asked.*

*"Then let's buy new computers," David suggested, thinking he was now going to get an even better deal.*

*"We don't want new computers, either. We want SMART Boards and projectors," Mary said. "It isn't just for senior projects. It's how some of us want to teach, especially since we have Internet access, and this equipment would give us interaction. Ask anyone who has taught a lesson using an interactive whiteboard. Kids get energized when they edit a document, highlight it, save the changes, and give copies to everyone before they leave class.*

*"Yes, but the more computers we can get, the more class time students will have to type their assignments. Every student should have a computer to use at school when they want it. Besides, who wants a SMART Board? Most of us wouldn't even know what to do with it, and some of us are too old to care," Carl shouted.*

*"It's easy. We can show you how to use it. Your students can type at home," Dennis Hunter argued back.*

*"You won't be able to get all of us a SMART Board and projector. But with this price we will be able to get a lot of computers," David stated emphatically.*

*"Dinosaurs," Dennis retorted.*

*Joe, who had watched this discussion go on way too long without Jerry stopping it, couldn't take it any longer. He stood up, not wanting to take the facilitator's job away from Jerry, but realizing that the group was stuck and there was no way to move them forward. Joe looked at Jerry and said, "I'll take over. Thanks Jerry."*

*Jerry nodded, glad to sit down. Joe looked at the group. "Again, I am sorry I am late. If I had been here, my intention was to have Dennis report what had been discussed and decided by the technology committee. I have already approved their recommendation, as has the booster club. This was only going to be an information item."*

*"Are you telling us that you have already decided to buy toys instead of computers—and pass up this great, once-in-a-lifetime price?" David challenged.*

*Jerry took a deep breath. He didn't like being put in this awkward position, especially with this group of teachers. "Yes, that's what I'm saying."*

*"It figures. You guys are always wasting our time. If you already decided what you were going to do, why did you let us go on for the last twenty minutes talking about it?" David shouted. "What a bunch of. . . ." He stopped himself, just in time, but everyone knew what he was thinking.*

*In a soft voice, Joe said, "I'm sorry I was late. Let's move on. The last item on our agenda is the new graduation requirements that are being tied to the statewide assessments."*

*David interrupted, "I bet you have already decided on that one, too. Just tell us what you did. You know our opinions don't count."*

*With that, there were loud "yeah" and "you tell him, David" comments that came from several of the teachers. Others simply nodded their heads.*

*"I was going to tell you that you do have an opportunity to influence the school board before they make their decision next month," Joe said.*

*(Continued)*

(Continued)

*"Yeah, just like last time when they decided to take out all of the vocational technical programs,"* Carl argued back.

*"That was different,"* Joe started, only to be cut off.

*"Yeah, right. That's what they always say. Just tell us what to do. Nobody wants our input anyway,"* Maria said in disgust.

*"I'm not going to stand here and argue with you. All I want to do is invite you to a meeting next Tuesday after school to meet with the superintendent, the school board chairperson, and several commissioners. This will be your opportunity to share with them your opinions about what they should do."*

*"What they should do is make kids take the assessments seriously and not let them graduate until they pass the tests. That will show them,"* David stated.

*"Yes, but if they do that we will have a lot of senior citizens running around the high school hoping to pass the test before they die,"* Maria chimed in.

*"Yes, but maybe their parents will take it seriously for a change and make them do their homework,"* Mary added.

Joe couldn't take it anymore. He could see the natives were restless, and he was getting nowhere. Over the top of the arguing, he shouted, enunciating every word, *"It is only an invitation to have a conversation about the issues before the district changes the graduation requirement policy. If you are interested, the meeting is next Tuesday afterschool at 3:00 in the library. That's it for today. Thank you everyone."*

With that, Joe walked to the back of the library, out the door, and headed straight to his car. *"I don't get paid enough to do this job,"* he thought to himself.

As he slid behind the wheel, turned on the ignition, and pulled out of the parking lot, Joe couldn't help thinking about the afternoon meeting. *"Why did the meeting take such a wrong turn?"* he asked himself. *"What am I going to do to get faculty to attend the meeting on Tuesday to express their beliefs and concerns about the new graduation requirements? How am I going to structure future faculty meetings so I don't find myself in such a hostile environment? How will I ever regain trust and credibility from faculty who saw me taking up their time to talk about something that was already decided?"*

As he turned into his driveway, Joe's head hurt. For once, he knew why.

## ■ WHAT IS COMMUNICATION?

Communication, in its purest form, is all about sending and receiving (encoding and decoding) messages from others. Whether we are speaking, writing, listening, learning, feeling emotions, or observing behaviors, we communicate with others by exchanging verbal and nonverbal cues and sound bites of information to create meaning and build rapport. Often the silence of what doesn't get said or done, or the tone in which messages are delivered, can be more powerful and have a greater impact on the organization than the words that are spoken. Thus, the old cliché, "Do as I say, not as I do." Or the importance found in the phrase, "Walk the talk."

Although communication is everyone's responsibility, the access, exchange, and transfer of information begins with the school leader. The leader is responsible for building rapport and trust, setting the tone, establishing communication channels, and determining what information gets shared, when, and by whom. The communication processes and structures that leaders build have the ability to cement relationships, build commitment, and inspire others to accomplish the school's mission. Likewise, when the communication processes and structures break down and become dysfunctional, they have the power to create a climate and culture that is lonely, vicious, fear-driven, competitive, and resistant.

Communication is the primary means by which people relate to each other. When effective, the means by which the adults in the school speak, listen, and learn from each other ensures that everyone understands the internal and external forces and issues that impact the school. It is from this shared understanding that teachers find meaning and purpose in the work they do and are inspired and motivated to contribute to and accomplish the school's mission. When the communication processes are ineffective, or adults within the school are inept in their use of appropriate communication skills, the work that the school leader hopes to accomplish can come to a dead stop.

For educators to work together to accomplish the school's mission, there must be clarity of purpose along with a shared and agreed upon vocabulary and definitions. There must be time during the school day for dialogue about the teaching and learning processes, as well as quality conversations that challenge assumptions, values, and beliefs and build consensus around those issues that matter. Most important, there must be time for educators to share their knowledge (tacit and explicit), talents, experiences, and expertise so they can continue to build capacity within the school system and learn from each other.

## ■ NEEDS MET THROUGH COMMUNICATION

This motivational factor is grounded in organization development (Schmuck & Runkel, 1994) and more recently by Senge (1990); Senge, McCabe, Lucas, and Kleiner (2000); and Sparks (2005a). It helps meet Maslow's (1998) esteem needs, Herzberg's set of motivators (as cited in Heller, 1998), Glasser's (1998a) choice theory, Deci's (1995) autonomy, Sagor's (2003) usefulness and optimism, and Perkins's (2003) feedback. (See Appendix A.)

## ■ WHAT COMMUNICATION IS AND ISN'T

Figures 5.1 and 5.2 (pages 92–94) will help to clarify effective communication. Figure 5.1 explains what effective communication is and what it isn't. Figure 5.2 compares the differences between a communication-supportive environment and a communication-deficient environment.

## ■ WHY IS COMMUNICATION IMPORTANT?

Before people become actively engaged and committed to the mission, they must first feel as if their ideas and interests are heard, understood, and respected by others. Within the entire school system, there must be a

**Figure 5.1** Effective and Ineffective Communication

| Effective Communication | Ineffective Communication |
|---|---|
| Sharing information with all key stakeholders in a timely manner. | Withholding information and giving it out on a need-to-know basis. |
| Giving and receiving constructive feedback. | Talking about others behind their backs. |
| Common language in the form of shared vocabulary, definitions, meaning, and purpose. | Unclear and ambiguous communication. Staff don't understand the message. |
| Immediate, specific, and accurate feedback. | Limited, general, and delayed feedback. |
| People are willing to work through conflicts and directly confront the situation/issues, not the person. | People are afraid to approach the person about the situation/issue, and gossip, backstabbing, tattling, and parking lot conversations are directed at the person. |
| People talk to and with others about the issue (face-to-face). | People talk about the issue to others (behind people's back). |
| Channels of communication are open, information flows both ways, and stakeholders are kept "in the loop" about matters that concern them. | Information is shared on a need-to-know basis. People are kept in the dark, and rumors run rampant as people guess about what is really going on. |
| Active listening—people feel their voices are heard and their ideas/opinions respected. | Distracting, diverting, minimizing, kidding, interrogating, ridiculing, or shaming. |
| Ability to suspend judgment and need for a specific outcome. | Judging, criticizing, disagreeing, blaming, and knowing the right answer. |
| Ability to listen to everyone and consider other points of view. | "Only my point of view or ideas are important. There is only one way to look at it or do it." |
| Ability to listen deeply to self and others for collective and shared meaning. | Listening and hearing only self and own ideas. |
| "Yes, and . . ." | "Yes, but . . ." |
| Respecting and accepting differences. | Knowing there is only "one right way." |
| Allowing all key people to participate in the processes that directly affect their work. | Ordering, directing, or commanding, "This is how to do it" or "We've always done it this way." |
| Allowing everyone in the room to have a voice, be recognized, and be heard. | Dominating the discussion, cutting others off, interrupting, or stopping the flow of conversation. |
| A willingness to separate the person from the issues. | Name calling, ridiculing, shaming, interrogating, judging, disagreeing, blaming. |
| Using effective communication skills to convey meaning and understand others (e.g., summarizing, paraphrasing, encouraging, asking open-ended questions, asking clarifying questions, checking perception). | Using ineffective communication skills that stop the conversations (e.g., judging, dominating the discussion, blaming, disagreeing, not paying attention). |

| Effective Communication | Ineffective Communication |
|---|---|
| Being present and focused on the speaker. | Thinking about other things, doing other things while the speaker is talking, side conversations. |
| Using "I" and "we" statements. | Using "you statements" to evaluate and criticize. |
| Initiating, contributing, elaborating, sharing opinions, energizing, and encouraging others. | Not acknowledging others. Remaining impervious and ignoring them. |
| Seeking opinions, seeking information, gate keeping, and observing others to understand them and their ideas/position. | Controlling or manipulating others. |
| Being aware of nonverbal cues. | Not paying attention to nonverbal cues. |
| Responding personally with "I," "our," or "we." | Respond impersonally by using "you," "it," or "they." |
| Expressing equality, collaboration, mutual trust, and respect. | Displaying superiority, using put-downs, being a show-off or know-it-all. |
| Directly reporting your own feelings. | Claiming to know how others feel. |

**Figure 5.2**  Structuring a Communication-Supportive Environment

| Communication-Supportive Environment | Communication-Deficient Environment |
|---|---|
| People have an established clarity of purpose, expectations, and boundaries. | People are confused, unsure, and do their "own thing." |
| There is a clear set of group agreements that form the norm and structures of collaboration and open, shared, honest communication. | There are no group agreements. The culture is one of isolation and closed communication, based on "need to know." |
| There is mutual trust and respect for others, especially as it relates to verbal and nonverbal communication. Leaders and others "walk their talk." | Communication is closed and one-way, Staff feels a lack of respect and trust. They question the honesty and integrity of the information or speaker. |
| All members will respect privacy and confidentiality. | Gossip, rumors, and back stabbing occur on a regular basis. |
| All members are willing to be candid, confront others when necessary, and give and receive constructive feedback. | People verbally attack others or talk behind their backs. |
| Conversations are centered on learning. | Conversations are centered on trivial and petty issues unrelated to learning. |
| Goals, expectations, performance, and feedback are clearly defined and communicated to all members. | Goals are fuzzy, expectations are unclear, and performance results and feedback are on a yearly basis at best. |

*(Continued)*

**Figure 5.2** (Continued)

| Communication-Supportive Environment | Communication-Deficient Environment |
|---|---|
| Leaders influence, inspire, and create meaning for others. | Leaders tell others what to do and how to do it. |
| Feedback is effective and provides learning and growth for individuals and groups. | There is no meaningful exchange found in feedback, and it often drives people apart. |
| Listen, listen, listen. Talk. Listen, listen, listen. | Talk, talk, talk. Talk, talk, talk. |
| Reflecting upon the conversations, paying attention to visual and mental notes. | When the conversation is over, forgetting it and moving on to the next conversation. |
| Asking clarifying questions, rephrasing statements, and checking perceptions to focus and further the conversations, understanding ideas, positions, and assumptions. | Ignoring ideas and suggestions. Casting them aside with just a word. |
| The focus of work-related conversations is on the mission and topics that make a difference. | The focus of work is on external forces that people can't control and blame for lack of results. |
| People are willing to share and challenge their own and other's assumptions, values, and beliefs. | People are closed and keep to themselves. They are uncomfortable talking about values and assumptions. |
| Probing others with questions to discover beliefs, assumptions, goals, and other ways of doing things. | "There is only one right way . . . mine!" |
| Ample time for teachers to have quality conversations on a regular basis during the school day. | No time during the school day to have quality conversations about the work teachers do. |
| Sufficient opportunities for teachers to share knowledge, talents, expertise, and continue to learn from each other during the work day. | No time during the school day to share tacit and explicit knowledge, expertise, talents, or to learn from each other. |
| Willingness to take risks, try ideas, offer suggestions. | "This is the way we have always done it." |
| Openness to ideas, suggestions, and feedback (positive and negative). Taking things seriously, discussing them, willing to compromise. | The only time people are given feedback is when there is something wrong. Feedback is negative. Unwilling to try new ideas or suggestions. |
| Quality of life is supported. | Quality of life is deficient. |
| Admitting when wrong, displaying flexibility and openness. | Expressing certainty, knowing all the answers, and taking sides. External locus of control and blaming others. |
| People are willing to collaborate with each other, make connections, compare and integrate ideas, and construct new meaning. | People are isolated, discourse is disconnected, there is no effort to connect ideas or to acknowledge other people's views. |

rapport based on both vertical and lateral trust and respect that has been built over time through honest, open dialogue. All members of the school must feel listened to and appreciated. When the channels of communication are open, and everyone is kept informed about issues that concern them by those at the top of the decision-making processes (i.e., superintendent to principals, principals to teachers, teachers to instructional assistants), people are more likely to feel included and thus become more willing and engaged in helping to accomplish the school's mission.

Effective, open, honest, reciprocal (two-way) communication is critical to the success of a school community. When communication is used effectively by school leaders, it has the ability to be a powerful spark and strong motivational and inspirational force. Great leaders use their voice to propel the mission, keep the vision alive, build passion and commitment, and sustain growth over time. Communication is the glue that holds the school community together and serves as the catalyst for moving it forward to achieve its goals. As many books on communication or organizational development and theory state, "Effective communication is essential for successful relationships and successful organizations" (Childre & Cryer, 1999, p. 82.). We need not say more.

## ■ STRUCTURING COMMUNICATION

School leaders with great communication skills integrate communication into everything they do. They are visible and accessible. They develop, clarify, and stay on message. They find ways to ask probing questions that open the door to further dialogue, discussion, and discovery. They stop rumors and gossip by addressing immediate concerns and issues, giving others relevant information as it becomes available instead of on a need-to-know basis. Most important, school leaders with effective interpersonal communication skills are active listeners. Whether listening comes from solicited probing questions or unsolicited spur-of-the-moment assertions, it is one of the most powerful strategies a school leader can use to motivate, lead, and inspire others. Often, teachers want nothing more than to have an administrator listen while they clarify their own thinking by hearing themselves talk or to have the administrator demonstrate that he or she cares enough about the teacher or their issue to listen and hear what is being said or felt. When asked, "What would you like me to do to help you?" many people will say, "Nothing. You just did it. I just wanted someone to listen."

Daniel Goleman (1998) describes communication as "listening openly and sending convincing messages." He says that people with this competence

- Are effective in give-and-take, registering emotional cues in attuning their messages
- Deal with difficult issues straightforwardly
- Listen well, seek mutual understanding, and welcome sharing of information fully
- Foster open communication and stay receptive to bad news as well as good (p. 174)

Effective school leaders find multiple ways to communicate with their staff and keep them informed by promoting the free flow of information. Many administrators do daily announcements (verbal and e-mail), weekly staff newsletters, common Web pages, and post information on bulletin boards in faculty rooms. They provide time for professional sharing during faculty meetings and common planning time. They find ways to have formal and informal conversations with staff members, ranging from planned faculty meetings and evaluation meetings to informal classroom observations and conversations over lunch. They keep their door open, except at times when they are dealing with confidential issues or deadlines that need their full attention. They are visible in the school; available when teachers, parents, and students need them; and follow through with issues they said they would investigate or promises of things they said they would do. When necessary, they use problem-solving strategies and facilitate conversations to help staff members work through constructive disagreements and conflict. Most important, school leaders model positive communication skills.

According to Bennis & Goldsmith (2003), schools, like most organizations:

> depend on shared meanings and interpretations of reality to facilitate and coordinate action. The actions and symbols of leadership frame and mobilize meaning. Leaders articulate and define what had previously remained implicit and unsaid; then they invent images, metaphors, and models that provide a focus of attention. (p. 124)

This essential communication process helps school leaders create meaning that emerges from thinking, challenges people's ideas of old conventions, and leads them to discover new directions, visions, and ways of doing business. According to Bennis and Goldsmith, this distinctive role of leadership is to help others "know-why" before they help them to "know-how" (p. 124).

Understanding the "why" comes first from building a shared vocabulary and shared definitions, so all people within the school setting are speaking the same language and their words have the same meaning. For example, pedagogical terms (such as mentors, closure, inquiry-based learning, technology, consensus, and the list goes on) have different attributes based on different interpretations, contexts, and uses. Once teachers have created a shared vocabulary and definitions, they can have the dialogues that build shared meaning and purpose and challenge and strengthen their assumptions, values, and beliefs. It isn't always easy for people to speak up, especially when core values, beliefs, and assumptions are on the table. Surveys show that 70 percent of people in the United States are afraid to speak up, and in other countries, it is even higher (Childre & Cryer 1999, p. 81). To do so requires a form of "authentic communication" which implies listening and speaking with "sincerity, security, and balance" (p. 81). Authentic communication requires that leaders and others first dig deep to discover and understand their own assumptions, values, and beliefs. Then, it requires listening deeply to what others think and feel and being willing to speak up and say what you really think. This is the only way to reach consensus and achieve a shared and collective meaning and purpose. Childre and Cryer (1999) suggest that to be effective there must be something much deeper than just effective communication. Leaders should develop the skills to use authentic communication to move their organizations from chaos to coherence. Authentic communication has the ability to "catapult speakers and listeners into a new dimension of clarity, resonance, and entrainment" (p. 82), thus causing something, some form of change, to occur.

The meaning and purpose created from authentic conversations, or what Sparks (2005a) calls "dialogue," is what leads to actions that have the ability to create deep and lasting change. This deep and lasting change is what Fullan (2005) and Marzano, Waters, and McNulty (2005) call second-order change, that is, the type of change that is needed to sustain school reform efforts.

In order to get to authentic communication, leaders need to be open to others in both how they send and receive messages. "Talking openly," according to Adam Kahane (2004), "means being willing to expose to others what is inside of us. . . . Listening openly means being willing to expose ourselves to something new from others" (p. 73). To do this is not always easy. One of the best techniques for suspending judgment, and really hearing what others are saying, is through the process of dialogue.

Dennis Sparks (2005b) makes a distinction between dialogue, discussion, debate, and argument. He says:

> Advocacy for a point of view is not part of dialogue, nor does it attempt to convince others that they are wrong. While these methods sometimes have their place, they often produce defensiveness, which is a barrier to the deep understanding and transformational learning that often accompanies dialogue. The assumption leaders hold as unquestionable truths often represent some of the most fruitful areas for dialogue because alterations in these assumptions can produce profound changes in behavior and relationships. When leaders listen with their full attention and truly honor a speaker's view and experience, relationships are deepened and individuals are profoundly changed. (p. 171)

Leaders can begin the dialogue process by posing their own assumptions and then asking others to think about what has been said in relation to their own assumption on a particular topic. This can be a powerful strategy for improving relationships, learning from each other, and creating shared meanings, purpose, and understandings. Leaders can use dialogue as the vehicle to structure professional development opportunities to engage all staff members in learning experiences about the things that matter most (i.e., what they believe, their assumptions, their values). This process doesn't, however, come easy for people, both in terms of opening up to each other and in terms of using the effective skills of dialogue. These effective skills of dialogue include:

> suspension of judgment, release of our need for a specific outcome, an inquiry into and examination of underlying assumptions, authenticity, a slower pace of interaction with silence between

speakers, and listening deeply to self and others for collective meaning. To those ends, we suggest focusing on shared meaning and learning, listening without resistance, respecting differences, suspending role and status distinctions, and speaking to the group as a whole. (Ellinor & Gerard, as cited in Sparks 2005a, p. 49)

Although people learn how to communicate with others from the moment they are born, effective communication is truly an art that takes a lifetime to perfect and achieve. As we all know far too well, there are many people who never have, or never will, become effective communicators. This is demonstrated by the number of dysfunctional relationships and communication breakdowns. Yes, unfortunately, even in the school setting.

Most school leaders have had classes and training in using "I-statements" and active listening exercises. We would suggest, however, that communication is much more than this. It involves emotional intelligences, especially that of empathy; multiple intelligences, especially interpersonal and intrapersonal relationships; and leadership skills, especially collaboration, conflict management, and decision making. Effective communication, primarily during meetings, requires planning the meeting and balancing the tasks with maintenance activities. We define the meeting *tasks* as the activities, projects, or work the group needs to accomplish. We define *maintenance* as the activities groups need to do to nurture, build, maintain, and sustain quality relationships. These include but are not limited to checking in (helping people feel welcome and included); summarizing the meeting; debriefing the group's effectiveness; consensus building; and team-building and community-building activities that help people feel a sense of identity, belonging, connectedness, and relatedness to the group. In other words, leaders need to hone and practice their skills to become adept at facilitating dialogue, planning and running effective and efficient meetings, communicating effectively with others in formal and informal settings, and using their interpersonal skills to help others build, develop, and sustain relationships.

We have provided a brief overview of the communication process. We believe it can be one of the most powerful tools for creating shared meaning and purpose and for inspiring, motivating and leading others to accomplish the school's mission. In this chapter, we have only begun to scratch the surface of ways to use communication to break down barriers and structure dialogue and meaningful conversations within the school setting. For further information, we have listed books we have found to be helpful in Appendix B.

## QUESTIONS FOR DISCUSSION

1. Think about the case study at the beginning of this chapter. It is obvious that communication among staff members is dysfunctional during the meeting. Before you read the rest of the chapter, decide what essential conditions are missing, and what, if anything, Principal Joe Smyth has the ability to change.

2. If you were Joe, what would you do to improve communication among staff members, especially during meetings, and rebuild the trust and credibility that Joe lost during the meeting above?

## ESSENTIAL CONDITIONS

There are several essential conditions that are not being met in the case study at the beginning of this chapter. Read along and see if you agree.

1. **Quality of life.** From the situation, it is difficult to tell what the quality of life is at the high school. What is apparent, however, is that teachers have little respect and trust for each other or for the administration. There are cliques of teachers who stick together as well as work against each other. The faculty is dominated by several people who rule in this culture, and whom others are afraid to speak up against. This most likely means that the essential conditions for quality of life and the basic needs of individuals, especially Maslow's (1998) security (i.e., risk-free environment) and social (collaboration), or Glasser's (1998a) choice theory (i.e., belonging, fun, power, and freedom) are not being met.

2. **Common language that utilizes a shared vocabulary and shared definitions.** It is clear that there is not a policy on the minimum specifications for accepting donated technology. If there were, it would provide the faculty with a shared definition and understanding of acceptable and adequate equipment that is capable of supporting teaching and learning. The faculty does not understand the cost involved in disposing of computers that are antiquated, nor do they understand how much time and support it takes to keep old equipment running. If they did, they would realize that the computers from Waldon are not a "good deal." There is also a communication breakdown between the technology committee and the faculty. The faculty have not been informed of the committee's work (i.e., minutes from the meeting).

3. **Clearly defined, articulated, and shared mission (including vision and goals) and understanding of boundaries, frameworks, standards, and expectations.** One of the most important responsibilities of the school leader, as well as a strong motivational strategy, is to "stay on message" by communicating the mission (the urgent, morally compelling, important work the school does) and helping people see the vision (what they can achieve and become) every chance he gets. Not once in this scenario did Joe or Jerry speak about the mission (including the goals and vision), nor did they use it to help the faculty understand the decision to purchase interactive technology. By simply telling the teachers that the decision was already made, without the rationale behind it (especially how the decision helps to further the goals and the purpose of their work), teachers view the decision as top-down. They do not understand why the decision was made to spend $45,000 on interactive technology, nor do they understand how it can help them achieve the school's mission. In addition to clearly articulating the mission, "All leaders need to be able to describe where they are going (vision), persuade people to come along with them (consensus), connect on a personal level (charisma), and demonstrate credibility, i.e., do what they say they will do (trust)" (Baldoni, 2003, p. xv).

4. **Honest, open, reciprocal (two-way) communication and access to essential information that allows staff members to do their work.** People need to feel that their voices are heard and their opinions are respected. By the end of the teacher's meeting, it is clear that most of the faculty do not feel that their voices are heard or their opinions respected. This is true, not just in this situation, but appears to be part of the culture of the faculty meetings, based on teachers rudely shouting out comments like "I bet you have already decided that one, too. Just tell us what you did. You know you don't want our opinions." It is obvious that Jerry and Joe did not speak before the meeting about how the meeting would progress. Jerry, who filled in for Joe, was obviously unclear what the goals were for each agenda item. This added to the confusion and stress of the teachers. If the faculty had been told up front which items were "action items" (and who would make the decision), or which items were for "information only," it would have eliminated the confusion and stopped the argument from happening during the meeting. In addition, the minutes and/or a report from the technology committee meeting were not shared with the faculty either before the meeting or at the beginning of the discussion. This also would have stopped the confusion and arguments. Sharing the minutes from the technology committee meeting would not only have kept teachers in the loop about the recommendations from the committee, but could serve as a means of educating faculty members about the use of computers, the minimum requirements, and how much technical support is needed to keep the equipment running. Finally, if the technology committee and the administration wanted to get teachers excited about interactive technology and/or to educate them on the possibilities of teaching with such technology, they could have set up a demonstration from a vendor or conducted their meeting in Dennis Hunter's classroom which was already equipped with a SMART Board and projector system. It is difficult to help teachers think about new possibilities without a model of what it could look like or how it could be used.

5. **A trustful (and trustworthy), respectful school culture with opportunities for everyone to express themselves through dialogue that is open and honest.** It is obvious that there was a lack of respect and trust among staff members. Only a handful of teachers spoke up, and some of those people were hesitant to do so, including Joe, the principal. The meeting was filled with shouting, rude comments, and arguments dominated by differing opinions. The free-for-all conversation was not structured in any way, nor was the technique of dialogue used to help people explore differing points of view.

6. **Freedom for all members of the school community to express themselves without fear and to be able to take risks and learn from mistakes.** Again, it appears that there is a culture that does not allow the majority of the faculty to express themselves or to speak up against the small, dominant minority without fear of retribution from those very vocal and controlling teachers. Although not stated, it would be difficult to take risks or try new ideas in a culture that is so oppressive.

7. **Norms of collaboration and a set of group agreements that all staff members hold sacred.** The way teachers spoke and behaved during the meeting demonstrated that there were no group agreements about meeting etiquette, especially in how they treated each other. Because of the lack

of respect that was demonstrated during the meeting, we suspect that most of the teachers simply close their doors and do their own thing rather than collaborating and working together to achieve the school's mission.

8. **Respect for divergent opinions and ideas.** The ability to suspend judgment, challenge assumptions and beliefs, and, when necessary, agree to disagree to achieve the school/district's mission. Again, there was no respect for divergent opinions. No one suspended judgment. There were numerous assumptions and beliefs about teaching and the use of technology that were left unexplored. Rather than agree to disagree, Joe simply stopped the conversation by stating that the decision had already been made, rather than helping to lead the group to understand why. In reality, because of how the meeting had progressed, the lack of shared information, vocabulary, and definitions (including how interactive technology could enhance instruction and engage students in learning), and the lack of defined minimum requirements for accepting used computers, it would have been difficult for Joe to do anything but stop the conversation by saying the decision had already been made. The way the meeting progressed, however, served to alienate the groups of teachers and move them further apart because of the way they spoke to each other. It further lessened the trust and respect for the administration because those teachers who argued for more computers (the losers in this situation) felt as if their time was wasted. They will be less likely to participate in future discussions and will be more likely to sabotage any efforts to use the interactive technology in the school because of their perceived loss.

## WHAT WOULD YOU DO?

1. After reading the above discussion about the essential conditions that need to be in place, do you agree? Is there anything else you would add?

2. Before you read the rest of the story, look back at what you said you would do if you were Joe Smyth. Is there anything else you would add to your list?

Read on to compare your list with what Joe chose to do.

## AND NOW FOR THE REST OF THE STORY

Joe sat in his office thinking about the meeting from the day before. It was a welcome relief when Mary Roberts poked her head into Joe's office. He knew he had a problem. He just wasn't sure what to do.

"Good morning, Joe. How's it going?" Mary asked.

"Not well," Joe sighed. "I am still upset with how the faculty meeting went yesterday. It wasn't good."

"No, it wasn't," agreed Mary as she walked into the office and sat down. "I can see that it is bothering you."

*(Continued)*

(Continued)

*"Yes, more than I even realized. I can't believe how badly people treat each other, and how few of them even seemed to care about anything, especially each other," Joe said. "It was like they were there only because they had to be."*

*"That's right, we did all have to be there. Most of them seem to have forgotten why we became teachers or what our school is all about," she said.*

*"Yeah, you're right," Joe sighed.*

*"And it didn't help that we just kept arguing about buying computers instead of interactive technology, when some of us already knew the decision was a done deal. Why didn't Jerry just announce that was how the money was going to be spent instead of letting people talk about it?" Mary asked.*

*"I guess I am to blame for that one," Joe said. "I was late because the assistant superintendent was in my office and I couldn't get away. Jerry and I didn't have time to go over the agenda before the meeting, so he was just helping out. I think, what I learned from this is that I need to make sure when the agenda gets typed up that I list what kind of item it is—whether it is an action item or information item—you know, what they teach you in your basic administration communication course." Joe saw Mary smile with recognition. "Have you taken that course, yet?" Joe asked Mary, knowing that she began the work on her administrative program during the summer.*

*"Actually, I am taking the course right now," she replied.*

*"I bet you have already talked about how to put an agenda together and run an effective meeting," Joe said, thinking back to when he took the course.*

*"Well, you're right. I think that was the second week of class," she replied. "You know Dr. Bailas, he moves right through his book. From what I hear, he doesn't change much from term to term. But he did talk about how important it is to spend twice as much time planning and structuring the faculty meeting than the actual meeting will take. Guess this is one of those times where, if you and Jerry had discussed the outcomes of the meeting before it got started, he would have known what you wanted to accomplish and done a better job of facilitating. I really don't think he knew what to do when everyone started shouting," she stopped. "Did he even know that the decision had already been made and that you were in the process of ordering the equipment?"*

*"Now that you mention it, no, I don't think he did," Joe said, with that "ah-ha" tone of recognition in his voice. "You're right. He didn't know."*

*"If I were him, I would probably be feeling pretty stupid and incompetent right about now," Mary said, speaking out loud. Then, just as quickly, she wished that she hadn't said it and bit her lip.*

*"You're right, Mary. I need to apologize to him for not finding the time to work with him more closely. I need to keep him in the loop about what is happening in the school outside his world of discipline. I should thank him for helping me out. We need to find a way to talk with each other more and work more closely as an administrative team." Joe thought for a minute. "Maybe it means building time into both of our schedules so that we meet every day."*

*"Every day would be nice, but is it realistic?" Mary asked.*

*"No, you're probably right. But we should be able to meet two or three times a week," Joe agreed. "What else have you learned from Dr. Bailas?"*

*Mary thought for a minute. "Oh," she said, "I know." Joe looked up at her. "Two weeks ago, Dr. Bailas did something he never did before."*

*"Well, that's a little out of character for him, don't you think?" Joe asked.*

*"Yes, I guess so. He is in the process of revising his communication book. Dr. Bailas has been reading about how corporations are using improvisation skills to enhance teamwork, leadership, and creativity. So, he invited actors from the Uptown Comedy Club to talk to our class about improv theater. They demonstrated how we could use some of the same skills they use in theater to help us be more effective administrators. It was really interesting and fun. Probably one of the best classes I have ever attended."*

"How so?" Joe asked curiously.

"Well, for one thing, they talked about several principles that improv teams use, such as a set of agreements and boundaries that they abide by. It looks unstructured when you watch them perform, but they trust each other to stay focused and within the moment of what is happening. They really listen and watch each other, especially the nonverbal cues. They have to really hear and see each other to be ready to accept the ideas that other people are offering to them in order to move the scene forward." She stopped, thought for a minute, and then said, "We played several different improv games during the night, but the most powerful lesson I learned was when we did an activity called "Yes, And."

Joe looked puzzled. "So, what was that all about?" he asked.

"It was simple. We got into groups, and they asked us to talk about an end of the term celebration we would like to have. Money was not an issue. We were supposed to take turns giving an idea about what we could do, but each time someone shared an idea, the next person had to start by saying 'no' and then give his or her idea for the party. So, the first person might say, 'Let's plan a dinner at Lenny's Cafe.' The next person could say, 'No, I want to eat at the Steak House.' The third person might say, 'No, let's have coffee and dessert at the Diner.'"

"Well, that doesn't sound like much fun," Joe said.

"You're right. But, after a few minutes, they stopped us and told everyone to do the same thing, only this time, each person needed to start by saying 'yes, but.' So, for example, I might say, 'Let's go to the Uptown Comedy Club for an evening of improv.' And the second person says, 'Yes, but if we do that, we won't be able to talk to each other.' And the third person says, 'Yes, but we really have nothing to say to each other, anyway.' And the fourth person says, 'Yes, but I wanted to show you pictures of my son's wedding.'"

"That doesn't sound like much fun, either." Joe said.

"You're right," Mary said. "So, the third time, they had us agree with whatever someone said and build off of it by starting with 'Yes, and.'"

"What do you mean?" Joe asked.

"I might say, for example, 'Let's go to dinner at the Olive Garden,'" and, the next person might say, 'Yes, and afterwards, let's go to the Uptown Comedy Club and watch an improv show.' And the next person might say, 'Yes, and afterward, we can invite the comedy club actors for a drink at the top of the Hilton . . .'"

At that point, Joe was getting into the conversation, and he interrupted with, "Yes, and, let's grab several bottles of champagne and have the limo driver take us around town to see the holiday decorations on our way to the Hilton."

"Wow," Mary said. "This is exactly what happened in class. The energy level during the first two rounds was dull and people were even getting upset with each other. But when we did the 'yes, and,' there was excitement and fun. Everyone added ideas. When they stopped us, we had a great party planned."

"I can imagine. I can't believe I jumped in and said that." Joe added.

"It's okay, it is kind of contagious," Mary said. "We know that when people begin with 'no' they are arguing. But it wasn't until I did this activity that I realized that when people say 'yes' and then add the word 'but,' they are really just saying 'no,' which in improv theater blocks any action, and in brainstorming and discussions stops the ideas from flowing." Mary hesitated for a moment.

"That is really powerful," interjected Joe. "I have never really thought about the fact that saying 'yes, but' means the same as saying 'no.'"

"Telling you this now has made me think that what we were doing at the meeting yesterday, when we were talking about how to spend the $45,000, was really a lot of 'yes, buts.' No wonder everyone was upset. We went round and round without accomplishing anything. We just got angrier and angrier at each other. When you stopped the conversation by telling everyone what had already been decided—well, I guess that was just the icing on the cake."

*(Continued)*

(Continued)

*"You're, right," Joe said thoughtfully. "I guess I owe some people on our faculty an apology, don't I?"*

*"That would probably help," Mary agreed.*

*"I wonder if it would help to go around and talk with people individually about how important it is for us to share our ideas with the school board and superintendent about graduation requirements."*

*"It couldn't hurt," Mary agreed. "At the same time, you might ask them what ideas they have about graduation requirements. That way you will have an idea before the meeting what they might say."*

*"That's a good idea. Plus, if they can't make it to the meeting, I can share their ideas." Joe hesitated and then continued, "I really hate to do this, but there are several outspoken teachers I need to talk to about their rude behavior at this meeting. No matter how frustrated or upset they were, their behavior at this meeting was unacceptable. I need to put a stop to it now, before it gets worse."*

*"You're right," Mary agreed. "It seems as if they are becoming more and more vocal at each meeting. Their yelling and rude comments are also making many of us feel uncomfortable . . ." She hesitated and then continued, "Quite frankly, many of us don't want to be at the faculty meetings or even in the same room with some of them!"*

*"I agree. Often, I don't want to be there, myself," Joe replied honestly. "Maybe it is time to develop some group agreements about meeting etiquette."*

*"Dr. Bailis would probably agree with you on that one," Mary laughed.*

*"Do you think members from the comedy club would share their improv strategies at our professional development day next month?" Joe asked.*

*"Hey, that's a great idea. I bet they would. I will get you their names and the phone number. I have their card back in my classroom. I was thinking about having them come and talk with my students. They said they did that kind of thing, so I bet they would work with our faculty. They had some really fun theater games to help people learn and practice dialogue skills, listening, being in the moment, accepting ideas, and supporting each other. All of this might even help us improve relationships—you never know, we could actually have fun on a professional development day—and maybe even start to like each other. Stranger things have happened!" Mary said.*

*"Great. I will stop by your classroom when I am out talking with faculty members today," Joe said. He stood up. "I think I will start with Jerry," he said. "I owe him, big time."*

*"Have a great day," Mary said.*

*"Yes, and," Joe paused for emphasis, then he smiled knowingly, "I'll see if I can get The Uptown Comedy Club actors here to work with our staff. Thanks again, Mary." She smiled back as she headed off to class.*

*Joe smiled, too, as he walked down the hall to find Jerry. He had learned an incredible lesson about planning ahead for meetings. He couldn't wait to call the comedy club and arrange to have them come and work with his staff. Joe was actually looking forward to learning improv techniques to help him improve communication and move his school forward.*

## CHAPTER SUMMARY

Communication is the primary means by which people relate to each other. Although communication is everyone's responsibility, the access, exchange, and transfer of information begins with school leaders. The communication processes and structures leaders establish have the ability to cement relationships, build commitment, and inspire others to accomplish the school's mission. Likewise, when communication breaks down and becomes dysfunctional, there is a strong potential that the climate and culture will become lethal.

For educators to work effectively together to accomplish the school's mission, there must be clarity of purpose along with a shared and agreed upon vocabulary and definitions. Dialogue can be a powerful tool to help educators share information and build consensus on issues that matter (i.e., assumptions, beliefs, and values). There are numerous books and resources, including organization development strategies and improv theater techniques, that can help school leaders improve the communication processes, build relationships, and facilitate effective meetings.

School leaders with great communication skills are visible, accessible, and use communication effectively to further the mission and keep the vision alive. They address concerns and issues immediately to stop rumors and gossip. They keep all key stakeholders involved and informed in decisions that matter to them. School leaders must be great listeners. At the same time, they must be open, honest, and share their voice, while helping others to find their own voices.

School leaders who use communication effectively to motivate their school community, *walk their talk,* and *talk their walk!*

## NEXT STEPS

1. Think about communication in your own school. What does effective communication look like, sound like, and feel like at your school? What would you like it to look like, sound like, and feel like?

2. Put a star by those things that are already in place in your school or system. Put a check by those things that you would like to implement or explore further.

3. Select one or two ideas that you checked above and list several strategies or changes that you can make to improve communication within your school.

4. Think about the barriers that may get in your way and list several ideas that can help you alleviate or decrease those barriers.

5. Decide on one or two things that you are going to implement at your own school or in your work because of this chapter. List them along with any notes to help you remember what you want to do.

6. Take a few minutes and reread "Picture This" at the beginning of the chapter. Highlight the "no's" and "yes, buts" you see in the text. Next time you are engaged in an informal conversation or meeting (e.g., lunch, IEP meeting, team meeting, faculty meeting, committee meeting, brainstorming session), pay attention to how many "no's" and "yes, buts" you hear. How do these words affect the outcome of the meeting or conversation? (For additional information and a full description of the activity you can use with others, visit www.optimalperformancemodel.com.)

7. If possible, discuss with others what you found interesting about this case study on communication and what you found challenging.

# 6

# Relationships

*Building the*
*Human Infrastructure*

■ **PICTURE THIS**

*As he left his office and walked down the junior high school corridor to the cafeteria, Austin Klien was hopeful. He had hired Dr. Judith Jenkins to help his staff build positive relationships with each other and develop the skills they needed to collaborate and work together.*

*Dr. Jenkins, a professor from the local university, had published several articles on collaboration and leadership that his superintendent, Bill Martin, had given to Austin last year to read. In a conversation during his final evaluation, Dr. Martin had highly suggested that Austin choose building a collaborative culture as his professional development goal for the coming year. Dr. Martin said he would like to see the Kennedy Junior High teachers develop collaborative, respectful relationships with each other. Dr. Martin believed that if the teachers were able to work as a team, it would go a long way toward helping to improve the overall climate of the school as well as the quality of teaching and learning. Dr. Martin had basically laid it on the line—either Austin would improve the culture of his school and the quality of working relationships among his staff or he would not be given tenure at the end of his third year.*

*This was Austin's second year as the principal of Kennedy. Even though he would not have an assistant principal for the school of approximately 450 students, he had been excited to take this position. He felt ready to be a principal. That is, until he began to interview each teacher before school started to get to know them and learn the culture of the school.*

*(Continued)*

(Continued)

*Austin quickly realized that every teacher had his or her own agenda. Each thought his or her subject was the most important. Teachers were willing to do only what they had to do. They didn't like innovation because, as most of them reported, everything that goes around comes around. If you wait long enough, "this, too, shall pass." Teachers didn't take risks and were hesitant to try new teaching strategies. They felt that student discipline was horrible, and they did not trust or feel supported by the administration. Information was shared on a need-to-know basis, and like so many public schools, resources were tight. The teachers talked about having to compete and beg for materials and supplies. Several teachers admitted that if they weren't so old they would change careers.*

*Austin didn't need to be reminded about how poorly his students scored on the statewide assessments. Last year, his school was the first in the district to be put on "the list" for failing to make adequate yearly progress in two cells, free and reduced lunch and special education. If only his teachers liked each other and treated each other with respect, he thought, as he entered the cafeteria. But maybe this was a turning point. If anyone could help them, he knew it would be Dr. Jenkins.*

*As Austin walked into the cafeteria and sat down next to a couple of his eighth-grade teachers, Dr. Jenkins smiled at him, even though she had expected him to attend the entire session. She knew it didn't bode well for the staff when they had to "sit and get" and the school leader was nowhere to be seen. She was, however, glad that Austin had finally decided to join them.*

*"Things appear to be going well," Austin thought to himself. Dr. Jenkins had set the agenda for the ten sessions she would be conducting with the school staff, established her expectations, and explained to the teachers that the goal was to structure collaborative study teams. She finished summarizing her overview of the differences between working in competitive, individual, and cooperative structures, and then announced that she had a cooperative group activity for the teachers to complete.*

*Before the session, she and Austin had assigned teachers to collaborative study teams. They had purposefully mixed up the staff, in order to break up the cliques, encourage collaboration, and build relationships across departments and grade levels. Dr. Jenkins read the names of the collaborative study teams and told the teachers they would be working together as a study group for the coming year. She suggested that they name their team. She formed the groups and asked each person to share three truths and a lie to see if their team could guess which of the four statements was the lie. Dr. Jenkins gave groups five minutes to complete the task before she asked groups to share. The comments were superficial at best, with most of the groups uncomfortable with the process. She heard a few snickers and jokes about this being "some kind of touchy-feely thing." The groups did not put much thought or effort into creating team names. One group even called themselves "The Undecideds" because they couldn't agree on a name. Dr. Jenkins told them that it was a starting place, and they could change their name anytime if they thought of something that fit better.*

*Dr. Jenkins then gave each group four articles to read, one for each member. She gave them twenty minutes to read their articles and highlight the important points about collaboration to share with their group. After each of the four articles had been shared, the teams were to develop their top-ten list of important attributes for how collaborative study teams work effectively with each other. During the process, they were encouraged to generate a list of questions they had along with important ideas or thoughts. Dr. Jenkins told the teams to be ready to report out to the entire group in ninety minutes.*

*With that, Dr. Jenkins took a deep breath, and began to watch as the whole group structure started to fall apart. Several teachers, including the entire Undecideds team, simply picked up their things and went to their own classrooms to work. Other teachers moved away from their groups but stayed in the cafeteria to read their articles. Only one group stayed intact while they read their articles independently. Austin, who had decided not to join a group, went back to his office to do some work. He figured he had ninety minutes until he needed to be back.*

*In all of her career, Dr. Jenkins had never experienced anything like this, but decided to sit back, wait, and watch the process. That is, until about a half hour later, when a couple of teachers came to her (like their junior high school students would do) and started complaining about the other two members of their group. Dr. Jenkins helped them get back on course by restating the group task. It wasn't long after that when another group became very disrespectful with each other and began shouting so loud that Dr. Jenkins felt she could no longer sit back and watch, but would have to step in and help. One of the teachers had grabbed the pencil and top-ten form. She had taken over the role of recorder and facilitator and was only recording the comments that she thought were important. It was clear that what she valued and believed about collaboration was not shared by the rest of her group. The other three members of the group were angry, and Dr. Jenkins had to intervene. She gave the team a new top-ten form and told them to use a "round table" structure in which each member of the team wrote two ideas that were different from the others on the list. If they could agree on the final two ideas, that was great. If not, their group would have only eight top-ten ideas about collaboration to report.*

*When the ninety minutes were up, only half of the teachers were back. Dr. Jenkins sent one person to the office to ask Austin to make an announcement to have all teachers return to the cafeteria. Austin made the announcement and, along with half of his teachers, dragged himself into the cafeteria.*

*The teams reported out, but Dr. Jenkins could tell that their hearts were not into the words they were espousing. It was a futile attempt at helping the teachers learn how to work collaboratively as a team. Dr. Jenkins could see the concern on Austin's face as each group shared their list. It wasn't so much what they said that was telling; it was what they left off their lists and didn't say.*

*The groups finished reporting. Even though Dr. Jenkins helped the teachers get through the content quickly, she had purposefully given each teacher a copy of the articles to put into their collaborative study team notebooks. She hoped that before her next visit, the teachers would review the articles.*

*Dr. Jenkins gave them one last assignment. She asked them to take a copy of the "People Search Bingo Card" she had pulled out of a notebook and duplicated while the teachers were working on the jigsaw activity. She told them that in order to play bingo and win some great prizes, the card had to be signed by teachers who could answer the questions in the bingo squares. Each bingo player needed to look for a teacher who could answer a question in one of the squares that did not already have a signature in it. If the teacher answered the question, he or she signed their name in the square. Bingo players continued looking for teachers to answer the questions until all the squares had a different teacher's signature. Teachers could only answer one question per bingo card, but they could answer the same question on a number of different bingo cards. In two weeks when Dr. Jenkins returned, players would need to be ready to share the answers each teacher gave to their questions, if they won a bingo. Dr. Jenkins wasn't sure how this group would react. Most people like bingo, especially if there are prizes. She hoped this group would be no different.*

*After she dismissed the group, she walked over to where Austin was sitting with his head in his hands. He was frustrated by what he had heard and decided he should start looking for a new job. There was no way he was going to get his teachers to collaborate. As Dr. Jenkins looked on, his face said it all.*

*Luckily for him, so did hers.*

## ■ WHAT ARE RELATIONSHIPS?

People need people. We all need to belong, feel wanted, and have a connection with others. Teachers are no different. They want to be contributing members of the school community. In fact, one of the most significant reform efforts is to increase the opportunities for educators to build and improve their relationships (Hargreaves, Earl, & Ryan, 1996) and work collaboratively and interdependently to accomplish their mission.

Until recently, most teachers have worked alone in their classrooms. All too often, they feel isolated, lonely, and disconnected from their colleagues, even within the same department or grade level. During the last decade, school leaders have worked hard to break down the barriers of isolation (Vojtek, 1993). The National Staff Development Council (NSDC, 2001), including a *Journal of Staff Development* columnist, Rick DuFour (1998, 2005) and NSCD member Shirley Hord (1997) have taken a lead in advocating for professional learning communities that provide collaboration and learning time for teachers embedded within the school day. Before staff members are willing and able to work, share, and learn from each other, school leaders must create the conditions that support cooperation, collaboration, collegiality, and shared decision making. For teachers to feel motivated to accomplish the mission of the school, they must feel united through a sense of belonging and purpose.

Just because we permeate the classroom walls (Vojtek, 1993) and structure time for teachers to meet, doesn't mean that educators want to work together, or even have the necessary skills to work cooperatively and collaboratively. School leaders must develop their own interpersonal skills in order to help others. They must also understand the stages of group development and build a repertoire of facilitation, team building, problem solving, and conflict management skills if they are to create and sustain a community of learners. School leaders must provide opportunities for all staff members to get to know each other, respect each other, and build a sense of affiliation so that there is "unity" within their school community and mutual trust among all staff members.

Trust and mutual respect do not happen overnight. It takes time, nurturing, and numerous interactions between people to build and sustain mutual trust and respect. Trust building happens one conversation or interaction at a time. Leaders must find ways to create the quality of life within their school, including a safe environment, so teachers are willing to have open, honest dialogues with each other to create shared values, goals, beliefs, and purpose.

School leaders must find a way to help teachers balance their daily work while simultaneously strengthening their relationships during small group, team, department, and whole school activities. One way to do this is to provide a regular meeting time, embedded within each school day, so teachers can work together in small groups to create, teach, and revise lessons. Collaborative planning, observing, coaching, and feedback helps teachers strengthen and build relationships while improving their teaching and instructional practices.

## ■ NEEDS MET THROUGH RELATIONSHIPS

This motivational strategy is based on Maslow's (1998) social needs; Herzberg's hygiene needs (as cited in Heller, 1998); Deci's (1995) relatedness; Glasser's (1998a; 1998b) love and fun; Sagor's (2003) belonging, usefulness, and optimism; Lundin, Christensen, & Paul's (2000) be present and make their day, and Covey's (2004) love. Fullan (2001; 2008) has also written a great deal on the importance of relationships as has DuFour and Eaker (1998). (See Appendix A.)

# ■ WHAT RELATIONSHIP IS AND ISN'T

Figures 6.1 and 6.2 on pages 112–113 will help to clarify relationship as a motivational factor. Figure 6.1 describes effective relationships that lead to collaboration and dysfunctional relationships that work against collaboration. Figure 6.2 compares the differences between a relationship-supportive environment and a relationship-deficient environment.

# ■ WHY ARE RELATIONSHIPS IMPORTANT?

Teachers, like all people, are motivated by the fundamental human need to be connected, to belong, and to be loved, recognized, and appreciated by others. In fact, through a meta-analysis of school leadership, Marzano, Waters, and McNulty (2005) have identified *relationships* as one of the twenty-one responsibilities of a school leader. They define relationships as the "extent to which the school leader demonstrates an awareness of the personal lives of teachers and staff" and suggest that "a case can be made that effective professional relationships are central to the effective execution of many of the other [21] responsibilities" (p. 58). During the current period of high-stakes accountability, with such a heavy emphasis on rewards and sanctions, the authors stress the importance of developing and using emotional intelligences to build strong relationships with staff members, especially through face-to-face interactions rather than through "bureaucratic routines." The most effective and "powerful incentives reside in the face-to-face relationships among people in the organization, not in external systems" (p. 59).

The research supports and emphasizes that teachers are more likely to learn when they work with others and "because of their interactions with others. . . . Teachers' attitudes, perceptions, behavior, and motivation to adopt new practices are affected by the quality of their connection to others—including students, school staff, and the larger community" (Dewey, 1958; Vygotsky, 1978; as cited in Jarrett-Weeks, 2001, p. 24–25). Numerous authors have written about the benefits of teachers working and learning together in study groups, through peer observations and coaching activities, collaborative inquiry, and action research. Fullan (1993) takes it one step further by suggesting that "There is a ceiling effect on how much we can learn, if we keep to ourselves" (p. 17).

"Recognition and satisfaction stem not only from being a masterful teacher, but also from being a member of a masterful group" (Little, 1990, p. 165). Professional learning communities are one powerful method of strengthening educators' commitment to reform and leading to continuous improvement in teaching and learning practices (Hord, 1997; DuFour, Eaker, & DuFour, 2005).

Collegial relationships strengthen and support teaching, learning, and school reform efforts while satisfying the basic human need of social interaction.

**Figure 6.1**    Effect of Relationships on Collaboration and Collegiality

| Effective Relationships That Lead to Collaboration & Collegiality | Dysfunctional Relationships That Work Against Collaboration & Collegiality |
| --- | --- |
| Teachers share resources and work cooperatively together to achieve shared goals and receive recognition. | Teachers work in isolation or compete against each other for resources, recognition, and achieving individual goals. |
| Teachers respect confidentiality and confront others about issues. | Teachers hold parking lot meetings, gossip about each other, and spread hurtful rumors. |
| Teachers move in and out of groups to achieve goals. | Cliques that form are ineffective as groups. They do not work with others outside their own circle. |
| Teachers are willing to deal with conflict to resolve the issues. | Conflicts stay hidden. Teachers are not willing to confront the issues. |
| There is a mutual respect among staff members. | There is a lack of tolerance for each other. |
| Teachers are able to separate the issue from the person to solve the problem. | Teachers are "nice" to each other. Problems get buried because they don't want to step on toes, hurt others, or make people angry. |
| Collaborative—willing to share and work together. | Competitive—trying to outdo and get "one-up" on each other. |
| Trust among staff members. | Lack of trust among staff members. |
| Honest, open, two-way communication. | Lack of honest, open, two-way communication. |
| Teachers are willing to work and share with all members of the school staff. | Teachers refuse to work or share with other members of the school staff. |
| Teachers share and challenge each other's beliefs, values, and assumptions. | Teachers withhold information. They do not listen to, share, care about, or challenge each other's beliefs, values, and assumptions. |
| Teachers help and share with each other. | Teachers work against each other. |
| All staff members feel included and connected to the school community and each other. | Staff does not feel included or connected to the school community and/or each other. |
| The school leader understands the stages of group development and helps staff work through the different stages. | The school leader lacks knowledge and skill to help others work through the stages of group development. |
| Staff members have developed knowledge, understanding, and skills of collaboration. | Staff members lack knowledge, understanding, and use of collaboration skills. |
| Strong interpersonal and collaboration (social) skills among staff members. People are willing to work together and put aside their differences in order to achieve goals and further the mission. | Ineffective interpersonal and collaboration skills among staff members. People are rude and are not willing to put aside differences to achieve goals or further the mission. |
| Teachers are willing to share and dialogue in meaningful ways about the things that matter most to them, including values, beliefs, and assumptions about curriculum, instruction, and assessment. | Teachers do their own work and keep to themselves. They are not willing to open up, dialogue about important issues, or share ideas. |
| Teachers genuinely care about each other. | Teachers either don't like or are neutral about their feelings toward each other. |
| School leaders genuinely like and care about their teachers. The feeling is mutual. | School leaders don't like or don't care about teachers. The feeling is mutual. |

**Figure 6.2**   Structuring a Relationship-Supportive Environment

| Relationship-Supportive Environment | Relationship-Deficient Environment |
|---|---|
| Quality of life is present. | Quality of life is missing. |
| Morally compelling school mission that all staff members can articulate, agree with, and share. | Lack of shared, morally compelling school mission staff members work to accomplish. |
| A clear balance of task and maintenance activities. | A focus on either task activities (work) or maintenance activities (too nice to each other). |
| Nurturing and supportive school climate. | Unfriendly and cold school climate. |
| Staff room, workroom, and other places where teachers can congregate are warm and inviting. | Teachers are afraid or do not feel welcome or comfortable in staff room or work room. |
| An established set of group agreements, and norms of collaboration and interdependence. | No set of group agreements, and a norm of competition or isolation among staff. |
| Individual and group accountability for achieving shared vision, mission, and goals. | Lack of accountability for achieving shared vision, mission, and goals. |
| Shared meaning and purpose. | Lack of shared meaning and purpose. |
| There is a strong school identity (e.g., slogan, mission, brand). | A sense of who we are and what we are about is missing (school identity and purpose). |
| Open, honest, reciprocal (two-way) communication. | Lack of communication. Information is shared on a need-to-know basis. |
| Appropriate resources, time, and structures to support and facilitate collaboration. | Lack of time, resources, and structures to support and facilitate collaboration. |
| Staff genuinely care and support each other. | Staff don't support or care about each other. |
| There is a balance between the tasks and maintenance activities. | People are so focused on the task they forget about each other or are so nice to each other they can't accomplish the goals. |
| Regularly scheduled times and processes to check-in with each other at the beginning of the meeting and debrief at the end. | Lack of structure or processes for checking in at the beginning of the meeting and debriefing at the end of the meeting. |
| Scheduled time for team-building activities and rituals, especially at the start and end of the school year, when people join or leave the staff. | No time for rituals or team-building activities. Team building is viewed as "touchy-feely" and a waste of time. |
| Teachers are recognized and feel that their contribution to the staff and the work they do is meaningful and important. | Teachers do not feel recognized, nor do they feel they make a contribution or feel their work is meaningful. |
| Teachers have opportunities to interact with each other inside the school, across the district, and beyond, to learn from each other and share successes and ideas. | Teachers work alone within their school, across the district, and beyond. They either do not have the opportunity or appreciate the opportunity to collaborate with others. |
| There is a shared interdependence and collective responsibility for working together to help "all of our students" learn. | Teachers are solely concerned with their own students and not interested in helping others deal with or teach "their students." |
| All staff members are engaged in decision-making and problem-solving issues that are directly related to the work they do. | Decisions are made and problems are solved by the administration with little or no input from staff. |
| Shared (group) focus on "getting the job done." | Individuals focus on "getting the job done." |

## ■ STRUCTURING RELATIONSHIPS

School leaders build and strengthen relationships—person by person, interaction by interaction, time after time. It is an ongoing, reciprocal process that takes a lot of work. Relationships don't just happen. Strong bonds won't last without purposeful maintenance.

From the first day on the job, school leaders must become aware of the personal needs of each teacher. Each staff member is unique, with his or her own set of knowledge, skills, experiences, background, and baggage. School leaders must get to know and come to understand each member of their staff like elementary teachers know and understand students in their self-contained classrooms. They must develop personal relationships with them by getting to know their families, the significant events in their lives, and personal issues within and outside the school setting (Marzano, Waters, & McNulty, 2005, p. 59). School leaders can do this simply by being visible, accessible, and by finding time each day to say "hello," and ask, "How is it going?" School leaders can also strengthen relationships by remembering staff members' birthdays and other special events in their lives; celebrating with them as they advance up the career ladder (e.g., degree, certification, tenure) or achieve personal success (e.g., marriage, baby); leaving positive notes when visiting classrooms; talking with them during lunch; and caring enough to listen deeply to what they have to say. These simple strategies work great for strengthening personal relationships.

In my (Rosie's) role as school administrator, I always think of myself as a "teacher of teachers." In this capacity, not only do I need to get to know each member of my staff on a personal basis, but I must also learn to recognize teachers' strengths and weaknesses. Only by getting to know each teacher will we, as school leaders, be able to encourage individuals to use their talents, interests, and strengths to refine those areas that aren't as strong. School leaders must work with teachers to achieve their individual goals, as well as working collectively with the entire school community, if we are to achieve our shared vision, mission, and goals. To do this, we must build the capacity and complexity of all staff members.

Collaborative relationships among staff members don't just happen. Just because administrators provide time and space for teachers to meet, doesn't mean that the teachers have *the will* (motivation) or *the skills* (competence) necessary to allow them to work together as an effective school team. To create conditions that support and strengthen collaborative relationships, school leaders must first create the conditions and provide the quality of life that we described in Chapter 3. Administrators must transform the school into a community of learners in order to successfully structure the opportunities that support and nurture the relationships that allow collegial learning communities to grow and flourish.

To "promote learning of high intellectual quality, a school must build the capacity of its staff to work well as a unit" (Newmann, 1996, p. 7). Often this requires school leaders to serve as facilitators or mediators when teachers find themselves in disagreements with colleagues. School leaders need to understand the stages of group development (i.e., forming, norming, storming, conforming, and performing), and build a repertoire of skills to help them facilitate collaboration, especially during the storming stages when members of the group try to fit in and keep their individuality while seeking to find a shared voice and influence within the group.

To help teachers build collegial relationships and develop skills for collaboration, there must be a strong balance between task activities and group maintenance activities. In Chapter 5, we define the meeting *tasks* as the activities, projects, or work the group needs to accomplish, and *maintenance* as the activities groups need to do to nurture, build, maintain, and sustain quality relationships. In order to build relationships, school leaders and teachers need to take time to check in with each other at the beginning of each day and/or the beginning of meetings. This doesn't need to be a long process, but simply a brief, "Hi, how's it going" conversation. If school teams and staffs are to get better at what they do, there must be a structured time throughout the year as well as at the end of meetings to provide feedback to each other by debriefing. School staffs, committees, or teams can do this by reaffirming what others are doing to move the school forward by making comments such as, "We appreciated it when you . . ." or "When you did ___ it really helped us to ____." They can also do this by posing questions such as, "What are we doing that is working well for us as a group?" or "What can we do to make our school or team work more effectively?"

The feedback teachers give and receive can strengthen and improve the group processes over time. Be forewarned, when teachers either don't get along with each other or are too nice to each other (they never reach that storming stage and are afraid to confront the issues because they might hurt another person), little will be accomplished.

In their book, *Why Teams Don't Work*, Robbins and Finley (1995) define a team as "people doing something together" and say there is "no single reason why teams don't work" (p. 10). Instead, Robbins and Finley list a number of problems ranging from poor leadership (e.g., confusing goals, bad policies, poorly structured procedures, unresolved roles, lack of vision, negative team culture, insufficient feedback, poor communication and lack of information, lack of resources, the wrong tools, ill-conceived reward systems) to interpersonal relationships (e.g., mismatched needs and personal agendas, personality conflicts, unwillingness to change, poor communication skills, lack of commitment, and lack of trust) (p. 14–15). The authors suggest that the first step is to identify the situation that is causing the team to be dysfunctional. Then leaders must take steps to understand and improve the team's effectiveness and build commitment and relationships. School leaders must build a repertoire of strategies they can use to help teams improve their *will* to work together and their *skills* to accomplish the task.

As we mentioned in Chapter 5, communication can build or destroy relationships, especially integrity and trust. School leaders must "walk the talk" and "talk the walk." In other words, to build and sustain mutual trust and respect, administrators must have a clearly defined message and stay on topic. What they say must be congruent and aligned with what they do if they are to be trustworthy and respected by their faculty and staff. Leaders must model what they expect others to be. To build relationships, it is important for school leaders to do perception checks as well as check for understanding. Robbins and Finley (1995) make the point that misunderstanding, or the "I know you think you understand what you thought I said. But I am not sure that what you heard is what I meant" syndrome, "often occurs for the simple reason that the individuals involved are communicating on two different wavelengths. How you communicate with others is influenced to a very large degree by what kind of person you are—by your behavioral style" (p. 52) They suggest that to prevent miscommunication, leaders must know their own behavioral styles as well as the styles of the people they are leading. Robbins and Finley state, "It requires that we relearn how to communicate with others in a way that is cognizant of their differing natures and sensitive to their needs" (p. 52–53). In other words, if school leaders are going to communicate effectively, they must develop those relationships that help them know and understand each adult working as part of the learning community.

Covey (2004) writes:

> When we seek to expand our influence and inspire others to find their voice [the 8th habit], we move into the world of relationships. Building strong relationships not only requires a character foundation of inner security, abundance and personal moral authority. . . . but it also involves stretching ourselves in developing vital new interpersonal skills that will make us equal to the challenges we will face with others. (p. 161–162)

Covey continues his discussion by saying that there is nothing faster than the "speed of trust." He says:

> When trust is present, mistakes are forgiven and forgotten. Trust is the glue of life. It is the glue that holds organizations, cultures and relationships together. Ironically it comes from the speed of slow. With people, fast is slow and slow is fast. (p. 162)

It takes time and effort to build and sustain relationships that lead to what Covey calls the "third alternative," what Fullan (2008) calls the "we-we solution" (p. 49), or what we call later in this book "positive interdependence"—the ability to discover "the we" and find the "middle position" that allows a learning community to use empathetic listening, to create synergy, and work together to accomplish a shared mission.

As you will learn in the chapter on positive interdependence, you can't "artificially force interdependency—it has to come naturally through people's getting to know and understand and trust each other" (Covey, 2004, p. 214). Then, Covey explains, people can become innovative and creative. Until the connection and relationships that are built over time happens, "people see interdependency as dependency" (p. 214). Ironically, leaders can structure the process by putting people together in the same room and provide time, but they can't force the relationships.

School leaders must help teachers build affection, or a genuine caring for each other. All members of the school community need to be included and connected to each other if the school is going to work to their optimal performance level and accomplish the school's goals. One way to help teachers feel that connection is by creating a shared identity centered around the school's mission, in much the same way as a manufacturer creates a product brand and slogan. Often, school leaders select a message and give staff members pins, mugs, bumper stickers, and even t-shirts to build identity and a sense of belonging.

For collaborative relationships (i.e., teams, groups, committees, departments) to be successful, school leaders must help all groups to create an identity and work cooperatively together. School leaders must understand the stages of group development and learn how to facilitate and nurture the group during each of the stages. They must also understand the importance of balancing the tasks of the group with the maintenance of the group. Successful groups aren't just "task oriented." They get the job done, but still structure time at each meeting to build, maintain, and sustain relationships. Most important, school leaders ensure that all adults within the learning community have a voice; feel included, equal, and important; and are essential, contributing members of the school community.

To do this, school leaders must build and strengthen relationships—person by person, interaction by interaction, time after time. They must also help the people they work with do the same.

## QUESTIONS FOR DISCUSSION

1. It is obvious that the relationships among staff members at Austin Klien's school are dysfunctional. Before you read the rest of the chapter, decide what essential conditions are missing, and what, if anything, Austin has the ability to change.

2. If you were Dr. Jenkins, what suggestions would you make to Austin? What does he need to do if he is going to improve the relationships and build a collaborative culture at Kennedy Junior High School?

## ESSENTIAL CONDITIONS

There are several essential conditions that are not being met in the case study at the beginning of this chapter. Read along and see if you agree.

1. **Quality of life (as defined earlier).** It is unclear from the scenario what the quality of life really looks like. It appears, however, that the basic needs of individuals are not being met, especially the social needs. The environment is not supportive, nor are there adequate resources. In fact, the superintendent, Dr. Martin, has said that unless Austin improves the culture, which for us is defined by the quality of life within the school, he will not earn tenure. This leads us to believe that Austin needs to begin by meeting the needs of all individuals as well as improving the climate and making the environment more supportive. Finally, he needs to build mutual respect and trust among all staff members.

2. **Morally compelling school mission.** Although not explicitly stated, this appears to be missing. There does not seem to be a morally compelling, clearly articulated and defined meaning and/or purpose for the important work that is shared and accomplished by all. In fact, most of the

teachers are only concerned about themselves and their own subjects or programs. Teachers are working in isolation, competing for resources, and little, if any, of the responsibilities for the work are shared.

3. **A balance between task and maintenance activities.** Although people go through the day-to-day tasks, we suspect that there are few maintenance activities. In fact, when Dr. Jenkins structures the activity of learning about their members and naming their group, some of the teachers snickered about this being "touchy-feely" stuff. If collaboration were the norm, the teachers would enjoy getting to know each other better.

4. **Open, honest, reciprocal communication.** It is stated that communication is on a "need-to-know" basis. We suspect that in this culture there is a lot of gossiping, backstabbing, and numerous parking lot conversations. Teachers had a difficult time discussing the content of an article and reaching consensus on the top-ten ideas. Can you imagine what might happen if they were to have a dialogue about topics that matter most (i.e., beliefs, values, assumptions)?

5. **Culture that is cooperative and conducive to collaboration.** The culture is structured to support independent teachers who compete for resources and accolades. There is no sense of interdependence. Teachers do not respect each other, nor do they want to work together.

6. **Interdependence.** There is no clear reason for teachers to feel compelled to work together, nor is there a structure for them to feel supported and drawn to help each other. In fact, from what was said or not said in the situation, the teachers probably closed their doors, did their own thing, and never had a reason to collaborate. We suspect that there have been few, if any, situations in which teachers worked together.

7. **Accountability that requires all members to work to achieve the mission.** Although test scores are low and the school is on "the list" for not making adequate yearly progress in two cells, Austin and his teachers do not seem to be concerned. So far there appear to be no consequences from above, and little effort on the school's part to improve student learning. Austin has not established high expectations, nor is he holding anyone accountable for achieving results. There is no compelling reason for teachers to work together to achieve school goals.

8. **Mutual respect, trust, and trustworthy school environment.** The case study explicitly described the lack of mutual respect or trust. It is clear that staff do not trust the administration or each other. We suspect because of this no one is viewed as being trustworthy either.

9. **Time, resources, and structures that support and facilitate collaboration.** This does not appear to be in place. Most of the teachers did not, for example, stay in a group to achieve the collaborative goal of creating a top-ten list. Even if time, resources, and structures had been in place in the school, it is clear that the teachers had not taken advantage of them and do not understand how to collaborate. In fact, based on the breakdowns among several groups, the teachers are probably lacking the skills (i.e., interpersonal, teambuilding, conflict management, and emotional intelligence) necessary to work well together. This is also true of Austin Klien. He did not model, nor did he participate, in the collaboration process.

## WHAT WOULD YOU DO?

1. After reading the above discussion about the essential conditions that need to be in place, do you agree?

2. Before you read the rest of the story, look back at what you said you would do if you were Austin Klien and/or Dr. Jenkins. Is there anything else you would add to your lists?

Read on to discover what Austin does and how Dr. Jenkins helps him.

## AND NOW FOR THE REST OF THE STORY

*Dr. Jenkins sat down next to Austin. He looked up at her. "So, what do you think?" he asked, afraid to hear the answer.*

*She hesitated, choosing her words carefully. "I see why you asked me to come work with your teachers. They haven't worked together much, have they?"*

*"I'm not sure what happened before I became principal, but it was difficult to get them into the same room, let alone talking to each other," he said.*

*"I can tell," mused Dr. Jenkins. "I don't think they know how to work together. I suspect it is because they have never had a reason to need each other. I can't tell if they don't like each other, or if they just don't know each other. I suspect the latter. What do you think?"*

*Austin thought for a second. "I don't know, either," he said. "I haven't really thought about it. They seem friendly enough, one-to-one, but most of them eat lunch in their classrooms. I seldom see them having friendly conversations."*

*"That's kind of what I suspected," Dr. Jenkins said. "They were cordial enough and on their best behavior during my presentation. But as soon as I put them into groups—well, you saw them. It didn't take long before they fell apart," she said. "Usually when I facilitate group activities, I have trouble getting the teachers' attention back. They don't have the luxury of getting to talk to each other. Most groups really take advantage of the time to share things about themselves or even ideas about the articles. From the beginning, your staff acted like they did it because they had to do it—not because they wanted to."*

*"You're right, I don't think they wanted to be here," Austin said.*

*"Part of the reason may be because . . ." and she stopped, bit her lip, took a breath, and then continued, "You didn't want to be here either, did you?"*

*Austin looked up. "What do you mean?"*

*"You didn't think it was important enough to be here either," she said.*

*"What makes you say that? I hired you, didn't I?" Austin asked.*

*"Usually when people spend 'big bucks' to bring me in to help them, they want to make sure that they have established the purpose for why I am here. They say so in their opening remarks. Today, I waited to get started, and finally, when I realized you weren't coming, I introduced myself. It was clear from the looks on the teachers' faces that they were here because it was a contracted, every other Tuesday afternoon, professional development day. But the teachers didn't know why they were learning about collaboration or the purpose behind the study groups. I tried to give them reasons, but they needed to hear it from you."*

*(Continued)*

(Continued)

"Oh," Austin said. "I knew what you were doing. I didn't think it mattered if I was here. The school was quiet, and I decided I could get something done."

"True, but in the scheme of things, what mattered most? Something I have learned from experience is that when the principal is involved, the activity is valued and believed to be important. For a principal to make a difference, he must be visible, build relationships, communicate the message, and model the behavior. Unless your teachers see you doing whatever it is that you are asking them to do, you can spend a bazillion dollars on staff development, and it won't make a bit of difference. As their school leader, they are looking to you for direction, meaning, and purpose. When they saw that you were in your office doing things that needed to get done, many of them followed your lead and used the ninety minutes in their classrooms to grade papers and plan lessons. When they didn't come back, and I had to send someone to get you to make the announcement, it put me in an awkward position. Even if it wasn't true, it left the impression that the work we were doing was just filling time and wasn't important. If that's the case, I am willing to let you out of your contract, and you can find someone else to come in and be your presenter." She didn't like saying it, but Dr. Jenkins knew that she had to lay it on the line.

Austin's face turned bright shades of pink. She was right. He could see his teachers didn't take this seriously. The entire effort to build a collaborative culture and collegial relationships had gotten off to a bad start.

"I am so sorry," he said, not able to let his eyes meet hers. "I had no idea that my absence from your presentation would have such an impact and carry such a hidden message. No wonder the teachers aren't willing to work together. I guess, as their leader, I am not very cooperative or collaborative either."

"Well, I didn't want to be the one to say it, but…" her voice trailed off.

"You aren't the first," Austin admitted. "I just don't know what to do anymore. I wasn't going to tell you, but my first year didn't go well. At my final evaluation, Dr. Martin told me he would not be able to offer me tenure if I didn't build a cooperative and collaborative culture at Kennedy. After reading several of your articles, I thought I could invite you in to work with the teachers, and you could fix everything. Guess it's not that simple," he said.

"You're right and you're wrong," she said. "Let me ask you a couple of questions. Try to be honest, and don't get defensive. I just want to try to help."

"Sure," he agreed, thinking he had nothing to lose.

"First, how well do you know your teachers? Who are their family members? Where did they grow up? What do they like? Who did they pick to win the World Series? What is their favorite food? Or hobby? Or vacation spot? What are they passionate about? Let's just take anyone on your staff, for example. How about Jack Snow, the science teacher. What do you know about him?"

Austin looked surprised. "I think he is married, but I'm not sure. He is probably excited by science; he's good at getting the students involved in hands-on experiments. But," he stopped. "Guess I don't know much about him, do I?"

"Let me ask another question. What is your typical day like?"

"I come in, turn on my computer, check my voicemail, e-mail, and pray there aren't any major problems from parents or students. Somehow, the morning just flies. There's always so much paperwork to do. I just can't seem to get out of my office. And by lunch, I have so many discipline referrals that I spend the rest of the day dealing with kids. By the time I leave school, most everyone is gone. Unless they stop by the office, I rarely see anyone," Austin admitted.

"As I thought," Dr. Jenkins said. "Let me ask you a couple more questions. Do you respect and like the people you work with? Do you trust them to do their jobs? Even more important, do you like being a principal?"

Her questions surprised him, and he really had to stop and think. "You know," he said, "there are times when I think that I am the luckiest person alive—to be a principal. When I took this job, I wanted so much to be able to make a difference for the students and teachers. I wanted to help get our test scores up and make sure that our students got the best education we could give them *so they can do whatever they want and lead successful lives. But, since I have been here, there isn't a day that goes by that I haven't wondered why no one else cares. I see the teachers coming to work every day, just like me. They go through the motions, and when I ask them, they talk like they care. But I feel like we just aren't doing it." He stopped, and then continued, "I haven't thought about whether or not I like the staff. I guess I just figured they work here, and that was that." He stopped. "I barely know them. I rarely see them, except during assemblies, or if I am doing an observation, or someone has a problem they want me to fix—and then it's like, whoa, slow down. They act like it's my job to fix everything."*

*"You're right. You can't fix everything, even if you are the school leader," she agreed. "You need to be a school community. It takes everyone, working together, if you are going to become a high-performing school. Let me ask you one more question. And please, don't just give me the answer you think I want to hear, because I don't care either way," she paused, and then continued. "Do you really want to be the principal of Kennedy Junior High? Not just do you want to get tenure. Do you really want to be the school leader and turn this school around?"*

*What a question. It sucked the breath right out of his lungs. It took him a few seconds to gain composure, and then he unequivocally said, "Yes. I want to be the principal and make a difference." It was the first time he said these words out loud, and it surprised him. "Is it too late? Can I turn this school around?"*

*Dr. Jenkins smiled. "You have the potential and the ability to be just what your school needs. But, as I said earlier, you are right and you are wrong about what I can do to help you. I don't have the power to fix anything," she paused, "but you do! I can help you change the culture, but you have to do the work."*

*"What do you mean?" he asked.*

*"Relationships can only be made between the people in the relationship. I can facilitate and mediate, but I can't build your relationships for you. You have to do that yourself. The first thing you need to do is get to know your staff. You may know them for the role they play at your school as teachers, but you do not know them as people. You need to get to know them by having frequent conversations with them—and let them get to know you, too. You need to give them reasons to trust you and find you trustworthy. You need to give them opportunities to prove that they are trustworthy, too. You need to show them that you respect them and appreciate them. Most important, you need to model for them what you want them to become.*

*"How do I do that?" Austin asked.*

*"You've asked the right person," Dr. Jenkins laughed. "I love this stuff. You probably wondered why I gave everyone that bingo card assignment."*

*"Yes, as a matter of fact. It wasn't something that we planned," he said.*

*"It's because I realized that your teachers don't know each other very well. You can't just put people together, into forced situations, and expect them to work together efficiently and effectively. They need time to get to know, trust, and gain respect for each other. So, I gave them the first of several team-building assignments, to help them get to know each other by finding out things they have in common," she said. "That is, unless you don't want to do this?"*

*"Oh, I do. I think it is a great idea," Austin said.*

*"I was hoping you would say that, because I want you to do it, too. In fact, I want you to get into the spirit of it and really make it fun! Even if you have all of your squares filled in, I want you to make sure to check in with each teacher to see how their squares are coming along. In fact, put out a special bulletin, on bright paper, and say that you will give a prize to the first three people who show you their completed bingo card. Then, when they show up with it completed, make a big deal as you give away the first, second, and third prizes. Have fun with it."*

*"But what can I give them?" Austin asked.*

*Dr. Jenkins could see that Austin had never done anything like this before. "It really doesn't matter," she said. "They are going to like anything. Give them a Starbucks gift certificate, chocolate, a six-pack of coke, or a duty-free pass."*

*"Or a 'leave when your student's leave' early bird pass," he suggested.*

*(Continued)*

(Continued)

*"You got it!" Dr. Jenkins laughed. "And now for your homework. Here is a pencil, write it down." She handed it to him. "Before I return in two weeks, I want you to have gone out of your way to do the following: (1) Begin every morning by saying 'hello' to each teacher and asking a question, such as 'What did you think of the game last night?' or 'What plans do you have for the weekend?' (2) On a staff member list, write at least three things that you have learned about each person by his/her name, so that you can share it with me when I come back. (3) Make sure to get into each teacher's classroom at least once. You do not have to stay long, five–ten minutes. But notice something special he or she is doing and leave a note on that teacher's desk telling what you saw, and how it is helping students learn. (4) Bring donuts or some kind of special treat to the staff room and leave a 'Just because of all the things you do' kind of note. (5) Make sure to have lunch in the staff room at least five of the next ten days, and spend time talking with the teachers and getting to know them on a personal basis. (6) If teachers are not eating in the staff room, or even if they are, pick a day and have pizza and salad delivered to your school. Watch how many teachers show up to eat. Make sure you are there during the lunch period and get to know them. (7) Think about the message you want to convey. It could be something like, 'Together, we can.' Whatever it is, make it your slogan for the year—what you want your school to become. "Teacher Appreciation Day" is in a couple of weeks. There are tons of catalogs and Web sites selling products with messages like this. Find a pin, a mug, a pen, or a tablet with the slogan on it. Give it to all of your staff members during that week. And, when you give it to them, publicly thank them in front of the students for all they do. You can do this at an assembly or just going around from class to class. (8) Finally, find time for meaningful conversations that focus on getting to know your staff and having them get to know you. The teachers may want to talk about students or things they need. That's okay. Just make sure that if you promise something, you follow through. That's how you build trust and gain respect. Can you do that?"*

*"I think so," Austin said. "It looks fun—like I am not really working."*

*"Oh, but you are. The most important thing for you to do right now is to build relationships with your staff. They need to see you as a person, and you need to see them in the same way. The biggest mistake administrators make is that they think they can put people together and they will collaborate. That is so not true! All too often, when you look closely at school teams, you see nothing more than forced collaboration. Leaders can't build a collaborative culture unless they have established relationships among staff members. People don't have to be best friends, but they have to be collegial, and they have to care about each other, and it really helps if they like each other. It also helps if they have a reason, like your low test scores, to put their heads together and figure out how they can do a better job of helping students learn. But that will come later. First we have to build the relationships that will get people talking with each other."*

*"I guess I jumped the gun by having us talk about collaboration." Dr. Jenkins thought out loud. "If it's okay with you, I would like to spend the entire next three-hour session working on team-building activities. What I will do is model some ideas they can use with their students. Between you and me, I am doing it as much for the teachers as I am for the teachers to use the activities with their students. After all, in order to teach it, you have to know it."*

*"I think that is a great idea," Austin said. He liked what he was hearing.*

*"Yes, and, there is one more thing I need to ask of you," Dr. Jenkins said.*

*"Sure, fire away," Austin said, grabbing his paper and pencil to write.*

*"I want you to introduce me at the next session, explain why I am here, and what you hope to accomplish. Not that you want to keep your job, but your vision for how you want your staff to work together. And when you are finished, I want you to stay and be a part of everything we do," she said.*

*"You got it. But I expect to win one of those bingo prizes," he laughed. In a serious tone, he said, "Thanks. I am looking forward to your next visit."*

*"So am I," said Dr. Jenkins, and she meant it.*

## CHAPTER SUMMARY

School leaders build and strengthen relationships person by person, interaction by interaction, time after time. It is an ongoing, reciprocal process that takes a lot of work. Relationships don't just happen. Ultimately, the only people who can build relationships are those people involved in the relationship. School leaders can structure the process by putting teachers together in the same room and by providing time for them to work together. But they can't force the relationship. Until leaders have built relationships among and between staff members, the best they can hope for is forced collaboration; instead of positive interdependence they will have dependence. Administrators must model the behaviors (e.g., trust, respect, reciprocal communication, trustworthiness) they want their staff to use. School leaders need to understand the stages of group development so they can facilitate and support group processes when necessary and as appropriate. The "speed of trust" is slow. Relationships built on mutual respect and trust take a long time to build. Time and effort are needed each day and at each meeting to build, maintain, and sustain relationships.

## NEXT STEPS

1. What do the relationships in your setting look like, sound like, and feel like? Define what you would you like to see, hear, and feel so that strong, effective relationships will be firmly embedded in your school community?

2. Put a star by those things that are already in place and a check by those things that you would like to implement or explore further.

3. Select one or two ideas and list strategies or changes that you can make to improve relationships in your current situation. What barriers may get in your way? Make a list of choices that can help you alleviate or decrease the barriers.

4. If possible, discuss with others what you find interesting about this case study on relationship building and what you find challenging.

# 7

# Accountability

*Creating Ownership and Mutual
Responsibility to Accomplish the Mission*

■ **PICTURE THIS**

*The warm, summer day was going well, that is, until Lynn Taylor, principal of a large K–5 elementary school, opened the mail and was once again reminded that her fourth-grade students had failed the statewide assessment in reading and writing. The fact that the same students were number one in the district, with over 85 percent of the students meeting the standards in mathematics, had no effect on the reaction from central office. David Preston, the superintendent, was livid, not just with Lynn's test scores, but with the entire district's performance. Just as school ended in June, the test scores were released by the state. Several days later, Lynn had been surprised with a visit from Dr. Preston. He flashed several unflattering graphs of her student's performance in front of her. His message was clear. Only 45 percent of her school's fourth-grade students achieved proficiency in reading and 56 percent achieved proficiency in writing on the state standards assessment. Although far from the bottom, for the first time since becoming the principal eight years ago, her school was not the top ranking school in the district. Dr. Preston said he expected her school's scores to carry the district. He blamed Lynn for the low district average. Dr. Preston demanded answers. Caught off guard, Lynn had none.*

*(Continued)*

(Continued)

*This was the third year since the district had begun the massive effort to create a comprehensive accountability plan that would, as promised by outside consultants, improve teaching and learning throughout the district. Now, heads were flying as central office reacted to the worst scores the district had seen in over five years. The school board was asking hard questions, especially after fighting the city so hard for funding. They had promised patrons that the millions of dollars spent each year on this massive restructuring and accountability effort would greatly improve student scores. After all, the new district mission, strategic planning, and stretch goals had been front-page news for the past several years as patrons debated the exact wording. The new accountability system was expected to bring incredible results and learning gains. Instead, as the latest headlines in the paper proclaimed, the district achieved just the opposite.*

*Dr. Preston was blaming Lynn and her teachers for bringing the district's average reading and writing scores down. As the letter she held in her hand stated, if Lynn and her teachers were not the top scoring school in the district in reading and writing on next year's statewide assessment, he would "move her and/or her teachers." She knew Dr. Preston was serious because, during the first weeks of summer break, he had already transferred several principals to different schools and was in the process of reconstituting another elementary school.*

*Lynn felt as if she had just had the wind knocked right out of her as she sat clutching the letter tightly in her hand. She worked so hard to build a culture in which the teachers helped their students achieve to their greatest potential. Lynn knew that the teachers respected each other and got along well with each other. They still tended to close their doors and work independently, but as long as each teacher made sure his or her students met the district benchmarks, Mrs. Taylor was content with the status quo. Until now, that had been the case.*

*Lynn's school community had been included in the district's process for creating the accountability system. Many patrons in the district, however, believed that even though a lot of time, money, and effort had gone into creating the document, it would have a shelf life of only a few years before it, too, passed away. Each summer, like all district administrators, Lynn wrote the yearly report and presented it to the school board at the August meeting. It was simply a part of her job, having very little meaning or impact, because until this year, Lynn's scores had remained steady and high for the district. It was simply a ritual that Lynn found to be "one more thing on her plate to do."*

*As Lynn thought back over the year, she knew in her heart that the latest test scores didn't reflect how hard individual teachers had worked each day to help their own students learn. Reading and writing were both target areas in the school's action plan. Last year the teachers had been trained extensively to use the newly adopted curricular materials in both areas, yet her students did not perform as everyone had expected. The school's motto, "Reach for the stars," summarizing the school's mission of setting high expectations and holding all students accountable for achieving to their greatest potential, was definitely not reflected in these latest test scores. How would Lynn face the parents? What would she say to the teachers and staff? Most of all, how would she lead, motivate, and inspire her teachers to improve student scores when morale all across the district was at an all-time low due to depressing test results, upheaval, and knee-jerk reactions from central office? How could she help the teachers when she wasn't even sure how to help herself?*

## ■ WHAT IS ACCOUNTABILITY?

Almost everyone you ask will tell you that schools should be held more accountable. But accountability means different things to different stakeholders:

For policymakers, accountability usually seems to mean that students perform well on tests. For teachers, it is often defined as working hard to meet the needs of students. For parents, it may mean simply that their wishes are listened to. For some educational critics, it means that if students are going to be held to higher standards, the public should provide the resources that give all students an equal opportunity to learn. Thus, while the accountability movement pushes forward with considerable fanfare, behind the scenes multiple perspectives and conflicting agendas are clashing, with uncertain results. (Lashway, 2001, p. 3)

Our purpose is not to debate the issue of accountability, but to explain how accountability can be used as a motivational strategy and is an essential condition for other motivational strategies (i.e., mission, empowerment, autonomy, results).

For us, accountability means that *educators take ownership and responsibility for successfully achieving their target goals to accomplish their school's mission. They hold themselves and each other responsible for student learning as measured by results that demonstrate student achievement.*

To be held accountable for teaching and learning, educators need feedback about their performance, which should come from a clearly defined and articulated evaluation process that includes self-reflection as well as outside observations, analysis, and feedback. They also need feedback about student learning, which should come from assessments that are objective, valid, reliable, and aligned with clearly articulated and shared standards and curriculum.

Being accountable means that school leaders hold themselves and others responsible for reaching target goals and achieving results. Leaders do this by clearly defining and articulating all of the elements of the school's mission. They create ownership, establish high expectations, share pertinent information just-in-time, provide adequate and appropriate resources and support, communicate feedback about performance, and ask others only to do what they are willing to do themselves. Most important, school leaders who use accountability as a motivational factor must clearly articulate the target (vision, goals, standards, and indicators of success) so others can see where they are going. They must stay the course and build momentum for the morally compelling purpose (mission) and help everyone to recognize and celebrate their successes when goals are achieved and results are actualized.

The literature is full of information about using data to make decisions. Many people equate statewide assessment results with accountability and even interchange the two terms (that is, assessment and accountability). They are not, however, the same thing. In fact, if administrators are going to use accountability as a motivational strategy, or as an essential condition for one of the other nine motivational strategies, they must fully understand what, why, and how to structure accountability.

Accountability (or the data from assessments that are used as measures of accountability) can be constructive or destructive, depending on how the data are used. It is destructive when educators feel afraid, victimized, or blamed for making a mistake because it can destroy morale, school climate, and motivation. We agree with Kurt Landgraf, president of Education Testing Service (ETS), who reportedly said, "We've got to stop using assessments as a hammer and begin to use them appropriately as a diagnostic learning tool" (as cited in Olson, 2005, p. 7). In addition, participants at the ETS 2005 Conference argued that, "Far more attention has been paid to using tests as an accountability tool, and to sort and classify students, than to shape what actually happens in classrooms" (as cited in Olson, p. 7). When it is used constructively, accountability can be a "key for increasing trust, reducing fear, and improving morale and performance" (Samuel, 2001, p. 23). Therefore, we will present several guidelines for administrators who are using accountability as a strategy to motivate staff.

First, *accountability begins with school leaders* who are responsible for helping teachers see and understand the big picture and share the morally compelling purpose that determines the work they do. Teachers won't take ownership or responsibility for something they don't know, understand, or feel competent in performing. School leaders must spend each day clarifying the vision, clearly articulating the mission, asking questions that provoke thinking and action, and linking research to practice. They must make sure teachers have the knowledge and skills necessary to perform the tasks. School leaders must define what success looks like so everyone recognizes and celebrates when it happens. School leaders are models of what they want others to be. They make time to roll up their sleeves, get their hands dirty, and walk the talk. When teachers fail to help their students succeed, school leaders need to first ask themselves "why" before they either blame others or become victims of their own lack of self-efficacy and locus of control.

Second, administrators need to be especially cautious when the only indicators of success are from summative, one-shot, high-stakes test data. Accountability plans must use *multiple sources of data to triangulate the results* if teachers and school leaders are to be held accountable for achieving gains in student learning. There are far too many variables involved in measuring student learning to base all of one's decisions on one set of data or test score.

Third, *data is not knowledge.* Simply creating a data-rich environment does not mean that one is using information in a deep, purposeful, and meaningful way to transform teaching and drive instruction. School leaders need to know what data are important to collect and analyze to avoid *analysis by paralysis,* a condition in which groups get bogged down with too much information, failing to make decisions because they can't agree on what to do (Samuel, 2001, p. 54). This, by the way, is taking its toll on teachers and administrators in much the same way that the comprehensive strategic planning process did in the early 1990s (Vojtek, 1993). As many educators can attest to, once strategic plans were completed, vision statements were hung on school walls and action plans were placed in beautiful binders on administrators' shelves like trophies collecting dust. Likewise, data are collected, recorded, and even analyzed, but the results are abandoned before they are used to inform instruction. Far too often, even before teachers have time to use the information they gleaned from the last data set, the process begins again by either reassessing the same information and/or assessing something different.

As Figure 7.1 illustrates, educators need to realize that raw data is simply that, raw. It needs to be digested through analysis to become information that can be transformed into knowledge to inform instruction and apply the wisdom that has been learned to accomplish the desired goals.

**Figure 7.1**   Data to Results

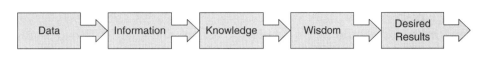

Recently, at a statewide administrative workshop, one administrator said to a group I (Rosie) was participating in, "If I hear about data one more time, I am going to pack—it—up." In their book, *Sustaining Leadership*, Hargreaves and Fink (2006) define "sustain" as "to hold up; bear the weight of; be able to bear (strain, suffering, and the like) without collapse" (p. 23). In many schools throughout the country, Hargreaves and Fink report, "The education standards bubble is about to burst. In fact, in a number of places—the United Kingdom, Australia, and many parts of Canada—it already has" (p. 10). One reason for its demise is that schools cannot sustain the overload of assessments and data that is collapsing an exhausted system of workers. In addition, school districts are discovering that they have exceeded their capacity of current data warehouse space and must reinvest in additional data storage.

To avoid analysis by paralysis, *less is best.* We have to get smarter about the number of goals we set, the data we collect, and how data is used. When teachers are overwhelmed with too much to do, they may not know where or how to begin. We need to help them prioritize and focus on the most important work first. One way to do this is with SMART goals. Conzemius and O'Neill (2006, p. 13) state that even though SMART goals have been used in other industries for over twenty years, educators are beginning to recognize their power and potential. Blanchard, Carlos, and Randolph (2001b) state:

> [T]hat for goals to be useful, meaningful, and motivating, each should answer five key questions that make goals SMART.
>
> S  = Specific: "What am I going to do?"
> M = Motivational: "What is in it for me?"
> A  = Attainable: "Can I reasonably expect to achieve it?"
> R  = Relevant: "Why am I doing this?"
> T  = Trackable: "How will I assess ongoing progress?" (p. 88)

There are different versions of what the SMART acronym means. We have included our favorites below. After the prioritized SMART goals are in place, teachers must find meaning in the data, making data actionable so that the information informs teacher practice and benefits student learning.

SMART Goals

S  = Specific, Strategic, Significant, Stretch
M = Measurable, Meaningful, Motivational
A = Attainable, Agreed-upon, Action-oriented, Achievable
R = Realistic, Relevant, Results-oriented, Research-based, Reasonable
T  = Time-bound, Timely, Trackable, Tangible

Once validated by results, this information becomes knowledge that transforms instructional practices and leads to optimal student and teacher performance. This knowledge is then shared with others across departments or grade levels inside the school and district and disseminated to a wider audience. To create deep learning and meaningful changes that lead to optimal performance, school leaders and teachers must have time within each school day to make meaning and sense of the data—transforming data into actionable information that leads to the knowledge and wisdom that furthers their mission.

*Slow is becoming the new fast.* Carl Honore (2004) reports there is a *slow* revolution taking place. Many people who are living on the edge of exhaustion as their hectic lives spin out of control are finding ways to slow down the pace and live healthier, happier, more productive lives. Like the tortoise, from an Aesop's fable story record of *Tortoise and the Hare* I listened to repeatedly as a child, said to the hare, "I may be slow, but I am sure." If teachers and school leaders are going to be held accountable for accomplishing their mission, the entire process must be slowed down. They must have time to analyze the data, learn from it, and use it to make informed decisions that transform practices before they are collecting data again. As many researchers and schools are discovering, "Results reach a plateau when speed matters more than substance" (Hargreaves & Fink, 2006, p. 14).

Finally, school leaders and teachers need *a better understanding of assessments.* They need to understand when and how to use formative assessments, or what Stiggins (2004) calls "assessment for learning," and when to use summative, or "assessment of learning." Formative assessment should be used as just that, to inform the teaching and learning processes each day. When teachers use formative (e.g., short, quick, mini-diagnostic) assessments everyday to make decisions about student learning, they realize and comprehend what their students know and are able to do. At the 2005 ETS Conference, James W. Pellegrino, a professor of cognitive psychology and education at the University of Illinois at Chicago was reported saying:

> If assessment is going to be particularly powerful in achieving enhanced learning outcomes, then it is at the classroom level that we need to focus our attention. . . . As instruction is occurring, teachers need information to evaluate whether their teaching strategies are working. (as cited in Olson, 2005, p. 7)

Teachers do not need to purchase formative assessments that are designed and produced by test companies and marketed as "assessments for learning" (Olson, 2005, p. 7). Formative assessments need be nothing more than a quick review at the beginning of each lesson or a quick check for understanding at strategic places within the lesson (e.g., several questions that relate to the learning objective; a review of the main idea, concept, or essential question; one or two sample math problems to see if they can perform the calculation or understand the process). Formative assessments, like quick Response To Intervention (RTI) probes, are not "trick" questions designed to stump and confuse students. Instead, formative assessments are carefully scaffolded throughout the lesson or unit to make sure students are "getting it." Teachers should begin each lesson with a brief formative assessment to review what students have retained and stop frequently during the lesson to check for understanding. When they do both routinely and effectively to inform their daily instruction, summative assessments can be just that—summative, like climbing a mountain, they describe peak (overall) performance.

Assessments of learning, or summative assessments, simply evaluate students after the learning has taken place, when it is too late to affect instruction. As Hargreaves and Fink (2006) suggest, we should reduce the "excesses of standardized testing" (p. 15) by using summative assessments as one component of an evaluation process. Doing so means that every student does not need to take every test. As in research, students can be randomly stratified to collect samples of student work to gauge how our systems are performing. When teachers use formative assessments to drive instruction on a routine basis, students are confident when they sit down to take summative assessments and educators are not surprised by the results.

Hargreaves and Fink (2006) contend that often it is the teachers that get in the way of understanding student learning. They write:

> Sometimes the biggest impediment to understanding learning is not peoples' fixation with testing but their excitement about teaching. After spending time sitting in the classroom of underperforming schools, Harvard professor Richard Elmore discovered that teachers are sometimes so excited about and committed to their teaching they don't really notice how or whether their students are learning. Teachers, he says, actually teach too hard! They give themselves no time or opportunity to step back, watch, and then respond to how their students are actually learning. (p. 32)

Hargreaves and Fink (2006) suggest that "A more sustainable strategy is to focus on learning first, then achievement, then testing, so we never lose sight of the learning that truly matters as we strive to increase students' achievement in it" (p. 32). In order to do this, they suggest two "elements of leadership for learning": (a) "deep and broad learning that satisfies our greater hunger for human growth and betterment," and (b) "slow knowing that curbs our tendencies toward being fast school nations" (p. 32).

## ■ NEEDS MET THROUGH ACCOUNTABILITY

This motivational strategy is the foundation of the standards and accountability reform efforts in education today. It helps meet the needs as describe by Maslow's (1998) esteem needs, Herzberg's set of motivators (as cited in Heller, 1998), Sagor's (2003) competence, usefulness, and optimism needs, and Covey's (2004) legacy. (See Appendix A.)

## ■ WHAT ACCOUNTABILITY IS AND ISN'T

Figures 7.2 and 7.3 on pages 132–133 will help to clarify accountability. Figure 7.2 explains what accountability is and what it isn't. Figure 7.3 compares the differences between an accountability-supportive environment and an accountability-deficient environment.

**Figure 7.2**   Effective and Ineffective Use of Accountability

| Effective Use of Accountability | Ineffective Use of Accountability |
|---|---|
| Taking ownership and responsibility for accomplishing the school's mission. | Feeling lucky or blaming others for accomplishing the school's mission. |
| Pride and accomplishment for work. | Apathy and indifference toward work. |
| High standards without standardization. | High standards and standardization. |
| Teacher behavior that is congruent with student learning and methods of assessment. | Lack of alignment between teacher behavior, student learning, and assessment methods. |
| Educators are empowered to make decisions that directly affect their ability to get results and held responsible for their actions. | Educators are told what to do and how to do it, and then held responsible for results |
| Evaluations support the school's mission and are based on criteria that are realistic, objective, clearly defined, and understood. | Evaluations are subjective and inconsistent, often based on whether or not the evaluator likes the evaluatees and/or their work. |
| Empowerment and sense of efficacy. | A "gotcha" feeling of powerlessness and being victimized. |
| Continuous feedback and knowledge of results is shared with all educators and students. | Feedback and knowledge of results is limited and/or nonexistent for educators and students. |
| Specific, immediate, authentic, accurate, and ongoing feedback. | Little or no feedback. |
| Clearly defined target with shared goals, expectations, and indicators of success. | "Guess what I want, and I will check to see if you are right and you reached the target." |
| Just-in-time training—resources, support, and competence to accomplish goals. | "Just do it" without training, adequate resources, or support to accomplish goals. |
| Interdependent structure—"we are all in this together," and a "together we can" attitude. | Competitive or independent structure—"I win and you lose" or "I lose and you win" attitude. |
| Sense of efficacy and internal locus of control—"we can and do make a difference." | Lack of efficacy and external locus of control—"it doesn't matter what we do." |
| Autonomy to do the work within clearly defined boundaries and framework. | Often given a script, pacing guide, and told what to do and how to do it. |
| Data is analyzed and information is shared. Knowledge is used to make informed decisions. | Data is collected with little or no effort to use it to inform decisions. |
| The school's mission is aligned with the district's mission. Resources, expectations, assessments, and evaluations are congruent. | Little if any alignment exists between the school and district missions. There are misinterpretations, misinformation, and misalignments between resources, expectations, and evaluations. |
| There is continuous feedback and support to all members of the school community based on data analysis and results. | Little if any information is shared or communicated to members of the school community based on data analysis and results. |
| Educators hold themselves and students to high standards without standardization. | When educators hold themselves to standards and expectations, they are usually unclear and subjective. |
| Communication is open, honest, and reciprocal. Information is shared with all stakeholders. | Information is tightlipped and on a need-to-know basis. |
| Everyone is responsible, individually and collectively, for the school's mission results. | No personal or collective investment or responsibility is held for accomplishing the mission. |

**Figure 7.3**   Structuring an Accountability-Supportive Environment

| Accountability-Supportive Environment | Accountability-Deficient Environment |
|---|---|
| Quality of life as defined in Chapter 3 is evident. The basic needs of all individuals are met, including adequate resources and support. | Quality of life is not present in the school. Basic needs of all individuals are not met, especially adequate resources and support. |
| The elements of school mission, as defined in Chapter 4, are aligned, clearly defined, articulated, and shared. | There is confusion, misunderstanding and lack of consensus or support for the school's mission. |
| The essential conditions for supporting a school's mission are present. | The essential conditions for supporting a school's mission are missing. |
| There is a shared passion and joy for accomplishing the school's mission. | There is apathy and/or no commitment for accomplishing the mission. |
| Interdependence and collaboration. | Competition and isolation. |
| A continuous improvement cycle is utilized with formative and summative assessments that collect quantitative and qualitative data. | No structure for continuous improvement. Data is collected without thought. There is data overload with analysis paralysis. |
| Ample embedded regularly scheduled time to collect, analyze, study, plan, implement, evaluate, refine, and celebrate interventions. | Data are collected, with little or no time to analyze, study, plan, and implement interventions before the new data is collected. |
| A climate of mutual respect and trust allows educators to take risks without fear of failure and retribution from mistakes. | People are afraid of making mistakes, taking risks, and failure. |
| There is explicit knowledge and understanding of expectations (vision and SMART goals) for achieving success. | There is confusion and lack of information about expectations (vision and goals) for achieving success. |
| Educators and students have explicit knowledge and understanding of the indicators of success (e.g., criteria, rubric). | The target (vision and goals) keeps changing with no indicators of success or mental picture of the desired results. |
| Communication is honest, open, and reciprocal. Information is shared with all stakeholders to make informed decisions. | Information is withheld and shared on a need-to-know basis. Rumors and gossip are the norm. Peopie are afraid to speak. |
| Just-in-time opportunities for real-time professional learning to insure competence. | One-size-fits-all models of staff development that often are events. |
| Professional development and learning that build capacity, complexity, and growth for the individual as well as the organization. | Inservice training that is planned by others because they "don't know what they need." |
| Educators take ownership and responsibility for their own professional growth and learning. | Staff development is planned by others, often central office, "to them, for their own good." |
| Collaboration time is regularly scheduled and embedded within the school day. | There is little, if any, time for sharing, learning from each other, or collaboration. |
| A collaborative culture that includes decision making, consensus, and interdependence. | The culture is competitive. Teachers feel isolated with little support from others. |
| Celebrations of success are frequent and efforts are recognized and appreciated. | People are not recognized and success is not rewarded or celebrated. |

## ■ WHY IS ACCOUNTABILITY IMPORTANT?

Accountability closes the gap between our intentions and our actions. When we take responsibility for our actions, resulting in either positive or negative outcomes, we come to understand that if we want different results, we need to choose a different course of action (Klatt, Murphy, & Irvine, 2003, p. 1).

Likewise, "People play differently when they're keeping score," (Covey, 2004, p. 284). No matter what sport or street game is being played, when players don't keep score, they often joke around, aren't as focused, and don't take the game as seriously as players who are keeping score. Covey says this happens at work, too:

> Without crystal-clear measures of success, people are never sure what the goal truly is. Without measures, the same goal is understood by a hundred different people in a hundred different ways. As a result, team members get off track doing things that might be urgent but less important. They work at an uncertain pace. Motivation flags. (p. 284)

Motivation is diminished.

Covey says also that a scorecard helps workers to establish clear measures of success and to see the results of their efforts. He describes the scorecard as a "tremendous motivating power." The scorecard provides

> [an] inescapable picture of reality. Strategic success depends on it. Plans must adapt to it. Timing must adjust to it. Unless you see the score, your strategies and plans are simply abstractions. So you must build a compelling scoreboard and consistently update it. (p. 284)

In schools, a school improvement accountability report or annual school report card serves in a similar capacity. The results on the report card or in the accountability report tell the story and the school's "score." It answers the question, "How are we doing?" Some districts in the state of Connecticut, for example, used a "Science Fair Model," in April 2006, to present their data and results on poster boards in a public venue cosponsored by the Connecticut Association of Schools and the Connecticut State Department of Education. Some Connecticut school districts, such as Bristol public schools, have also used this model to communicate their progress toward achieving their accountability goals in a public forum to patrons of the district.

Marzano, Waters, and McNulty (2005, p. 55–56) report that the most powerful single motivation, and the simplest prescription for enhancing and improving education, is *feedback.* They list twenty-one responsibilities of school leaders, the core of which is to create a system that monitors and evaluates the "effectiveness of school practices in terms of their impact on student achievement" (p. 55). They state that school leaders must "continually monitor the effectiveness of the school's curricular, instructional, and assessment practices" (p. 56) and be "continually aware of the impact of the school's practices on student achievement" (p. 56).

Feedback about performance and knowledge about the results of an individual or group's efforts is a powerful motivational factor. Madeline Hunter (1967, p. 27) defined knowledge of results as feedback that answers the question, "How am I doing?" or "How are we doing?"

"The answer," Hunter said, "has a powerful influence on our state of motivation. . . . The more specific the feedback we get, the more we become motivated to improve our performance" (p. 27). This feedback from an objective, clearly articulated and agreed upon evaluation process should be constructive, continuous, and timely. It should provide information to teachers about what they are doing well and how to refine their current practices to make them even more effective. Teachers should be given ample and appropriate opportunities to collaborate within and outside the school setting, build their capacity and complexity through professional learning activities that support their individual growth as well as that of the collective group of teachers. Each time teachers learn a new skill or implement a new intervention strategy, they must be given sufficient time to practice and become proficient before being evaluated.

Many educators think of accountability as being something that is imposed on them from the outside. But when educators take responsibility for creating a clearly defined, articulated, understood, and shared mission as defined in Chapter 4 and accept ownership and responsibility for successfully accomplishing their mission, the important work they do becomes purposeful and meaningful. School leaders and teachers become vested in their ability to accomplish their shared mission. The accountability becomes internalized, from the inside-out, because the educators own it. As the leadership becomes distributed, the culture becomes one of collaboration and interdependence. Through self-reflection and self-evaluation, teachers hold themselves and each other accountable for doing their part. When the data is relevant and timely, it becomes valuable information that informs decisions and provides the knowledge teachers use to transform teaching and learning. Success breeds success, and momentum builds from the synergy and joy of achieving successful results. Accomplishing mission goals provides encouragement, confidence, and gratification. "Data and results can be a powerful force for generating an intrinsic desire to improve" (Schmoker, 1999, p. 39). Schmoker also says, "Data make the invisible visible, revealing strengths and weaknesses that are easily concealed" (p. 44).

Educators need and want a process in place that provides immediate, specific, and accurate information about their progress toward accomplishing their schoolwide mission. This feedback can come from administrators in the form of evaluations and from school leaders and peers as they collaboratively review and reflect upon the data from their goals and analyze their results. It can also come from self-evaluation and reflection about their work. The power of using accountability as a motivational factor is that accountability is "a promise and an obligation, both to yourself and to the people around you, to deliver specific, defined results" (Klatt, Murphy & Irvine, 2003, p. 1); and, we would add, accountability brings joy, satisfaction, a sense of accomplishment, and gratification when the goals of the shared mission are actualized and celebrated.

# ■ STRUCTURING ACCOUNTABILITY

As in business, accountability in education is inevitable and here to stay. "The choice for educational leaders is not whether to have accountability. Instead, these leaders must decide how to make this slippery concept effective and fair" (Reeves, 2002, p. xiii).

In his book, *Accountability in Action,* Doug Reeves (2000) writes:

> Accountability must mean more than a recitation of data. Accountability must also include the elements of "conduct" and "actions." Moreover, accountability must involve the acceptance of responsibility. Educational "accountability" systems that merely describe test scores are not worthy of the term. Instead, comprehensive accountability systems contain multiple measures of student achievement. Ultimately, only systems that include effects, causes, conduct, actions, and yes, responsibility, can earn the label accountability. In the end, every element of an effective accountability system must be evaluated by one and only one criteria: did it help students learn and achieve more than they might have without the system? (p. 1)

There are several different models that are popular for structuring accountability plans, including the work by Doug Reeves and The Leadership and Learning Center (http://www.leadandlearn.com), Mike Schmoker (1999 & 2001), and Richard DuFour and Robert Eaker (1998). In addition, the early work of Schmuck and Runkel (1994) provides strategies for both macro- and microintervention plans, evaluation processes, and other organizational development tools and techniques. Evaluation experts, such as Tom Guskey (1999) and researchers like Robert Marzano (2003) and Marzano, Walters, and McNulty (2005) provide strategies and tools that educators can use with their accountability plans. Fullan (2005) and Hargreaves and Fink (2006) provide strategies for sustaining the momentum to achieve results. Although the comprehensive development and implementation for creating, implementing, and evaluating accountability plans is beyond the scope of this book, we have listed several useful resources in Appendix B.

Accountability is not, however, just about detailed plans. You are more likely to clarify the expectations and achieve whatever you put down in writing. However, like strategic planning in the 1990s, there is a danger that you can become so consumed in designing the process that you have burned out before you begin to do the work.

In Chapter 4, we defined *mission* as *the morally compelling, important work you do.* It isn't the written document that sits on your shelf or the posters on the wall, but the *walk you talk* and the *talk you walk* every single minute. Accountability works like that, too. Accountability isn't the document you create, but the fact that you hold yourself and each other responsible for achieving the desired and agreed upon results from the purposeful work you do.

After having worked with districtwide accountability systems and school accountability plans, we have come to realize that the real power and results come from the dialogue, problem solving, and collective decisions that are made *in the moment*. It is while teachers and leaders focus on student work, learning, and achievement that teachers and leaders have those powerful "ah, ha" insights that lead to deep learning and, ultimately, results. When educators own and take responsibility for student learning and the daily work they do, accountability becomes an intrinsic force that drives action.

## ■ ACCOUNTABILITY IS A CONTINUOUS PROCESS

The accountability plan must be a living, working document. As such, it must remain flexible, adaptable, and changeable. Within carefully defined boundaries, teachers must be empowered to take the initiative and have the autonomy to make decisions and choices to complete their mission. Ultimately, the power of accountability comes from moving through a continuous improvement cycle as a means to hold yourself and others responsible for accomplishing your mission. Figure 7.4 illustrates the continuous improvement cycle.

**Figure 7.4**  Continuous Improvement Cycle

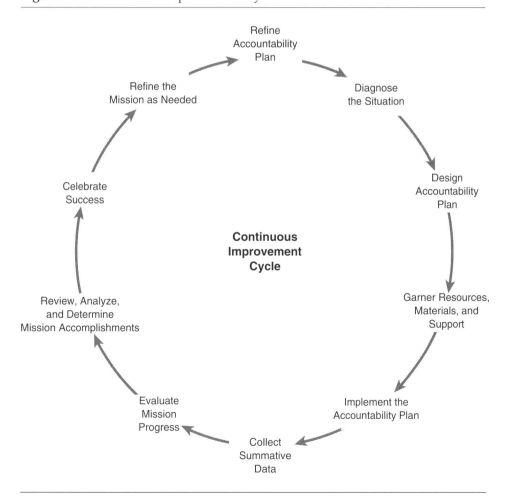

We define use of the continuous improvement cycle as moving through the following phases:

1. Diagnose the situation by collecting and analyzing data based on needs, progress, and results toward accomplishing the school's mission (i.e., vision, assumptions, goals, indicators of success).

2. Design an accountability plan (including intervention strategies) based on data-driven decisions that include knowledge from research and best practices to accomplish the school's mission. The accountability plan is based on the mission goal(s), intervention (action) strategies, people responsible, resources needed, timeline, and indicators of success.

3. Garner resources, materials, build competence/capacity, and support as needed to implement the accountability plan and mission. This must include time for teachers to meet, analyze formative data on a regular basis, gain additional knowledge and skills, celebrate successes, build on successful strategies, and refine the intervention strategies as necessary.

4. Implement the accountability plan and intervention strategies using frequent, informal teacher-generated, formative assessments (i.e., review, check for understanding) to determine student progress toward learning. Refine intervention strategies (e.g., pedagogy, structures, processes, procedures) as necessary to meet needs of all individual students.

5. Collect summative assessment data that is specific, purposeful, and accurate (i.e., reliability, validity, sustainability).

6. Evaluate mission progress at scheduled intervals using supportive data from multiple sources, both qualitative and quantitative, that can be triangulated to determine how well you are progressing toward accomplishing the vision, goals, and achieving success as determined by your indicators of success.

7. Determine mission accomplishments, including the specific results of the accountability plan.

8. Celebrate successes by recognizing progress and appreciating efforts of students, teachers, and staff members.

9. Refine the mission as needed by establishing new goals, by revising existing goals to reflect progress that has been made, by extending and updating the vision by moving further on the horizon, or by making changes that occur because of new information, research, or understandings of best practices. Gain additional knowledge and skills as appropriate. Make sure that your mission and accountability plans, especially the intervention strategies, are aligned with district and state curricula and standards, district and school policies, procedures, norms, and structures.

10. Refine the accountability plan and intervention strategies based on summative diagnosis and evaluation of previous work and results.

Once you return to where you started, continue the process, moving from phase to phase through the cycle.

You may begin anywhere in the process if you already have a clearly defined school mission and accountability plan in place. It doesn't matter which model you used to develop your accountability plan, strategic plan, or school improvement plan. You can use the continuous improvement cycle with any document or plan that is aligned with your school's mission.

If, however, your school community has not clearly defined your school's mission or developed a school improvement or accountability plan, begin the cycle at the top. Once you have gathered data to diagnose your situation, you will need to refer back to Chapter 4 to begin the process of defining your mission. At the very least, you need to establish a vision, goals, and indicators of success to define what teachers are trying to accomplish (the target and goals). This is crucial to your success so you will know the results when you see them. As we stated earlier, we have listed several helpful resources in Appendix B.

The danger of presenting a continuous improvement cycle as a model for structuring accountability is that at any given moment, based on the complexity of your work, your school and/or individual teacher teams or departments may not be at the same place within the cycle. But that is okay and to be expected. Change is messy! Although creating a timeline is important, it should not be rushed, and should, in fact, provide ample time for implementation and reflection as noted earlier. After all, it is the conversation and deep learning that come from analyzing and triangulating meaningful and purposeful data from multiple sources within the moment and context of the work that will have the greatest effect on teaching and learning and lead to informed decisions that produce desired results.

Accountability is a powerful intrinsic motivator that leads to optimal performance when information is communicated to all stakeholders and teachers are empowered within a culture of collaboration and interdependence to accomplish the school's mission. School leaders must make sure that teachers are supported within a quality of life that affords them time and the resources they need to build their confidence, competence, and complete their work. Within the defined framework and established boundaries, school leaders and teachers must be given the autonomy to make informed decisions that impact their work, based on the context, conditions, and needs of their unique situation. Most important, mistakes must be viewed as learning opportunities, results must be celebrated with efforts recognized and appreciated, and educators must take ownership and responsibility for successfully achieving their target goals to accomplish their school's mission. Above all, they must hold themselves and each other responsible for student learning as measured by student achievement results.

## QUESTIONS FOR DISCUSSION

1. It is obvious that the district and school have invested a great deal of time, effort, expectations, and funding into creating a districtwide accountability plan. Before you read the rest of this chapter, decide what essential conditions the school has in place and what essential conditions are missing to help teachers take ownership and responsibility for accomplishing the school's mission.

2. Morale is low. Lynn Taylor and the teachers are being blamed for the poor test scores. Most of them are fearful of what the central office is going to do next. How would you handle the situation if you were Lynn? Where would you begin? What would you say to your teachers and staff? How would you make sure that all of your students are prepared for the statewide assessments next year?

3. In this authentic situation, it would be easy to feel victimized, lose your sense of efficacy, and blame the low test scores on external factors. How can Lynn help her staff to find the positive forces hidden within all the negative press? How can the staff capitalize on their inner strengths to regain their confidence and put forth the energy they need to accomplish their mission?

## ESSENTIAL CONDITIONS

There are several essential conditions that are not being met in the above case study. Read along and see if you agree.

1. **Quality of life.** From the scenario, it is unclear if all the basic needs of individuals within the school community are met. It is likely there is support for teachers and adequate materials. We say this because traditionally the fourth-grade students performed well on their statewide assessments, the district invested a lot of time, money, and effort in creating a new accountability system, and the school's math scores are still high. Lynn says her teachers get along and respect each other. Teachers work to help students achieve their potential.

2. **Establish the Mission. Lynn says the school's motto, "Reach for the stars," summarizes the school's mission.** There is a districtwide accountability system that has been implemented. It is not apparent how well the plan has been articulated to all stakeholders or how much ownership and buy-in teachers and other stakeholders have in the process. It sounds as if the teachers and perhaps even Lynn herself see this latest "accountability fad" lasting only a few years. Therefore, it appears as if the commitment to the accountability plan and perhaps even to the school's mission may, in fact, be weak.

3. **Open, honest, reciprocal communication.** The superintendent has shared his negative reactions with Lynn about her school's test scores. He has not, however, recognized her staff and students' high achievement in mathematics. The teachers and building administrators are feeling depressed and afraid after seeing their colleagues being transferred to different schools, with one school being reconstituted based on the recent statewide assessment scores. There appears to be direct communication from central office with little or no reciprocity. Teachers and administrators throughout the district are most likely feeling a lack of support, respect, and trust. Dr. Preston paid a visit to Lynn and blamed her and her teachers for the poor test scores. He caught her off guard as he flashed several unflattering graphs of her students' performance in front of her. She had nothing to say. We suspect that she was feeling victimized and did not feel that she had the freedom to speak without fear of retribution and sanctions.

4. **Competence.** Even if there was a structure in place to provide teachers and administrators with the time to fully analyze, understand, and reflect upon the data, we suspect that because the students traditionally scored high on statewide assessments, Lynn and her teachers simply went through the motions without much effort or deep learning taking place. One could hypothesize that the district had entered an "implementation dip" (Fullan, 2001) where things get worse before they get better,

based on the massive effort of developing an accountability system. It could be that the schools did not have enough time, training, or resources to implement new strategies and innovations before the assessments were given. It could be that the standards, curriculum, and assessments were still in the process of being aligned. It could be that teachers still needed more time, collaboration, coaching, and training to build their competence and confidence in using the new reading and writing programs.

5. **Interdependence with individual accountability.** Although teachers get along with each other, it does not appear that strong relationships have been established so that teachers feel a sense of belonging and support from their colleagues. It also does not appear that the school's culture supports norms of collaboration, cooperation, and collegiality. It appears that the teachers may have been told to work together to achieve the shared mission. Even though teachers are willing to do their fair share, there does not seem to be a coordinated effort. Teachers work in isolation, taking responsibility for their own students' learning.

6. **Empowerment and autonomy.** Although the teachers and administrators were involved in developing the accountability system, it is unclear if everyone within the school feels empowered to do the work or able (autonomous) to make the necessary decisions that will directly impact their work and achieve desired results.

7. **Curriculum alignment and support.** Within the last year, the teachers were given a new reading and writing program along with training and support in using that program. It is unclear how well the newly adopted curricular materials are aligned with instructional practices and procedures—or with the teachers' values, beliefs, and assumptions. It is also unclear if there is alignment between the district curriculum, new materials, state standards, and state assessments.

8. **Recognition, celebration, and refinement of results.** The superintendent was quick to find fault with reading and writing test results. He did not celebrate, appreciate, or recognize Lynn and her staff for helping 85 percent of the same students achieve the state math goal on the statewide assessment. If Dr. Preston had thought about this, he might have realized the strange disconnect between students who were able to read math problems and explain their answers to achieve the goals in math, yet not good enough to achieve the desired goals in reading and writing. This, more than anything, should have raised the red flags and prompted conversations and further data analysis to determine what is really happening.

## WHAT WOULD YOU DO?

1. After reading the above discussion about the essential conditions that need to be in place, do you agree? Is there anything else that you would add?

2. Before you read the rest of the story, look back at what you said you would do if you were Lynn Taylor. Is there anything else you would add to your list? Read on to compare your list with what Lynn chose to do.

## AND NOW FOR THE REST OF THE STORY

*The snow was gently falling around her as Lynn walked to her car at the end of the day. She didn't feel the February depression from another cold, winter snowfall. Instead, Lynn was ready to explode from sheer happiness and could hardly contain the screams of joy that were overflowing inside of her.*

*Lynn began the morning in a technology committee meeting, knowing full well that today was D-day. Before she left the central office, she stopped in to see the district assessment coordinator, who had just received the statewide assessment results from the late September administration and was madly entering the scores into her database. Lynn wanted to know the results, yet she was afraid for her life. Everything rested on this one set of test scores.*

*There wasn't a day that went by that Lynn didn't think about that summer day when she opened the letter from the superintendent and realized that she and/or her teachers had fallen from grace with one set of low test scores. The superintendent had made it clear that out of all twenty-one elementary schools in the district, her students needed to be number one in reading. She knew it was possible. After all, her school had been number one in reading many times before. But, somehow, when last year's test scores had arrived, four months later than predicted because of internal problems at the testing company, the passion and zeal for the job had been sucked out of her and her staff. Where Lynn once felt confident and competent in her leadership position, she now lacked self-confidence, self-respect, and self-esteem. She felt sorry for herself, her staff, and for the other administrators and teachers who had been moved so abruptly. Every day she said her prayers and wished for a miracle. Today was no exception.*

*As she stood watching the assessment coordinator enter data, the last several months flashed through her mind. The first thing she had done was to write a letter to her staff, asking anyone who was available on an early July morning to come to the school to analyze what had happened and create a plan to jumpstart their students and make sure they were ready in September for the next round of assessments. Every teacher and a few of the special education building aides had shown up, without pay, ready to work. That meant a lot to Lynn and said a lot about the dedication of her staff.*

*Lynn remembered the look of fear in the teachers' eyes as she read them the letter reprimanding her and the teachers for the low test scores, with the threat of being transferred to another school if their students were not number one in reading next year. She let the teachers vent and listened as they all talked about what they had done to help the students prepare. They questioned what they could have done better or differently. When some of them began to blame the parents, the students, themselves, and each other, Lynn interrupted the conversation.*

*"Let's not blame each other, our students, or their parents for what has happened. Blaming and feeling victimized is not going to get us anywhere. Trust me, we all feel horrible about what has happened! But blaming ourselves isn't going to do us any good. Who knows what caused the low test scores in reading and writing. I ask myself that question every day. Could it be the construction crew was still putting on the roof during the time our students took the test? I can't remember when they finished, but maybe the smell of tar got to our students? Maybe we slacked off, not doing the job the best we could, knowing our students always 'get it' and score high? Or maybe it was because our student assessments were not scored accurately—especially after all of the trouble the testing company had internally with scoring. I don't know what it was, and perhaps we never will. But we can do better than this!" Lynn stopped, giving them time to think about what she had just said.*

*"I had an insightful conversation earlier this summer at one of my son's softball games. I talked with Dr. Daniels, our writing consultant. She was shocked. Dr. Daniels works with students all over the state to improve their writing, and she couldn't believe that our students would score so poorly on the assessments. Dr. Daniels was as surprised as I have been, especially since 85 percent of our students*

*passed the math portion of the assessments, and yet, out of that same group of students, only 45 percent achieved the reading standards and 56 percent achieved the writing standards. In order to meet or exceed the math standards, students have to be able to read the math problems, and they have to be able to explain their answers in writing. It just doesn't make sense. Dr. Daniels suggested that we resubmit our students' assessments to be rescored. I talked with Dr. Preston, and he has begrudgingly resubmitted them. I will let you know as soon as I hear what happens," Lynn said, as she stopped to take a breath.*

*"We can't wait for the results to come back, and we can't worry about what has happened. We have to learn from it, take responsibility for what we can change, and never let it happen again. We have to step up to the plate and take control. We can do it! After all, 85 percent of our students passed math! You should all be proud. We can't forget that fact! We all need to work together and develop a plan. I call it the 'all hands on deck' plan, because it is going to take you, me, all of us, to pull this thing off. We are all in this together, sink or swim."*

*"Looking at the calendar, we will have fourteen school days to prepare our students before the testing begins. We need to really look at all of our student data to determine where our students are doing well and what skills we need to work on so they are prepared for the assessments. Everyone—special ed, literacy, ELL, previous teachers—you all have information that can help us get our students prepared. We don't have a lot of time to get them ready for the next round of assessments. And when the assessments are over for this year, we can't just relax. We will need to continue to work with our students and help them master all the skills they need, because, as you know, there will be another round of assessments the next year."*

*Lynn took a deep breath. "I can't promise you, even if our scores come back and we are vindicated, or even if our students achieve number one this year, that Dr. Preston won't move me or you. After all, if he continues to move people around, as he has this summer, trading poor teachers for good teachers, none of us will be held harmless. But we can't worry about that now. We have an urgent job to do—we must accomplish our mission, which means that we must make sure all of our students are ready for the statewide assessments."*

*That summer day with the teachers seemed like such a long time ago. As she waited for the test results, Lynn smiled a worried smile remembering how she and her teachers had earnestly begun working together during the rest of the summer to develop a profile of strengths and weaknesses for each student in the fourth grade who would be taking the statewide assessments in September. The teachers met with Lynn and each other on a regular basis. In fact, there wasn't a day during the summer that several teachers didn't show up at the school to work. Together, they looked at how each student had performed in third grade. They also looked at the students who took the tests the previous year, to see their strengths and weaknesses on the tests. They noted that students had a difficult time with critical stance, written response to text comprehension questions, and editing and revising. From this information, the teachers grouped students according to what they knew about them from district summative reading and writing assessments, teacher-made formative assessments, and other teacher observations. Lynn worked with the literacy teacher to create a reader's club, where students made their "minutes count." They could do this by reading to others or listening to someone read to them. Lynn even talked the PTA into buying prizes, including club t-shirts for everyone who logged in over 6,000 minutes.*

*On the first day of school, the fourth-grade teachers hit the ground running. Special ed, literacy, ELL, teachers, and aides had developed a schedule to work in each of the five classrooms for thirty minutes each day with small groups of students on specific skills. Even Lynn got involved and worked with one group of students each day. After school all of the teachers met to strategize on what they would do the next day. They each took responsibility for developing different lessons from fiction and nonfiction stories. They asked students to read and respond in writing to questions like those found on the statewide assessments and then gave students specific feedback about what they were doing*

*(Continued)*

(Continued)

*well and how they could improve their work. Throughout the process, Lynn kept the group focused on the mission by asking questions, sharing and listening to observations and experiences, and finding ways to push their thinking and actions further.*

*The school held their curriculum night earlier than usual. Lynn began the evening by sharing with parents the test results. She showed the parents that even though only 45 percent of the students were proficient in reading, 85 percent of the same students had met or exceeded the math goal. In addition, after she and the teachers had analyzed the district reading assessment results from the spring, they realized that the same group of fourth-grade students had scored better on the reading and writing assessments than any of the other twenty-one elementary schools in the district. It didn't make sense that her fourth-grade students could be the best on the district assessments and score so low on the statewide assessments. Lynn explained to the parents what the teachers were doing to prepare the students. She asked the parents to help make sure their children were ready for the assessments that would begin in eight days. She also explained the reader's club and encouraged everyone to participate. As parents moved to their child's classroom, the teachers did the same, stressing ways that parents could reinforce skills, increase student vocabulary, and most important, stress the importance of the assessments without creating too much anxiety for the students.*

*Lynn jumped and then quickly snapped back to reality when she heard Jill McLaughlin, the testing coordinator, ask, "Do you want to see the results?"*

*"I think so," Lynn said, slowly easing toward Jill's computer. "If it's good news, that is," her voice trailing off as she mentally said a quick prayer.*

*Jill put her index finger on the row where Lynn's scores were. Lynn's eyes darted across the line as it focused on the numbers. "What does it mean?" she asked. "Is it good? Are we okay?" Lynn crossed her fingers.*

*Jill smiled. "You did great! Look at this; you have 84 percent of your students proficient in math, 83 percent in reading, and 90 percent in writing!"*

*"Yes, but are we number one in reading?" Lynn held her breath.*

*"Yes, you're number one," Jill said, as she looked at Lynn who was still holding her breath, in a state of shock. "You're also number one in math and writing!"*

*Lynn couldn't believe it. "Pinch me, I have to be dreaming," she said. "Are you sure?" Her voice was quivering with excitement and disbelief.*

*"I'm sure. You did great."*

*"Wow! Wow! Wow!" Lynn shouted with jubilation and danced to her car, not paying attention to the snow. With every step, she said a prayer of thanks.*

*All the way back to her school, she wondered what she could do to recognize and show her appreciation to the teachers. How would she tell them? She thought about buying a cake, but knew that her staff didn't really like cake. Besides, it felt more like they should be standing in the locker room pouring champagne over their heads after winning the Super Bowl, than eating cake.*

*As she walked up to the front door of her school, carrying a large box filled with test results, her custodian saw her, opened the door, and said, "You look like you have just seen a ghost. Are you okay?"*

*Lynn laughed. "More than okay. I guess I was just deep in thought," she said as her custodian took the box from her and led her to her office. Lynn grabbed the secretary and as the custodian set the box of test results on the table, Lynn closed the door, and swore them both to secrecy. She told them about the results, and how she wanted to do champagne, but didn't know what to do.*

*Her custodian asked, "Why not do sparkling cider?"*

*"In champagne glasses," suggested the secretary.*

*"Yes, that's it!" Lynn laughed. "It's perfect."*

*After lunch, Lynn sent her custodian to the local supermarket to buy sparkling cider, plastic champagne glasses, and cookies. Five minutes before school let out, Lynn got on the intercom and said that she needed to see all staff members, certified and noncertified, in the library for a short meeting right after school. If teachers were on duty they needed to join the staff meeting as soon as possible. Of course, the school was abuzz with teachers wondering what was going on? Did Lynn get transferred? Or find another job? No one could blame her. Was someone sick? Did someone die? The gossip and rumors were rampant.*

*When everyone had assembled, Lynn took a deep breath. She cleared her throat and, in a somber voice, began, "I asked you all to be here today because I have some news . . . news that affects every one of us in this room." She paused, took a deep breath, and continued, "As you know, last year, our test scores were the worst they have ever been. Even though we had our tests rescored last year, as you know, our scores were better, but they still weren't as good as they had been in the past. We don't know what went wrong, and we probably never will."*

*"Today, we got our statewide assessment results. I'm not sure where to begin." She checked the faces of the staff members. They all looked frightened and so vulnerable. "I guess I'll start with math. As you remember, last year 85 percent of our students met the state goal. This year, we only had 84 percent of our students meeting goal in math." As she paused, she could see teachers slinking down into their chairs, bracing themselves for what was to come. "I guess I'll do reading next. Last year, we had 45 percent of our students who met the standards in reading. This year, we had" she paused, took a deep breath, and said, "83 percent. We're number one!"*

*Cheers of joy, shouts, and hugs broke out all over the room. Just as she said it, both of her custodians came dancing into the room, one with a white towel over his arm like a wine steward, carrying a cookie pan filled with glasses of sparkling cider and the other pushing one of the kitchen carts draped with a checkered table cloth, trays of assorted cookies and bottles of sparkling cider.*

*When the pandemonium stopped, Lynn told the teachers that not only were they number one for reading, but they were also number one for writing and number one in math.*

*"I wanted to do something really special for each and every one of you to show my appreciation for all of the work and effort you put into making sure our students were ready for the statewide assessments. I didn't know what to do—all I could think of was that it feels like we have just won the Super Bowl, and we should be pouring champagne over our heads. Of course, we can't do that, so Jeff, Steve, and I," pointing to the two custodians who were still enjoying the role of waiters, "decided this would be the next best thing. If anyone wants to 'twist a lid,' be my guest. You deserve it and a whole lot more. I can't thank you enough for all you have done to help our students learn and to accomplish our mission! Just know, your work is greatly appreciated and keep on doing what you are doing, because it works! Thanks, everyone!"*

*With that, roars of cheers rang out as teachers and staff members stayed late into the afternoon, basking in their glory, and recounting all of the pent up feelings of defeat, fear, and frustration.*

*As Lynn left the school that night, she knew that the work was far from over. She knew there would always be another group of students that they would need to prepare for the next round of state assessments. She wished that her staff didn't have to live from test score to test score and that the district's accountability system used multiple methods to measure schoolwide success and individual student progress. But out of the tragedy of low test scores she realized that her school had finally found a sense of urgency for accomplishing their school's mission. Within that urgency, the staff had learned to work together, using their own strengths and talents to analyze data, design and implement intervention strategies, evaluate their effectiveness, and accomplish their mission.*

*Lynn hadn't heard from the superintendent. She hoped he would congratulate the staff on a job well done, even though that wasn't his style. In the meantime, Lynn knew she and her staff would tell stories about this day for a long time. They knew Lynn recognized and appreciated their efforts.*

*Lynn knew that this moment would leave a lasting legacy as it became part of the oral history and culture of the school. The days had been painful and the results of their work were a long time coming. It felt rewarding to know that the work they had done together made a difference in their students' achievement!*

## SUMMARY

Accountability closes the gap between our intentions and our actions. To be accountable means that educators take ownership and responsibility for successfully achieving their target goals to accomplish their school's mission. They hold themselves and each other responsible for student learning as measured by results that demonstrate student achievement. To be held accountable for teaching and learning, educators need time to reflect and analyze their own work, as well as to garner feedback about their performance, which should come from a clearly defined and articulated evaluation process. Teachers also need feedback about student learning, which should come from an assessment process that is objective, valid, reliable, and aligned with clearly articulated and shared mission, as well as standards and curriculum goals. Knowledge of results or feedback about their performance is a powerful motivational strategy as well as the most powerful and simplest prescription for enhancing and improving education.

To use accountability as a motivational strategy we provided several guiding principles: (1) Accountability begins with school leaders; (2) Accountability plans must use multiple sources of data to triangulate the results; (3) Data is not knowledge and must be transformed—from data to information to knowledge to shared wisdom—if collegial learning communities are to achieve desired results; (4) Less is best; (5) Slow is becoming the new fast; and (6) Educators need a better understanding of assessments, including how to use that data to inform instruction.

The accountability plan must be a living, working document that remains flexible, adaptable, and changeable. The power of accountability comes from moving through the continuous improvement cycle as a means to hold one's self and others responsible for accomplishing the school's mission.

## NEXT STEPS

1. How did Lynn use accountability as a strategy to improve student learning and motivate her staff?

2. Think about how accountability is used in your current situation. What does accountability look like, sound like, and feel like when it is used as a motivational strategy? What would you like accountability to look like, sound like, and feel like? Make a list. Put a star by those things that are already in place in your school or system and a check by those things that you would like to implement or explore further.

3. If possible, discuss with others what you found interesting about this case study on accountability and what you found challenging.

4. Select one or two ideas that you checked above. List several strategies or changes that you can make to improve the accountability within your own school. Think about the barriers that may get in your way, and list choices that you can make to help you alleviate or decrease those barriers.

5. Decide on one or two things that you are going to implement in your current situation because of this chapter. List them along with any notes to help you remember what you want to do.

# 8

# Competence and Capacity

*Generating the Confidence to*
*Successfully Achieve the Goal*

## ■ PICTURE THIS

*Slam! The office door flew open, crashing against the wall! Stomp, stomp, stomp! Slam, slam, bam!*

*Donald Costello was sitting at his computer, facing away from the door as he edited a report that was due to the superintendent before the end of the day. Just as he swung around and literally jumped out of his chair (and skin), he heard a loud thud as he watched the mounds of paper on his desk being flung every which way by a tall stack of computer spreadsheets. In front of him stood three of Rockville High's teachers, hands folded across their chests. In the background, his secretary, Mrs. Tatum, was running down the hallway from her desk, screaming in her high-pitched, nervous voice, "You can't just barge into Mr. Costello's office like that! Mr. Costello needs to get his monthly attendance...."*

*She stopped at the door. It was too late. "I'm sorry, Mr. C.," she said sheepishly. "I tried to stop them!" She bowed her head, afraid to look at their eyes, and like a puppy about to be scolded, slowly began to inch her way back to her desk.*

*Don turned his attention to the three teachers who were standing in front of him. He could see that they were boiling over with anger. Ironically, these were not the usual offenders. In fact, these were three of his best and most conscientious teachers: Keith Gegesky, the mathematics department chair; Nancy Roux, science teacher; and Marty Kubeck, English teacher.*

*(Continued)*

147

(Continued)

*"What is the meaning of this?" he asked, his voice louder than normal, but then he was still caught off-guard from the sudden interruption. "You can't just barge in here like this. You nearly scared me half to death!"*

*Keith Gegesky, the math chair, was the first to speak. "I'm sorry ... but we have had it! Our online grade book and the new report card are despicable! I don't know how this district expects us to be able to do our grades when the programs don't work, and there is no way to import the grades into the report card."*

*"Not to mention that you type in the numbers for the comments that you want, and they don't align with the comment you wanted to make—that is, if you get that far. Then, when you print out the student report, none of the comments are what you wanted. I have students who are getting As and their comment reads 'they didn't complete their project' instead of, 'always prepared for class' or 'actively participates in science labs,'" Nancy Roux stated emphatically.*

*"Listen to her complain. At least she has grades. Look at this. These are the print-out copies that show I have entered all the student grades into the grade book program. But only part of the grades show up here," Marty shouted, definitely agitated, "but not here!" He held up other papers. "Then, some of my grades are saved and printed on this paper, but I can't get them to show up on this paper, let alone transfer them into the report card program."*

*"I've tried to help him," Nancy added, "but even when I do for him everything I did for me, we can't get some of his grades to show up in the grade book."*

*"Half the teachers can't even remember their passwords to get into the report card program, because remember, in August when they trained us, there was a problem, and they were going to get back to us. Well, if they did, I sure don't remember seeing anything come across my desk," chimed in Marty.*

*"We are only three of your teachers, but we are representing everyone. I don't know anybody who is going to have their grades ready for you by Friday," Nancy said.*

*"Yeah, as you can see, we are angry. But at least we are still speaking in a somewhat normal tone, without superlatives," Marty said.*

*"You probably don't want to leave your office today. It is hell out there in the trenches. Nobody had a good weekend! In fact, your ears should have been ringing all weekend from the smoke that was coming out of all the teachers' chimneys as they had war with their computers and that report card program! You have a revolt on your hands. We want our old report cards back. None of us are able to do our report cards this way," Keith stated emphatically, then continued. "In fact, none of us are going to do it this way, even if we could. If we don't get our old report card system back by the end of the day, our union is going to file a grievance for this change in working conditions."*

*"Wait a minute," Don tried to say calmly. "Why is it that no one has said anything before this? You all had a full day of training in August so that you would be able to do your report cards. Now, here it is, November, and you are telling me that it can't be done? Why did you wait until the last minute? Marty, you should have known before this that your grades weren't printing in your online grade book. I don't understand. If you entered and then saved them, why aren't they showing up?" Don asked, hearing his voice becoming more and more agitated.*

*"We didn't have all our grades until this weekend, so it didn't make sense to try to use the report card program until now. But for those of us who could get into the program, it was so slow and cumbersome that a lot of teachers just gave up. Nancy needs to be commended. She stayed with it, and look ... the comments don't match up with what she tried to say," Keith explained.*

*"Yeah, can you imagine what the parents are going to think—or say, when they see that their A student didn't attend class or that their D student completed all of his work on time? Do you know how many phone calls I am going to get?" Nancy argued.*

"Well, one thing's for sure," Keith said, laughing, "Caryl Marcos isn't going to have to worry. I doubt she even remembers how to turn on the computer, let alone use it to enter grades. That workshop was so far above her head, it's no wonder she is planning to retire this year! In fact, this may push her so far over the edge that she may just decide not to come back after Thanksgiving."

Don knew Keith was right. Caryl had been teaching health at Rockville for thirty-one years, and as far as he knew, she had never touched a computer in her life.

"Yeah," Marty chimed in, "I heard she offered to pay Josh Wilcox, the kid teaching computers, to do her grades, but he said she didn't make enough money to pay him for the time it would take him to get through the—I won't say what he called it—program."

"Poor Caryl," Nancy sighed. "She is such a nice person. She would do anything for you. You know it is bad when Josh won't even take the money to help!"

"I don't know what to say," Don said, looking at the mess of papers on his table. "Grades have to be in by Friday because report cards go out next Wednesday. You have known about this deadline all along. This was not my decision. The school board and superintendent are requiring us to use this grading and report card system because it is tied to our student information data system. We will have access to a wealth of data when it is fully implemented," he said, then bit his lip, realizing he said more than he should have.

"Fully implemented!" the three teachers shouted, almost in unison.

"What else are we going to have to do?" Keith said out loud, even though the other two were thinking the same thing.

Don took a deep breath and continued. "You are all highly qualified teachers. You have been doing report cards for years. You were trained in August to use this program. There is no reason why you can't get it done. But . . ." Don Costello stopped. Then, as an afterthought added, "I will call Doug Powell, the technology director, and Karen Shea, the curriculum and instruction director, and get them over here this afternoon. You and the rest of the teachers can tell them your problems. It's the best I can do at this late date."

The three teachers stood staring at Don. "If that's the best you can do. . . ." Keith's voice trailed off.

"Yes, at this moment, that's the best I can do," sighed Don, shrugging his shoulders.

The three teachers picked up their piles of paper and left. It was only 9:30 in the morning, and already Don knew it was going to be one long, hard week. What is wrong with these teachers? A simple thing like an online grading program and report card system should not be causing him this much grief. Especially since the district had supported them by bringing in a company expert and dedicating a full day of professional development time at the beginning of the school year for this important training.

"You would think," Don muttered to himself as he sank back down into his chair and turned his attention back to his attendance report, "that I could get at least one technologically savvy teacher working at his school. What's wrong with this picture? What's wrong with these teachers?" he asked himself as he put on his armor and prepared to make the phone calls downtown to let the superintendent, technology director, and curriculum director know about the storm that was brewing at Rockville High.

## ■ WHAT IS COMPETENCE?

Competence can be a powerful motivational strategy when educators perceive themselves as being capable and adept at helping all students learn by actualizing the goals of their school mission. Competence can be found at two levels: the individual (i.e., administrator, teacher, staff member); and the school community. Often, when people talk about staff development opportunities, they talk about it in terms of developing the individual and developing the organization (e.g., school, department, grade level, or districtwide initiative).

When we talk about *competence,* we are talking about individuals, and when we talk about the competence level of an entire grade level, department, school, district, or organization, we are talking about *organizational capacity.*

We define *competence* as *having the knowledge, skills, dispositions, and perceptions of one's selves, which afford individuals within the school organization the ability and/or capacity to successfully meet the level of challenge to accomplish the task, goal, or mission of the school.*

We define *organizational capacity* as a group's *collective competence (i.e., knowledge, skills, dispositions, and perceptions of themselves), which affords the school organization the ability and/or capacity to successfully meet the level of challenge to accomplish the task, goal, or mission of the school.*

For educators to perform at optimal levels and to feel good about what they are doing, they must feel competent about their knowledge, skills, dispositions (i.e., attitudes toward curricula, pedagogy, student learning), and perceptions of themselves (i.e., self-esteem, efficacy, locus of control, assumptions) in relation to the challenges of their work. At the same time, the challenge of the tasks must be at the correct level of difficulty; that is, not too easy and mundane to create stagnation, apathy, and feelings of boredom; and not so difficult as to overwhelm with worry, fear, stress, and anxiety. When educators perceive that their knowledge and skills afford them the ability to successfully meet the level of challenges to accomplish their mission, they are happy, confident, focused, and in control of the teaching and learning process.

In Chapter 1, we defined this state as *optimal performance* and said that the more motivational strategies are embedded in the culture, the more likely educators will be to find themselves performing at optimal levels.

**Figure 8.1** A Balance for Optimal Performance

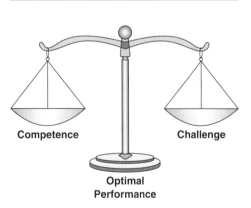

Competence · Challenge

Optimal Performance

As illustrated in Figure 8.1, the scale weighing teacher competence and/or organizational capacity and the challenges of their work must be balanced for competence to be an effective motivational strategy that allows educators to accomplish the school's shared mission.

When teachers perceive the challenge is too difficult or when they lack competence (knowledge and skills) to complete the task, as illustrated in Figure 8.2, they feel anxious. When stress and anxiety becomes too great, as in the case at the beginning of this chapter, people give up.

As illustrated in Figure 8.3, when teachers are overqualified and the challenge of their work is perceived as too easy (they could do it in their sleep) they become bored, uninterested, and simply go "through the motions."

As we have mentioned before, there are many different ways to define the euphoric motivational state or condition in which individuals or organizations are engaged in an action, work, or activity; and people are able to complete the task and achieve the goal to their highest level of potential. We define that state as *optimal performance,* Sears (1985) calls it *the zone,* Maslow (1998) calls it *self-actualization,* and Csikszentmihalyi (1997, 2003) calls it *flow.*

Csikszentmihalyi (2003) says a good flow activity is "one that offers a very high ceiling of opportunities for improvement— playing the piano, for example, provides almost infinite challenges. Thus it invites growth" (p. 63). We believe that teaching is also such a skill. No matter how much knowledge, skill, or years of experience teachers have acquired, there is always room for additional growth. The knowledge, practice, and experiences teachers bring to their work is equal to their level of competence and complexity. To perform at optimal levels (or stay in a level of flow), a person "must progress and learn more skill, rising to new levels of complexity" (Csikszentmihalyi, 2003, p. 63). When this doesn't happen, teachers become bored and tired with what they are doing. "Ultimately, each person has a significant degree of control over how many challenges she deals with. Even the simplest task, if carried out with care and attention, can reveal layers and layers of opportunities to hone one's skills" (Csikszentmihalyi, 2003, p. 66).

Education is a profession with a relatively flat hierarchy. The only vertical movement is to be an administrator. It is critical, therefore, that teachers and admin-

**Figure 8.2**   An Imbalance When Challenge Outweighs Competence

**Figure 8.3**   An Imbalance When Competence Outweighs Challenge

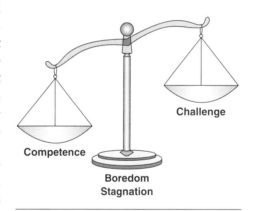

istrators are provided with opportunities to improve their skills and develop complexity. One such way is to distribute leadership by providing teachers with leadership roles and opportunities to become actively engaged through collaboration and shared decision making. This includes involving teachers in problem-solving processes to find solutions to issues that directly affect their work—especially making sure that all students achieve the school's high expectations, learning goals, and shared mission. As in the medical field when doctors find flow by being able to perform difficult operations successfully, so too, can teachers enter a state of flow when they are able to help any student achieve (ranging from those with learning disabilities and socioeconomic disadvantages, to the gifted). School leaders have only to listen to teachers describe their greatest student success story, usually a situation in which "the light bulb went on" and the student "got it," to understand how motivating and powerful feeling competent and performing at optimal levels can be for them. After all, this is why they became teachers.

All too often in the ever-increasing fast-paced world, the challenges from higher expectations, social and political agendas, and new innovations are being hurled at educators so quickly that teachers don't have time to digest it and feel competent in their teaching abilities. As Hargreaves and Fink (2006) explain:

> Educators . . . have reported how the rapid, relentless, and pervasive spread of standardization in educational reform has . . . undermined teacher confidence and competence as the pace and priorities of reform have left teachers with no time or flexibility to respond to their students' needs or even mark their work in a timely manner" (2006, p. 11).

Educators become anxious and fearful when their expertise is challenged. They resist the new innovation by becoming aggressive (saboteurs) or passive aggressive (quiet resisters). In situations like this, school leaders need to pay attention to the symptoms and slow down the change process, providing teachers with the ability to increase their skill level to match the challenges of the new innovation, if they want the innovation to become successfully institutionalized within the culture of the school.

Csikszentmihalyi (2003) uses the piano player analogy to describe the dynamics of flow (the experience that "occurs when both skills and challenges are high") in relation to competence and complexity. Csikszentmihalyi says that a beginning piano player with basic skills slowly learns how to play songs for enjoyment. As the piano player's skills improve and the songs he has learned become easier to play, boredom sets in. The piano player gets tired of playing the same songs over and over. He has to make a decision, either to continue to play the songs he knows better, or to learn more difficult songs to play. This makes playing the piano more engaging, and his interest and involvement increases. As that happens, the piano player eventually becomes adept at playing the new songs, thus once again finding himself getting bored and tired of the repetition. He needs even higher challenges to keep enjoying his piano playing (p. 66–67).

Alternatively, this process of learning to play the piano can lead to anxiety, "as when the beginner is asked to play a piece that is too difficult. The challenges are suddenly too high, and the only way to return to flow is to increase skills quickly to match. In either case" [learning new skills because the challenge is too easy or too difficult], "the result is the same: The individual moves to a plane of higher complexity" (Csikszentmihalyi, 2003, p. 66-67). This issue of complexity is important because, as Csikszentmihalyi writes, it

> is the central feature of personal development. . . . Many people go through life never quite finding a way to match their talents to what is expected of them. They feel either that life is passing them by— marooned in loneliness, their talents remain useless or undeveloped—or that they are being crushed by excessive demands from relatives and bosses, never able to find time for themselves. . . . Adults who are more often in flow are not only happier, but they spend significantly more time at work actually working instead of gossiping, reading the papers, or surfing the Web. (p. 69)

To increase their level of competence, capacity, and complexity, all members of the school community, certified and noncertified, must have the time and resources to learn and grow professionally, both individually and collaboratively, if they are to remain current in their use of new technologies, new curricula, and research findings. For educators to be motivated to learn, they must find the professional learning activities personally meaningful. What they learn and practice must be beneficial to them because of the effect it has on helping them and their students perform effectively and efficiently at higher levels. Like all people, when teachers are motivated to learn, especially when the learning comes "just-in-time," they utilize skills (i.e., attend more carefully to instruction, take notes, rehearse and memorize material, reflect on their understanding, and ask questions) that contribute to a higher degree of retention and application.

On their Web site, the National Staff Development Council (NSDC) (2008) defines the rationale for their *learning standard* by saying:

> It is essential that staff development assist educators in moving beyond comprehension of the surface features of a new idea or innovation to a fuller and more complete understanding of its purposes, critical attributes, meaning, and connection to other approaches. To improve student achievement, adult learning under most circumstances must promote deep understanding of a topic and provide many opportunities for teachers and administrators to practice new skills with feedback on their performance until those skills become automatic and habitual. Such deeper understanding typically requires a number of opportunities to interact with the idea or procedure through active learning processes that promote reflection such as discussion and dialogue, writing, demonstrations, practice with feedback, and group problem solving" sec. 3, para. 3).

For educators to find their work meaningful, purposeful, and satisfying, they must feel competent about the work they are doing. They must continue to increase their levels of complexity and work interdependently to build organizational capacity. If they are going to be able to perform at optimal levels, there must be a balance between the knowledge, skills, dispositions, and perceptions of themselves and the challenges they face to insure that all students achieve high standards.

Competence can be a powerful motivational strategy when educators find meaning and purpose and see the benefits from new levels of learning. All members of the school community play an integral role in working to accomplish the school's mission. To do so, each person must be committed to becoming a lifelong learner to achieve his or her own personal learning goals as well as those to help the school achieve its mission. There must be time for all staff members within the school day, each day, to engage in continuous, quality professional learning activities that are based on adult learning theory (andragogy), and take into account adult learning styles, previous knowledge, experiences, and career stages.

# ■ NEEDS MET THROUGH COMPETENCE

This motivational strategy is grounded in staff development, professional learning, and adult learning literature and research. It addresses the needs as defined by Maslow's (1998) esteem and self-actualization, Deci's (1995) competence, Glasser's (1998a) freedom and fun, Sagor's (2003) competence, and Covey's (2004) growth and development. In addition, it contains critical attributes of the flow-experiences (Csikszentmihalyi, 1997), and an important component of confidence (Kanter, 2004). (See Appendix A.)

# ■ WHAT COMPETENCE IS AND ISN'T

Figures 8.4 and 8.5 will help to clarify competence. Figure 8.4 explains what competence is and what it isn't. Figure 8.5 compares the differences between a competence-supportive learning environment and a competence-deficient learning environment.

**Figure 8.4**  Competence Defined

| What Competence Is | What Competence Isn't |
|---|---|
| Capability to do the work and accomplish the mission. Everyone is a teacher and learner. | Inability to do the work and accomplish the mission. Learning by command and control. |
| The educator feels proficient in his/her knowledge and skills in relation to the quality of his/her work. | The educator feels bored, anxious, frustrated, and inadequate in relation to the quality of his/her work. |
| There is a clear balance between the challenge of the task and the knowledge, skills, and experiences of the people doing the work. The work is optimally challenging for a person's capacities. | The challenge of the tasks is either greater than the knowledge, skills, and experiences causing educators to feel overwhelmed and frustrated; or the knowledge, skills, and experience level of the task provides little or no challenge and the educator is bored. |
| Lifelong learning and enjoyment of personal and professional growth. | "I'm too old to learn," or "been there done that" resistance to learning. |
| Accepting and adapting to change. | Resistance and hostility toward change. |
| Feelings of confidence, self-esteem, and efficacy. Educators know that what they are doing makes a difference. | Lack of confidence, self-esteem, and efficacy. Educators blame others and have externalized their locus of control. |
| "Success is from what I know/do and my effort." | "I am successful because of luck." |
| The ability to develop and increase the capacity of personal and organizational learning goals. | The inability to develop and increase the capacity of personal or organization learning. |
| Positive emotional energy increases. | Emotional energy is sucked out of the school. |
| Self-determination and autonomy. | Control and dependence. |

| What Competence Is | What Competence Isn't |
|---|---|
| Learning goals and mission work are successfully achieved or accomplished. | Learning goals and mission work are not successfully completed or accomplished. |
| Diversity of ideas is valued. | Homogeneity of ideas and thoughts are valued. |
| Specific, accurate, and timely constructive feedback emphasizes improvements and progress toward agreed upon criteria and goals. | Feedback is limited, nonspecific, and often focuses on deficiencies and mistakes. |
| Feedback is informational and respects autonomy, builds competence, and encourages personal responsibility and self-motivation. | Feedback is perceived as controlling and intended to direct or change behavior; little or no explanation or rationale for change. |
| Teachers connect their prior knowledge, skills, and experiences to new ideas and expectations. | Teachers are unable to make connections between new and old programs and practices. Often new innovations are not aligned and are incompatible with current practices. |
| Unleash the talent of individuals/teams and promote ingenuity, creativity, and innovation to solve problems and improve instruction. | Teachers use teacher-proof materials, are told what, when, and how to teach. There is little room for creativity, ingenuity, and innovation. |
| Willingness to share tacit and explicit knowledge through mentoring, coaching, and networking, and give back to the profession. | Lack of time or commitment to share ideas, mentor, coach, or network. The culture is competitive and teachers work in isolation. |
| Frequent dialogues that question and challenge assumptions and values that lead to deeper understandings and build transformational learning. | Little or no involvement in dialogues or conversations that challenge assumptions and values. When they happen, it usually causes conflicts and tensions among staff members. |

**Figure 8.5** Structuring a Competence-Supportive Environment

| Competence-Supportive Environment | Competence-Deficient Environment |
|---|---|
| Quality of life is established, including a safe climate, mutual respect, and trust. | Basic needs are not met. People do not feel safe and lack mutual respect and trust. |
| The school's mission is clearly defined, aligned, articulated, and shared. | Everyone has different ideas about what work (i.e., mission, vision, goals) is important. |
| Communication is honest, open, reciprocal, and multidirectional (up, down, sideways). Information is shared with all stakeholders. | Communication is on a need-to-know basis. Information is defensive, limited, withheld, and/or misinterpreted. |
| Communication is used to engage all stakeholders in solving problems. | Command, control, and coercion from the top are used to solve problems. |
| Teachers have a choice and voice in identifying and selecting improvements and changes. | Teachers are handed externally driven and mandated adoption of new programs and pedagogical strategies. |
| Teachers share in the decisions that directly impact their work through consensus. | Teachers receive top-down decisions and mandates with little input. |
| The climate is conducive to risk taking and the culture encourages people to be creative and try new and innovative ideas. | There is a climate that is fearful and a resistance to change, risk taking, and exploring new and innovative ideas. |

*(Continued)*

**Figure 8.5** (Continued)

| Competence-Supportive Environment | Competence-Deficient Environment |
|---|---|
| Within explicitly stated boundaries, educators are given autonomy to make professional decisions that directly affect student learning. | Boundaries are not clearly defined. Educators are often handed teacher-proof materials with little latitude to make decisions. |
| Educators have developed strong professional relationships. There is a norm of collaboration and a culture of interdependence. | Educators are isolated and disconnected from one another. There is a culture of competitiveness and doing what is best for "my" students while working alone. |
| Teachers are provided with time to share knowledge, skills, experiences, and to network with others during the school day. | There is no time or expectation to collaborate or share knowledge, skills, and experiences; or to network with others. |
| Educators have input into planning their own professional development based on their own needs, levels of concern, experiences, and levels of competence. | Educators have limited input into planning their own professional learning. Most staff development opportunities are top-down, one-size-fits-all, training events. |
| Materials and resources are adequate, provided, and readily available during and after training. | Materials and resources are limited. Often training occurs before resources are available. |
| Professional development is job-embedded within the school setting and school day. | Professional development is a pull-out model, often outside of the school day. |
| Professional learning is based on the standards like the National Staff Development Council. | Staff development planners know what will work best and plan events accordingly. |
| There is an array of purposeful, just-in-time professional growth opportunities, including follow-up support, which take into account adult learning styles, appropriate level of difficulty, demographics, and needs. | Inservice training and events are orchestrated and scheduled. There is little flexibility. All teachers are expected to attend the same sessions, learning the same things, in the same way. There is little, if any, follow-up support. |
| Teachers are provided with training and support to feel competent in the knowledge and skills needed to accomplish the mission and held accountable for student learning. | There is no direct relationship between teacher learning, teacher accountability, and accomplishing the school's mission to help all students achieve school goals. |

## ■  WHY IS COMPETENCE IMPORTANT?

A person's worst nightmare is often when he finds himself in a situation where he needs to perform a task and soon discovers that he doesn't have the knowledge and skills to do it. There is nothing more frustrating, if the task is minor, or more fearful, if it is something urgent or crucial.

As many people have learned the hard way, being "highly qualified" because they have earned a degree, or several degrees, does not always mean they graduate having the skills that enable them to complete the task successfully and competently. Nothing has proven this point more to us than when interviewing potential teachers. We have been surprised on many occasions, when a candidate looks great on paper, but can't answer the questions, can't explain how she would set up her classroom, establish the classroom climate, describe a typical day, or plan and teach a quality lesson to students at the school. Likewise, many administrators have been burned when they hire a teacher who looks great on paper and perhaps even aces the interview questions, but once hired doesn't have a clue how to set up his classroom, manage his day, teach a quality lesson, or help all students achieve their learning goals. Not only are situations like this frustrating and costly for administrators, but they can also be devastating for teachers who find themselves in way over their heads.

The field of education, like the world, is changing rapidly. For highly qualified educators to remain competent and to keep up with the latest technological advances and pedagogical research-based knowledge, teachers and school leaders must become lifelong learners. To do so means that educators must be intrinsically motivated to learn and have numerous quality professional learning opportunities, such as those that are defined by the *National Staff Development Council's Standards for Staff Development* (1995) and based on andragogy (adult learning theory) best defined by Knowles, Holton, and Swanson (1998). Without motivation and opportunities to learn, grow, and build competence and complexity, teachers and school leaders will not increase their content and pedagogical knowledge or improve their instructional practices by increasing their repertoire of skills. Without continuous professional learning opportunities and support, educators will not be able to continue to reach higher levels of complexity (the ability to perform tasks using advanced skills), nor will they be able to continue to build the capacity of the school.

Any change in behavior requires some new learning, "ah, ha," or way of thinking about current practices followed by a new action or way of performing the old behavior. Often, teachers are energized and revitalized after spending time learning together and from each other. This can take place in traditional forms of staff development such as trainings, workshops, or conferences when the learning goals of the session are perceived as valuable and meaningful to the teacher, at the correct level of difficulty and complexity, and are aligned with what the teacher needs to know or do to help his students learn (i.e., just-in-time).

In recent years, new models of staff development have emerged in which teachers collaborate, study, share ideas, and solve problems with each other. Teachers are often even more excited and energized about new ideas or key learnings when they are able to work and study together in teams or professional learning communities. Constructing their own knowledge, by analyzing data, scoring student work, designing units, lessons, or common assessments; and sharing ideas and strategies with each other, is both powerful and motivating. Whether teachers are engaged in studying issues together, analyzing data, designing lessons or interventions, the work they are constructing together becomes meaningful and purposeful to them. They see the value in what they are doing, take ownership of the problem or situation, and have a vested interest in the outcome. In fact, often the knowledge and skills teachers gain during collaboration time is seen as more powerful and beneficial to them than the more traditional "sit-and-get" forms of professional learning.

The school community is more likely to perform at optimal levels and accomplish the shared mission, when individuals are competent, schools and districts have built capacity, and the deep learning of both move the organization to act on the new knowledge and skills they have gained.

# ■ STRUCTURING COMPETENCE

In 1994 at the National Staff Development Council Conference in Orlando, I (Rosie) called my session, "The Principal as Staff Developer." I wish I hadn't, because, all too often, when the principal becomes the staff developer, he or she provides learning opportunities as traditional, "sit-and-get, one-size-fits-all" training events. Although, at the time "sit-and-get" learning was not my intention, I should have called my session, "The Principal as a Teacher of Teachers" to get across the idea that teachers are a diverse group of learners, just like the students in their school. When principals view themselves as staff developers, they are more likely to provide traditional, "one-size" inservice activities to "develop others," by "doing things to them," because, as many staff developers report, "we know best what they need" (Vojtek, 1993). When principals view themselves as instructional leaders and teachers of teachers, however, they are much more likely to provide quality professional learning opportunities that personalize the learning experiences while meeting the precise learning needs of each teacher.

For decades, administrators and staff developers have been providing one-size-fits-all, sit-and-get, fly-in learning opportunities for teachers, most of which have met the needs of very few. In the fashion world, the rich and famous gravitate toward the designers because they know that this is the only way to get a garment that is personalized—one that will precisely fit their bodies. The rest of us aspire to find a designer original, off-the-rack, that fits our personal body shapes. Sometimes we get lucky—most of the time we don't. Thus, tailors over the years have made a fortune. The bottom line is that most of the time we have a really difficult time finding something that fits really well off-the-rack, even when it has been "sized." Needless to say, the fashion term one-size-fits-all congers up in our minds, at least, a huge t-shirt that, at best, fits me as a nightshirt and is still extra large on Bob. Most retail stores offer a variety of sizes (e.g., x-small to x-large). Yet, even with this offering, to get the perfect fit, there still must be the work of the tailor or, in our case, the teacher of teachers who customizes the learning to fit the individualized needs of each teacher. If school leaders or staff developers are to meet the unique individual learning needs of teachers, they must find ways to customize (and personalize) their learning experience, just as a designer carefully crafts the garments for celebrities.

What staff developers need to remember is that educators, certified and noncertified, each bring unique abilities, talents, and experiences to every situation. School leaders, like any great teacher, know that if they want their students to be successful, they must differentiate the curriculum and learning activities to meet the individual needs of the learner with whom they work. In addition, school leaders must distribute the leadership by empowering teachers to make choices and decisions about what they need to learn to help them meet the needs of the students in their classrooms. We are convinced that to provide quality learning experiences for all staff members, school leaders should, first and foremost, think of themselves as a "teacher of teachers." Next, they need to know their teachers and find ways to customize the learning so that it is just-in-time and tailored to fit their needs.

When school leaders structure professional learning opportunities using a "teacher of teachers" model, there are six principles that must be followed. These are: (1) establish and sustain the essential conditions,

(2) implement and practice andragogy (adult learning needs), (3) differentiate the learning, (4) engage in mutual learning opportunities, (5) employ a virtuous teaching cycle model, and (6) create sustainability. A brief description of each follows.

## 1. Establish and Sustain the Essential Conditions

Building the competence and capacity among all staff members requires that school leaders make sure that the school culture and climate support the quality of life we discussed in Chapter 3. The school's culture must be conducive to learning. This means that there is a climate of mutual respect and trust, and one in which mistakes are viewed as opportunities for learning. "A certain level of challenge is needed for continued personal and professional development. But too much pressure, and settings that are too controlling, can lead a person to drop below her optimal level of challenge. . . . Optimal growth and development necessitates feeling safe" (Jarrett-Weeks, 2001, p. 22).

Likewise, communication must be open, honest, reciprocal, and such that it encourages problem solving. The basic needs of all individuals within the school must be met. There must be adequate and appropriate resources, including time and support for all individuals. Professional learning opportunities must be "just-in-time" and job-embedded. The culture must support collaboration and interdependence, and everyone must understand and share the school's important mission. Most important, all staff members must take responsibility for their own professional learning and share the responsibility for building the capacity to accomplish the school's mission.

In addition, there must be time during each school day for teacher collaboration and networking. There must be ongoing follow-up and support in the form of mentoring, coaching, and feedback, through the use of a supervision (formative) model, not an evaluation (summative) model. Teachers must be given adequate resources and materials to support their new learning. Most important, teachers must have a clear understanding of the school's mission, vision, goals, and boundaries, so that within their own classroom contexts, they are empowered to make daily pedagogical decisions about when, how, and with whom to use their newly acquired knowledge, skills, or curricular materials. Once teachers become competent in using the new knowledge and skills (i.e., having moved through stages of mechanical to routine use), administrators must hold teachers accountable (through evaluation) for using their skills to achieve the desired results.

## 2. Implement and Practice Andragogy

The traditional "sit-and-get, one-size" model of staff development is based on pedagogy rather than andragogy. It treats adults in much the same way that adults have traditionally taught captive audiences of children who have no choice but to "sit-and-get." Even the best of these (i.e., workshops that model for participants how to use the instructional strategy with students, or how to effectively teach the content), all too often do not take into account the unique needs of adult learners (i.e., just-in-time needs and interests, life-centered orientation to learning, analysis and reflection of their own experiences, self-direction and autonomous needs, learning styles, and individual differences that increase with age). Knowles, Holton, and Swanson (1998) make an important distinction between the concepts of pedagogy and andragogy. They write:

> The pedagogy model, designed for teaching children, assigns to the teacher full responsibility for all decision making about the learning content, method, timing, and evaluation. Learners play a submissive role in the educational dynamics. In contrast, the andragogical model focuses on the education of adults and is based on the following precepts: adults need to know why they need to learn something; adults maintain the concept of responsibility for their own decisions, their own lives; adults enter the education activity with a greater volume and more varied experiences than do children; adults have a readiness to learn those things that they need to know in order to cope effectively with real-life situations; adults are life-centered in their orientation to learning; and, adults are more responsive to internal motivators than external motivators. The pedagogical model is an ideological model that excludes the andragogical assumptions. The andragogical model is a system of assumptions that includes the pedagogical assumptions. The andragogical model is not an ideology; it is a system of alternative sets of assumptions, a transactional model that speaks to those characteristics of the learning situation. (p. 72)

If school leaders are to actively engage and intrinsically motivate teachers and other staff members through the power of professional growth and learning, they must be cognizant of the core principles of andragogy. These core principles take into account the unique individual growth, learner differences, situational differences, and subject matter differences of each teacher. Based on the work of Knowles, Holton, and Swanson (1998, p. 4), the core adult learning principles are: (1) learner's need to know (i.e., why, what, and how); (2) self-concept of the learner (i.e., autonomous, self-directing); (3) prior experience of the learner (i.e., resources, mental models); (4) readiness to learn (i.e., life related, developmental task; (5) orientation to learning (i.e., problem-centered, contextual); and (6) motivation to learn (i.e., intrinsic value, personal payoff).

To build competence and organizational capacity so that it can be used as a motivational strategy that leads to optimal levels of performance, we must help teachers gain deeper understandings, build transformational learning, and provide them with the resources and support to translate their knowledge and skills into a continuous stream of powerful actions. We must help each individual unleash her unique talents and passions, while at the same time building the competence and capacity to accomplish the school's mission.

## 3. Differentiate the Learning

As a teacher of teachers, a leader must visualize the needs of all staff members in much the same way you would if they were students in your classroom. School leaders must discover who each person is (i.e., their strengths and weaknesses, their likes and dislikes, their unique talents and abilities) and what they want to know or do. Take time to ask each person, "Where do you see yourself five or ten years in the future?"—in other words, "What kind of a legacy do you want to leave?" The role of the school leader then becomes helping everyone continue to build upon their individual strengths, hone their weaker skills, use their knowledge and skills to help their students achieve high standards, find ways to encourage and support each person to develop their leadership abilities, and take responsibility for collaborating with others by learning together and sharing the important work they do. Most important, school leaders must take time and find ways to recognize, encourage, thank, and support each staff member for their important role in helping the school accomplish its mission.

No matter what professional learning activities a school leader chooses to use, adult learning needs (including readiness levels) must be assessed through a variety of characteristics (i.e., previous knowledge, background, years of experience, career stages, learning styles, interests, needs of students). In addition, school leaders need to listen to teachers (e.g., what they say, the questions they ask) to determine where they fit within the change process, using models such as the concerns-based adoption model also known as CBAM (Hall & Hord, 2001) or Schlechty's adoption model (Schlechty, 1993, p. 46–51).

By listening to teachers and asking questions, school leaders can help them choose what mode of learning will best meet their needs. For example, if teachers are at the initial stages of change and simply need to find out "what it is" and "how it will affect them," school leaders need to help develop an awareness and then help teachers to build their knowledge base about the new innovation (e.g., program, practice, process). School leaders can do this through a number of staff development models, including study groups, workshops, courses, institutes, curriculum development and adoption processes, inquiry, action research, and examining student work. If, however, teachers are asking questions about how to manage all the materials or how to plan and schedule their time, they are focused on the task and need help understanding how the innovation gets translated into practice. All too often, school leaders misinterpret this stage and give teachers more of the "why they should use it and how it works" leaving them frustrated because their questions weren't answered.

Teachers who are task-oriented need to see models, make visitations, hear what others are doing, and work with colleagues to practice using the innovation through peer coaching, or with a mentor or coach providing effective feedback (i.e., what works and why). Once teachers begin to use the innovation, they become more impact-oriented and need to know how the innovation is affecting their students. At this stage, teachers need time to examine student work, collaborate and network with others, and discuss the findings with a coach or mentor who can provide additional insights and feedback. Once teachers become comfortable with the innovation, they want to know how they can improve on the innovation so all students are successful and/or tweak it to make it their own. This can be done through staff development models such as networking, collaboration, coaching, mentoring, examining student work, case explorations, action research, reflection, and self-evaluation. Based on where educators are during the implementation of any new program or innovation, they will be faced with different learning needs. Figure 8.6 illustrates the questions educators may

**Figure 8.6** The Change Process—CBAM

**Levels of Concern, Stages of Concern, Levels of Use, and Modes of Learning**

| Change Process | Level of Concern | Stages of Concern | Level of Use | Comments of Concern | Modes of Learning |
|---|---|---|---|---|---|
| Renewal. | Concern about impact. | 6. Refocusing. | VI. Renewal. | How can I modify this for students? What if I (we) try ___? Next time let's try ___. | Higher level learning (analysis, synthesis, evaluation) through: reading (e.g., book, journal, research); writing for publication or self-reflection; presentations; networking; and collaboration. |
| Implementation and evaluation. | Concern about impact. | 5. Collaboration. | V. Integration. | Am I doing this right? Are we on the same page? How did you do ___? What works best with your students? | Collaboration with: team or department work; data-team analysis, including student work; study group; action research; interdistrict and intradistrict meetings; and online networking. |
| Implementation and practice. | Concern about impact. | 4. Consequence. | IVa. Routine use. IVb. Refinement. | How is this helping my students learn? Why are my students so far behind previous classes? How well did my students learn ___? Does this really work? | Practice and application with: self-reflection (e.g., journaling, blogs); feedback from supervisor, coach, or mentor; data analysis of student work; action research; and collaboration with grade level or department team. |
| Implementation and learning. | Concern about task. | 3. Management. | III. Mechanical use. | What do I do with all of this stuff? Why does it take so much time to get everything ready? How do I keep track of all the materials? I can't keep it all straight! It takes too much time! | Training by: workshop; course; online course; book; coaching; mentoring; just-in-time; peer observations; study group; outside consultant; explore models; school or classroom visitations; online discussion group; and networking. |
| Readiness and learning. | Concern about self. | 2. Personal. | II. Preparation. | What does using this mean for me? How will it affect my teaching? How does it align with what I already do? Will I be able to do this? | Training by: workshop; course; online course; book; computer tutorial; coaching; mentoring; peer-observation; seminar; just-in-time; study group; outside consultant; etc. |
| Initiation and readiness. | Concern about self. | 1. Informational. | I. Orientation. | Tell me more about ___? How can I find out more about ___? What is it? | Information gathering by: reading (e.g., journal, book, research, web search); conference; presentation; workshop; course; video; conversations. |
| | Unconcerned. | 0. Awareness. | 0. Nonuse. | I'm not interested. I don't care about ___. | |

SOURCE: (Adapted by Vojtek & Vojtek based on Hall & Hord, 2001)

ask at different stages of the change process and the types of learning experiences that can be used, while they are at that level or stage of concern, to build individual competence and/or organizational capacity.

No matter what new innovation educators are learning about (e.g., practice, program, or process)—based on their own previous background, knowledge, skill, disposition, and perceptions of themselves—individuals quickly find themselves in different stages of the change process. This is why teachers are frustrated with most staff development activities that rely on "one-size-fits-all" learning events. As you can see from Figure 8.6, workshops and presentations to large groups of teachers work well at the initiation and readiness stages of change when teachers do not know much about the change initiative. But as teachers gain more knowledge and skill, they will learn and apply the new skills at different rates (moving in and out of the various CBAM levels and stages of changes). Because of this, professional learning opportunities need to be personalized and differentiated to fit each teacher's needs and learning styles and just-in-time when they need to use it. To be the most effective, they should also be job-embedded within the context of the school or classroom. All too often, however, time and money win out, and school leaders opt for a "pull-out, one-size-fits-all" workshop, hoping to meet the needs of all learners. Unfortunately, by the end of these traditional "sit-and-get" workshops, teachers are no more comfortable with the learning innovation than they would be if everyone wore the same "one-size fits all" swim suit to the end of the year school picnic.

Likewise, Schlechty's (1993) model, which uses a frontier metaphor to describe how individuals adapt to change, lists five roles that "become activated in the restructuring process" (p. 47). These roles are: (1) *trailblazers*—people who are out in front; (2) *pioneers*—people who are right behind the trailblazers; (3) *settlers*—people who need to know where they are headed and what is expected of them; (4) *stay-at-homes*—people who will only change when the present conditions are intolerable or when the results are worth the effort; and (5) *saboteurs*—people who are actively engaged in stopping the change.

When helping to build teacher competence and organizational capacity, school leaders must be cognizant of the CBAM model, other models for adaptation, such as Schlechty's frontier model, and theories on change. They must understand the individual needs of each teacher and use this knowledge to plan meaningful, just-in-time, job-embedded differentiated learning experiences.

## 4. Engage in Mutual Learning Opportunities

School leaders must be a model for lifelong learning and set the tone and importance of mutual learning by embedding and structuring learning opportunities for all staff members into every school day. School leaders do this for their staff by finding those teachable moments and asking reflective questions that cause deep conversations and help to create the "ah, ha" moments.

When describing great leaders (such as Jack Welch from General Electric and Roger Enrico from PepsiCo) who use teaching as a way of leading others instead of "command-and-control," Noel Tichy and Nancy Cardwell (2002) write:

> Great teachers are also great learners. People who value knowledge enough to put the time and effort into communicating it well to others also value it enough to want to keep acquiring it for themselves. They are as avid about learning as they are about teaching, which leads them to see everyone they meet as a potential teacher and every situation they experience as a learning opportunity. (p. 58)

## 5. Employ a Virtuous Teaching Cycle Model

A virtuous teaching cycle model, as defined by Tichy and Cardwell (2002), is one in which leaders structure teaching and mutual learning situations into everyday operations. In other words, we are talking about job-embedded, just-in-time, ongoing mutual learning activities that help educators to create new meanings and deeper understandings through the important work they do. These activities range from formalized study groups, data-team meetings, coaching, collaborative planning, coteaching, and peer observations to informal shared planning times, copy machine room, and/or lunchroom conversations.

To help better define what they mean by a virtuous teaching cycle, Tichy and Cardwell compare and contrast it with what they call, "a vicious cycle" or the opposite end of the spectrum. They describe the vicious cycle as:

> Organizations that deplete their intellectual capital and actually become less smart, less aligned, and less energized every day. These are organizations that are caught in vicious nonteaching cycles where there is little or no knowledge transfer, intelligence is assumed to reside at the top, and everyone below senior management is expected to check their brains at the door. Not only do these organizations waste valuable information by not getting it to the people who need it, but they alienate workers and destroy their self-confidence, so that they stop thinking that they have anything to offer and stop trying to be contributors. (2002, p. 53)

On the other hand, in a virtuous teaching cycle, Tichy and Cardwell write:

> Each act or event of teaching improves the knowledge and abilities of both the students and the teachers and spurs them both to go on and share what they have learned with others. It creates a cascade of teaching and learning where, eventually, everyone is always playing the dual roles of recipient and imparter of valuable knowledge. Virtuous Teaching Cycles work to make people smarter every day, align them around shared goals, and give them a sense of self-confidence as valued and contributing members of the community. (2002, p. 53)

Although Tichy and Cardwell define the "virtuous teaching cycle" as being "how great leaders teach their companies to win," we visualize the virtuous teaching cycle as one in which school leaders help all staff members to increase their competence, complexity, and build capacity to achieve their mission. Using this model, the school leader develops a teachable point of view (based on what it will take to achieve the mission), while at the same time acquiring an omnivore-type commitment to learn. School leaders set the stage for mutual learning by reducing the hierarchy, thus becoming a teacher and learner during the interactive collaborative processes that they structure during the work day. Simultaneously, the school leader is committed to helping others develop their own teachable points of view so that they too can become teachers (i.e., mentors, coaches, data-team leaders, study group facilitators) by fostering deep conversations and sharing what they have learned with others.

The school leader helps others build their self-confidence to learn and teach by modeling and engaging in mutual learning activities. Tichy and Cardwell (2002) write that when organizations use the virtuous teaching cycle, they have more leaders because there is "conscious effort to teach people to be leaders. And they have better leaders because in order to teach, people must think through their ideas and develop the ability to communicate them, both of which hone their own leadership abilities" (p. 53). This happens when leaders are able to construct their learning with others, develop their point of view, and, in turn, teach it to others. We are not, however, talking about school leaders watching a PowerPoint lecture on "how" or "why" to do something at a district level and then being held responsible to deliver that same PowerPoint message to teachers back at their schools or in their departments. The virtuous teaching cycle means that school leaders take time to engage in quality conversations and meaningful activities about student learning that lead to deeper understandings and shared experiences. They, in turn, are able to teach what they have learned to their faculty or colleagues, while at the same time learning and making new connections with and from those they are teaching.

## 6. Create Sustainability

For such new behaviors to be sustained over time, school leaders must develop "deep learning that spreads and lasts" (Hargreaves & Fink, 2006, p. 17). This requires building individual competence while simultaneously building the capacity of the school to accomplish its shared mission. In order to engage in a cycle of continuous improvement, all educators must be committed to deep learning. They must gain the knowledge, skills, dispositions, and perceptions of themselves as individuals and as members of the collective school group. This is the only way they will be able to accomplish their shared mission.

School leaders need to help their school communities identify the knowledge and skills to achieve the goals, hone their talents and unique abilities, and build the capacity of all staff members. In order to sustain the effort over time, school leaders need to have clarity of purpose, stay the course, and make sure that the unique talents and expertise of individuals as well as those of the group are utilized. Sustainability "requires improvement, adaptation, and collective problem solving in the face of complex challenges that keep arising" (Fullan, 2005, p. 22). To help their school become an adaptive organization that can sustain change initiatives over time, administrators and school leaders must provide the culture and climate that is built on mutual trust and respect and views mistakes as opportunities for learning. There must be time for all members of the school community to engage in quality professional learning activities; meaningful conversations; and to explore new ideas, techniques, and practices. In addition, learning opportunities must be "just-in-time" when educators need to use the knowledge or skills. As many school districts have learned the hard way, when you train people to use a new software program, either before they have access to it or before they need it, by the time people need to use it to complete a task, they have forgotten what they learned and need to be retrained. Thus the saying, "if you don't use it, you lose it" couldn't be truer!

As veteran staff developers know all too well, teachers (and administrators) can be forced to attend workshops, use a particular curriculum, or complete tasks in a particular way. But they cannot be forced to be fully present during a training session (their minds can be a million miles away), nor can we control the portion of themselves they give or bring to a task, or to what degree they embrace a new innovation or idea. But by creating and sustaining the essential conditions that allow for quality professional learning, including a virtuous teaching cycle, we: help educators understand the purpose; empower them to take responsibility for learning; provide just-in-time experiences that are life-centered; and help educators realize that their results are worth their effort, and we are much more likely to intrinsically motivate them to increase their level of competence, increase their complexity, and build organizational capacity. "Feedback on competence and support for autonomy work hand in hand to promote self-motivated behavior—one ceases to exist without the other. While positive feedback can boost motivation, that alone is not enough. Studies show that a noncontrolling atmosphere is also essential to promote competence" (Jarrett-Weeks, 2001, p. 18).

We have just brushed the surface of what it takes to structure professional learning opportunities for all educators in such a way that school leaders can build the competence of individuals and the capacity of the organization. To go into greater depth is beyond the scope of this book. We do, however, suggest several valuable resources in Appendix B that we hope readers will use to help them differentiate the learning, distribute and build leadership, while becoming a teacher of teachers.

## QUESTIONS FOR DISCUSSION

1. In the case study at the beginning of this chapter, it is obvious that the district and school have invested in the technology and training for teachers to be able to use an online grading and report card system. Before you read the rest of this chapter, decide what essential conditions are in place and what essential conditions are missing to help teachers feel competent and have the ability to use the new report card grading system.

2. Don Costello obviously feels that his teachers should have the knowledge and skills to be able to use the report card system. He also feels that the training they received in August was adequate. After having read the above discussion, do you agree or disagree that teachers have been adequately trained? What would you say to Don? What would you suggest he do?

## ESSENTIAL CONDITIONS

In the case study at the beginning of the chapter, there are several essential conditions and principles of a "teacher of teachers" model used to build competence and organizational capacity that are not being met. Read along and see if you agree.

1. **Establish and sustain essential conditions.** It is difficult to tell from the scenario at the beginning of this chapter whether or not there is a culture and climate that is conducive to mutual respect, trust, and collaboration. It is also unclear how honest and open the communication process is, or if teachers felt safe to take risks, although the three teachers did let their guard down and barge into Don's office to share their frustrations with him. It is difficult to say whether or not there were adequate and appropriate resources available to meet the needs of individual teachers. The district did, for example, provide training in the use of the new online grading and report card system. It did not, however, differentiate the learning for individuals, nor offer training and support "just-in-time" when the teachers needed it. Likewise, there was no follow-up coaching and support that teachers needed to be successful with the transition between the old way of doing grades and report cards and the new system requirements. Although teachers were told they needed to use the new grading and reporting system, until Don let it slip, they did not understand the vision of what the district was trying to accomplish by creating a more complex student database system that would house all student records and provide educators with access to student information. Therefore, it would appear that communication is on a "need-to-know" basis. In situations like this, teachers are simply doing what they are told to do (if they can figure out how to do it) without understanding the reasons for the change. When teachers understand why there is a change, they are more likely to feel empowered to make professional decisions about student learning to achieve the shared school mission.

2. **Implement and practice andragogy.** Even if this were a hands-on workshop in a computer lab rather than just a PowerPoint demonstration to provide teachers with the knowledge and skills they would need to use the software to record grades and complete student report cards, it did not take into account the principles of adult learning. Specifically, the training did not help teachers understand the big picture—why it was important, how this process integrates with the larger, complete student database information system, and how it can help them make more informed decisions about their student learning. It was a "sit-and-get" experience in August, long before teachers needed to think about student grades and report cards. Therefore, because of the gap between when they learned how to use the software and the time they needed to use the software, most of the teachers had forgotten what they needed to do. Likewise, the district did not pay attention to prior experience, readiness, orientation to learning, or motivation to learn when putting together the training for the high school teachers. The district simply brought in a consultant who delivered the training so teachers would know how to do their grades and report cards using the new system.

3. **Differentiate the learning.** The workshop did not take into account the prior experience and competence of the learners. For example, Caryl Marcos, the health teacher who had taught at Rockville High for thirty-one years, yet never turned on a computer, found herself in the same workshop session as the rest of the teachers. Because everyone needed to do grades, they all got the same information about how to use the software at the same time and delivered by the same consultant. It is highly unlikely that the district considered the human side of this change effort, such as where teachers were as far as their comfort level with technology, their levels of concern, or their abilities to adapt to change.

4. **Engage in mutual learning opportunities.** Although it is not explicitly stated in the scenario, since he was not involved with grades and report cards, it is highly unlikely that Don Costello or any of the other administrators attended this workshop. He did not realize what the teachers were going through—or even what it was like "in the trenches" that morning as he sat behind his closed door, working on his attendance report.

5. **Employ a virtuous teaching cycle model.** In this situation, all of the teachers attended the same "sit-and-get" workshop, getting "one-size" knowledge and skill development training. It was a one-time event, without follow-up, job-embedded coaching, or support. There was no attempt to collaborate, develop leadership, build capacity, or share expertise. In fact, even Josh, the computer teacher, wasn't willing (even for money) to help Caryl, the health teacher. In this scenario, it is clear that teachers and administrators have not taken on the dual roles of recipient and imparter of valuable knowledge to help each other achieve the goal of using the online grading system, nor is there a culture of interdependence. It is obvious that the school leaders were not helping teachers build their self-confidence or competence in using the online grading program. In fact, because everything was thrown at the teachers in August, without follow-up coaching and support, it is clear that the learning was not broken down and scaffolded so that all teachers could be successful in entering their grades and completing their report cards. Overwhelmingly, the challenge of entering grades in the online program and completing the report cards in the new system was greater than the skill level of the teachers. There is no way that the teachers will be able to achieve optimal performance levels when they are anxious, frustrated, and have all but given up on using the new system to record student progress and grades.

6. **Create sustainability.** One can ask, what is left to sustain? The teachers have decided they are not going to use the online grading program because it is too difficult and time consuming. They want their old report cards back. Citing a change in working conditions, the teachers are ready to file a grievance if they don't get to do their grades and report cards the way they have always done them.

## WHAT WOULD YOU DO?

1. After reading the above discussion about the essential conditions that need to be in place to help teachers build competence, do you agree? Is there anything else that you would add?

2. Before you read the rest of the story, look back at what you said you would do if you were Don Costello. Is there anything else you would add to your list?

Read on to compare your list with what Mr. Costello chose to do.

## AND NOW FOR THE REST OF THE STORY

*Just as Don Costello was signing his name to the printed version of his monthly attendance report to the superintendent, there was a knock at the door. Don looked up, smiled, and said, "Come in." It was Karen Shea, the curriculum director, and Doug Powell, the technology coordinator. Don looked at his watch. It was only 1:30 P.M. The emergency staff meeting wasn't supposed to start for an hour. But Karen and Doug had promised to stop by before the meeting so they could get the issues before walking in front of the firing squad.*

*"Thanks for coming over," Don said, putting his sealed report into the manila envelope to be sent that afternoon via the district courier.*

*"So, what's up?" Karen asked. "Since we hadn't heard anything from the high school after the August training, we figured no news was good news."*

*"Yeah, that's what I thought, too," Don said. "That is until today!"*

*"They sure don't give you much warning, do they?" Doug laughed nervously, not sure what to expect.*

*"You can say that again," Don said.*

*"So, just what are the issues?" Karen asked, taking out a legal pad and getting ready to script.*

*"It's like this," Don said, cutting to the chase. "We trained the teachers in August on how to do their grades and report cards. That was when the consultant from Classroom Grade Book could do our training. We decided that August would be okay because it would give teachers a couple of months to play with the program before they had to do their report cards. Trouble is, nobody played!"*

*"What do you mean?" asked Karen.*

*"I mean," said Don, clearly frustrated, "that because we didn't tell them they had to start entering their grades in the program or make them do their midterm reports using the new report card system, nobody did anything with it. They did their grades and their midterm reports just like they did last year. It wasn't until this past week, and especially this weekend, that most of the teachers decided to start entering their grades into the program. I guess that is when the frustration started. It seems that some of them couldn't get into the program because they didn't have a password."*

*"Nobody said anything to me about that," Doug shrugged his shoulders.*

*"They didn't say anything to me, either," Don said. "I guess they were too embarrassed to say anything—or else they just thought if they waited long enough, something would happen. I guess it did, because as the teachers who could get into the program started saving their grades, they realized that some of what they did got saved and some didn't."*

*"What do you mean?" asked Doug.*

*"I'm not sure, but Marty Kubeck, one of our English teachers, showed me pages of grades he had entered, saved, and printed. When he logged in to add more grades, the grades he thought he put into the system weren't there."*

*"Were they using different computers?" Doug asked.*

*"I don't know. But," he asked, "why would that make a difference?"*

*"If they used different computers and didn't save their work to the server, then their grades would only be saved on the hard drive of the computer they were using. The next time they logged on, the grades they entered wouldn't be on the server, unless that is where they saved them.*

*(Continued)*

(Continued)

*Unless they work on the same computer each time, or store their grades in a file on the server, like the consultant told them to do, they won't have access to the information. Make sense?" Doug asked.*

*"Yeah, that's probably what they did. But what about Nancy Roux, one of our science teachers? Miraculously, she got her grades entered and imported into the report card system, but when she typed in the numbers to make comments, the comments were all messed up."*

*"That's because we told them not to use the numbers on their old comment list. We told them they would have to scroll down to find the comment they wanted to use. The Classroom Grade Book programmers didn't use our old numbering system. They put them in alphabetically. We told the teachers that—but I guess we should have given them a shocking pink cheat sheet to wake them up enough so they wouldn't forget!" Doug laughed.*

*"And, of course, there is Caryl Marcos and several other dinosaurs like her. You know Caryl. She has never used a computer in her life, and if she had her way, she probably never would. Talk about computer challenged! She makes everybody's life miserable. It is just one catastrophe after another when it comes to any kind of technology, including the old filmstrip projectors—if she still has one hidden in her room! Even Josh Wilcox won't help her any more! He says it's not worth any amount of money. Actually he said a lot more than that when I talked to him at lunch—but you really don't want to go there."*

*Hearing that, Doug sat down at the table and buried his head in his hands. "And if that isn't enough," Don continued, "the teacher's union is going to file a grievance—change in working conditions, if we don't let them use the old report card system to do their grades." As he said it, he shot one of those "if looks could kill" glances at Karen.*

*"Don't shoot the messenger," she said. After a long pause, Karen said, "I guess we should have done the training on our inservice day in November, like we wanted to do. Especially since the teachers didn't use the last couple of months to get comfortable with the program, anyway."*

*"When you don't use it, you lose it," Don mumbled under his breath. "So, what are we going to do?"*

*Doug looked up. "For starters, I need to talk with the teachers who have used the programs to find out exactly what went wrong. But since grades are due by Friday, and before I can do anything substantial, it will be Tuesday. There isn't much time."*

*Karen picked up the phone and called the superintendent. The three of them explained the situation to Dr. Jenkins. As they talked it through again, it became clear that there were several issues, which Karen had begun framing. "First," she explained, "there is the issue of the software not functioning the way it is supposed to function."*

*"I will meet with the teachers, do some trouble shooting, and find out where the glitches are," Doug suggested. "If I need to, I will get the Classroom Grade Book technology reps over here to help us fix the bugs in the program. But that may take a few days, depending on what we find," he told the group. "In addition, I will get a couple of my tech guys to go through the program and create screen shots, and make a step-by-step guide that we can post on our Intranet as well as make a printed tutorial that teachers can use." He looked at Karen and said, "If you can interview the teachers to find out what their questions are, we can create a "frequently asked questions" and answers section on our Web site, so no matter when teachers are entering their grades or working on report cards, if they get stuck, they can look there for answers. I just need to know what their questions are, and then we can get to work on giving them the answers."*

*"I can do that," Karen said, then added, "Is there a way that you could do a streaming video that explains what they need to do? Or, at the least, maybe we could put audio directions with the screen shots, so teachers can listen if they don't want to read while they follow the steps. It will be good to have several different ways to help the teachers learn how to use the software."*

*"No problem—anything for you, Karen," Doug said, winking.*

*"What if we do a training session tomorrow after school, once I know where the glitches are," Doug suggested. "We can record the training session and then burn it to DVDs that people can take home and watch."*

*"It sounds like you have a plan,"* the superintendent said from the other end of the conference call line.

*"Yes, it is a beginning,"* Don said. *"But we haven't talked about the real issue."*

*"Which is?"* asked the superintendent.

*"The teachers want to use their old report cards. Even if we hold tight to making them use the new report card system, Doug and his tech guys aren't going to have everything ready to go in time for the teachers to get the report cards done by next Wednesday,"* Don stopped.

*"What would you like to do?"* the superintendent asked.

*"I have a suggestion,"* Karen joined in. *"The teachers are in different places using the report cards. Some of them, like Nancy Roux, are almost finished. Others, like Caryl Marcos, have not even started. Do you agree?"* she asked Don.

Don shook his head, *"yes."*

*"Once we know who the teachers are that have been successful, let's bring them and the department chairs together and make sure that they all feel competent using the program. Doug, can your tech guys help with that training?"*

*"You got it."*

*"Good. Then I can get subs to cover classes, so that the department chairs and some of the teachers like Nancy can coach the struggling teachers during their prep times and guide them through the process."* She stopped. *"But it is still going to take time—more time than we have. What if,"* she said, talking out loud, *"we send a note home to parents and post it on our Web site, saying something like, there was a computer glitch and grades will be delayed an extra week? Is that something we could do?"* she looked at the phone, waiting for a response from the other end.

*"I don't see why not. Stuff like this happens. I would much rather help the teachers learn to use the program, give them the support they need to get through this, and use the new report card system rather than going backwards."* The superintendent paused. *"What do you think, Don? You are the one who will have to sell this idea to your teachers."*

Don thought for a moment. *"I think it just may work. Yeah,"* he said confidently, smiling for the first time all day. *"I like it. We messed up when we didn't scaffold the learning by providing time for the teachers to practice entering grades and requiring that their first midterm report be done with the new program. We didn't take into consideration that the comfort level using the computer program would be different for different teachers and that some of them would be more adept at using the computers than others. Because they didn't use the program until the last minute, we didn't know that there would be technical difficulties that they would encounter. And, we didn't give them access to technical support 'just-in-time.'"* Don stopped, pausing long enough to give a great sigh of relief as he continued saying, *"What I really like about this, is that instead of just using Doug's guys to do all the training, we will use his guys to help build tutorials that people can refer back to 24/7 when they get stuck. But we are also using them to train in-house experts, that is, our department chairs and a few other trailblazers, so they can coach other teachers through the process and help to answer questions along the way."* Again he stopped. *"I only regret one thing,"* he said.

Karen and Doug looked up at him. The superintendent on the other end of the phone line asked, *"What is that?"*

*"I wish I would have thought through this process more last summer when we planned the workshop. If I had known my teachers better and had anticipated the ongoing help and support they would need, we could have had all of this in place, so that the teachers wouldn't have had to struggle like they did to do something that was designed to make their life and workload easier."*

*"One more suggestion,"* the superintendent said without stopping for a response. *"I suggest that the three of you meet with the department chairs and tech guys periodically to troubleshoot the glitches and brainstorm the solutions so that the rest of the year goes even more smoothly. These will be the people that you will want to use to become your data-team leaders, as we continue to add to our new database system and access the information to help us make informed decisions about student learning."*

*(Continued)*

(Continued)

*"Great idea,"* Nancy said. *"It will really help to have those resident experts serving as coaches for the rest of the teachers."*

*"Yeah, who knows, maybe Caryl Marcos will decide that computers aren't so foreign after all and keep teaching for another ten years!"*

*"You never know,"* Doug said as he stood up just as the bell rang signaling the end of another day. *"Let's go talk with the teachers, find out what the issues are, and let them know what we are going to do to help them."*

*"I'm with you,"* Don said, this time not afraid to face the firing squad.

## CHAPTER SUMMARY

The feelings educators have about their own level of competence is a powerful motivational force. This force can manifest itself in both positive or negative forms. When a person has the capacity and capability of meeting the challenge of the task, he or she is more likely to experience flow and achieve optimal levels of performance. When a person lacks the knowledge and skills to successfully achieve the demands of the challenge, he or she feels anxious and overwhelmed. When a person's knowledge and skills are greater than the challenge, he or she becomes bored.

In order to stay motivated, each person must continue to build complexity by increasing his or her own knowledge and skills. Likewise, for the organization to continue to work at optimal levels, it must build the collective capacity of the group by first building individual competence toward achieving the school's goals, ultimately increasing the levels of complexity and the groups' capacity to achieve the school's mission.

## NEXT STEPS

1. What do competence and capacity look like, sound like, and feel like in your situation? What would you like them to look like, sound like, or feel like? Make a list. Put a star by those things that are already in place in your school or system. Put a check by those things that you would like to implement or explore further.

2. If possible, discuss with others what you found interesting about this case study on competence and building capacity and what you found challenging.

3. Select one or two ideas and list several changes you can make to improve the competence and build capacity within your own school. What barriers may get in your way? List choices that you can make to help alleviate or decrease those barriers.

4. Decide on one or two things that you are going to implement in your current situation because of this chapter. List them along with any notes to help you remember what you want to do.

# 9

# Autonomy

*Leveraging the Freedom*
*Within Articulated Boundaries*
*to Make Informed Decisions*

## ■ PICTURE THIS

*Kit Johnson looked up. She saw third-grade teacher, Gina Berry, standing at the door of her office with her hands on her hips, face flushed, and frustration written all over her face.*

*"I can't do it! I can't teach this spelling program anymore," Gina blurted out. In five minutes the bell would ring, lunch would be over, and the third graders would be returning to class. Once again, it would be time for them to take out their whiteboards and practice words from the new scripted spelling program.*

*Kit knew that Gina didn't like the spelling program the district had adopted. Kit was glad that Gina had volunteered to represent their school on the committee because of her expertise and passion for language arts. But after her ideas were virtually ignored by central office, Gina said she would never serve on another district committee. Kit hoped that Gina would change her mind, but right now, it didn't look like that would happen anytime soon!*

*Gina and her colleagues had wanted each grade level to develop a core set of spelling words related to the district curriculum and aligned with state standards. Given time, Gina felt the teachers could develop a stronger spelling program than any available for purchase. Ultimately, the decision came down to a change in philosophy. Central office administrators strongly opposed spelling tests. The teachers disagreed. The conflict was never resolved, just overruled.*

*(Continued)*

(Continued)

*In early September, all primary teachers were pulled out of their classrooms for half-day training, with the mandate to use the program for thirty minutes each day, no matter what. The teachers were told this new program would replace the traditional way of teaching spelling. There would be no more spelling lists or Friday spelling tests. Principals were told to make sure teachers followed the program. Kit and the other principals were given a checklist of what to look for when they observed teachers using this program. This checklist was to be part of the formal evaluation process and included in each teacher's file.*

*Kit had observed all of the teachers in her school using the program. All of them, including Gina, had complied with the mandate and, as far as she could tell, were doing the best they could to implement the program.*

*"What can I do to help?" Kit asked hesitantly, afraid to hear the answer.*

*"I can't stand the smell of those markers another day! My students are not spelling as well as they did last year at this time. I look at their papers, and I feel like we are wasting our time with this spelling program. The words don't match what we are teaching. The pace is so fast, I can't see every student's whiteboard each time they write a word; I know they are practicing some of the words wrong. I hate it! I just hate this spelling program!" Gina blurted out, then stopped.*

*Gina sat down in a chair by the door. In a softer voice, she said, "I'm sorry. I shouldn't have come in here like this. I have been trying so hard to do what I am supposed to do. But I am just so frustrated teaching something I don't believe is helping my students learn."*

*Although students were excited to use whiteboards and markers in September, after seven months of use, they were tired of the activity. Kit knew the district bought cheap whiteboards and smelly markers that left streaks when students erased their writing, making them hard for teachers to read. She also knew that most of her teachers had purchased markers that didn't smell and whiteboard cleaner they used once a week, after school, to clean the streaks.*

*Even though the bell just rang, Kit knew that Gina did not want to go back to class and read the words from the scripted program, while students wrote the words as fast as they could, saying the word, spelling the word, erasing the word, ready to write the next word. She knew Gina was right. It didn't matter that the words were too easy, too difficult, or even words third-grade students used in their writing. The premise was that if Gina followed the script, her students should learn. The reality was that "one-size-fits-one," if you are lucky!*

*Kit felt helpless and frustrated. On several occasions, Kit had looked the other way as Gina and other teachers in her school shut their doors when they thought no one was looking. If she asked, she knew that Gina would say she just wanted to help students practice spelling words in a different way and to challenge them to spell some of their third-grade vocabulary and content words "just for fun." Because Kit knew that Gina was a conscientious teacher, she didn't have to ask to know that when Gina closed her door, she felt guilty.*

*Kit looked at Gina. "I have an idea," she said. "Let's meet in the library after school. Invite the other third-grade teachers to join us and bring your students' literacy portfolios."*

## ■ WHAT IS AUTONOMY?

As we said at the beginning of the book, the world of teaching is much different since the standards and accountability movement began in the 1990s. Although some would argue that teacher education programs are still not preparing our teachers for the challenges they find in the classroom, the reality is that teachers are more prepared than they have ever been for their life-long careers. In most states, they are required to have a bachelor's and master's degree to be certified. Currently, many teachers now earn credits beyond a masters, including a fifth year degree, a doctorate, additional certifications in specialty areas (i.e., special education, literacy, administration), as well as accumulating numerous required hours of professional development credits for recertification. In fact, many state universities now offer an EdD, where in the past they were only able to offer a master's degree. Other universities also offer educators an EdD, as well as or instead of the traditional PhD. This trend is making a doctorate degree for educators more appealing, affordable, and attainable. With so many educators earning their EdD, one of our friends commented the other day that it appears as if a "doctorate of education" is becoming the "new master's." We strongly believe it is time that teachers and administrators are recognized as professionals and are respected as "knowledge workers."

Because educators make numerous professional decisions each day, they must be given the autonomy to make the best possible decisions, in the moment, to ensure their students' academic success. Autonomy is the ability to make choices that provide for authenticity and self-determination. Rather than controlling people and requiring them to act in a particular way, autonomy is about giving educators the latitude, within clearly defined and articulated boundaries, to make professional, informed decisions and choices that are aligned within the structure and framework of the morally compelling mission of the school or district.

Using autonomy as a strategy can be a powerful motivational catalyst for building and sustaining school improvement efforts. In the book, *Learning Through Knowledge Management*, authors Ahmed, Kok, and Loh (2002) define autonomy as "having control over means as well as the ends of one's work" (p. 92). We define *autonomy* as *the freedom and latitude within clearly defined, aligned, and articulated boundaries for all educators to make informed professional decisions that directly impact student learning and promote the accomplishment of the school's mission.*

Our definition is based on the two types of autonomy, strategic and operational, as described by Ahmed, Kok, and Loh (2002, p. 92). Like them, we believe there must be a balance between both strategic and operational autonomy. Ahmed, Kok, and Loh define *strategic autonomy* as "the freedom to set one's own agenda"; and *operational autonomy* as "the freedom to attack a problem, once it has been set by the organization, in ways that are determined by the individual." They write:

> Operational autonomy encourages a sense of individualism and promotes entrepreneurial spirit, whereas strategic autonomy is concerned more with alignment with organizational goals. Firms that are most successful emphasize operational autonomy but retain strategic autonomy for top management. In these companies top management specify ultimate goals to be attained but thereafter provide freedom to allow individuals to be creative in the ways they achieve goals. The opposite approach, giving strategic autonomy, ultimately leads to lower strategic alignment. The result of strategic alignment is an absence of guidelines and focus on effort. In contrast, having too little operational autonomy also has the effect of creating imbalance. Here the 'roadmaps' become too rigidly specified, and control drives out innovative flair leading eventually to bureaucratic atmospheres. (p. 92–93)

For those reasons, Ahmed, Kok, and Loh state that a balance between operational and strategic autonomy is the most desirable combination.

Our definition of autonomy uses a balance between both strategic and operational autonomy. A balanced approach means that top-level administrators (which could also include the board of education), through whatever decision-making model they choose, use strategic autonomy (i.e., top-down, committee consensus) to define, align, and clearly communicate the standards and policies. Once that is in place, they afford school leaders and teachers the ability to use operational autonomy, within clearly established and communicated boundaries and frameworks, to make decisions at the building, department, grade, or individual level. For operational autonomy to work, administrators must clearly communicate the mission, provide the appropriate levels of support, and hold teachers accountable for accomplishing student learning goals. At the same time, teachers must perceive themselves as working in an environment that is balanced and aligned with a shared, collective, morally compelling purpose, including mission, vision, and goals, and have the ability to use professional judgment to make sound professional decisions within the unique context of their classrooms (e.g., student learning needs). Teachers must have the freedom to use creativity and intuition to put their own signature and style into the pedagogical process. The balance between strategic and operational autonomy will allow educators to balance the art and science of pedagogy, selecting each at appropriate times.

Teachers can act more autonomously when they understand what motivates them and then find ways to do their jobs, while at the same time meeting their own needs and the needs of their students, within the clearly established boundaries. For teachers to become self-motivated, their willingness to act in one way or the other must come from inside the person rather than from external factors. Autonomy does not mean that teachers, schools, or districts are simply allowed to shut their door and do what they want. To build support for any new task, activity, or innovation, school leaders must build interest, ownership, and support by effectively communicating the purpose for the change with all members of the school community. These changes must be aligned and viewed as necessary to achieve that mission.

For autonomy to be a powerful motivational strategy that leads to optimal performance, all teachers must be committed to the mission. They must be willing to interact vertically and horizontally to collaborate and learn with other teachers. School leaders must be committed to interact laterally with other school and district leaders if they are to continue to learn, improve, and achieve optimal results. Ultimately, for autonomy to be effective, educators must take responsibility and be held accountable for accomplishing the school's mission to achieve student learning goals.

## ■ NEEDS MET BY AUTONOMY

The motivational strategy of autonomy helps to meet educator's needs, as defined by Maslow's (1998) esteem and self-actualization needs, Herzberg's hygiene needs and set of motivators (as cited in Heller, 1998), Deci's (1995) autonomy, Glasser's (1998a) power and freedom, and Sagor's (2003) potency. (See Appendix A.)

# ■ WHAT AUTONOMY IS AND ISN'T

Figures 9.1 and 9.2 will help to clarify autonomy. Figure 9.1 explains what autonomy is and what it isn't. Figure 9.2 compares the differences between an autonomy-supportive environment and an autonomy-deficient environment.

# ■ WHY IS AUTONOMY IMPORTANT?

For years, administrators and staff development leaders have been frustrated by how difficult it is to change teacher behavior and reform classroom instruction. Each year, districts spend thousands of dollars to bring in dynamic speakers, provide training sessions that are filled with engaging and stimulating activities, and give teachers resources designed to change their behavior and improve student learning. All too often, administrators

**Figure 9.1**   Autonomy Defined

| What Autonomy Is | What Autonomy Isn't |
| --- | --- |
| Interdependence. Members of a school community who share the responsibility for achieving its morally compelling mission. | Independent. Mavericks who do what they want in their classrooms without regard for others or alignment with the school's morally compelling mission. |
| A sense of ownership, pride, and responsibility for one's actions. | A sense of "who cares" because "I just do as I am told." |
| Interest and commitment based on purpose and needs for the new task, activity, or innovation. | Mandated participation and/or use of the new task, activity, or innovation. |
| Self-determination. | Learned dependence. |
| Authenticity. | Compliance. |
| Shared decision making and problem solving. | Micromanagement. |
| A menu of options for pedagogical and curriculum decisions. | Prescribed, teacher-proof curriculum. |
| Latitude to think, act, and make professional decisions using creativity and ingenuity to meet the individual needs of students. | Restrictions and mandates on when, how, and what should be taught, often prescribed using pacing guides and scripted programs. |
| Actions that are aligned and congruent with the system's mission, vision, goals, and values. | Loosely-coupled suborganizations within the building that are not aligned or congruent with the system's mission, vision, goals, and values. |
| A sense of correlation and direct benefit between what administrators and teachers do and the outcomes for staff and students. | No correlation or sense of benefit between what administrators and teachers do and the outcomes for staff and students. |
| Freedom and latitude to do one's work to achieve the shared mission. | Told this is what, when, and how to do one's work. |

**Figure 9.2**    Structuring an Autonomy-Supportive Environment

| Autonomy-Supportive Environment | Autonomy-Deficient Environment |
|---|---|
| Choices are made freely within clearly defined boundaries. | Choices are nonexistent or imposed from above. |
| Clear understanding about the purpose, role, and power to make informed, professional decisions about issues that directly affect individual and group work. | Multiple perceptions of the purpose, authority, structures, and processes about individual and group work. |
| Efficacious educators with an internal locus of control. A sense of "we make a difference." | Educators without efficacy with an external locus of control. "There is nothing we can do" or "It is all their fault." |
| Principal as entrepreneur. | Principal as middle manager. |
| School has control of budget and resources. | All essential materials and resources are provided by the district. |
| Educators treated as professionals and respected knowledge workers. | Educators treated as blue-collar workers with the perception of "just a teacher." |
| School has adequate and appropriate resources, including time and professional learning. | Resources are limited, often duplicated, and there is little time for collaboration and professional learning. |
| Professional learning that provides time to network and collaborate with others (inside and outside one's own school or system) to create meaning, question assumptions, and build deeper understandings about one's work. | Professional learning that engages educators in activities that are "done to them for their own good." |
| Informed professional judgment. | Informed prescription. |
| Ownership of the problems with time to design solutions by those closest to the situation. | Outside forces that provide innovations that are perceived to meet the needs of the school or system. |
| A feeling of empowerment. | A feeling of coercion and being controlled. |
| Accountability with members sharing and accepting responsibility and ownership. Internal decisions garner results. | Accountability with understanding cause and effect. External forces cause results. Often educators feel victimized and blame external forces. |
| Everyone has access to information that is openly and honestly communicated. | Information is tightly controlled and shared only as needed with others. |
| People feel that their voices are heard and their opinions are respected. | People feel that "no one listens, hears, or cares about what I think." |
| A climate that is conducive to risk taking, creativity, and problem solving. Members feel trusted, respected, and are provided with sufficient resources to do their work. | A climate in which people feel afraid to experiment and try new innovations for fear of failure. Members feel a lack of trust and a sense that they are being controlled. |
| Evaluators utilize self-reflection and self-evaluation as part of the evaluation process. Feedback and support is frequent and ongoing, formal and informal. | Evaluators provide formal feedback about performance on a yearly cycle without input from subordinates. "I know best about what you should be doing." |

discover months or years later that the resources and materials are sitting in a closet on a shelf, collecting dust, still bound by the original shrink wrapping. Once the teacher returns to class, she simply closes the door and does what she has always done.

When a teacher chooses not to comply, school leaders may think that the teacher lacks motivation. We, however, do not believe that teachers are unmotivated. Teachers are either willing (or motivated) to do what we have asked or they are not. Their refusal to do something, whether they choose to do nothing or choose to do something else instead, is a motivated act.

Trying to *make* teachers change their behavior, love an idea, or share the enthusiasm for an innovation has frustrated many school leaders. Instead of leveraging a teacher's motivation, commitment, involvement, and need for continual growth, far too often, school leaders increase their control (often through coercion) over teachers to change their thinking, behavior, or attitudes. Even when the administrator has the best of intentions to help improve the teaching and learning process, too much outside pressure and control will undermine the teacher's performance and professional growth. Most administrators have worked with or know teachers who have responded in a situation like this by closing their doors and doing what they have always done. In fact, teams of teachers often decide to circle their wagons to protect their territory, at which time a stand-off occurs, usually until either a frustrated administration gives up and goes away or a new innovation is born to take its place. (Thus the term, *this, too, shall pass.*)

Teachers who are given the freedom to make informed, professional decisions and choices that directly impact teaching and learning are likely to be efficacious and have internalized their locus of control. They will believe that they can and do make a difference in the lives of their students. They take ownership, pride, and responsibility for their choices and actions. Teachers who are given latitude to make choices often tend to be more creative, more willing to take risks, find their work more satisfying and fulfilling, and have a higher sense of self-worth (Deci, 1995). Because teachers believe that what they are doing is best for their students, they have a vested interest in student assessment results and are compelled to put forth whatever effort it takes to make sure their students achieve the benchmarks and develop to their greatest potential.

## ■  STRUCTURING AUTONOMY

School leaders must create an environment that supports autonomy. That is, they must actively encourage self-initiation, experimentation, creativity, ingenuity, and responsibility—all within established guidelines and appropriate boundaries. For teachers to make professional choices and participate in decision making, they must have ample resources (e.g., time, flexibility, access to information). Likewise, for teachers to make choices about how they will teach the required curriculum there must be a variety of supporting structures, technologies, and materials that allow teachers to differentiate the learning activities and help them acknowledge individual learning styles and needs of their students. Creating a positive environment with norms conducive to collaboration, trust, open communication, and shared decision making is important. Teachers must have a clear understanding of the boundaries if leaders are to promote responsibility without undermining authenticity.

Because of the standards movement of the 1990s, for example, states have determined the curriculum standards, frameworks, and assessments. Educators have an explicit understanding of what students need to know and be able to do to achieve state and district benchmarks. At no other time in the history of education has the teaching and learning process been so clearly defined and articulated. Because the content and processes are so clearly defined and the accountability so high for all members of the school community, teachers have a moral obligation to teach and insure that all students achieve the desired goals and outcomes. Within the district's structure and framework, and as long as their students reach defined benchmarks, teachers should have the freedom to make informed, professional decisions about how to best help their students learn. When schools or districts are underperforming, outside agencies (e.g., district, state, province) have a moral (if not legal) obligation to intervene (Fullan, 2005). This should not, however, be in a fear-induced, punitive way, as defined by NCLB legislation, but through positive assistance, additional resources, and support that is grounded in the ten strategies that lead to optimal performance.

When teachers choose a grade level or a subject area, they are, in fact, choosing the content they will teach. Their job is to make sure that all of their students are able to achieve defined curricular and learning goals. When school leaders allow teachers to select the pedagogical methods used during instruction that will help them meet the learning needs of all students in their classroom, they are, in fact, giving them autonomy. Many districts provide a menu of options from a variety of sources that teachers use to help students learn. Rather than using pressure and control to manage and motivate teachers, school leaders must find ways to encourage, inspire, and support innovation and risk taking, provide a forum for teachers to be problem solvers, and give them a voice in decision making.

Likewise, central office must establish the same structure and framework, thus giving building administrators autonomy over the school. Ouchi (as cited in Fullan, 2005) says that we must "uproot the top-down way of doing things and replace it with huge, revolutionary change" (p. 79) in which "every principal is an entrepreneur" and "every school controls its own budget" (p. 79). Fullan (2005) adds that:

1. The district has a critical role in helping to develop *school capacity* to act in more autonomous ways.

2. Successful districts . . . foster cross-school (and beyond) learning—lateral capacity building which has powerful benefits for individual schools and the systems as a whole (indeed, this is one way in which "systems" change toward sustainability).

3. Local school autonomy does not guarantee that underperforming schools will improve—districts have a moral (and increasingly legal) obligation to intervene in these schools. (p. 80)

For teachers, schools, and districts to work autonomously in the manner that Fullan describes, there must be an autonomy-supportive environment that is open, honest, and conducive to risk taking and experimentation. Communication must be two-way for feedback and trust to be established. Building administrators must be the conduit in which all communication flows. They must serve as a sieve that is able to effectively buffer external pressures and outside interferences, while communicating all pertinent information with stakeholders in a timely manner. District administrators must work in the same way to buffer external pressures from state and federal officials while communicating pertinent information to all stakeholders within the school system. Ultimately, schools must have autonomy if they are to be held accountable for results. School leaders and faculties must still be accountable for their actions and behaviors when they are given freedom to make strategic and/or operational autonomous choices.

## QUESTIONS FOR DISCUSSION

1. The case study at the beginning of this chapter suggests that teacher morale and motivation are impacted by the new spelling program. Before you read the rest of the chapter, see if you can identify the issues causing low teacher morale and what power, if any, Kit Johnson has to help Gina and the other teachers change.

2. What essential conditions were in place to support autonomy? Are there essential conditions missing that need to be in place for Kit to give autonomy to the teachers? If so, what?

3. Kit is going to be meeting with the teachers after school. They will be bringing their literacy portfolios. If you were Kit, what strategies would you use to motivate the teachers to create "buy-in" and support for the spelling program? Is there a way to give teachers more autonomy and still keep to the integrity of the scripted program?

## ESSENTIAL CONDITIONS

Within the case study there are several essential conditions that are missing that have decreased teacher motivation and stifled their autonomy. The following is a discussion of the essential conditions raised in the case study, with an explanation of the critical issues as we see them. Read along and see if you agree.

1. **Quality of life.** It is obvious that the basic needs of teachers within this district are not being met. There is a lack of trust and mutual respect. The social and emotional structures do not support and encourage risk taking and innovation or provide for what Fullan (2005) calls *cyclical energizing* (p. 27), which includes positive energizing forces as well as energy recovery rituals. Teachers do not have quality resources and materials that

allow them to do their jobs. As in this case, when teachers are given inferior tools and equipment, they feel compelled to purchase the necessary materials to adequately accomplish the required tasks. Within reason, teachers should not have to purchase their own materials to do their work, especially supplies that are mandated. They should also have some choice in selecting the type of materials that work best for them.

If schools are to be held accountable and responsible for their decisions and actions, they must have adequate funding and resources available to them. Principals must have control of their own budgets, especially when it comes to acquiring and purchasing the tools and supplies necessary to do their work. When group purchases are available, rather than taking the funds away from the schools for such purchases, schools should be given the choice to opt in or out based on their own perceived needs. Far too often, well-intentioned central office managers look for bargains (that may or may not meet the schools needs) and make purchases without input from those using the supplies. Or, in their haste, they make last minute decisions about how to spend grant money at the end of the cycle before they lose it and purchase materials or supplies that the school either doesn't want or doesn't need.

Because money for resources is tight, schools need autonomy to make budget decisions and then be held accountable for their decisions and results. If, however, the school finds itself in trouble due to inadequate student gains or budgetary issues, central office must step in and help the struggling school. But until that happens, schools must have the freedom to make decisions about what they need in order to achieve their mission.

2. **Mission.** In order to provide teachers with autonomy, there must be a district and school mission that is clearly articulated, understood, and shared. These missions must be aligned and based on core values and beliefs. School leaders must clearly communicate the vision, goals, and indicators for success. Teachers must have an explicit understanding of the boundaries within which they can operate, including clearly defined knowledge and understanding of the curriculum standards, frameworks, policies, structures, procedures, and norms. In the scenario above, it is obvious that the spelling philosophy was changed without addressing the core values and beliefs held by teachers. This has caused friction among teachers because it challenges their basic assumptions without having provided them with opportunities to dialogue and develop the deep learning needed to create buy-in and support for decisions made by the central office administrators that require teachers to change their core values and beliefs if the new program is to be implemented effectively.

3. **Communication.** Only teachers on the committee had an opportunity to dialogue and process the philosophical changes for the new spelling program. After all the meetings, the teachers on the committee walked away feeling like no one had listened to them. They perceived the new program as one more top-down decision without bottom-up buy-in and support. After studying the problem, Gina and other teachers on the committee felt that with time, energy, and vertical and horizontal work groups, they could develop a core list of spelling words for each grade level that would be congruent with their grade-level curriculum. These

lists could be individualized for students based on their reading levels and would be a better alternative than any product on the market. Ultimately, central office made the decision. The teachers felt as if the committee was a farce because no one listened or heard what they had to say. For everyone to feel as if the committee work is authentic, the group must be informed of, and agree to, the rules, the process, the purpose, and the boundaries within which the committee will operate at the first meeting.

Because most of the teachers in the district were not involved with the committee's work, they learned about the new spelling program during a half-day training session. Without much warning (if any), these teachers found out at the beginning of the new school year that there would be no more traditional spelling tests because the district had changed the philosophy of how to teach spelling. Instead of helping teachers understand the purpose and rationale of the new approach, allowing time for them to dialogue and process these changes, teachers were simply told to use this new spelling program. Because teachers didn't understand the change in philosophy, they felt coerced and controlled. Often in this type of situation, teachers become compliant and simply sit back in their chairs, "suck it up," and "do what they are told to do," or they become passively or aggressively resistant, and even defiant. "When spoken by teachers and principals, the phrases, 'There's nothing I can do' and 'Tell me what to do' are two of the most damaging and disempowering unintended consequences of school reform efforts" (Sparks, 2005a, p. xii).

4. **Empowerment.** Gina feels helpless and frustrated because she is following a mandated program that does not empower her to make professional decisions to meet the individual needs of her students. She grows more frustrated each day as she watches her students practice spelling some of the words incorrectly. With each new dictated word, there is not enough time for Gina to scan the room and see all of the words written by the students on their whiteboards. Because the pace is so quick, she can't determine which students are writing the word correctly and which students are misspelling the word. She does not feel empowered to slow down the pace and take time between words to stop and help those students who need more time to practice writing the word correctly or to speed up the pace or use more challenging words for those students who can already spell the words correctly. Gina knows that, once a student learns to spell the word incorrectly, it will be harder to relearn it correctly. She also believes she is wasting the time of those students who can already spell the words. Gina wants to help all of her students succeed but feels powerless to change the system by slowing down the pace or modifying the words or process for students who are either struggling because the words are too difficult or bored because the words are too easy. Gina complies with the mandate and does what she is told to do.

Likewise, Gina feels guilty as she becomes resistant and noncompliant by closing her door to do what she feels is best for her students. She knows that her students love to be challenged to spell difficult words. Gina wants to put the joy and fun back into helping her students learn to spell. Even though Gina knows she is breaking the rules and worries that she may get caught, she closes her door and challenges her students to spell some of the words that are part of their third-grade vocabulary and curriculum. We suspect that Kit Johnson feels guilty because she knows the teachers are doing this and thus far has chosen not to address the issue.

5. **Accountability.** There is always a higher level of concern when teachers are held accountable through the evaluation process for using a new program or instructional strategy effectively. In this scenario, "principals were told" that they need to make sure all teachers used the mandated, prescribed spelling program each day. They were to use a checklist to evaluate teacher performance and include it in the teacher's professional file. Not only are teachers being controlled by central office and held accountable, so too are the administrators. Deci (1995) makes it clear that "if the managers themselves [in this case, the principals] do not feel competent, autonomous, and related to others, they will not be autonomy-supportive and involved with their subordinates" (p. 185).

When administrators, in their eagerness to achieve results, pressure teachers to produce these results, a paradox occurs. The more the administrators put pressure on the teachers, Deci says

> the more controlling the teachers become, which as we have seen so many times, undermines intrinsic motivation, creativity, and conceptual understanding in the students. The harder the teachers are pushed to get results, the less likely it is that the important results will be forthcoming. The same is true for managers and others in one-up positions. The more they feel pressured to get results from their employees (or children, or athletes, or students) the harder they push. Unfortunately, in the process, they typically sabotage their own efforts. (p. 158)

Not only are Gina and her colleagues feeling the pressure of the change, so, too, is Kit Johnson. Any time teachers are given a new program or strategy, there must be ample time for practice and learning before they are evaluated on their effective use. When a teacher learns a new skill, it takes approximately twenty-seven times to practice that skill before it becomes part of her routine and she feels comfortable using it. In addition, for a program or innovation to become institutionalized within a school setting, it takes three–five years. Teachers need to feel supported, especially during the first year of implementation. There needs to be a climate that is conducive to risk taking, experimentation, and learning. Even though this is a scripted, teacher-proof program, we still disagree with administrators using a checklist to evaluate teachers during the first year of implementation. We would argue instead for a supervision and/or coaching model rather than an evaluation model. The district could use expert teachers, consultants, or staff developers to encourage and support teacher understanding, growth, and development (e.g., coach, mentor, model, observe).

6. **Competence.** Deep, philosophical changes, even as simple as how one teaches spelling, take time to digest and process. Teachers need to have time to create their own meaning and to gain a deep understanding about the sudden change of direction. It may have seemed like a long process for central office administrators and the teachers who sat on the language arts committee. But to teachers, hearing about the changes for

the first time during a three-hour training session in September, the change in philosophy can be sobering and shocking. Teachers need to have time to question their own values and assumptions, as well as work through their own philosophical differences and/or personal concerns with the change process.

7. **Collegiality and interdependence.** Sparks (2005a) explains:

> The most successful schools are "innovation machines" in which students and adults continually invent better ways of achieving their purposes and that amplify the best practices across the faculty. Teachers in such schools tap research and best practices, but they do so as peers and partners with researchers and policy makers who recognize and value their contributions and talents. Unless such appreciative and respectful relationships are in place, we cannot create schools in which all students and teachers learn and perform at high levels. (p. xiii–xiv)

In this case study, the central office administrators missed the opportunity to unleash the talents of their teachers. Through their experiences of teaching diverse students, Gina and her colleagues have gained the professional knowledge (tacit and explicit) and skills necessary to help students learn how to spell words that are aligned with their grade-level curriculum and at their correct level of difficulty. Yet, the central office did not recognize or appreciate the work the teachers had done or could do. Instead of honing in with precision to create a program that is personalized to meet the individual and collective needs of students (Fullan, Hill, & Crévola, 2006, p. 16–17), the district chose to adopt a prescriptive program.

The district could easily have validated teachers as professional knowledge workers and unleashed the talents of teachers (along with continuing to build momentum, commitment, and support for the new philosophy) by having grade-level teams work vertically and laterally to create a list of words that teachers view as important for students to master. This, by the way, could be an excellent professional learning opportunity that builds competence and organizational capacity among teachers. Once the lists were generated, teachers could develop and share strategies to help students learn and apply the grade-level specific words without relying on Friday spelling tests. Or the district could adopt the program as planned and use the teacher generated list of words to supplement or enrich the program.

8. **Results.** Gina is frustrated with the results in student learning after implementing the district mandated spelling program. The "one-size-fits-none" spelling program requires thirty minutes out of an already too short day. Because it is a scripted program, based on words *typical* third-grade students need to spell, it does not address the individual needs and abilities of each student in her class. Gina sees no direct benefit for her students because the words they practice are unrelated to the curriculum she teaches. The words are either too easy or too difficult for most students. Gina has decided that this program is a waste of time. Because she is

mandated to follow the program, she feels controlled and helpless. Her integrity is being challenged because there is no longer a sense of authenticity for the work she is doing.

In addition, Gina's students are not making the same gains students have made in previous years. Veteran teachers worry when they do not see their students making similar progress to students in previous years. They compare themselves and their students by what they have been able to accomplish before. It is difficult for Gina to feel efficacious when she perceives the mandated program isn't working. Gina finds herself victimized. She finds it easier and easier to externalize her locus of control, blame the district, and refuse to take ownership for her students not being able to spell. Instead of enthusiastically supporting the program, she simply closes the door or goes through the mechanical process of teaching spelling.

## WHAT WOULD YOU DO?

1. Now that you have had a chance to read what we think are the essential conditions necessary for autonomy to exist and the major issues that Kit Johnson is facing as a school leader, do you agree? Are there other issues that we didn't mention that you feel are important?

2. Before you read the rest of the story, look back at what you said you would do if you were Kit when you met with the teachers after school.

After reading our discussion of the issues, is there anything else you would like to add?

## AND NOW FOR THE REST OF THE STORY

*As soon as Gina left, Kit made a phone call to central office. She asked for the names of several schools where the program was working successfully and arranged for the language arts supervisor to meet with teachers during their next grade-level team meetings. Kit called several principals and talked with them about their spelling program. One of the principals volunteered to let Kit bring her teachers to visit, which she scheduled for the following week. Finally, Kit asked her secretary to order scentless markers and better quality whiteboards so that teachers would have ample and appropriate spelling supplies in the future.*

*Kit met Gina and the other teachers in the library as soon as school was dismissed. She brought iced tea, pretzels, and chocolate to eat while they worked.*

*"You know that our state assessments are in a month," she began. "We must make sure that all of our students are proficient at writing and can achieve the state benchmarks. Our mission, whether we like it or not, is to make sure our students have learned everything they will need to know and do to pass the state assessments. Our own building goal is for 100 percent of our students to be proficient at writing." Kit stopped and took a deep breath. "Gina, you told me that you are frustrated with our spelling program. You said that our students are not making the progress that students in previous years have made. Show me what you mean."*

*Kit listened carefully to what her teachers were saying as they looked at a variety of writing samples from student work and compared them to some samples from student work in previous years. Kit saw that her teachers were correct in their assessment of student spelling errors. She asked teachers if they saw any patterns in the errors students were making. The teachers had not looked at this, so Kit asked the teachers to analyze student writing to see if there were consistent errors or patterns in the way students were spelling.*

*Kit told the teachers she had arranged for them to visit another school. She said that the language arts supervisor would be meeting with them next week. In the meantime, Kit suggested the teachers talk with other third-grade teachers across the district to find out what strategies (within the boundaries of the program) they were using to improve student learning and retention in the areas in which students struggled. She also suggested they talk with special education teachers and the gifted coordinator to see if there were some ways to differentiate learning, even while doing whole group instruction.*

*Most important, Kit acknowledged that she knew the teachers were frustrated. But she also reminded teachers that they could not stop using the mandated spelling program the district had implemented. If, however, Gina and the others could analyze the data and demonstrate skills that students were lacking, they might be able to convince central office administrators that a supplement to the program was needed. Worst case, if central office administrators didn't want to supplement the spelling program, the teachers could incorporate the skills they had identified were missing into their guided reading programs, writer's workshop mini-lessons, or specific content area vocabulary lessons.*

*Kit asked the teachers to generate a list of questions they wanted to ask teachers when they visited the school. She suggested that one of the questions might be how they differentiated instruction and another question might be how they kept their students excited about practicing spelling words in the same way each day. Or had they found other strategies?*

*Kit suggested that the teachers have their spelling analysis done before the following week when they would meet with the language arts supervisor. She wanted them to show the supervisor samples of student work and get feedback from her about how they could help their students become more proficient spellers.*

*Before the meeting adjourned, Kit and the teachers scheduled a time to meet before the language arts supervisor met with them to look over the findings from the analysis of student work. Kit also scheduled time in each of the three classes to teach spelling so she could see firsthand, before they visited the other school, what teachers were talking about and perhaps generate questions of her own. She gave her teachers permission to select three–five core words from their third-grade vocabulary list to have students practice at the end of each spelling lesson just for fun. This brought smiles to their faces, but not as big as the cheers she received when she told them she had ordered scentless markers and better quality whiteboards and would distribute them as soon as they arrived. As the teachers picked up their things to go home, Kit smiled and thought to herself, "It's those little things that really do make a difference."*

## CHAPTER SUMMARY

We define autonomy as *the freedom and latitude within clearly defined, aligned, and articulated boundaries for all educators to make informed professional decisions that directly impact student learning and promote the accomplishment of the school's mission.* Our definition is based on the idea that there must be a balance between strategic and operational autonomy.

If a school is going to have an autonomy-supportive school environment, the school leader must make sure that everyone is committed to the school's mission and clearly understands his or her role and responsibilities for helping the school community to achieve their mission, vision, goals, and high expectations. There must be a clearly articulated, shared, and understood set of boundaries and a solid framework that includes an action plan based on high standards, SMART goals, and criteria for success.

Quality of life as we have defined it must be firmly established. The school leader must be able to trust and empower the staff to do their work. Communication structures that allow teachers to access all information that pertains to them must be strongly embedded within the school culture. Communication must be honest, open, direct, and timely.

Teachers must be given a menu of options from which to work. There must be sufficient and appropriate resources available for teacher use. All educators must be respected as professionals and recognized as *knowledge workers*. They must have the freedom to make professional decisions and choices, based on pedagogical knowledge, within the context and framework of strong boundaries and high expectations. School leaders can help teachers to feel efficacious, with a strong sense of internal locus of control, by pointing out ways in which they can and are making a difference. The culture of the school must be conducive to risk taking, creativity, problem solving, and innovation.

School leaders become entrepreneurs as they carefully and skillfully manage the school's budget, taking responsibility for how the money is spent. School leaders and their faculties must be held accountable for the decisions that are made to insure all students achieve high standards. If, however, the school does not achieve their realistic goals and students do not make sufficient progress, the district has a moral obligation to intervene. Likewise, if the district does not make adequate progress or demonstrate sufficient growth, the state has a moral obligation to intervene.

Ultimately, autonomy only works when all educators hold themselves and each other accountable for accomplishing their school's mission and helping all students achieve learning goals.

## NEXT STEPS

1. What does autonomy look like, sound like, and feel like in your current setting? What else would you like to see, hear, or feel? Make a list.

2. Put a star by those things that are already in place in your school or system. Put a check by those things that you would like to see implemented further.

3. If possible, discuss with others what you found interesting about this case study on autonomy and what you found challenging.

4. Select one or two ideas and list several strategies or changes that you can make to incorporate these ideas into your current situation. What barriers may get in your way? What can you do to remove or decrease those barriers?

5. How will you know that these changes are working effectively? How will you define success?

# 10

# Empowerment

*Delegating the Responsibility*
*That Affords Educators*
*the Authority to Do Their Work*

■ **PICTURE THIS**

*It was finally 3:30 P.M., as the last bus was pulling out of Lincoln Elementary School's parking lot. Margaret McGuire realized, as she watched it drive off, that once again she had not made it out of her office all day, except once to use the bathroom. It was no wonder that her head hurt. She hadn't had anything to eat or drink all day. Her office was a revolving door, and she felt as if she needed one of the deli "take-a-number" ticket machines just to keep track of who was next in line. She wasn't sure how many students had passed through her office during the day, but she knew it was far more than should have.*

*Just as she began to head back into the school to get her lunch and something to drink, she heard Shelby Young, one of her fourth-grade teachers, walking in the breezeway, hollering, "Mrs. McGuire! I didn't know you were here today! I have something I need to ask you."*

*"What do you mean, you didn't know I was here today?" Margaret shouted back, walking toward Shelby.*

*"None of us saw you all day, so we figured you were off at another meeting," she said, in a normal tone, since she had caught up to where Margaret was standing.*

*(Continued)*

(Continued)

*"This has got to be the last straw," Margaret thought to herself. "It is exactly like the superintendent said last week during her mid-year evaluation meeting. She had tried to explain to Dr. Zarrilli that she hadn't been away from her building as much as he might be thinking. In fact, she was rarely gone. But he had said that the teachers at her school were complaining because she was never there. Margaret couldn't understand how he could say such a thing, but now it was becoming clear. Since she never got out of her office because all she did, all day long, was discipline student after student, the perception from the teachers was that she was never at school. In part, she guessed that was true, but whose fault was it? She didn't ask to have kids stacked up like books on a shelf outside her door, day after day. In fact, every time she went into a classroom to do an observation, she came back to her office only to discover that the number of students waiting to see her had doubled—or even tripled.*

*Just then she heard Shelby finish her sentence, "and we thought maybe you could do something to stop it."*

*"Stop what?" Margaret asked, realizing that she had been deep in her own thoughts and missed whatever it was the Shelby was asking about. "I'm sorry, Shelby. I was thinking about something else. What did you say?"*

*"No problem. I was telling you that the girls have trashed the bathroom again. They have used their fingernails, or something sharp to carve four letter words into the paint. I just had a call from April Hernandez's mother. April went home crying because some of the girls had scratched some really horrible, nasty things about her on the bathroom stall. I went in and checked it out. She's right. It's a big mess. Her mom said she wants it taken care of, now! Mrs. Hernandez sees this as a form of bullying and said if we don't take care of it, she will call the superintendent. So, I am asking if there is something you can do to stop it?" Shelby finished repeating the story.*

*"Have you done anything about it?" Margaret asked, knowing the answer.*

*"No, because I found out about it after school. I did tell Jerry, the night custodian about it, but he said he couldn't do anything unless you told him what you wanted him to do." Shelby stated, then added, "so I thought maybe you could take care of it for me."*

*"Shelby, don't take this the wrong way, but I can't do everything around here. I have already suspended three boys today for bringing knives to school. I had to settle five fights on the playground after the lunch recesses. Every time I try to step out of my office, someone has sent me three more kids—kids who need pencils, who won't stop talking in class, who are copying somebody else's papers ... it doesn't stop! I am at the end of my rope! No wonder this school has had three principals in the past four years. It is time for somebody else, besides me, to take some responsibility for how the students are behaving at our school!" Margaret blurted out, and then felt as if she had said way too much.*

*"I'm sorry," Shelby said. "Just tell me what you want me to do, and I will take care of it."*

*"That's just it," Margaret said, looking right at Shelby. "I shouldn't have to tell you what to do. I shouldn't have to be the one to tell Jerry to sand the scratches off the bathroom walls and paint over them. I shouldn't have to be the one to tell the teachers to monitor the bathrooms during recess and to talk with students about destroying property. I shouldn't have to be the one ..." she caught herself.*

*"Look, Shelby," Margaret said, in a more friendly tone, "I'm tired, I'm hungry, and I'm thirsty. I haven't been to the bathroom since ten o'clock this morning. I don't mean to be cross, but I can't do any more than I'm already doing. The norm at this school is for teachers to send anyone they don't want to deal with to the office. Mrs. Grey is getting tired of babysitting all day long. I don't know how she answers the phone and gets all of her other work done." Margaret stopped, then added, "Thank goodness for the weekends, because if I didn't have them, I would never get anything done, either," she said, as she thought about all the Saturday and Sunday afternoons she had spent at the school instead of at home with her family. "And, to think that the teachers' perception is that I am never here. If they only knew," she thought to herself.*

*Shelby stood looking at her. Margaret knew she had to say something. "Look Shelby, you are not the problem. You rarely send me students from your classroom, but you are the exception, not the rule. I will find a way to deal with this problem. But right now, I just want to go to the bathroom, get a drink, and a couple of aspirins. I think they call this 'Excedrin headache number 93' because that's how many days I have been working at this school as your principal. Maybe, in my next life, I will get a job working in advertising," she laughed. "I'll think of it all tomorrow ... After all, tomorrow is another day," Margaret thought as she walked away remembering the famous words spoken by Scarlet O'Hara at the end of* Gone With The Wind *(Mitchell, 1936, p. 1024).*

*"If only it were so easy—to have this whole thing—gone with the wind!"*

# ■  WHAT IS EMPOWERMENT?

To empower others is to give the power to the people who are doing the work. But as Harvey Seifter (Seifter & Economy, 2001), the executive director for the Orpheus Chamber Orchestra, writes, few leaders do more than give lip service to empowerment:

> In recent years, most managers have become very familiar with the mantra of empowerment. According to this mantra, employers who give every worker the responsibility for performing meaningful tasks and the authority to get jobs done are rewarded with an empowered workforce composed of contented and loyal employees, who in turn make their customers happy as well. However, while many companies have taken on the symbolic trappings of empowerment by trimming multiple levels of management and giving nonmanagerial workers new titles and job descriptions, how many have granted employees real, meaningful power?
>
> The truth is that few employees—even among so-called empowered corporations—have any say in setting the goals and directions of the companies they work for. In most organizations, authority to decide what products and services to provide to customers, and how best to provide them, still remains closely held by management at levels far removed from either products creation or service delivery. A Gallup survey of twelve hundred U.S. workers demonstrates that the reality of worker empowerment is quite different than the story touted by today's "enlightened" businesses. While an impressive 66 percent of survey respondents reported that their managers asked them to get involved in decision making, only 14 percent felt that they had actually been given real authority. Apparently, it's one thing to talk about empowerment, but it's another to give it. (p. 19)

It is easy to give people the *responsibility* to do their work (and even hold them accountable). It is another thing to grant them *authority* to accomplish it.

As in business, the world of education has given lip service to empowering teachers and administrators for decades. But as many of us have witnessed throughout the years, there have been far more examples of micromanaging teachers than empowering them. There are numerous examples ranging from "teacher-proof" programs and materials to management structures that support isolation, command, and control. Many educational leaders, who appear to not trust teachers to know how to do their job, are notorious for planning inservice workshops for teachers "for their own good," often leaving very little creativity in their wake (Vojtek, 1993).

It is not uncommon in this era of standards and high-stakes accountability for district or school leaders to dictate what teachers need to know and be able to do, including when and even how to do it. In many school districts, for example, teachers have been given curriculum maps, scripts, and pacing guides with the expectation that no matter which school or classroom someone enters, teachers in like-grades, teaching like-subjects, will be using the same materials in the same way, even going so far as to be on the same page on the same day. Well-intentioned central office administrators and school boards implementing such procedures do so hoping that when students move from school to school within their district, there will not be gaps in student learning, and that the quality of education (and fidelity of instruction) will be held to the same standard no matter who the child has for a teacher. In situations like these, the teachers' goals are to cover material and make sure students finish assignments by a certain date, often at the expense of learning. Covering the materials has nothing to do with learning because it is calendar driven. In addition, policymakers forget that one-size-fits-all curriculums rarely meet individual student's needs. Worse still, teachers, who have been programmed like robots, become dependent upon such edicts. After years of learned dependency, they simply throw up their hands and say, "Just tell me what to do and how to do it."

Even after the best laid plans have been actualized, students may, in fact, not achieve the test scores that the administrators expected. This is when *the blame game* begins. Administrators lash out at the teachers, blaming them for poor results. After all, they gave the teachers everything they needed to ensure their students achieve high standards. They posit that teachers must not have been doing what they were told to do. After all, the curriculum was "teacher proof."

Teachers, on the other hand, feel the daily frustration of teaching students as if they are on a factory conveyor belt that moves at the same pace, day after day, whether or not the pieces of learning are connected, transferred, or stored in a location in students' brains where key concepts and processes can be easily accessed, comprehended, and applied successfully. The teachers feel victimized and blame the administrators because they don't listen or trust teachers to make informed, professional decisions. Although teachers are given the responsibility to make sure that all students achieve the high standards and either meet or exceed state or district learning goals, often they do not have the necessary authority to make informed decisions allowing students to achieve success (such as deviating from the pacing guide to reteach a skill that some students didn't understand the first time, selecting materials at the correct level of difficulty for individual students from a menu of options, or using a hands-on problem-solving approach). Eventually, teachers no longer feel ownership for what they are doing, and the passion and excitement for the teaching and learning process is diminished. Many teachers throw up their hands, do what they are told to do, and wait for retirement.

Yes, there is a time and place for directives, and in some circumstances, such as if a student brought a weapon to school, command and control is imperative. A crisis situation demands immediate action from someone who is in charge. But schools are seldom in a crisis mode. School leaders are able to garner many benefits from staff members when they are able to trust the people closest to the work to make the best decisions. Habitual overcontrolling debilitates people (Dreher & Tzu, 1996, p. 144), often to the point of paralysis from "fear of being their best. Most organizations are set up to catch people doing things wrong rather than to encourage and reward them for doing things right" (Blanchard, Carlos, & Randolph, 2001a, p. 14). Teachers need to be proud to show what they can do and not afraid to use their knowledge, skills, and experiences to help students learn to the best of their ability. School leaders can do this by unleashing the talent in their staff and empowering them to do the job they hired them to do.

When describing what that power might look like in the business realm, Seifter and Economy (2001) suggest that it is allowing a "measure of authority over such areas as setting work schedules and environment, developing and executing budgets, hiring and firing employees, determining what products and services will be developed and sold, and participating in the development of mission, strategy, and goals" (p. 21). Rewards for doing this, they say, improve worker morale; increase trust, innovation, and commitment; and decrease absenteeism and turnover among employees. We believe that empowering educators provides similar results.

We define *empowerment* as *delegating the responsibility and granting the authority that affords educators the freedom and latitude to do their work and achieve their mission.* For educators to use their creative inspiration and professional judgments to make informed decisions that lead to optimal performance, they must be empowered with freedom and latitude to do their work and then be held accountable for accomplishing the goals of the school's morally compelling mission.

Theodore Roosevelt once said, "The best executive is the one who has sense enough to pick good men to do what he wants done, and self-restraint enough to keep from meddling with them while they do it" (as cited in Maxwell, 1998, p. 125). Delegating the responsibility and granting the authority is not as easy as one might think. To do so, school leaders must view their faculty and staff as being competent. They must treat staff members as professionals and trust them to do the job they hired them to do. Administrators must clearly define their high expectations; establish the necessary framework and boundaries; provide staff members with the knowledge, skills, and resources; discover and unleash their unique talents; and then get out of the way and watch them do their work.

Vince Lombardi, Jr. (2001) writes that his father had a "three-pronged approach to building accountability among his players" (p. 257). His steps, Lombardi recounts, were as follows: (1) He told his players exactly what he expected of them, and why; (2) He gave his players all the tools they needed to do their job; and (3) He got out of the way. In other words, Lombardi's rule was to, "Paint the picture, provide the tools, and get out of the way" (p. 259). According to his son, the older Lombardi knew that once the game started it was out of his hands. This is the epitome of empowerment, especially when school leaders use empowerment as a motivational strategy.

When explaining the "8th habit," Covey (2004) describes the four roles of leadership (i.e., modeling, pathfinding, aligning, and empowering) that inspire others to find their voice and shift the paradigm from the four chronic organizational problems found in today's industrial age control model (i.e., rules, misalignment, efficiency, and disempowerment). To empower others, Covey says one must "focus on talent and results, not methods," and then "get out of people's way and give help as requested" (p. 112–114). He says empowerment "is where the rubber meets the road" (p. 119). It unleashes human potential without external motivation and produces cultural moral authority (p. 272).

School leaders, for example, put the power and control into the hands of the teachers when they: (1) delegate responsibility to them to insure that all students are able to achieve the learning goals defined by the state's standards, district's curriculum, and school's mission; (2) give them tools and resources (a menu of options); (3) grant them the authority to use their knowledge and professional judgment to make informed decisions to best meet the needs of the individual learners in their classrooms; and (4) get out of their way and trust them to do the work. Csikszentmihalyi (2003) says that "control" is the feeling, "that if the occasion requires it, the individuals involved have the necessary skills to set new strategies to reach the ultimate goal" (p. 136). This is precisely the latitude of control that should be available on the job for employees to be in flow and perform at optimal levels. They should be able to feel that they have a choice over how to perform their job, and that they are trusted to come up with the best approach that a given situation requires.

In education, the ultimate goal is to ensure that all students achieve the established learning goals to accomplish the school's mission. We agree that if teachers are to achieve levels of optimal performance, they must be trusted and given the latitude of control that allows them to use their professional judgment to choose the best approach to help individual students achieve in all areas (e.g., physical, mental, cognitive, social, emotional). Teachers are much more likely to take ownership and responsibility for the results they are held accountable for when they have a voice in the methods used to achieve the goals. The results from empowerment are "far greater because [they are] multiplied and fueled by passion" (Secretan, 2004, p. 40).

Empowering educators to do their work cannot be accomplished with an antiquated industrial-age command and control accountability model that uses a carrot-and-stick, do-as-you-are-told system of controlling employees. Instead, school leaders who want to empower their faculty and staff to do their work must focus individual and collective talents and efforts on achieving the desired results, rather than on the methods they will use to get the job done (Covey, 2004, p. 114). Empowerment is a different paradigm from the industrial-age command and control accountability model that has plagued business and education for decades. When school leaders hold teachers accountable for *doing things the right way,* they maintain the status quo. By holding teachers mutually accountable for *doing the right thing* and achieving the desired results as defined by the morally compelling school mission and openly sharing information and having ongoing quality conversations about the progress being made toward the efforts, administrators are free to empower teachers by delegating the responsibility, autonomy, and authority to do their work.

From experience with the Orpheus Chamber Orchestra, Seifter and Economy (2001) warn that:

Delegating authority without feedback mechanisms can quickly lead to disaster, especially if workers find themselves too far down the wrong path and fail to seek help when serious problems arise. Proper delegation involves more than just giving employees authority; it also requires setting up appropriate mechanisms for obtaining and integrating feedback, such as milestones, regular reports, status meetings, and other methods of communication. The best tools provide exactly the quantity of genuinely valuable information managers and other employees need, at a frequency that doesn't lead to employees spending more time preparing reports or attending meetings than doing their jobs. (p. 39)

In this age of accountability, is easy for us to become overwhelmed and burdened with too many meetings and too much paperwork. Administrators must not allow their schools to become so bureaucratic, data-driven, and overloaded with paperwork and reports that educators find themselves in a state of analysis paralysis. Data-driven, yes! We should be collecting information that is meaningful to guide the decisions that will provide knowledge and wisdom to improve performance and achieve the desired results. Authentic feedback and evaluative reports, yes! We owe it to our school community to provide meaningful feedback and reports on results that make a difference. But energy and time are finite, and we must respect and use them both wisely.

Covey (2004) suggests another idea to "keep score" and inform others about our results. He uses a soccer stadium or baseball arena scoreboard metaphor as a way to "display information so that everyone in the entire arena knows exactly what is happening" (p. 278). Doug Reeves (2000, 2002) suggests a data-fair (science-fair) model to display important and meaningful results related to a school's accountability plans and tier goals (www.leadandlearn.com). Whatever the means, all staff members, as well as patrons of the school and district, must be kept informed of student progress. Likewise, teachers must have access to information that helps them to make meaningful and purposeful decisions.

## ■ NEEDS MET THROUGH EMPOWERMENT

Basic needs that are met with this motivational strategy include Maslow's (1998) esteem and self-actualization needs; Herzberg's set of motivators (as cited in Heller, 1998); Deci's (1995) autonomy; Glasser's (1998) control theory, especially power, freedom, and fun; Covey's (2004) "8th habit"; Csikszentmihalyi's (2003) flow; and Sagor's (2003) potency. (See Appendix A.)

## ■ WHAT EMPOWERMENT IS AND ISN'T

Figures 10.1 and 10.2 on pages 196–197 will help to clarify empowerment. Figure 10.1 explains what empowerment is and what it isn't. Figure 10.2 compares the differences between an empowerment-supportive environment and an empowerment-deficient environment.

**Figure 10.1**   Empowerment Defined

| What Empowerment Is | What Empowerment Isn't |
| --- | --- |
| Lateral organizational structure and culture that leads to collaboration among staff. | Hierarchical organizational structure and culture that leads to competition among staff. |
| Delegated and shared responsibility management practices. | Command and control management practices. |
| Opportunities for individuals to develop and use talents and abilities. | Few if any opportunities to develop and use individual talents and abilities. |
| Shared decision making with input in decisions that affect one's own work. | Top-down decision making with no input in decisions that affect one's own work. |
| Responsibility to accomplish goals and the necessary authority to make it happen. | Responsibility to accomplish goals without the necessary authority to choose how it happens. |
| Leaders share responsibility, authority, and accountability with others, even when the tasks are delegated. | Leaders dictate responsibility and/or authority. They don't necessarily hold themselves accountable, yet hold others accountable. |
| Taking responsibility, accepting accountability, and acting to make it happen. Asking, "What else can I do to get results?" | Waiting to be told what to do before doing anything (give responsibility). Blaming others when results aren't achieved. |
| Leaders ask, "How can I support you and be of service to you?" | Leaders provide service to others by telling them what to do and how to do it. |
| Power from a shared commitment, purpose, and desire to make a difference. | Power from fear. |
| Liberating others and allowing them to use their knowledge, skills, experiences, and talents to achieve a clearly defined mission. | Controlling others and making sure they do things right and achieve the mission. |
| Giving teachers clearly defined curriculum frameworks (especially standards and learning goals), the latitude to choose from a menu of options (e.g., materials and instructional practices), and holding them accountable for student academic performance and success. | Giving teachers curriculum frameworks, with a one-size-fits-all curriculum (including scripts or pacing guides that make sure everyone covers the same material in the same way on the same day), and holding them accountable for student academic performance and success. |
| Autonomy within specific boundaries and limits to make decisions to achieve the mission. Accountability for actions and results. | Autonomy with no clearly defined boundaries or limits. Freedom to do what one wants and thinks is best without accountability. |
| Tools, resources, and support are provided for educators to do their jobs. | Tools, resources, and support are withheld and/or inadequate for educators to do their jobs. |
| Accepting challenges, ownership, and responsibility for finding solutions to problems. | Letting someone else solve the problems. |
| A person not afraid to be creative and think outside the box for innovative ideas and solutions. | A "yes" person. "Just tell me what to do, and I will do it." |
| Looking for, recognizing, and accepting opportunities that will make a difference. | Maintaining the status quo—not wanting to "make waves" and afraid to do anything without permission. |

**Figure 10.2**    Structuring an Empowerment-Supportive Environment

| Empowerment-Supportive Environment | Empowerment-Deficient Environment |
|---|---|
| All members of the school/district have access to important and essential information necessary to do their jobs. | Information is shared on a need-to-know basis. |
| Communication is honest, open, and a reciprocal two-way process. | Rumors and misinformation are rampant. Communication is top-down and one-way. |
| People take responsibility for making decisions and are given the authority to actualize their efforts. | People are held hostage by indecision and inaction when they have the responsibility without the authority to actualize efforts. |
| Leaders trust others to make professional decisions to help accomplish the mission. | Leaders tell others what to do. They do not trust staff members to make professional decisions. |
| People feel that their voices are heard, their input is listened to, and their ideas and opinions are valued and respected. | People feel that their voices and input are not listened to and their opinions and ideas are not valued or respected. |
| Mission (including vision, values, goals, and assumptions) are clearly articulated, communicated, and understood, by all. | No clear mission (including vision, values, goals, and assumptions) and people are confused about purpose. |
| Standards and expectations are high. Everyone clearly understands and is responsible and holds themselves and each other accountable for achieving the desired results. | Standards and expectations are confusing, especially when the target keeps changing or isn't clearly defined. People aren't sure what success is and are surprised when they are held accountable for something they didn't know they were responsible for. |
| Morally compelling mission is clearly defined, articulated, understood, and shared. | Morally compelling mission is not clearly defined, articulated, understood, or shared. |
| Boundaries and limits are clearly established, defined, articulated, and understood. | Boundaries and limits are not established, defined, clearly articulated, or understood. |
| Adequate and appropriate resources to accomplish day-to-day tasks and mission. | Inadequate and/or inappropriate resources to accomplish day-to-day tasks and mission. |
| Staff members feel they are respected and treated as professionals. | Staff members feel victimized. There is a lack of respect and trust. |
| Quality of life (as defined earlier) is supported within the school and/or district. | Quality of life is not supported within the school and/or district. |
| Opportunities and support for all staff members to build individual competence and organizational capacity based on their own perceived needs and interests. | Lack of opportunities and/or support for all staff members to build individual competence and organizational capacity based on their own perceived needs. |
| Leader gives power to others (authority and responsibility) to achieve desired results. | Leader uses power to command and control others to get desired results. |
| There is a culture of collaboration and interdependence. All members of the organization share the responsibility and accountability for achieving the mission. | Teachers work in isolation and take responsibility for only their own students' learning and achievement. Little if any collaboration time is provided. |
| There is a culture that is conducive to learning, creativity, innovation, and risk taking. | People are afraid to take risks by creating or trying new innovations or strategies. |

# ■ WHY IS EMPOWERMENT IMPORTANT?

When you manage people like things, they become dependent instead of independent thinkers and doers. Codependent workers maintain the status quo by simply doing as they are told to do. They "stop believing that leadership can become a choice. Most people think of leadership as a position and therefore don't see themselves as leaders" (Covey, 2004, p. 16).

Teachers who work with students who will become the information/knowledge workers of the future need to be empowered to utilize twenty-first century skills such as leadership, creativity, innovation, and problem-solving strategies in their classrooms if their students are to be prepared for the unknown future. Teachers, as knowledge workers, must be granted the authority to make the professional decisions they were trained to make if they are to be motivated to achieve at levels of optimal performance. "Teachers who are empowered to help make decisions about their school will structure their classrooms to empower students in the learning process, encouraging students to take greater responsibility for their own education" (Evans, 1996, p. 232).

Over time, when teachers, like all people, are controlled and managed with the carrot-and-stick philosophy, they begin to "believe that only those in positions of authority should decide what must be done" (Covey, 2004, p. 16). Even when people recognize that action should be taken, they wait. "They wait to be told what to do by the person with the formal title, and they respond as directed," Covey explains. "And they are thanked for their 'cooperation and support'" (Covey, 2004, p. 16–17). We see this far too often in schools today. Educators comply by jumping on the latest bandwagons and are rewarded for following the latest mandates.

John C. Maxwell (1998) writes:

> The people's capacity to achieve is determined by their leader's ability to empower. Only empowered people can reach their potential. When a leader can't or won't empower others, he creates barriers within the organization that people cannot overcome. If the barriers remain long enough, then the people give up, or they move to another organization where they can maximize their potential. (p. 126)

If we, as school administrators, are going to retain the highly qualified, competent, and caring teachers we have spent so long training and recruiting, we must unleash their talents and believe in their abilities and worth to do the job we hired them to do. We must also support their efforts and then get out of the way and let them do the work. "The latest, most up-to-date management concepts and techniques won't help if you've neglected the basic principles that empower people and organizations to turn in exceptional performances" (Connors, Smith, & Hickman, 2004, p. 9).

It is hard to hold yourself accountable for situations over which you have little or no control. For teachers to take ownership and responsibility for accomplishing the goals of the school's mission, they must have the authority to control the situation and the freedom and latitude to make informed decisions about the important work they are doing. Teachers can't do this with scripts and pacing guides that establish the parameters of what, when, and how they teach. In situations like these, many teachers simply cover the material and make sure students complete the assignments. There isn't much hope of achieving optimal performance and accomplishing the school's mission unless school leaders change this paradigm so teachers can meet the individual needs of each learner every day. Teachers must be able to differentiate instruction. As Bill Spady, a leader of the outcome-based education movement, once said, "All students can learn and succeed, but not on the same day in the same way."

School leaders must, therefore, provide teachers with clear expectations; the boundaries within which to work (i.e., state standards, district curriculum, school mission and goals); the autonomy (freedom and latitude) to make professional decisions about what, how, and when to teach concepts and skills to the students in their classroom; and the authority to do their work. When teachers use their knowledge and skills to differentiate the learning so all students achieve to their fullest potential on any given day, they take pride in their accomplishments for a job well done. They are also more likely to accept responsibility and be held accountable for achieving the school's mission. Empowerment gives the power to those who are doing the work and, in the process, provides the motivation that energizes and inspires them to make a difference.

The boundaries and frameworks provide the direction and guides, while periodic measurements against the indicators of success provide a way to measure teacher effectiveness and student results. Achieving desired results, as you will see in Chapter 12, is motivating and invigorating. Celebrations of learning become electrified when teachers realize that they have become entrusted and empowered to make the choices that can and do make a difference. Empowerment, therefore, plays a vital and significant role in helping teachers accomplish their school's mission and achieve optimal levels of performance.

The literature is full of reasons why empowering employees is motivating (Blanchard, Carlos, & Randolph, 2001a, 2001b; Csikszentmihalyi, 2003; Covey, 2004; Deci, 1995; Seifter & Economy, 2001). To summarize, we have adapted a list of those benefits for all employees and work teams by making them specific to empowering teachers and empowering collaborative school teams. Our list includes: increased job satisfaction and worker morale; increased level of trust; more creativity and innovation; an attitude change from "have to" to "want to"; greater commitment to accomplishing the school's mission; better communication between the administration, faculty, and staff; more efficient decision-making processes; a sense of ownership; more willingness to accept responsibility; less absenteeism and turnover among employees; and improved teacher performance and student learning.

There are a couple of quotes that summarize for us the benefits of using empowerment as a motivational strategy. Harvey Seifter (2001), executive director for the Orpheus Chamber Orchestra summarizes it best when he says:

> Empowering musicians was—and still is—a radical innovation in the orchestra world. After nearly thirty years of experience, we can summarize the extraordinary results as follows: empowerment gives us the ability to maximize the talents of highly skilled individuals throughout our organization, and it improves our performance across the full spectrum of our activities. (p. 22)

Likewise, Covey (2004) states:

Synergy in the Knowledge Worker Age enables Third Alternatives to be created. It's an 8th Habit kind of communication, where people's voices are identified and aligned with the organization's voice so that the voices of different teams or departments harmonize together. (p. 278)

What more could we, as school leaders, ask for than that?

## ■ STRUCTURING EMPOWERMENT

Even if you aren't a Green Bay Packer or Washington Redskins fan, Vince Lombardi's ten-season record as a head coach is impressive: 105 wins, 35 losses, and 6 ties. As touched upon earlier, his son, Vince Lombardi Jr., attributes his dad's six World Championships and two Super Bowl wins to his approach to life and his philosophy of leadership (Lombardi, 2001, p. 3). Lombardis philosophy is the epitome of empowerment.

School administrators wear multiple hats during each day of their careers, sometimes switching so fast that the gray hairs on their heads stand on end from the static electricity of the quick changes even on calm days. At this crucial time in education, there is no hat more significant or influential than the hat of a coach for motivating others through empowerment to become a winning team.

If school leaders are to achieve optimal performance, they must become the Vince Lombardis of education. With their coach's hats on, they must empower others by *delegating the responsibility and granting the authority that affords them the freedom and latitude to do their work and achieve their mission.*

Simply by hiring faculty and staff, we give them the responsibility for the work we hired them to do, but not necessarily the authority to carry out the work. We have upped the anti even more since we entered the era of No Child Left Behind (NCLB) that gives all educators the responsibility to make sure no child is left behind and achieves the high expectations set forth by the law. Unfortunately for educators, authority does not necessarily come with that responsibility. It is, therefore, up to the school leaders to grant the authority that allows faculty and staff to do their work. Then, like Lombardi, if the school team is going to win at the NCLB game, the administrator becomes the coach on the sidelines (a difficult task, but a crucial one nonetheless), making sure that all teachers have the knowledge, skills, and resources they need to achieve their mission.

Empowerment, as we noted at the beginning of this chapter, isn't easy. Lip service is the easy part; granting the authority to do the work, and then standing back and letting it happen, is difficult for many leaders. To empower others and give them the freedom and latitude to do their work effectively and efficiently means that school leaders must create the conditions that allow them the ability to step back and trust that staff members will achieve the high expectations necessary to accomplish the school's mission. Empowerment that produces quality work from a winning school team occurs only after a strong culture to support it is in place.

## Understanding Authority

Let's be really clear, leaders cannot suddenly decide to grant authority. Cold turkey doesn't work! School leaders will be, at the very least, pleasantly surprised by the outcomes and consequences of their actions, or lack thereof. Even under the best of circumstances, administrators can find themselves surprised.

Early in my career as an administrator, I (Rosie) learned a powerful lesson. I had to meet with a parent and knew I would be late for a weekly school improvement team meeting. Earlier in the day, I told the teacher chairperson that we had $10,000 to purchase materials and resources for the library. I didn't care what the group decided, thinking they would purchase books, computers, or software. What a surprise, when I arrived thirty minutes late to the meeting and discovered that the school librarian had talked the rest of the team into purchasing several laserdisc players for teachers to use (this was before DVD players). Even though I disagreed with the decision, I could not renege on my word without losing trust from the school improvement team. My mistake was not to think through all the possible choices the school improvement team might select.

When working with groups, school leaders must carefully analyze the situation and then determine what level of authority they are comfortable giving to the group. When school leaders do not know the members of the group well and are not sure of all the possible choices they might make, they will want to choose to grant less authority to the group. Once administrators grant the authority, as I learned, you can't take it back without consequences. As Covey (2004) writes:

> There are times of great chaos, confusion, and survival when the strong hand of formal authority needs to be used to get things back on track, to a new level of order and stability or to a new vision. However, in most cases when people use their formal authority early on, their moral authority will be lessened. Again, remember that when you borrow strength from position, you build weakness in three places: in self, because you are not developing moral authority; in the other, because they become codependent with your use of formal authority; and in the quality of the relationship, because authentic openness and trust never develops. (p. 301)

Before empowering others, it is imperative that the school leader grants a level of authority on par with the level of confidence he has in the ability of the group to make effective choices. The school leader must look at the skill level of his teachers along with his own level of trust and comfort with the decisions to be made. The school leader should not feel guilty for giving some teachers or groups more authority to make decisions than others. Different teachers and groups will be in different places. It, therefore, becomes important for the school leader to put on his coach's hat and either scaffold the levels of authority by modeling the process for teachers or by offering boundaries with more structure and guidelines within which teachers or teams can operate. School leaders must be comfortable with the level of empowerment they grant to others. After all, the buck stops with the school administrator!

If you are new to the idea of empowerment, or if you are making decisions in new and unfamiliar territory, take it slowly. Remember, as the administrator, no matter how much authority you may grant in one area (such as the supplemental resource materials teachers want to use while teaching the district math curriculum), you do not need to grant that same level of authority for everything (such as how the math department plans to use the $3,000 they received from their business/school partner). Each committee, group, teacher, or situation does not need to be granted the same level of authority. This is a time when knowing your faculty and staff is crucial to your success in motivating and working effectively with teachers.

Before granting authority, make sure it is yours to grant. In addition, make sure that the decisions that will be made will not conflict with board policy, safety issues, or school procedures. Most important, start small. Begin with the first levels of authority, being more specific about the boundaries. As staff members begin to earn your trust, and as you teach them how to use data to make effective choices, you can provide them with less structure and more freedom and autonomy to make the decisions. Rather than telling them what they can't do (e.g., signing-off on everything teachers want laminated or copied for their classrooms), give them guidelines and latitudes within which to work (e.g., a budget for laminating or the number of copies they can make each month). As teachers gain experience in decision making, let the boundaries provide the latitudes and guide the actions.

Encourage responsible action by helping teachers learn how to make informed decisions. A clear value, for example, such as open and honest communication with parents about how well their students are doing, guides the actions of teachers, but does not constrain them from taking appropriate action in any given situation. "This philosophical difference is a critical one for both leaders and team members to understand. Think about what people need to accomplish, make that clear, and allow them the freedom to use their talents to achieve those goals" (Blanchard, Carlos, & Randolph, 2001b, p. 80–81).

There are two types of decisions that educators need to make: *strategic* and *operational.* Even the most empowered school and district situations call for administrators (often central office administrators and school board members) to make the *strategic decisions* (e.g., district curriculum, policies, financial matters, the school year calendar, hiring of staff members, contractual issues). These decisions may or may not call for input and advice from faculty and staff. It is in the daily operations of the school and classrooms where administrators can empower teachers to decide on *operational issues,* beginning with less complex and less involved decisions (those related specifically to the work they do with little or no impact on others) and then moving toward the more complex and involved decisions (those related to the school at large, such as the schedule or activities for field day).

## Levels of Authority

As school leaders begin to think through the process of empowerment, they must consider the level of responsibility and authority they are willing to grant in relation to their own comfort level and the ability of the group to make sound, effective decisions. Although there are different models for the level of authority (sometimes known as the levels of decision making), we have identified five levels of authority that leaders need to consider before delegating responsibility and granting the authority to empower teachers. They are:

1. *Top-down authority.* The school leader makes the decision without any input or regard for others. Confidence (trust) levels in teachers' abilities to make effective decisions vary. It could be low and the leader makes the decision. It could also be high, but this is a crisis situation, or teachers do not want to be bothered because the decision does not affect them. Example: The school leader decides how to spend $2,000 from a building grant to improve student assessment scores.

2. *Top-down authority with consultation.* The school leader consults with individuals and/or groups and considers their input before making his decision. The confidence (trust) level is limited. Teacher skill level is limited. Example: The school leader asks for ideas from teachers and then decides how the $2,000 is to be spent to improve student assessment scores.

3. *Top-down empowerment with constraining boundaries.* The school leader solicits ideas, suggestions, and opinions from individuals and groups. She then decides on several ideas or suggestions. The confidence (trust) level is average, and the teachers' decision-making skills are average. The school leader is still reluctant to give up more control. Teachers select how they want to spend their $2,000 from the list generated by the school leader. Example: After listening to teachers describe what they need to help students improve their assessment scores, the teachers select how the money will be spent from the school leader's list of possibilities.

4. *Empowerment with boundaries that guide the action.* The school leader lets teachers know that they have $2,000 from a building grant to purchase materials to help their students improve their assessment scores. The confidence (trust) level is above average, and the teachers' decision-making skills are above average. The school leader controls the decision by establishing the guidelines (boundaries) and focus on how to use the money—but not the specific items. Example: The school leader tells teachers they may decide how they spend the money as long as they use it to purchase books and materials that will help them to improve their students' abilities to read nonfiction, comprehend it, and respond in a written format on assessments. The teachers decide what books and materials they will purchase.

5. *Operational empowerment.* The school leader gives the teachers $2,000 and lets them decide how they will use the grant funds to improve student assessment. The confidence (trust) level is high and the skill level for the teachers is high. Or the school leader simply doesn't care, which is its own issue. Example: Teachers examine all pertinent data. From their analysis, they decide to hire a consultant to work with them on strategies to improve fluency, build vocabulary, and ask higher-level questions that generate quality conversations and written responses, by modeling lessons and coaching teachers as they plan and teach lessons.

Figure 10.3 illustrates the five levels of authority and the considerations school leaders must make when granting authority to others.

As you read through the levels of authority, notice the amount of information that is available to the teachers as they make the decisions. Having no authority, teachers in level one are simply given the additional resources from the grant funds by the school leader along with the expectation and

**Figure 10.3**   Levels of Authority

| Level of Authority | Decision-Maker | Trust Level | Teacher Skill Level | Factors Considered | Example |
|---|---|---|---|---|---|
| 1. Top-Down. | Leader makes decision alone. | Low. | Varies, but most likely low or doesn't directly affect the group. | Group doesn't have skill level, it is a crisis situation, or decision doesn't directly affect teachers. | Leader spends $2,000 on books to improve test scores. |
| 2. Top-Down Authority with Consultation. | Leader consults with others, makes decision alone. | Low or very limited. | Most likely low. | Group doesn't have skill level, or leader doesn't want to give up control. | Leader gets advice from others and then makes the decision to spend $2,000 on books. |
| 3. Top-Down Empowerment/ constraining boundaries. | Leader solicits input, provides a list of options, teacher/ group select from list. | Average: leader has some experience with group, but is afraid they may still not make best decision. | Average: Leader is learning, but still feels the need to scaffold the process/ choices. Leader still helps teachers practice skills—afraid to let go completely. | Group doesn't have adequate skill level, or leader still afraid of group decision or doesn't feel comfortable giving the full control. | Leader works through the process with teachers, examining data, soliciting input, and providing a list of options. Teachers choose from list how to spend $2,000. |
| 4. Empowerment/ boundaries guide action. | Leader provides the guiding boundaries and conditions; group or individual makes the decision. | Above average: leader still wants to set the parameters. | Above average: leader still wants to guide (coach) the process. | Group wants to make sure that teachers "get the best bang for the buck." | Leader doesn't care how money is spent as long as teachers use it to improve students' abilities to read nonfiction. |
| 5. Operational Empowerment. | Leader provides the freedom and latitude to teachers to make informed decision. | High. | High. | Confident that teachers will use data and all information available to them to make best decisions. | Leader gives $2,000 to teachers. Teachers decide how best to use it to improve student achievement. |

responsibility (accountability) from the leader that assessment scores will improve. Level five teachers, on the other hand, have access to student data, which they can align with their own level of competence and resources. By taking responsibility for improving student assessment scores, and from analysis determining what they need in order to improve their student learning, teachers are able to make informed decisions that will give them the best "bang for their buck." Through empowerment, these teachers are more likely to feel the ownership for their decision and use, in this case, the consultant's coaching strategies to improve their own teaching practices.

Teachers will be much more likely to accept responsibility and accountability for their own actions as they self-monitor, evaluate, and reflect upon their students' achievement on various assessments. As Seifter and Economy (2001) explain:

> Worker empowerment only succeeds if employees assume personal responsibility for following through on assigned duties and for the decisions they make. [Administrators must hold teachers] to a high standard of accountability; [Teachers] must hold themselves to an equally high standard. This doesn't mean punishing workers whenever they drop the ball, but it does mean helping them learn from their mistakes and giving them the training and support they need to do the job right the next time. (p. 40)

Training with ongoing follow-up and support is critical to the success of empowering individuals or groups. School leaders must assume the role of teacher and coach as they skillfully move teachers through the levels of empowerment. One word of caution, context is important! Like all motivators, the use of empowerment is situational. There will be times and places when the school administrator will want to make his own decision or is put into a situation in which he must make the final decision. Most likely, these will be strategic decisions or decisions made when the school is in crisis mode.

Just as with all ten of the motivational strategies in this book, leaders must know the people who work for them. Some faculty and staff will be highly motivated and challenged by being part of the decision-making process, while others will shy away at first. These staff members may need additional coaching and scaffolding until they gain competence in making informed decisions and the confidence that helps them feel good about being empowered to do their work.

## QUESTIONS FOR DISCUSSION

1. It is obvious that the teachers and staff do not feel empowered to help control student behavior. Before you read the rest of the chapter, decide what essential conditions are missing, and what, if anything, Margaret McGuire has the ability to change.

2. If you were Margaret, what would you do to empower your teachers and staff to improve student behavior at Lincoln Elementary School?

## ESSENTIAL CONDITIONS

In addition to understanding the levels of authority, the following nine essential conditions must be in place for a school leader to be able to structure empowerment effectively. Read along to learn about the essential conditions and to decide if you agree which conditions are missing at Lincoln Elementary.

1. **Recruiting and retaining the best.** From our own experiences, in far more instances than the media and those out for political gain acknowledge, the world of education has attained a new breed of professional teachers—those who can and want to teach! Unlike many teachers of the past, the new breed of teachers (knowledge workers) has chosen to make teaching their career and profession. As teachers retire, we must recruit this new breed of teacher. Likewise, school administrators must find the courage to weed out the few teachers remaining who are uncommitted and/or unwilling to dedicate their professional lives toward achieving the morally compelling school mission. Once school leaders have recruited competent and committed teachers, they need to find ways to retain them. This begins by treating them as professionals and recognizing and respecting their expertise by allowing them to do the work they were hired to do.

In the case study at the beginning of this chapter, it appears that the teachers have been at Lincoln Elementary for many years, or at least longer than Margaret, the newest principal. Since there have been three new principals in four years, it appears as if the superintendent may need to do some recruiting and/or make some changes in staffing in order to change the toxic culture of the school.

2. **Trust and integrity.** One of the most difficult barriers to granting authority is not trusting the people you lead to do the work you hired them to do. Most of us, at various times in our lives, have found the work easier to do ourselves than to let go and delegate it to others. Often, leaders feel as if the only person they can trust to get the job done right is themselves. But this is where the school leader must first put on his hat as a teacher of teachers to make sure that he has communicated his high and explicit expectations as well as all the important information about the task to staff members. Staff members must be provided with the knowledge, skills, and the resources to do the work. School leaders do not build trust and integrity through the hierarchical, top-down structures of telling teachers what to do and how to do it. Building trust and integrity takes true grit from getting your own hands dirty. School leaders have the most credibility and impact on the quality of teaching and learning when they work side by side with teachers in the trenches. It is by serving as a teacher who models the strategies and sets a good example, and by serving as a coach who articulates the mission and manages the systems to stay the course, that school leaders are afforded the ability to lead with integrity (by walking the talk) and to trust faculty and staff to use their knowledge, skills, talents, and professional judgment to get the desired results. When you work side by side, you know the teachers and what they can do. In return, they know you and what you are about. As this happens, both parties build a trusting and trustworthy relationship.

Although it is not explicitly stated, there appears to be a lack of trust at Lincoln Elementary. The teacher's perception of Margaret is that she is never at the school or there for her teachers. It is clear that Margaret needs to get to know her teachers better if she is going to empower them to help her improve student behavior.

3. **Commitment to achieve the mission.** All faculty and staff members must be committed to the morally compelling mission of the school. Lombardi Sr. says it this way, "I'd rather have a player with 50 percent ability and 100 percent desire because the guy with 100 percent desire is going to play every day, so you can make a system to fit what he can do. The other guy—the guy with 100 percent ability and 50 percent desire—can screw up your whole system because one day he'll be out there waltzing around" (as cited in Lombardi, 2001, p. 109). As we discussed earlier in this book, school leaders build commitment to achieve the mission by clarifying the vision, goals, values, and indicators of success so everyone knows and understands the expectations and work necessary to achieve the desired results. Everyone must have had a voice in the development of the mission, agree to accomplish it, and be willing to put forth the effort required to achieve it.

There does not appear to be a morally compelling mission at the school. The culture appears to be one in which the teachers simply send the students they don't want to deal with to the office. Everyone, including the principal, appears to be simply putting in time on the job, rather than making a difference through the important work they do.

4. **Clearly defined, articulated, and understood expectations, frameworks, and boundaries.** For school leaders to have the confidence and courage to let go and allow teachers the authority to do their work, they must first make sure that everyone knows, understands, and agrees to the boundaries and frameworks for achieving school goals. As we have said, at no other time in the history of teaching and learning have standards, curriculum frameworks, and desired results been so clearly defined and articulated. Even though teachers may not always know what questions are going to be on state assessments or how each question is weighted because the rules keep changing, they do have a deep understanding, from state and local frameworks, about what students need to know and be able to do. When the school's morally compelling mission is clearly articulated and in place, school leaders can let go and give teachers the freedom and latitude to do their jobs. Boundaries—those that express the latitude teachers have in making informed professional decisions about how best to help students achieve their learning goals—unleash teachers' talents, affording them the ability to be creative and innovative. Boundaries defining latitudes, giving teachers room to maneuver, are established in such a way that they define what is possible, rather than what teachers have to do or can't do. If we want teachers to be able to use student data to build knowledge and collective wisdom to help all students succeed, we must be willing to grant them the autonomy and empower them with authority to make professional decisions on how best to meet the needs of all learners.

In the situation at the beginning of this chapter it is clear that there are no rules, let alone boundaries or latitudes within which teachers work—at least not any that have been established by the principal. If there were, teachers would be doing more than simply sending students to the office when they no longer want to deal with them. One can assume from this description of what is happening with discipline that there are probably no clear expectations, boundaries, or frameworks for improving student achievement either.

5. **Accountability for results.** It is clear that the teachers have no concept of how the principal is spending her time each day. For example, they have no idea of the number of students she disciplines each day. Even if each teacher was only sending one or two students out of her classroom each day, with twenty classes in the school, the numbers add up very quickly. Likewise, the principal has not communicated her expectations about student behavior to the students or the faculty, nor is she holding teachers accountable for helping her to improve student behavior (such as working toward a goal of decreasing the number of student referrals to the office or the number of fights after lunch). It appears that teachers have not seen data on the number of discipline referrals, which leads us to believe that they probably are not collecting and analyzing other important information to determine the results of their work.

6. **Access to information.** Even though it isn't fair, all too often, school leaders hold teachers responsible and accountable for things they don't know or for information they didn't have access to. Nothing undermines trust and integrity, or creates a culture of learned dependency, more quickly than holding educators accountable without communicating the knowledge and essential information necessary to accomplish the task. Everyone doing the work must be in the know. It is imperative that school leaders establish open, honest, two-way communication structures that provide access to the pertinent information, just-in-time. To create buy-in, ownership, commitment, and support from faculty and staff, this information must be communicated accurately and in a timely manner. When it is not, school leaders find themselves using structures of learned dependency while their faculty and staff play the blame game.

Again, Margaret has not shared information with the teachers about how she spends her time each day or even about the number of students she sees each day because of discipline related issues.

7. **Quality of life.** The quality of life within the school setting is the foundation on which empowerment is built. As we described earlier, unless the basic needs for all individual staff members are met, and without the supportive structures and climate (including mutual respect and adaptation) in place, all of the best intentions from school leaders will be misguided and for naught. Empowerment results from a quality of life that is conducive to delegating responsibility and granting the authority and cannot be achieved without it.

From the case study at the beginning of the chapter, we are not sure what the quality of life is for teachers or students. We do know, however, that Margaret is not getting her basic needs met (e.g., lunch, drinks, bathroom use) nor is the secretary able to do her work without babysitting students. If the quality of life is like this for the administration, we suspect that it is not much better for the teachers and their students.

8. **Competence and capacity.** For school leaders to be able to let go and empower others, they must have the confidence that their teachers are competent and that the school has built the capacity for everyone to

successfully do the work and achieve the shared goals. It is as simple as that. As we said earlier, it is difficult for a leader to delegate a task that he does not believe others can do as well or efficiently as he can do himself. Therefore, it is vital that school administrators provide opportunities for teachers to gain the knowledge, skills, and dispositions they need to achieve the compelling school mission. This does not mean providing "one-size," pull-out, sit-and-get trainings. To build competence, school leaders must become a teacher of teachers who knows and understands the individual and collective strengths and weaknesses of each staff member. Likewise, administrators must serve in the trenches with teachers, working side-by-side as their coach, supporting their actions and strengthening their skill levels. School leaders must provide opportunities to help each person increase his or her own complexity through differentiated and meaningful professional learning experiences. Learning should be just-in-time and job-embedded as much as possible.

To build the capacity of the school, administrators need to examine the goals of the school's mission and make sure that all staff members have the knowledge, skills, and dispositions to collectively achieve the desired results. In addition, school leaders must make sure that the policies and structures are aligned and in place that support quality professional learning. Then, like coaches, school leaders must provide ongoing follow-up, feedback, and support to faculty and staff even as they let go and empower the group to do its work.

It appears that either the teachers do not have the knowledge and skills they need to deal with the student behavior issues at the school, or they have chosen not to use their knowledge and skills to do the job. We suspect, however, that because of the increasing social and cultural issues and pressures on students and communities today, that the teachers, especially if this is an aging staff, have not had professional learning opportunities to keep abreast of some of the current demands on educators (such as learning how to deal with autistic and emotionally disturbed students or violence and gang related issues). Schools are much different places today than they were even ten years ago. Administrators need to continue to build their own competence as well as the school's capacity for dealing with students' social, emotional, and behavioral issues if they are going to make the academic achievement gains required by NCLB.

9. **Interdependence.** There must be a culture that is conducive to collaboration, along with the structures for interdependence firmly in place, if school leaders are to have the confidence that their school team will be able to perform at optimal levels and accomplish the morally compelling mission. Not only must there be the recognition, understanding, and structures in place to make sure teachers can answer, "What's in it for me," there must also be a norm of interdependency among all staff members that is firmly entrenched within the school's culture that says, "We are all in this together" with a synergy that says, "Together we can" and that "None of us is as smart or does the work as well as all of us together." If school leaders are going to have the ability to let go and empower others, they have to know, first and foremost, that everyone is playing the same game, on the same field, with the same rules, and the same strong desire (passion) to win. Then, like Lombardi's rule number eight, for motivating the team to extraordinary performance, school leaders can "go where the

wisdom is." Administrators can have the same confidence in their staff that Lombardi had in his team and accept that their "people want to help you and the organization succeed. It motivates them" (as cited in Lombardi, 2001, p. 216). When this happens, you have a collegial learning community more likely to achieve optimal levels of performance.

It is clear in the case study at the beginning of this chapter that the teachers and principal are not empowered to work together interdependently. There appears to be nothing holding the school together except the four walls of the building. Each person, teachers and administrator, appears to be working in isolation and without regard for each other. It is clear that the teachers want to see their principal and are frustrated that they don't. It is clear that Margaret wants to get out of her office and do something besides disciplining students. But just wishing for things to change or wanting to work together doesn't create the positive interdependent structures that allow people to work as a collegial learning community.

## WHAT WOULD YOU DO?

1. After reading the above discussion about the essential conditions that need to be in place, do you agree? Is there anything else you would add?

2. Before you read the rest of the story, look back at what you said you would do if you were Margaret McGuire. Is there anything else you would add to your list?

Read on to compare your list with what Margaret chose to do.

## AND NOW FOR THE REST OF THE STORY

"It is hard to believe that this is the same school I was working in a year ago," Margaret thought to herself as she sat outside the superintendent's door waiting for her midterm evaluation. So much had happened since that day that became a turning point for Margaret and her school.

"You can go in now," Mrs. Johnson said, smiling at her. "Dr. Zarrilli is ready to see you."

"Thanks," Margaret caught herself saying as she stood up and began to move toward the door.

Dr. Zarrilli opened the door and greeted her warmly. "Come on in, Margaret. It's good to see you," he said, extending his hand to shake hers.

"It's good to see you again, too," she said, this time sincerely meaning it.

"Can I get you a cup of coffee, a soda, or something—a little water, maybe?" he asked in a friendly tone as she sat down at his conference table.

"No, thank you. I am fine," she said, smiling. "I just had lunch."

"Glad to hear you are eating again," he said smiling, thinking back to how tough it was for her the year before, when she barely was able to get out of her office to use the bathroom, let alone have a chance to eat lunch. Then Dr. Zarrilli added, "You have had quite a first year and a half in our district."

"That's right," Margaret said, remembering. "I can't thank you enough for all you have done to mentor me during my first year as a principal. I know I wouldn't have survived without your help," she said warmly. "I can't thank you enough for all of your help and advice."

"It was quite a year," he said, again laughing. "But my advice wouldn't have done you any good if you hadn't taken it and run with it. You had to want to be the best principal you could be, or you wouldn't have been able to weather those storms—and there were some pretty tough storms, if I remember correctly." He laughed, then sobered himself quickly saying, "I had no idea that things had gotten so far out of hand. But you never gave up. You just kept focused, stayed the course, and look what you have accomplished. From what I can see, you have really turned Lincoln Elementary School around."

"Thank you. It does feel like a different school now," she said.

"Let's see," Dr. Zarrilli said, as he opened up his folder and began to read the goal statement and indicators of success that she and he had agreed upon a year ago. It seemed like such a short time ago, he thought to himself, as he remembered driving to the school to talk with Margaret after Mrs. Hernandez had called to complain about her daughter's name being carved on the bathroom walls. Mrs. Hernandez had told Dr. Zarrilli other things as well, about the students' behavior in the classrooms and how her daughter, April, said that Margaret didn't care about the school because "Mrs. McGuire was never there." Mrs. Hernandez went so far as to say that April wasn't even sure what Margaret looked like because she never saw her.

That is when Dr. Zarrilli had paid Margaret a surprise visit, only to learn from Mrs. Grey, her secretary, what a zoo her office was. Thank goodness Mrs. Grey liked Margaret and felt sorry for her because she had let Dr. Zarrilli have it! Mrs. Grey was pretty fired-up and had lit into him for "putting someone with so little experience into a tough, inner-city school like Lincoln—expecting her to know what to do." And from everything he could see as he quickly evaluated what was happening at the school, both Mrs. Grey and Mrs. Hernandez were right.

After school let out that day, Dr. Zarrilli had called Margaret up to his office, where the two of them had sat for several hours, the first of many such sessions. Margaret had told Dr. Zarrilli everything that was going on at Lincoln, and, for the first time, he understood why so many principals had left the school during the past several years. That day, Dr. Zarrilli had made a promise to himself, that he was not going to lose another principal, nor was he going to let this quality educator leave the field of education, which is what she had told him she was ready to do.

As they talked, Dr. Zarrilli had remembered how one of his education leadership professors had told him, "You can put a bad person in a good school, and they will be able to survive, and perhaps even get better for it. But when you put a good person in a bad school, the system will eat them up every time." He remembered looking at Margaret that February afternoon a year ago, and he saw that she was just about fully cooked.

After Dr. Zarrilli had listened to her side of the story, he told her that he was there to help her take control of her school. He was not going to let her go down with the ship, nor was he going to let the ship sink. He also told her that she was going to have to step up to the plate, and that it wouldn't be easy, but if she was willing to work hard, he could help her turn the school around.

Even though Margaret had walked into his office that day ready to quit and never go back, she walked out of his office with a goal and a plan in place.

Dr. Zarrilli cleared his throat and began to read, "It says here that your goal for the second half of last year and this year is to empower your teachers to help you create and implement a school-wide discipline program that will improve the school climate at Lincoln Elementary so that it is conducive to learning. The indicators of success are that: (1) the teachers will take responsibility for creating, implementing, and monitoring a discipline program that everyone will agree with and follow; (2) the number of discipline referrals will be reduced by at least half; (3) the percentage of suspensions will be significantly reduced; and (4) you and the teachers will implement a schoolwide character education program. The ultimate outcome is a change in teacher and student behaviors at the school. Is that correct?"

"Yes, that's correct," Margaret heard herself saying.

"So, how do you feel about what you have accomplished?" Dr. Zarrilli asked.

*(Continued)*

(Continued)

*"I feel so much better today, walking into your office, than I did a year ago," she said, smiling. "I actually had time to do an observation today, listen to several students read, work with our library clerk to help her find a website that gave information about the latest NASA space mission, and eat lunch with some of the teachers. Not bad, considering it is only 1:30 in the afternoon."*

*Dr. Zarrilli was clearly pleased with what he was hearing. "I'm not surprised by what you are saying," he said. "In fact, I stopped by your school earlier this morning. Mrs. Grey said she thought you were in one of the classrooms. It was about 10:15. There were no students in your office, like a year ago. Things were quiet. In fact, Mrs. Grey was so involved with her attendance that for the longest time she didn't even know I was standing there. She was never like that before. Mrs. Grey always seemed so frazzled," he commented.*

*"I know," laughed Margaret, remembering what it used to be like before she and Mrs. Grey had collected data to share with the school improvement team.*

*"So, tell me what you have done during this past year to get your school to function the way it is now, and how you know that things are going well," Dr. Zarrilli said.*

*"Where do I begin," Margaret thought to herself. Then she said, "It started right after you and I created the goal to empower the staff to create a discipline plan and take responsibility for implementing and monitoring it. You were right. Until I got the teachers to take responsibility for their students' behavior, I was never going to get out of my office. The best thing we, Mrs. Grey and I, did was to keep a list of whom I saw, from which classroom, for what reason, along with the time I saw them. We collected that information for two weeks. We filled at least three pages in her notebook everyday. After two weeks, you can imagine how many names I had. I took them to my school improvement team meeting and said something like, 'I know that you are all frustrated. You would like me to be in your classrooms, working with you and helping to support what you are doing. I want nothing more than to be doing that, too. I know that you think I am never here, but let me show you what I have been doing for the past two weeks.' That is when I showed them all of the data," Margaret laughed and looked at Dr. Zarrilli as she remembered. "They were so surprised. Not just at the number of students who I saw each day, but that I saw them for such stupid reasons like not having their homework, talking out in class, not sitting in their seat, getting in a fight after recess over who won the soccer game, and the list went on and on. They were also surprised that I saw some of the kids three and four times a day, sent by the same teachers. It was a real eye opener." Margaret stopped, then continued.*

*"Once they saw what I was doing each day, and how I never got to leave my office, they, most of them, were ready to do something about it. I told them that unless they helped me with discipline and getting our students' behavior under control, I wouldn't be able to help them. It was a two-way street. Luckily for me, they agreed and were willing to help. Or at least most of them."*

*"So, thanks to you," Margaret continued, "I called that professor, Dr. Iverson, you had told me about, who had written the classroom management book for teachers. I told him exactly what was going on, and he agreed to come talk with us in March for our half-day inservice. I have to thank you and the director of instruction for helping me find the money to pay to bring him in to work with our teachers last year and again this year. He is great! He listened to the teachers talk, or I should say vent, about student behaviors in their classrooms and around the school. I guess that is when I realized that they, or I should say most of them, were as upset and frustrated as I was. Dr. Iverson told them it didn't have to be that way, and then he gave them several strategies to try. He had them practice the strategies and then came back to our next half-day inservice in April. He answered questions, and I have to tell you, he had them hooked—eating out of his hand. What he told them, worked!"*

*"I told you he was good," smiled Dr. Zarrilli. "But I still don't understand how you got them all to attend his course in the summer," he said.*

*"I'm not sure either," Margaret said, "but what he told them worked and they just wanted to know more and more after our initial meeting. Regardless, it was the best thing that ever happened to us. It helped that one of our teachers retired. And, you moved two other teachers,*

*you know who, to other schools. It really has made a difference having them gone. Plus, it also helped that you backed me up when they called you to complain. I really appreciate your help and support."*

*"Sometimes the only thing you can do is move people and hope that they take advantage of the fresh start in a new place. With those two teachers, if they don't make the changes that we have told them they need to make, I will make sure that they find a different profession," Dr. Zarrilli said. "You can't make people change if they don't want to change. You can help them think about what they need to do in order to improve their own performance. And you can help them make those changes if they are willing to work at it. But if they aren't going to give 100 percent to their job, then maybe it is time to leave," he said thoughtfully.*

*"How are they doing?" Margaret was almost afraid to ask.*

*"Actually, they are both doing very well in their new schools," he said. "In fact, you would never even recognize Dick Bowen," he laughed. "That guy has really turned it around. Maybe he needed to be at a middle school after all. He is teaching history and geography and has the students doing all kinds of interesting projects. In fact, you can see a lot of them on his website."*

*"That's wonderful," Margaret said, really meaning it. "I am so glad that he found his niche."*

*"So, back to the class. I think one of the biggest reasons that Dr. Iverson was able to work so effectively with your faculty is because you, as the school leader, sat right there with your teachers," Dr. Zarrilli stated emphatically.*

*"It would never have crossed my mind not to be there," Margaret said.*

*"You would be surprised how many administrators send their teachers to 'sit-and-get' and then wonder why things never change. The fact that you were there every day demonstrated to teachers how important this learning was for all of you. Margaret, what you were doing was not only 'walking the talk' and validating this process, but you were also a coach and a teacher for your teachers. From what Dr. Iverson told me, you were asking the right questions, reinforcing the key elements, and helping your teachers to analyze and reflect upon what you all were learning. Most of all, you helped your teachers fit the key elements they were learning into the context of your school so that you could make it your own unique program," Dr. Zarrilli paused for a moment. "How do you see that this experience has turned your school around?"*

*"During the week we spent with Dr. Iverson, we learned so much—about motivation, teaching strategies, logical consequences, being consistent and fair. We all grew so much during that course. What he had to say was just-in-time for all of us, me included. I would never have predicted it, but on several afternoons, most of the teachers stayed after class so he could help us develop our discipline plan, including the rules and consequences for not following the rules. He also helped us decide on the traits we wanted to target for our character education program and gave us a lot of resources that we could use, including a list of teachers and principals in different districts who were doing similar things in their schools. We divided the list. After interviewing people on the list, the teachers reported back at our summer meetings about what they learned. We tried several of the ideas. Each time we try something and it is successful, the enthusiasm among the teachers—well, they just go wild! I don't think I could have stopped the train if I had wanted to. Every time I saw them during the summer, they had something else to show me or something else they wanted to try. I guess all I could do at this point was stand back and watch them go! I am so proud of all the things they have tried this year. Not everything works like we want the first time, but that's okay. We are learning. Each month, for example, when we do our sharing assemblies, about the different traits, we keep getting better and better at it."*

*"I do have to say, that all of the posters and student artifacts that are hanging up around the school certainly make a statement about what all of you expect of your students. Having them write about the character traits, and demonstrate the different character trait of the month at your assemblies, has also helped them to internalize what you are teaching them. I have really enjoyed the couple of assemblies I have been able to attend," Dr. Zarrilli commented.*

*(Continued)*

(Continued)

"Do you want to know what has made the biggest difference?" Margaret asked.

"Sure, what?"

"The biggest 'ah, ha' for us was when we were looking at the data and discovered that we had the most discipline problems, especially fights, on the playground right after lunch. Almost every day I had students being sent to my office because they were fighting over stupid things, like who won the soccer game or what day of the week it was. It was ridiculous; it didn't matter, even to the kids. But everyday it was the same thing." Margaret said.

"So, what did you do?" he asked.

"We flipped the lunch around. Now the students all play outside first and then eat second. I rarely have any fights after lunch, because nobody wants to sit in the principal's office and miss lunch with their friends," she said smiling, proud of the discovery they had made by looking at the data. "Look," she said, holding up one of the charts she had brought to show him. "You can see that a year ago it was not uncommon for me to see ten to fifteen kids every day after the three lunch recesses were over. Now look, I haven't seen ten kids in a month, since October. In fact, look at the number of referrals and suspensions during this year compared to last year. It is hard for even me to believe that our numbers could be this good!" Margaret said, feeling very pleased with what she and her teachers had accomplished.

"That is a significant change. I bet your students are calmer when they return to class after eating."

"Their behavior in the cafeteria is better, too, because after playing they are hungry, so they eat," Margaret said.

"I thought you were going to tell me that the best thing that happened was that you have so many more parents volunteering at your school. I was really surprised the last couple of times I stopped by to visit. I even saw some of your Spanish-speaking parents working at your school," Dr. Zarrilli commented.

"It is great, isn't it?" Margaret said. "It surprises me, too, how many of them are willing to come and help now that you and the school board have hired a couple of teacher aides who can help translate, and we got the grant to help teach parents how to speak Spanish and English, in a two-way bilingual class. It is fun to watch the parents ask each other questions in the opposite language."

Dr. Zarrilli looked puzzled, so Margaret explained, "Spanish parents have to ask English parents a question in English, such as 'Where does your daughter take dance lessons?' or 'Who is your son's soccer coach?' Then, English parents have to answer the question in Spanish. The teachers help them practice communicating and asking questions. At the same time, parent, teachers, and even me, are getting to know each other. It is a great community building activity. It helps the parents and teachers build relationships and a sense of community."

"What I can't understand," Dr. Zarrilli said, "is how you have gotten so many of your parents to come back to school at night for your activities. We have been trying to do that in this district for a long time," he said.

"Oh, that," Margaret laughed. "It was Jen's idea. We were brainstorming ideas last summer during the class about how we could get families more involved. Jen said that every time her church had an event, and they wanted to get as many people there as they could, they did a couple of things. One thing was that they made sure they had enough people there to help interpret what people wanted to say to each other. Another was that they had to have free food, so we have been working with some of the local restaurants and chains to donate food, like our back-to-school hot dog barbeque or our spaghetti supper. Instead of trying to make money, we just try to get the food donated so we can offer to give them a free meal. It really surprised me when one of our more affluent parents said that she always felt that she was 'giving, giving, giving to the school, and that it was nice when the school gave something back' to her. It really surprised me that she would say something like that, because all she was getting was a hot dog dinner that she was helping to cook," Margaret said. "Guess you just never know how you touch people."

"People are full of surprises, that's for sure," Dr. Zarrilli replied.

*"The other thing that gets parents to come to our school is when we have them bring their kids and do some kind of an activity, like a father-son soccer game, mother-daughter craft night, or a hands-on family literacy or math night. Oh, and I almost forgot, we always try to do a drawing, so people get door prizes. It doesn't have to be much, but people like to win. It makes them feel good, I guess." Margaret laughed. "We don't usually give away much, but when we had the PTA meeting with the youth officers and the gang prevention council, we gave away some sports equipment and clothes from one of the local sporting stores, and we had a full house. Plus, it really helped us to have the parents learn about violence prevention and how to keep their children safe. Now our parents are helping us implement our discipline program here at school. They no longer argue when we tell them what their children are doing. Instead, they are supporting us and doing everything they can to make sure their children follow the rules and act respectfully and responsibly."*

*"I can see that you and your teachers have really begun to turn Lincoln around. I see that you have some other documents. Is there anything else you would like to show me?" Dr. Zarrilli asked.*

*"Oh, yes, I almost forgot," Margaret said, beaming. "I asked the teachers, parents, and students to fill out a survey for me. It was only a couple of questions about whether they felt our school was safe, what they liked best about the school, and what we could do to make our school even better. There is no way I would have done this last year—well, you know what it was like. But here are the surveys. I will leave them with you so you can read them," Margaret said, handing him the bundle.*

*Dr. Zarrilli did a quick scan of several of them. Then he read one that caught his eye. "Mrs. McGuire truly cares about our students. She has made our school a safe place for everyone to be."*

*"Here is another one," he said, reading, "I did not like the idea of making my son wait until after recess to eat his lunch. But it is the best thing that has happened to him, because this year, he is not getting into so many fights."*

*"But this one," Dr. Zarrilli said, "this one says it all. I think it is from one of your teachers, too, Shelby Young? She wrote, 'A year ago I was so frustrated with everything. I never saw Mrs. McGuire and I didn't think she cared. The students were completely out of control. But I just want to say thank you for everything you have done, Margaret. You have empowered me to be the best teacher I can be. You have given me and the rest of the teachers the freedom to try out new ideas to help make our school a better place. Thanks for believing in us and for being our principal."*

*With that, Dr. Zarrilli looked at Margaret, extended his hand to shake hers as he said, "Well done, Mrs. McGuire. Keep up the great work!"*

## CHAPTER SUMMARY

We define empowerment as *delegating the responsibility and granting the authority that affords educators the freedom and latitude to do their work and achieve their mission.* There are several things that school leaders should do if they want to increase the likelihood that empowerment will be a powerful motivational strategy for all educators.

First, school leaders should understand the stages of authority in decision making. As their teachers become skilled at making informed and effective decisions, and as leaders become more confident in their teachers' ability to make professional decisions, leaders can let go and grant authority. When school leaders begin to empower staff, they must communicate clearly to teachers their expectations and the latitude for the decisions. Once this is in place they can allow faculty and staff the freedom and latitude to make professional decisions that directly impact the teaching and learning process as well as hold teachers accountable for their choices and the work they do to achieve the mission.

When administrators empower others, they will unleash the knowledge, skills, talents, and experiences of staff members to create partnerships that build ownership, responsibility, and accountability toward achieving the school's morally compelling mission. Although at times it is difficult, instructional leaders must be visible. To do this means administrators must schedule time to be in the trenches with teachers, in their classrooms, discussing student work, examining assessment data, etc. When school leaders build relationships with and among their staff members, they are more likely to trust their decision-making abilities. School leaders must be role models for staff members, jumping in at times to do those things they ask teachers to do.

School leaders must find ways to structure time during the day (job-embedded) for school teams (e.g., grade level, content level, interest, site council, data teams) to meet on a frequent and regular basis. Leaders should coach these teams to become self-directed and help them make, implement, evaluate, and refine the decisions that impact their work. Likewise, they must hold the teams accountable for their decisions and the results they achieve. The more leaders coach teachers like Lombardi coached his team, the more likely they will be to empower them. Leaders put the power and control into the hands of the teachers when they: (1) delegate responsibility to them to insure that all students are able to achieve the learning goals defined by the school's mission, (2) give them tools and resources (a menu of options), (3) grant them the authority to use their professional judgment to make informed decisions to best meet the needs of the individual learners in their classrooms, and (4) get out of their way and trust them to do the work. In other words, Lombardi's rule was to "Paint the picture, provide the tools, and get out of the way," which is the epitome of empowerment (Lombardi, 2001, p. 257–259).

## NEXT STEPS

1. Think about empowerment in your school and your comfort level in delegating responsibility and granting authority to others. What does empowerment look like, sound like, and feel like in your current situation? What would you like it to be? Make a list. Put a star by those things that are already in place in your situation. Put a check by those things that you would like to implement or explore further.

2. If possible, discuss with others what you found interesting about this case study on empowerment and what you found challenging. What ideas would you like to try?

3. Select one or two ideas and list several changes that you can make to feel more comfortable empowering your teachers to make decisions. What barriers may get in your way? List strategies or choices you can make to help decrease those barriers.

4. How will you know that the strategies you are using to empower your staff are working effectively? What are the indicators of success?

# 11

# Positive Interdependence

*Interacting in Ways
That Promote Each Other's Success*

■ **PICTURE THIS**

*"Why me?" Michael Tomassetti asked himself again, as he pushed open the staff room door. It didn't surprise him that he found the Blue House teachers engaged in a conversation about the latest March Madness college basketball statistics instead of using their weekly scheduled common planning time to discuss student progress toward curricular goals. Being the assistant principal of Holcomb Middle School meant doing all the things that the principal, Dr. Bill Evans, didn't want to touch. This was one of them, and Michael could see why. "If only they cared as much about their students' performance as they cared about the number of rebounds that were made during each quarter, or the number of times the referee didn't call the foul," he thought, as he shut the door behind him, walked over to the table, and sat down.*

*"I couldn't believe it when Duncan passed the ball to Crammer and just before the half-time buzzer, slam, dunk. Oh, my gosh—did you see them take the lead? With one second left! I couldn't believe it! I wanted to go to bed so bad, but I couldn't move!" Donna Slowik exuded such excitement recalling the game.*

*"And, we aren't even to the sweet sixteen, yet," Dan Martin laughed.*

*"I know. Can you imagine, if they are this tight already, what the final four will be like?" Ray Bradley said, almost salivating with anticipation.*

*(Continued)*

(Continued)

*"I can't wait—especially if Duke makes it," Pete Landis said.*

*"Yeah, but those Huskies . . ." crooned Dan.*

*"Can you imagine if the Blue Devils get to play the Huskies?" Kurt Phillips chimed in.*

*"Way too cool!" Julie Manning wailed.*

*"Stop, already!" Michael heard himself shouting above the group to get their attention. Heads turned, and for the first time, they noticed him.*

*"What's up?" Dan asked in his usual cocky manner. "You look like you have something for us."*

*"And it doesn't look good," Kurt murmured, then added, "Maybe you should go out and come in again with better news."*

*Everyone laughed except Michael. As he nervously shuffled the pile of papers, he asked, "Did you see the statewide test results?"*

*They all stared at him with blank looks on their faces. "Sorry," Dan finally spoke for the group. "I didn't have time to go to my mailbox. I figured if there was something we needed to see, somebody would bring it to us."*

*"Well, once again, this is your lucky day," Michael said, forcing a laugh as he tried to keep the conversation light. "I just happen to have a copy for everyone." Michael kept a copy for himself and passed the rest out.*

*When everyone had a copy, Michael cleared his throat, and then began. "Statewide testing starts in four weeks. Dr. Evans and I have split up. We are each taking two of the houses. I have you and the Yellow House. He has the Red House and the Green House."*

*"Lucky you–you get us!" Ray said, smiling smugly.*

*"If he only knew," thought Michael. Out loud, he said, "I have just given you all of the students who fall into the cells that the state will be looking at to determine AYP. We have it graphed, so you can see the entire sixth, seventh, and eighth grades first. Then we graphed the data by house." He paused. "As you can see, we have a number of students on free and reduced lunch that are struggling in all of the core subjects. When you look even closer at the list of students in each cell and their latest end-of-the-term grades, you will see that a large percentage of those students are in the Blue House."*

*"It figures," said Ray. "We've always known that the Blue House is the dumping ground for our school. We should just call ourselves 'Animal House.'"*

*"Yeah, or the 'sweat hogs,'" agreed Kurt, remembering* Welcome Back, Kotter, *a TV show from the '70's.*

*"It doesn't matter what you call yourselves," Michael said, drawing a line in the sand. "Your students aren't making the grade, and if they don't make it, we don't make it!" he said emphatically.*

*"Yeah, yeah," mimicked Pete Landis. "Try teaching math to some of the boneheads I have. They don't know a positive number from a negative number. It's all the same to them—until they take their stash to ole Jake down the street. Then they know if they are getting ripped off or not."*

*"And it doesn't matter who they ripped off before they got to him," chimed in Dan Martin. He understood exactly what Pete was talking about. The same students couldn't do calculations in science, either. But street smart—that was another story.*

*"The way I look at it," said Donna, "is that most of these kids belong in special education or ELL anyway. We can't expect them to do any better than they already are. In fact, look," she said, pointing at two students in her English classes, "these two girls have gotten 4s on their writing prompts. Sarah's reading on a third-grade level, and Cristina can't even speak English—let alone write it. After all, she has only been in America for a little over a year. A 4 for them is darn good—but does anybody care about that?"*

*"It doesn't matter," Michael tried to say calmly. "The public will only see the numbers—that is, the number of students who do not meet state standards. We have more than forty students in each of our ELL, free and reduced, and special education cells. We have to help our students become proficient. I'm here to talk with you about what we can do to make sure all of our students make AYP."*

*"Only in your dreams," murmured Ray. As the guidance counselor, he knew better than anyone what the Blue House was up against.*

*"Take it from me," Dan said. "Read my lips! They aren't going to make it! There is nothing more we can do. It isn't our fault. Every day, we all go into our rooms, close our doors, and teach until we are blue in the face. But, they don't care. They don't come prepared with their homework. They don't have a pencil. They lost their book."*

*"And their dog ate their homework, and they had to babysit their three little brothers while their old lady cleans houses and their old man's sitting in some jail cell keeping the place full," added Kurt. "We'd all like to help you out, but Dan's right." He stopped, ran his finger down the list of kids, and then said, "Take Jared . . . you see him in your office at least once a day, unless you suspended him or buried him in detention for the day. When that kid, and all the other kids like him, show up in my classroom, all they do is cause trouble. Why? Because they don't want to be here in the first place. They could care less about how World War II got started. But ask them about justice and the law. They can tell you more than you ever wanted to know about the juvenile system."*

*"It's like this, Mr. Tomassetti," Donna said, leaning toward him, but speaking slowly and emphatically, so that each word was enunciated and easily understood. "We are all here to teach. If they want to learn, great! We want to teach them. But when they don't, and they have just come to make our lives miserable because they have nowhere else to go, then just get them out of my classroom. It isn't fair to the others who have to sit and listen to the stuff that comes out of their mouths." Then she stopped. "If you really want to help these kids learn, then you need to stop including them in classes with everyone else. You need to send them back to Special ed and ELL, where Julie and Regina can try to help them. After all, these are not our kids—it's up to the two of you to fix them," Donna said, pointing her finger first at Julie Manning, the special education teacher, and then at Regina Cheyney, the ELL teacher. "We should not be responsible for teaching any student until they are working on grade level. It isn't fair to us, and it isn't fair to the rest of the students."*

*"I don't know what the answer is," Michael said, thinking out loud. "But Dr. Evans has given us our marching orders. The Blue House is at the bottom of the heap, no question about it. But your students are not any different from the students in the other three houses. All our kids come from the same neighborhoods, and they have been split equally among all four houses. Isn't that right, Ray?"*

*"Yeah," Ray whispered, knowing Michael was right. All of the students were assigned to the four houses as heterogeneously as possible.*

*Michael continued, "And, when you take time to look at how the students are doing, you will see that the only house that is bringing our school down, is your house. Dr. Evans wants us to come up with a plan to improve the academic performance of the students in your house that are at risk for not making AYP."*

*Michael paused. He looked at their faces. It was clear that they didn't get it. The teachers were masters at playing the "blame game." And, it was clear that the Blue House students were losing—big time! Michael knew he had to turn it around.*

*"March Madness is over in three weeks," Michael said catching their attention. They all looked up at him, quizzically, just as the bell rang, signaling that their common planning time before school was over and it was time to face another day.*

*"About the time March Madness ends, the statewide testing begins."*

*"Did you have to remind us," Pete moaned.*

*"I know you all saw the game last night. So, consider this the final two minutes of the game. Consider you are down by 10 points. Consider this your time-out and that you better huddle together and come up with a plan. Consider while you huddle together that your plan better be good because your future depends on it! Consider that from now on you better get back out there and kick butt," Michael paused for emphasis, "because if you lose, you lose more than just a game! Need I say more?"*

*Without a word, the Blue House teachers filed out of the staff room, one by one, with Ray stopping to pause as he shot Michael one more quick look before walking out and shutting the door, leaving Michael sitting there alone, staring at the empty room. It hadn't gone well, but then, what did he expect? They didn't care. Nobody cared. Why should he?*

# ■ WHAT IS POSITIVE INTERDEPENDENCE?

The walls of isolation may be crumbling, but in their place, within the rubble, stand structures of collaboration, many of which have been forced. In far too many school systems, educators sit together, often because they "have to," in meetings to learn, share lessons, double score student work, analyze data, and discuss results. Although their bodies may be physically present, their hearts and minds may be thousands of miles away, daydreaming about tomorrow. When the bell finally rings, the clock strikes the end of the contractual day, or the teachers are excused, they leave, only to go back to their classrooms still just as lonely, isolated, and disconnected as they were before the walls came tumbling down. Administrators, left cleaning up the mess, stand gaping at the empty room, asking why their teachers are still doing "their own thing" behind closed doors.

Although it *looks* like collaboration, and sometimes may even *sound* like collaboration, without positive interdependence, the *feel* and results just aren't the same. In many instances, "that which we call a rose, by any other name would smell as sweet" (Shakespeare, 1859, p. 30), but not so when people are forced to collaborate. All the meeting time in the world will not change the group dynamics—even when groups of educators sit knee-to-knee, eye-to-eye, face-to-face—unless the skills of collaboration and structures for positive interdependence have been built within a strong foundation, or what we call quality of life.

How educators perceive each other and interact with each other has been lost in the shuffle of school reform and accountability. After all, they are adults, and they are being paid to work together. So, why can't they get along? Why don't they like each other? Why aren't they willing to share ideas and strategies with each other? Why is it that they are here for only "their kids" and not those other kids down the hall? Why can't I make them want to work together?

We, as school leaders, have several strong forces working against us as we attempt to tear down the walls of isolation and rebuild collaboration and collegiality among our staffs. First, beginning with the one room schoolhouse, teachers have spent decades working in isolation. Educators have always known teaching is a lonely occupation. As a first-grade teacher, I (Rosie) remember looking out at my students on numerous occasions, thinking, "It's only them and me." As a middle school teacher, one of my colleagues was hospitalized for an emergency appendectomy. I didn't find out about it until a week later. Ask any teacher, both of these examples are far too common in our schools today. Even though our schoolhouses are no longer one room, teachers and administrators often feel just as lonely.

Second, let's face it, as much as educators have tried to make their classrooms and schools cooperative learning environments, there has always been a competitive force that is hard to reconcile. It is everywhere: in grades, in sports, in the arts, in college entrance requirements, and even in merit-pay for teachers. In fact, when I first began teaching, although merit-pay had been dropped from the teacher salary schedule, the dark clouds of merit-pay still loomed over our school and reared their ugly heads each time one teacher had an idea or project for her students to do and someone else "copied" it. Likewise, we have all been in classes in which we were put into groups to complete a task and, even though some of us did all the work, everyone, including the freeloaders, got the credit. When this happened, how did you feel? Or worse, what about being in a class, put into a jigsaw group, knowing you have important information others need, but the conflict of sharing it hangs over your head as you realize that you are competing against your group members for an A, knowing only 5 percent of the class will achieve that grade? Do you share everything? Or keep the important information to yourself? In a similar way, as students in one class are being measured against students in another for achieving standards and learning goals, how many teachers, who are rewarded because their students scored higher than the class next-door, are going to be willing to share "trade secrets" with their colleagues? As a school administrator, if you are told by your superintendent that your students need to be number one in reading again next year, will you share "trade secrets" with your colleagues? If not, why?

Third, in classrooms, educators call the instructional strategy for group work *cooperative learning.* For adults, group work or teamwork is often called *collaboration,* or some derivative. But in doing so, have we lost the cooperative aspects of group work? All too often, educators find themselves in situations of forced collaboration. Then, when the group isn't productive, leaders ask why?

Finally, we as educators spend most of our college prep work and inservice activities engaged in learning about classroom management issues, curriculum issues, instructional strategies, and recently, data analysis, accountability, and school improvement. Little time has been devoted to the skills of collaboration, and unfortunately, many educators do not understand interdependence. David and Roger Johnson (1989) explain:

> Because we are immersed in it, social interdependence can escape our notice. Whether it is quite personal or so impersonal that we are barely aware of it, we regularly underestimate the role that social interdependence plays in human life. Since we can barely imagine its absence, we do not often consider its presence. (p. 1)

Occasionally, teachers may learn about how their students should relate and interact with each other, but rarely do adults spend time learning how to interact with each other. In fact, David Perkins (2003) says:

> It's a rare team that at the onset has all the knowledge and skills needed to carry a complex initiative forward. Learning, not just doing, is part of the game. Areas of learning may include technical knowledge about the mission, broad perspectives on its place in the larger scheme of things, process skills, patterns of working comfortably with one another, and more. (p. 170)

Seldom do educators spend time learning "process skills, patterns of working comfortably with one another, and more" as Perkins suggests. In fact, he goes even further by saying that to "treat learning as a peripheral part of the process is again to fail in one's collaborative citizenship" (p. 170). In most administrative courses and certification programs, little if any time is spent on how to structure teacher-to-teacher interaction patterns or cooperative and collaborative reciprocity for school, department, or team activities. We just expect people to "do it!"

Social interdependence, or when the outcomes of individuals are affected by each other's actions, evolved from Kurt Lewin's field study in 1935 (as cited in Johnson & Johnson, 1989). According to Johnson and Johnson:

> Kurt Lewin stated the essence of a group is the interdependence among members, which results in the group being a "dynamic whole" so that a change in the state of any member or subgroup changes the state of any other member or subgroup. For interdependence to exist, there must be more than one person or entity involved, and the persons or entities must have impact on each other in that a change in the state of one causes a change in the state of the others. In addition, Lewin stated that individuals are made interdependent through their common goals. (p. 7)

Johnson and Johnson go on to say that Lewin and his colleagues found that all individuals are motivated by the three different goal structures (i.e., cooperative, competitive, or individual), which make up the three types of interdependence (i.e., positive interdependence, negative interdependence, and no interdependence, respectively). Within any situation, educators may choose to work together to achieve shared goals (cooperative—positive interdependence); compete to see which one of them is better (competitive—negative interdependence); or work by themselves without any interaction with others (individual—no interdependence).

Johnson and Johnson suggest, "how social interdependence is structured determines how individuals interact within the situation which, in turn, affects outcomes" (p. 5). More specifically, *cooperation* exists when *positive interdependence* (e.g., we are in this together, sink or swim) is structured into the group activity, causing individuals to interact "in ways that promote each other's success" (p. 5). This interaction "generally leads to higher productivity and achievement, more positive relationships among individuals, and greater psychological health and wellbeing" (p. 5–6). *Competition* (e.g., I win and you lose, or you lose and I win) occurs when *negative interdependence* is structured. When competing against each other to achieve the goal, individuals obstruct each other's successes, which usually leads to lower productivity, achievement, negative relationships, and lower psychological health and well-being. *Individual* goals exist when *no interdependence* structure is in place. As Figure 11.1 illustrates, because there is no interaction among individuals, there tends to be lower productivity and achievement, more negative relationships among individuals, and lower psychological health and well-being.

Because the relationships between social interdependence and the interaction patterns are bidirectional, one can cause the other. This creates what Johnson and Johnson (1989) have labeled the "spiral of cooperation" and the "spiral of competition." They write:

> There is a *spiral of cooperation* in which cooperation promotes trust, trust promotes a greater cooperation, which promotes greater trust and so forth. People tend to trust their collaborators but also to seek out opportunities to collaborate with those they trust. There is a *spiral*

*of competition* in which competition promotes limited communication with opponents, which causes greater competition, which promotes even more limited communication, and so forth. People tend to hide information from competitors and tend to compete with those from whom they are hiding information. (p. 168)

**Figure 11.1**   The Relationship Between Social Interdependence Goal Structures and Their Interaction Patterns

| Goal Structure | Which Causes . . . | Characterized By . . . |
|---|---|---|
| Negative Interdependence: Competition. | Oppositional interactions. ("I hurt you; it helps me."):<br><br>• Obstruction of each other's goal achievement efforts.<br>• Ineffective and misleading communication.<br>• Destructive management of conflict.<br>• Distrust. | • Perceptions of negatively-linked fates.<br>• Striving for differential benefit.<br>• Having a short-term focus on personal benefit.<br>• Building a relative identity of superiority or inferiority.<br>• Recognizing that performance is mutually caused by own and other's ability and effort. |
| No Interdependence: Individualistic. | No interactions. ("All for one; I did it by myself.")<br><br>• Me-centered.<br>• Looking out for number one.<br>• Only interested in self.<br>• Isolation and disconnected from others.<br>• Don't care what anyone else is doing.<br>• Lack of engagement or willingness to share or communicate with others. | • Perceptions of individual fate.<br>• Striving for self-benefit.<br>• Focusing on short-term individual performance.<br>• Building an individual identity based on actual-ideal comparisons.<br>• Recognizing that performance is caused only by one's own ability and effort. |
| Positive Interdependence: Cooperation. | Promotive interaction. ("We sink or swim together."):<br>• Mutual help and assistance.<br>• Effective communication.<br>• Constructive management of conflict.<br>• Trust. | • Perceptions of a common fate.<br>• Striving for mutual benefit.<br>• Having a long-term perspective.<br>• Having shared identity.<br>• Realizing that performance is mutually caused by own and others ability and energy. |

SOURCE: Created by Vojteks, from Johnson & Johnson, 1989, p. 167–170.

NOTE: The relationship between social interdependence and the interaction patterns are bidirectional. Each can cause the other.

After completing a meta-analysis of social interdependence, Johnson and Johnson (1989) concluded that although there are times when competitive and individual goal structures are appropriate and effective, the most important of the three is cooperation. All three goal structures were measured against the benefits (i.e., achievement and productivity, relationships, and psychological health). Because Johnson and Johnson frequently found that the research situations were "implemented in ways that reduce efforts to achieve and created animosity and divisiveness among participants," (p. 169) it was difficult for them to determine exactly which goal structure works best in which situation. They did, however, suggest conditions under which each goal structure would be more likely to be successful. To be effective, competitive or individualistic efforts *must occur* within an overall context of cooperation (p. 169). One way to do this is to play down the competition element involved in the activity, and instead, stress the learning and fun participants have working together. Another is to build individual accountability into group activities to avoid hitchhiking or to use outside force interdependence, both of which are discussed further in this chapter.

In Figure 11.2, we have synthesized the elements that need to be in place to increase the likelihood that each goal structure (i.e., cooperative, competitive, individual) will allow educators to work successfully to achieve their goals. Note that under the cooperation goal structure, we have added two elements from the work of Kagan & Kagan (2009): (1) *equal participation*, and we have added equal responsibility (although distribution of participation is never equal—when some people do more than others, it leads to negative feelings and alienation); and (2) *simultaneous interaction* (the more all people are actively engaged in the activity, the more likely they will be to feel that they have made a significant and worthy contribution to the group). In addition, we have added *quality of life,* which we have defined earlier in this book. We also have renamed "social skills" to "skills of collaboration" for purposes of this book. Although the need for social skill development with students is similar, there are additional and more complex collaboration skills that must be developed and used by adults. These eight elements from the cooperation goal structure become the eight basic elements for collegiality that we discuss later in this chapter.

For a school to maximize its productivity and achieve its mission, all members of the faculty and staff must be working to the best of their abilities and skills. Productivity and the ability to achieve the morally compelling school mission are dependent upon the physical and psychological energy that all staff members are willing to commit toward accomplishing the goals. There are many other factors that contribute and impact success as well. Some of these factors include the alignment of the school's goals with that of the district; the nature, background, skill level, and desire of the members; the unique match between the administrator and staff; the leadership skills and style of the school leaders; the quality of technology and materials being used; the nature of the situation; and the culture (e.g., norms, processes, procedures, and structures) within the school setting. Johnson and Johnson (1989) argue that all of these factors, and many others that come into play in various situations, make it difficult to determine which goal structure will work best in which situation. Having said that, however, they would still assert that the evidence for cooperation, which engages a school community in a positive interdependent goal structure, is overwhelmingly "effective for a wide range of goals, tasks,

**Figure 11.2**   Social Interdependence Goal Structure

| Goal Structure & Type | Cooperative Goal Structure (Positive Interdependence) | Competitive Goal Structure (Negative Interdependence) | Individual Goal Structure (No Interdependence) |
|---|---|---|---|
| Conditions under which goal structure is more likely to be effective. | Eight essential elements: To avoid negative interactions among members of the group (e.g., freeloading; unwillingness to help or share; lack of social, interpersonal, and small group skills, which include lack of decision making, problem solving, leadership, and communication skills), cooperative situations need to be carefully operationalized using the following elements:<br><br>1. Positive interdependence.<br>2. Face-to-face promotive interactions.<br>3. Training in social, interpersonal, and small group skills [skills of collaboration**].<br>4. Group processing.<br>5. Individual responsibility and/or accountability.<br>6. Equal participation* [and equal responsibilities.**]<br>7. Simultaneous interaction.*<br>8. Quality of life.** | Nine essential elements: All competitors must:<br><br>1. Correctly perceive their negative interdependence.<br>2. Be able to audit the progress of each other.<br>3. Be working on a simple, over-learned, and nondivisible task.<br>4. Have their interactions with each other strictly controlled.<br>5. Believe that they have a chance of winning (homogeneous matching).<br>6. Believe it is relatively unimportant whether they do so or not.<br>7. Have a clear beginning and ending that allows participants to be ranked from best to worse.<br>8. Possess the competitive social skills necessary to play fair; be a good winner or loser; enjoy the competition, win or lose.<br>9. Monitor progress of competitors, and not overgeneralize the results. | Seven essential elements: Individual goal structures must include:<br><br>1. Meaningful and important goal(s) or task.<br>2. A perception that individual efforts are independent and unrelated to the efforts of others.<br>3. No interaction with others (isolation).<br>4. Clear accountability for individual.<br>5. Clearly articulated and understood procedures and required skills.<br>6. Access to all necessary materials and resources—which must be readily available to all participants.<br>7. Individual skills and ability to complete goal or task by self. |

SOURCE: Created by Vojtek & Vojtek from Johnson & Johnson, 1989.

NOTE: To be effective, competitive or individualistic efforts must occur within an overall context of cooperation.

*From Kagan & Kagan (2009).

**From Vojtek

technologies and individuals of different achievement levels, backgrounds, and personalities" (p. 170). Johnson and Johnson base their conclusion on the fact that "since 1898 there have been over 378 studies that have investigated the relative impact of cooperative, competitive, and individualistic efforts on achievement and productivity" (p. 170).

Based on the social interdependence research and our work with cooperative learning and organization development theories during the past decades, we believe that positive interdependence is a critical motivational strategy that is missing from much of the community building, team building, and professional learning community (PLC) literature that is found in education today.

We define *positive interdependence* as *the relationship that connects members of a group in such a way that everyone's contribution is vital to the success of the group, and the work that is done mutually benefits everyone.* As a principal, the way I (Rosie) have explained this concept to my staff is that, "Together, we can! We, as a staff, are all responsible for all of the students at our school. None of us is as smart as all of us together. We are all responsible for the success of our students and the success of ourselves as a school community." Each day, we all strive to "be the best we can be" (our school motto). Over the years, I have purchased different pins and banners, all of which carry a similar message—we are in this together. In addition, I take every opportunity to make sure to thank each person for making a difference and being a vital, contributing member of our team. I let them know that without their help, we would not be able to do the great job we are doing for all of our students.

Unfortunately, in most schools, the positive interdependence structure competes against the longstanding tradition of a teacher working alone with groups of students in his classroom (individualistic goal structure). More recently, with the arrival of accountability and the standards movement, teachers and schools are finding themselves in a competitive goal structure, where their data and scores are being rewarded and sanctioned, pitted one against another, often in the same school (teacher v. teacher), across district (principal v. principal), or across state (superintendent v. superintendent). As we said above, depending on the situation, there are advantages for using competitive or individualistic goal structures. But to be used effectively, they must be used under the umbrella of a positive interdependence (cooperative) goal structure. When the tasks of daily work are not structured properly, isolation and/or negative interaction patterns develop among members of the school community that lead to lower levels of achievement, productivity, psychological health, and dysfunctional relationships.

## ■ NEEDS MET BY INTERDEPENDENCE

This motivational strategy helps to meet the needs defined by Maslow's (1998) social needs, Deci's (1995) relatedness, Glasser's (1998a) love, Sagor's (2003) belonging, and Covey's (2004) love. In addition, it is grounded in research on cooperative learning (Johnson & Johnson, 1989; and Kagan & Kagan, 2009) and organization development (Schmuck & Runkel, 1994). (See Appendix A.)

## ■ WHAT INTERDEPENDENCE IS AND ISN'T

Figures 11.3 and 11.4 will help to clarify positive interdependence. Figure 11.3 explains what positive interdependence is and what it isn't. Figure 11.4 on page 228 compares the differences between an interdependence-supportive environment and an interdependence-deficient environment.

**Figure 11.3**  Positive Interdependence Defined

| What Positive Interdependence Is | What Positive Interdependence Isn't |
|---|---|
| Collegiality. | Feeling or contrived collaboration. |
| "We all win" (win-win). "When we work together, we assist each other to succeed." | "I win, you lose. You win, I lose." "When we compete, we obstruct each other's successes." "I hurt you, it helps me." |
| Feeling valued, appreciated, and respected as a contributing member of the school community. | Feeling lonely, isolated, and disconnected from others in the school community. |
| "Together we can, because we are in this together." "Sink or swim." | "I can do my job better by myself." |
| Reciprocity. | Competition or isolation. |
| Shared mission, vision, values, and goals with a commitment to work together to achieve them. | Mission, vision, values, and goals may be visible, but not always shared with a commitment to work together to achieve them. |
| Cooperation, where individuals interact in ways to promote each other's success. | Independence, where individuals have no interaction. "All for one, I did it by myself." |
| Having a shared identity while striving for mutual benefit. | Having an individual identity (independence) or having feelings of superiority or inferiority (competition). |
| Performance and outcomes are mutually caused by own and others' ability and energy (synergy of the group). | Performance is caused only by one's own ability and effort. |
| Groups identify and work together to solve their own problems of practice. Groups take ownership of the problem. | Groups work on problems defined by others. Groups have no ownership of the problem—they go through motions. |
| Perceptions of common fate. | Perceptions of negatively-linked fates or individual fate. |
| Mutual help and assistance. | Obstruction of each other's goal achievement efforts. |
| Open, honest, and reciprocal communication. | Ineffective, limited, and misleading communication. |
| Constructive management of conflict. | Destructive management of conflict. |
| Trust. | Distrust or no trust. |
| Information is shared with all key stakeholders just-in-time. | Information is hidden and kept from others. Knowledge is power. |
| Members are valued and respected. Equal participation—the workload of the group is distributed as equally as possible among all members. | Some members are respected more than others. Unequal participation—not all members of the group are included or participate fully with workload responsibilities. |
| Everyone's contribution is vital to the success of the group. | "I am right, and my ideas are important to the success of the group." |
| The work done by the group or individuals mutually benefits everyone. | The work that is done by the group or individuals benefits only those doing the work at the expense of others. |
| Group efficacy. "Working together we make a difference." | Competition and individual successes are recognized. When things go wrong, groups blame each other or external factors. |
| Shared group identity. | Isolation and disconnection from the group. |

**Figure 11.4**    Structuring an Interdependence-Supportive Environment

| Interdependence-Supportive Environment | Interdependence-Deficient Environment |
| --- | --- |
| The eight basic elements of collegiality are purposefully structured in all group activities and embedded into the culture of the school. | Few elements of collegiality are visible. Most teachers work in isolation and/or compete against each other to achieve individual goals and success. Likewise, schools within the district compete against each other to garner resources and achieve individual school goals. |
| Groups are empowered to make professional decisions that affect their work, while at the same time holding themselves and each other accountable for achieving the goals. | Groups are told what to do and how to do it. Although they may be held accountable for the results of their efforts, they do not take the responsibility for achieving the mission. |
| The eight basic elements of collegiality are used to structure group/team/committee work. | Groups are formed with little or no attention to who serves or how groups are structured. |
| Mutual trust and respect, reciprocal relationships, and risk-free supportive culture. | Lack of trust and respect. Individuals feel disconnected and afraid to fail or try new ideas. |
| Quality of life as defined earlier in this book. | Not all basic needs of individuals are being met as defined by the quality of life. |
| Multiple opportunities for all staff members to build their competence and the school's capacity to achieve shared goals. | Little opportunity for individuals to build their competence or for groups to build their capacity to achieve goals. |
| Staff members willingly commit their physical and psychological energy to support group efforts to achieve individual and shared goals and rewards. | Staff members commit their physical and psychological energy to support their own efforts to achieve individual goals and rewards. |
| The school's mission, vision, values, and goals are aligned with the district and shared by all members of the school community. Members have a vested interest in results. | There is little or no purposeful alignment of the school's mission, vision, values, and goals. Nor is there a vested interest in the results. Individuals work to achieve their own goals. |
| There is evidence in all of the school's processes, procedures, structures, and norms that it supports a cooperative (interdependent) goal structure. | The school's processes, procedures, structures, and norms do not support a cooperative goal structure. Isolation and competition exist, even during times when groups, departments, committees, and teams must work together. |
| There is evidence that the school balances, encourages, and supports individual professional learning to build competence and collaborative learning and increase capacity for both content knowledge and pedagogical skills as well as to develop skills of collaboration. | There is little or no evidence of support for quality professional learning of individuals to build competence or for groups to increase capacity and improve their skills of collaboration. Most staff development is one-size, sit-and-get, one-shot activities. |
| The school leaders make sure to spend time building relationships and creating group and/or team spirit and identity. | The school leaders make little or no effort building relationships and creating group and/or team spirit and identity. |
| All staff members feel included and an integral part of the school team. There is a shared sense of "Together, we can!" | Staff members feel no sense of belonging or inclusion. Staff members feel isolated, lonely, and disconnected from each other. |

# ■ WHY IS POSITIVE INTERDEPENDENCE IMPORTANT?

Teachers who know, understand, and have used the basic elements of cooperative learning to structure lessons (i.e., individual accountability, positive interdependence, social skills, group processing, face-to-face promotive interaction, equal participation and responsibility, simultaneous interaction) are keenly aware of how these elements enhance cooperation. The method in which the basic elements are integrated throughout the group activities determines how successful students will be in achieving the desired goals. Likewise, how school leaders structure teacher-to-teacher interactions will determine how successful the faculty will be toward achieving the school's mission as well as the quality of working relationships among all staff members.

The social interdependence that exists within the group dynamics determines how individuals interact within a given situation. This in turn affects the outcomes and success of the group's efforts. The research reported by Johnson and Johnson is very clear. When positive interdependence is structured into the group activity, the interactions among group members generally lead to higher productivity and achievement. In addition, Johnson and Johnson (1989) report more positive relationships among group members along with greater psychological health and well-being (p. 5).

There is a synergy that comes from working together, when all members of the school community understand and internalize that one of us, or a few of us, are not as smart as all of us, and that we are *all* responsible for the learning and achievement of *all* our students and *each* other. When school communities are working cooperatively in a positive interdependent goal structure, there is a contagious spirit and a positive school environment that is difficult to describe but easy to recognize. From their meta-analysis Johnson and Johnson (1989) describe the benefits of positive interdependence this way:

> Groups become cohesive by formulating and working together on issues that are specific, immediate, and realizable. As cohesiveness increases, absenteeism and turnover of membership decrease, member commitment to group goals increases, feelings of personal responsibility to the group increases, willingness to take on difficult tasks increases, motivation and persistence in working toward goal achievement increases, satisfaction and morale increases, willingness to endure pain and frustration on behalf of the group increases, willingness to defend the group against external criticism or attack increases, willingness to listen to and be influenced by colleagues increases, commitment to each other's professional growth and success increases, and productivity increases. Cohesiveness within a group, team, department, business, classroom, or school is determined by how well members like each other as people and colleagues. . . . The successful chief executives create a "family" within which members care deeply about each other and the mutual goals they are striving to achieve. (p. 10)

Although they published their meta-analysis twenty years ago, Johnson and Johnson (1989) wrote the following as a reason for structuring positive interdependence into the school setting:

> We now live in a complex, interconnected world in which cultures collide every minute and interdependencies limit the flexibility of individuals and nations. . . . Understanding the nature of [i]nterdependent systems, how to operate effectively within them, and how to manage conflicts are essential qualities of future citizens of all countries and societies. (p. 176–177)

This message is even more relevant today. For all of the reasons we have mentioned, we believe strongly that positive interdependence is one of the most useful and powerful motivational strategies that a school leader can use to lead the school community, accomplish the morally compelling school mission, build collegial learning communities, and achieve levels of optimal performance.

## ■ BUILDING COLLEGIAL LEARNING COMMUNITIES

It is easy to assign teachers to collaborative groups; it is difficult to structure them so that people work together cooperatively, rather than in contrived situations where the collaboration is forced. Pam Robbins and Harvey Alvy (2004) write that there are many cultural factors that attribute to how well a school faculty will be able to collaborate as a professional learning community. Among these, they mention "Leadership, the history of professional development experiences of the staff, and existing norms, values, and beliefs" (p. 78–79). These factors, they suggest, will determine how quickly a school community will be able to move through the three stages from congeniality, to cooperation, to collaboration.

In an interview by Tracy Crow (2008), Judith Warren Little states that there must be "leadership that supports collective attention to problems of practice, to [help] people develop sophisticated instructional knowledge and skills" (p. 54). She warns, however, that:

> [W]hen district or school leaders take the initiative in the current policy climate to promote and establish collaborative groups, such efforts may be experienced by what Hargreaves described as "contrived collegiality"—that is, people are brought together to do work that is defined by others. They're brought together to do particular tasks of data analysis, looking at evidence, mapping out standards, aligning curriculum and assessment. All of that may be really valuable work. The question is who owns it. (Little, as cited in Crow, 2008, p. 54)

We agree with Little and the factors that Robbins and Alvy (2004) list as helping school communities to work more collaboratively. But unless the social interaction patterns that build relationships and structures of

positive interdependence are strongly in place, along with a solid foundation that provides the quality of life in which all members have their basic
needs met and the resources they need to do the work, school leaders will
continue to see a forced collaboration rather than authentic collegiality.

To Robbins and Alvy's stages of progression from congeniality,
to cooperation, to collaboration, we would interject *forced collaboration*
(or what Hargreaves [1993] calls *contrived collegiality*) prior to the stage
of collaboration and end with a stage of authentic collegiality or what
we refer to as a collegial learning community. Groups begin by moving
from congeniality (which to us means being pleasant and cordial to
those you work with) and pass through the stages of cooperation, on to
forced collaboration (they have to work together to do work defined by
others), to collaboration (people may work together to get the job done,
but do not necessarily care about each other). The stage of an authentic
collegiality or collegial learning community exists when there is a solid
quality of life foundation and members of the group have developed a
mutual trust and respect for each other (reciprocal relationships); a
vested interest in the outcome (shared mission); a voice in the decision
making (communication, autonomy, and empowerment); competence
and capacity for accomplishing the work; and a shared sense of responsibility for themselves and each other (accountability) for working
together (positive interdependence) to achieve the desired results.
Figure 11.5 illustrates the progression from congeniality to collegial
learning community.

**Figure 11.5**   Congeniality to Collegial Learning Community Continuum

*The American Heritage Dictionary* defines collegiality as "shared power
and authority vested among colleagues" (p. 362). Colleagues are "a fel-
low member of a profession, staff, or academic faculty" (p. 362). To this,
we would add working together to achieve a shared goal, purpose, or
mission. Therefore, we define *collegiality* as *a group of professional educators
who have a vested interest and take responsibility for achieving their shared
goals, purpose, and/or school mission.*

Taking this one step further, we define a *collegial learning community* as
*one in which a group of professional educators within a department, school, or
district, hold themselves and each other accountable for working together to
achieve their shared goals, purpose, or school's mission through positive interdependence, reciprocal relationships, shared decision making, professional learning,
and mutual responsibility.*

In her book *Community, Collaboration, and Collegiality in School Reform*,
Nina Dorsch (1998) suggests three important elements for collegiality to
exist: interdependence; reciprocal relationships that are stable and evolving;

and democratic communication that is dynamic, deliberate, and on-going (p. 1–3). Dorsch writes:

> These principles of interdependence, reciprocity, and democratic communication find a unifying voice in a discussion of community by Robert Bellah et al. (1985): "A community is a group of people who are socially interdependent, who participate together in discussion and decision making, and who share certain practices that both define the community and are nurtured by it" (p. 333). It is this sense of community, collaboration, and collegiality that I believe is at the heart of the relationship deemed essential to many reform efforts. A collegial community is characterized by reciprocal relationships between the community and its individual members—each must promote the growth of the other. (p. 2)

When implemented effectively, collegial learning communities are able to build and sustain the competence and capacity (skills) along with responsibility, accountability, and motivation (will) to perform at optimal levels to successfully achieve the compelling school mission. Collegial learning communities, however, don't just happen. They require careful and thoughtful planning, structuring, nurturing, and reflection. As Little (1990) states, "Tenacious habits of mind and deed make achievement of strong collegial relations a remarkable achievement; not the rule, but the rare, often fragile, exception" (p. 167). But it can be done!

To successfully create collegial learning communities, school leaders must understand the ten motivational strategies presented in this book and purposefully embed the essential conditions for each to exist within the culture of their school. As we have stated before, the quality of life within the school organization is itself a motivational strategy, while at the same time remains one of the essential conditions and foundation for the other nine motivational strategies found in the book. As Figure 11.6 illustrates, quality of life is at the heart of what makes a house a home and what makes a school a collegial learning community.

**Figure 11.6** House Is To Home

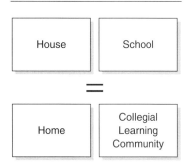

Without a strong foundation that provides for quality of life, school leaders will not be able to create the conditions that build collegial learning communities that perform at optimal levels and achieve the school's shared mission. Likewise, without structuring positive interdependence, building reciprocal relationships, providing professional learning opportunities that build competence and school capacity, and communicating a shared mission and purpose (including vision and goals) that all educators hold themselves and each other accountable for achieving, school leaders will be left with teachers who feel lonely, isolated, and disconnected from each other. "Just as collaborative opportunities do not assure collegiality, acknowledging interdependence does not guarantee opportunities to work together for mutual benefit" (Dorsch, 1998, p. 3).

In order to create collegial learning communities, school leaders must create the conditions for positive interdependence. This doesn't happen overnight. To begin with, school leaders must make sure that the basic needs of all members of the staff are being met. This includes an environment conducive to learning, as defined by the quality of life. Likewise, there must be structures that support effective communication, accountability, empowerment, autonomy, competence and capacity, and results, along with a strong, morally compelling mission with a shared commitment for achieving the school's vision and goals. Most important, before you can build positive interdependence, you must develop reciprocal relationships that help people care about each other as well as feel included and like an integral member of the group, team, committee, or school community.

## ■ WORKING THROUGH THE STAGES OF GROUP DYNAMICS

To help build reciprocal relationships and the skills of collaboration, all groups must learn to work effectively within the stages of group development. It is important that school leaders understand how to facilitate each stage, so groups can successfully navigate through the processes necessary to move into the performing stage, or where we find collegial learning communities working to achieve optimal performance.

There are three phases that all groups pass through during the life cycle of the group: (1) inclusion, (2) influence, and (3) community (Gibbs, 2001, p. 21). Although we have listed them as three phases, groups move in and out of each phase, and there is really no order or hierarchy.

### Inclusion

The phase of "inclusion" consists of the formation of the group, *forming stage,* and the establishment of group agreements, *norming stage.* For example, each time new members join the group, the group finds itself back in the initial forming and perhaps even norming stages. The duration of the initial inclusion stage is significantly affected by the number of people joining the group.

### Forming Stage

To help everyone feel included, members must take time to get to know each other, respect each other, and build trust. During the forming stages of the group, very little work is accomplished. Instead, it is important that leaders engage members of the group in a variety of team-building activities, from simple "share something about yourself" activities to complex (ropes course type) team-building activities. The formation of a group (forming stage) occurs when the group is first organized, when new members join the group, and at the beginning of each meeting. It is important that group members take time to "check-in" with each other at the beginning of the meeting to build rapport, trust, and respect, and strengthen relationships among members of the group. Maintenance activities (those activities that satisfy the human needs of the group) must be balanced with task activities (the work done by the group). For members to feel included, they must have opportunities to: (1) introduce themselves and get to know each other (e.g., talents, interests, feelings, special qualities); (2) express their interest, and share their hopes and expectations for the group work; (3) feel acknowledged by the group by feeling welcomed, heard, and appreciated; and (4) self-evaluate how well they are effectively working together as a group. Logan, King, and Fischer-Wright (2008) call the maintenance process "an oil change" (p. 178). Three questions help the group talk through the oil change: What is working well? What is not working well? What can the team do to make the things that are not working well, work? Gibbs (2001) complements this notion by explaining, "Balancing persons and tasks" is what "makes a big difference in how people finally are able to work together" (p. 79–80).

### Norming Stage

Once the group is formed, whether purposeful or not, the members of the group enter the norming stage. Norms are the ways in which the group operates as well as how members work with each other. Norms are based on the values, structures, processes, and procedures of the group. It is, in other words, the way in which the group members function to complete the tasks. Norms will be formed by every group, even if the group doesn't take the time to define and agree upon how it plans to work together. Norms of any group are present, even if they are not explicit. In fact, once norms are brought to the level of consciousness, made explicit, and agreed upon by members, they become part of the list of group agreements. For a group or team to become productive and eventually be able to work cooperatively and interdependently, it is important for each group to create their own set of group agreements. This list must include all of those elements that the group agrees to hold sacred. It can include, but is not limited to, such ideas as: the meeting will start and end on time; there will be no side conversations during the meeting; there will be no parking lot conversations after the meeting; what gets said during the meeting remains confidential; consensus will be used to reach all decisions; all members of the group will treat each other with respect; and all members of the group will equally share the responsibilities of completing the tasks. Group agreements should be reviewed by the group on a regular basis as well as agreed upon by new members as they join the group. All members of the group are responsible for upholding the group agreements. In this way, the group agreements eventually become the norms that determine how the group operates in any situation.

## Influence

During the second level, "influence," members of the group must work through the *storming stage* in which they engage in conflict, vie for leadership roles, and engage in conversations that get at the heart of beliefs, values, assumptions, and diversity, in order to achieve the *conforming stage* in which they come together as a group through shared behaviors, standards, core values, and expectations.

### Storming Stage

During the storming stage, members of the group explore how they fit into the group (e.g., what is their role; what and how will they contribute to the group; how will they influence the decisions of the group; how do their unique qualities, individual values, and assumptions fit with other group members; how will leadership be shared so all individuals are able to contribute resources and unique talents to achieve to their fullest potential).

All groups at one time or another find themselves engulfed in conflict. Most often, conflict arises as individuals attempt to influence others by putting forth ideas and suggestions about what the group should do (e.g., goals, tasks) or how the group should accomplish their work. Often conflicts surface as groups confront diverse feelings, beliefs, values, and assumptions while making decisions and solving problems.

There are many tools and strategies that school leaders can use to facilitate the group processes as they move through the storming stage. It is important that a school leader has a variety of these strategies and tools in her repertoire and uses them appropriately to help groups resolve the inevitable conflicts that will occur. These include facilitating communication processes through dialoguing, asking questions, clarifying issues, summarizing, checking perceptions, and providing constructive feedback; distributing leadership by assigning roles and responsibilities; using the basic elements of collegiality to build individual accountability, skills of collaboration, and positive interdependence; and using organization development tools to manage conflict, facilitate decision making, and solve problems of practice.

School leaders will also want to provide opportunities for group members to learn and practice the skills needed for successful collaboration. Such skills include interpersonal and communication skills, especially those skills related to dialoguing. Other skills include building trust, reaching consensus, expressing and accepting diverse opinions, feelings, and positions, and other participatory methods for decision making and problem solving. By providing opportunities for group members to learn, practice, and debrief their use of collaboration skills, groups will become more efficient and productive as they grow into the conforming and performing stages. Although the storming stage is difficult for leaders and members to endure, it is vital that groups struggle with, adapt to, and conform cohesively as a group.

### Conforming Stage

This is the stage in which team members achieve harmony, trust, and cohesiveness. Group members accept the group agreements and norms and become comfortable in their roles and responsibilities. Information flows freely among members as they contribute their unique talents and resources to help the group achieve its goals. As the group becomes more cohesive, the team is able to define its work by communicating effectively and reaching decisions through a consensus decision-making process. Ultimately individuals must feel the group cares, values, and appreciates their role in achieving the group's success. The more a person feels included as an important contributing member, the more he will be motivated, engaged, and committed to completing tasks and working to achieve the group's goals and shared mission.

## Community

In order for any group to achieve the third level, "community," all group members must have helped each individual group member feel as if he or she is a vital, contributing member of the group and have worked through all of the conflicts that arise as members seek to influence the group's decision-making processes. Once groups begin to work together to achieve their goals, they take on the characteristics of a community. At this level, groups reach the *performing stage* in which they are able to complete their tasks and achieve their goals.

### Performing Stage

Gibbs (2001) summarizes the five indicators of a successful, performing community as follows:

*Capacity:* Communities are built upon recognizing the whole depth, the strengths, weaknesses, and the unique capacities of each member.

*Collective Efforts:* Communities share responsibility to achieve goals for the common good and engage the diversity of individual talents and skills to do so.

*Informality:* Transactions of value are based on consideration; care and affection take place spontaneously.

*Stories:* Reflection upon individual and community experiences provides knowledge about truth, relationships, and future direction.

*Celebration:* Activities incorporate celebrations, parties, and social events. The line between work and play is blurred as people enjoy both at once. (p. 83)

As groups begin to work effectively together, they take on the five characteristics of a community. We would like to stress the importance of frequent celebrations, recognitions, and opportunities for groups to appreciate the work, efforts, and talents of individual members as well as those of the collective group. In addition, it is imperative that groups find time to change their oil (Logan, King, & Fischer-Wright, 2008) by debriefing their work and reflect upon what is working, as well as how they can refine what they are doing and/or how they can work together to become even more productive.

## Moving Through Group Development Stages

Often it is a struggle to help groups move from the inclusion phase to the community phase. As much as school leaders would like to avoid the storming and conforming stages of the influence phase, all groups must work through their own set of issues and conflicts to be able to successfully accomplish their goals. Far too often, we have seen groups, with the best of intentions, fail. Sometimes it is because the members are afraid to "step on anyone's toes" and do not want to "make waves." Sometimes it is because people really don't care and are forced to be a part of the group. For any number of reasons, these groups remain "congenial" to each other, never addressing the deeper issues that will get them through the storms to the other side. They undoubtedly have a good time but rarely accomplish anything meaningful or worthwhile. If the group stays together, it is for social reasons or because of forced collaboration. Over time, there becomes an unwritten, unconscious agreement (norm) not to bring up those issues that might wage conflict.

Likewise, groups who enter the storming stages without the skills of collaboration necessary to manage the conflicts, distribute the leadership, and reach consensus on issues that matter will quit long before they are able to work together productively and effectively. Many school leaders who find themselves engaged in change efforts—especially second order, deep change efforts—without the necessary facilitation skills to weather the storms of conflict and help their teams move out of the phase of influence into the phase of community give up and return to the status quo.

Finally, just because groups become productive during the performing stage does not mean that they won't revert to any of the previous stages. There are many reasons for this, including accepting new members, members leaving the group, new information, change in direction, communication breakdown, lack of trust, or unequal participation. School leaders must understand the stages of group development in order to recognize the needs of the group when they struggle to move through the stages to be able to perform. Leaders must be prepared to facilitate the group process using tools and strategies that address the specific needs appropriately and just-in-time.

## ■ STRUCTURING POSITIVE INTERDEPENDENCE

Earlier in this chapter, we defined *positive interdependence* as *the relationship that connects members of a group in such a way that everyone's contribution is vital to the success of the group, and the work that is done mutually benefits everyone.* Not only is positive interdependence an effective motivational strategy, but it is essential for building and sustaining a collegial learning community. School leaders can structure positive interdependence using either *positive outcome interdependence* or *positive means interdependence* (Johnson & Johnson, 1989, p. 25).

### Outcome Interdependence

When outcome interdependence is structured, group members realize they share a common fate, have a shared identity, strive for mutual benefit, and perceive that shared long-term productivity is more important than short-term individual advantages. There is a recognition that what helps other group members benefits oneself and what promotes one's own productivity benefits the other group members (Johnson & Johnson, 1989). Outcome interdependence can be structured in various ways, as follows.

### *Positive Reward Interdependence*

All members of the group receive the same reward for successfully completing a joint task or achieving the shared goal. The group is rewarded, based upon the performance of all group members. Example:

All members of the school community strive for and achieve blue ribbon success. The school community implements an afterschool program that receives an outstanding program award from the governor.

### Positive Goal Interdependence

All individuals within the group are working toward accomplishing a mutual set of goals. Individuals perceive that they can attain their goals only if other members of the group or school community attain their goals. Example: Working toward achieving accountability or school improvement goals.

### Positive Identity Interdependence

The school community or group establishes a mutual identity through its name, mission statement, brand, etc. All group members share the identity and purpose of the group. Example: A school community uses its name, colors, motto, or brand to create school spirit and pride. A middle school house may create their own identity within a school by giving itself a name, colors, flag, motto, etc. so that it is easily recognizable.

### Outside Force Interdependence

Groups are placed in competition with each other under the umbrella of cooperation. Example: The superintendent may tell a school that it needs to make sure all students perform better than the students in other schools within the district in reading. Or the robotics team in one high school may decide that they want to win the state robotics competition.

### Environmental Interdependence

Groups are bound together by the physical environment in some way. Example: Members of the school community share the same environmental space and therefore make up the school community. In larger schools, there is often a school within a school, thus even though the two schools share the same name, they may define themselves as a subgroup or an entire school community based on the physical boundaries of the school and/or the purpose of the task.

## Positive Means Interdependence

Positive means interdependence exists when group members perceive that the only way they can complete the task is when two or more individuals are needed to complete the task and/or coordinate their efforts. There are four ways to structure positive means interdependence, as follows.

### Positive Resource Interdependence

Each member of the group has only a portion of the information, resources, or materials. In order to successfully achieve the goal or complete the task, group members must share the information. Example: A grade-level data team in which each individual has information about how their own students scored on a mathematics assessment. Or a jigsaw is used to facilitate conversation during a professional learning activity.

### Positive Role Interdependence

Each member is assigned a leadership role for the duration of the project, task, or meeting. These roles are such that each member of the group has specific responsibilities that are interconnected and necessary for the group to complete the shared task. Example: During each meeting every person on the data team assumes the responsibility for taking on a specific role, such as facilitator, recorder, time keeper, data-entry person, or process observer. Roles may be rotated after each meeting.

### Positive Task Interdependence

A division of labor is created so the actions of one member of the group must be completed or combined with the work of other members. Each member of the group must contribute a part of the task if the group is to successfully complete the joint project or shared goal. Like an assembly line, the overall task is subdivided and each individual's part must be added to complete the project in a specific order. Or, when task specialization occurs, each group member is responsible for a unique part of the group's work, and order doesn't matter. Example: Each classroom teacher is responsible for entering the number of minutes his or her students read outside of school to measure the number of total minutes everyone in the school reads each month. Or the school-improvement team decides to divide up the accountability plan goals and each month create or update their graph for the school's data wall.

### Fantasy (Simulation) Interdependence

This is usually used in role playing or simulations used during professional learning and organization development activities. This task requires imagination (pretending to be in a given situation). Example: During a study group session, teachers use a case study to role-play and explore classroom management strategies that will lead to improved classroom climate and higher levels of student achievement.

In order to create the conditions that lead to working together as a collegial learning community, members of the group must perceive that they are connected with others through positive interdependence. Positive interdependence is the most important factor in structuring situations cooperatively (Johnson & Johnson, 1989, p. 29). When positive interdependence is structured effectively into group work, individuals recognize that in order for them to be successful everyone's contribution is necessary and important. As Blanchard, Bowles, Carew, and Parisi-Carew (2001) state, "None of Us is as Smart as All of Us" (cover). Personal responsibility and individual accountability are actualized as members of the team and/or collegial learning community realize that the successful accomplishment of the task or goal means the efforts of everyone are shared and required. "When feedback mechanisms for determining the level of each person's efforts are added, social loafing, the diffusion of responsibility, and the refusal to provide help and assistance are usually avoided" (Johnson & Johnson, 1989, p. 29).

## ■ EIGHT BASIC
## ELEMENTS OF COLLEGIALITY

To effectively structure group work for adults, school leaders must use the same eight basic elements of cooperation that are found in the cooperative goal structure (see Figure 11.2). Thus, the eight basic elements of the cooperative goal structure become the eight basic elements of collegiality. From our research and work, we contend that the more school leaders are able to structure the following eight basic elements into adult group work, the more likely the groups will be to successfully achieve their goals, and the more likely the teams will be to take on characteristics of a collegial learning community. Therefore, we list the *eight basic elements of collegiality* as follows.

### Positive Interdependence

As we stated previously, there are ten different ways school leaders can structure positive interdependence. The more administrators are able to embed positive interdependence throughout the school day and especially among the work the adults are doing to help students achieve the schools' mission, the more likely everyone will be to work together to achieve the morally compelling mission.

### Individual Accountability

Not only is it important for all staff members of the school to share in the responsibilities of accomplishing the shared mission (interdependence), it is also vital that all members are held individually accountable and responsible for doing their part. School leaders can build the individual accountability by distributing leadership roles and responsibilities, assigning task responsibilities to individuals or smaller groups, and utilizing a regular goal setting and evaluation process. They can also empower educators by delegating the responsibility and granting the authority for them to do their work; and giving them the autonomy they need to do their work by providing them with the freedom and latitude. Educators must then hold themselves and each other accountable for achieving the school's mission.

### Skills of Collaboration

It is important that all adults within the school setting have the opportunities to learn, practice, and reflect upon a variety of social skills, processes, and tools. As noted above, these include skills that improve communication (especially dialogue), interpersonal skills, conflict management, leadership, decision making and problem solving. Advocating for social skills (or what we call the skills of collaboration), Johnson and Johnson (1989) write:

> Working together to get the job done increases participants' social skills. To coordinate efforts to achieve mutual goals participants must: (1) get to know and trust each other; (2) communicate accurately and unambiguously; (3) accept and support each other; and (4) resolve conflicts constructively. Interpersonal and small group

skills form the basic nexus among individuals, and if individuals are to work together productively and cope with the stresses and strains of doing so, they must have a modicum of these skills. (p. 11)

## Group Processing

At the beginning of every meeting or work session, group members need to take the time to "check-in" with each other. This maintenance activity is important because it helps everyone to feel included, acknowledged, and like a contributing member of the group. In addition, it helps the group to continue to build caring relationships with each other. At the end of the meeting, it is equally important that groups take time to debrief and reflect upon their work—in other words, do an oil change (Logan, King, Fischer-Wright, 2008). They can do this in relation to how productive they were on the tasks (did they accomplish what they hoped to accomplish), how well they functioned and worked together as a group (maintenance issues), and how well they used collaboration skills. For example, they can focus on a skill, tool, or strategy they just learned or on skills they used during the meeting that worked well or needed to be refined.

Unless groups take time to debrief and reflect upon what is working or not working, the groups will never gain proficiency nor will members be able to work more efficiently and effectively together. In fact, when teaching cooperative learning courses and workshops, I (Rosie) always tell participants that if their groups don't take time to debrief after cooperative learning activities, they will have the same group issues and levels of productivity in June that they have in September. This is true for teacher collaboration activities well.

## Face-to-Face Promotive Interaction

Promotive interaction is defined by Johnson and Johnson (1989) as

individuals encouraging and facilitating each other's efforts to achieve, complete tasks, and produce in order to reach the group's goals. It is characterized by mutual help and assistance, mutual influence, the exchange of needed resources, interpersonal feedback, intellectual challenge and disagreement, the advocacy of committed efforts to achieve, and lower anxiety about performance. It is through promotive interaction that collaborators get to know each other as persons. (p. 29)

Group members must have the time to work together on a regular basis, during the school day, in face-to-face close proximity. We agree with and commend The National Staff Development Council (2008) for taking a strong stance on this position by calling for every educator to engage in effective professional learning every day so every student achieves. Without the time and resources necessary to collaborate on a regular basis (e.g., peer coaching, mentoring, data teams, study groups, grade-level teams, school-improvement teams, department teams), it will be very difficult to help teachers build the interdependence (as well as the competence and capacity) needed to collectively share the responsibility of achieving the school's mission. Likewise, as educators move outside the school walls to join district, state, and even online networking groups, they must also find consistent and regular times to connect with others (be there and be present) if they are going to be able to build positive interdependence and create collegial learning communities.

### Equal Participation and Responsibility

All members of the group share in the responsibilities of the group work equally—or as equally as possible. All members of the group feel responsible for doing their part and hold themselves and others accountable for doing the same. Hitchhiking and Freeloading are not allowed!

### Simultaneous Interaction

All members of a group are working at the same time to achieve the group's goals. Or different subgroups within a school community (e.g., grade-level teams, departments, committees) are working simultaneously to achieve the school's mission.

### Quality of Life

As defined in Chapter 3, the quality of life represents all of the essential conditions that must be in place for a school, district, and/or system to support the effective work and efficient learning opportunities for all individuals within the school community. These conditions include meeting the basic needs of all individuals, support for the individuals, a supportive school environment (including positive school climate), adequate and appropriate resources, supportive structures, supportive culture, respect for educators as professionals, and mutual adaptation and support.

School leaders should use all eight basic elements of collegiality to structure the group processes when working with base groups (e.g., grade-level teams, departments, school-improvement teams); work groups (e.g., committee, task-force teams, focus groups, study groups); or flexible groups during staff meetings or ad hoc committees. As we have said, the more these eight elements are used to structure the group work, the more likely the groups will be to successfully achieve their goals, and the more likely the group will be working together as a collegial learning community. In Appendix B, we have listed some of our favorite resources to help school leaders effectively structure and facilitate group work.

## ■ STRUCTURING POSITIVE INTERDEPENDENCE WITH AUTONOMY

In their book, *Good Work,* Gardner, Csikszentmihalyi, and Damon (2001) write:

> Optimal development of a person involves fulfilling two potentials that we all have: differentiation and integration. A differentiated person is competent, has character, and has achieved a fully

autonomous individuality. This is the highest goal of the Western cultures. An integrated person is someone whose goals, values, thoughts, and actions are in harmony; someone who belongs to a network of relationships; someone who accepts a place within a system of mutual responsibilities and shared meanings. In many Eastern cultures, it is integration that is held to be the highest goal of human development. A future worth striving for, in our opinion, is one where a person can develop both differentiation and integration to their fullest extent. (p. 243)

In the same book, Gardner, Csikszentmihalyi, and Damon also write, "It is difficult to look in the mirror and like what we see unless we can combine—in our lives, in our work—the full development of individual potentials with commitment to a greater whole" (p. 244).

There is no higher aspiration for structuring positive interdependence into a school setting than to provide opportunities for individuals to develop both their differentiation and integration potentials to their fullest.

Art Costa and Robert Garmston (1994) write about the importance of developing autonomous individuals who "exercise membership in holonomous systems" (p. 129) (the term holonomy which comes from the Greek: *holos* which means "whole" and *on* which means "part"). They write:

Autonomous individuals set personal goals and are self-directing, self-monitoring, and self-modifying. Because they are constantly experimenting and experiencing, they fail, frequently, but they fail forward, learning from the situation. But autonomous persons are not isolated or mechanical in their work; rather, they also participate significantly in their organization. They operate in the best interests of the whole while simultaneously attending to their own goals and needs. In other words, they are at once independent and interdependent—they are holonomous. (p. 129)

A collegial learning community is made up of holonomous educators—each able to work autonomously (see Chapter 9) as well as interdependently, and each able to develop both differentiation and integration to their fullest extent. Costa and Garmston argue that "the most effective teachers are autonomous individuals—self-asserting, self-perpetuating, and self-modifying. However, teachers are also a part of a larger whole—the school—and are influenced by its attitudes, values, and behavior" (p. 4). They continue to argue that there are two reasons for developing holonomy: (1) "to support people in becoming autonomous and self-actualizing"; and (2) "for members of the school community to function interdependently, recognizing their capacity to both self-regulate and be regulated by the norms, values, and concerns of the larger system" (p. 4).

"Interdependence," write Costa and Garmston, "is an essential state of mind for effective schools" (p. 140). It's as simple as people working together to achieve shared goals. A metaphor that Costa and Garmston use to describe positive interdependence is that of a two-way street with one person giving help, another receiving help; one influencing others and one being influenced (p. 141).

# ■ A RUBIK'S CUBE METAPHOR

Our favorite way of visualizing positive interdependence is with a Rubik's cube, the mathematical puzzle invented by Erno Rubik in 1974 (http://www.rubiks.com). The Rubik's cube is based on group theory, dealing with symmetry and mathematical relationships in their most abstract form. The cube itself is subdivided into twenty-seven individual subcubes, twenty-six which are visible to the eye. The center subcube is completely surrounded by the other subcubes, and forms the mechanical base. Each individual subcube is part of the whole Rubik's cube and can be visualized by a $3 \times 3 \times 3$ matrix. To solve the puzzle, players can make "face turns" or "quarter turns" by flipping subcubes, using one or more at a time. Depending on how the Rubik's cube is sliced, players can work with individual subcubes, corners, horizontal, or vertical groupings, until the puzzle is solved by getting all of the subcubes on each of the Rubik's cube back to their original (same) color.

A collegial learning community is like a Rubik's cube. The principal, as the school leader and skillful facilitator, becomes the center mechanical piece, around which all other staff members work together to form the whole. Each staff member, like each subcube, is autonomous and unique to the group, yet remains positively interdependent and connected to the group as a whole. Each subcube has its own properties, interactions, and mathematical relationships to the other subcubes. Various structures and combinations are necessary to solve the problem. Likewise, each staff member's unique characteristics and abilities play an integral role in helping to accomplish the school's mission.

A skillful school leader unleashes the unique talents and abilities of individual staff members and empowers and supports them to work autonomously and interdependently to achieve the school's morally compelling mission. To this endeavor, the school leader can facilitate group processes by aligning various staff members in either vertical (heterogeneous) team structures (e.g., across subjects or departments, vertical grade-level groupings) or in horizontal (homogeneous) teams (e.g., same subject area, departments, grade level). Just like flipping the subcubes can create different patterns, interactions, and relationships, so, too, are the results when leaders create different structures and teams within and among staff members.

To solve the puzzle successfully, Rubik's puzzle solvers need to understand and use both the autonomous and interdependent characteristics and relationships of the various subcubes. School leaders, if they are to be successful at motivating and facilitating staff members to accomplish the school's mission, must also understand and structure situations in which staff members develop their individual competence and build the organizational capacity during professional learning activities. Likewise, they must empower teachers to use both their individual talents and abilities, as well as the synergy and collective capacity from the group as a whole— that is, if they are to share the "wisdom of the crowd" (Surowiecki, 2004). Each individual staff member becomes vital to the success of the entire school community. Everyone's focus needs to be united by striving to achieve the same school goals, just as a Rubik's cube can't be solved if one square isn't aligned.

In his book, *The Wisdom of Crowds*, *New Yorker* columnist, James Surowiecki (2004) uses the case of the U.S. Scorpion, a submarine that disappeared on its way back to Newport News after a tour of duty. He writes:

> What is astonishing about this story, is that the evidence that the group was relying on in this case amounted to almost nothing. It was really just tiny scraps of data. No one knew why the submarine sank, no one had any idea how fast it was traveling or how steeply it fell to the ocean floor. And yet even though no one in the group knew any of these things, the group as a whole knew them all. (p. xxi)

Using many different examples, Surowiecki builds the case for the power and wisdom that can be found in groups, as long as there is still autonomy (independent thinking) when intelligent, complex decisions are being made (the opposite being that of group-think). He believes that "collective decisions are only wise when they incorporate lots of different information" (p. 65) and lists two reasons why, even when group members are interdependently connected with each other, it is still important for them to remain autonomous in their thinking, especially when making important decisions. Surowiecki writes:

> First, it keeps the mistakes that people make from becoming correlated. Errors in individual judgment won't wreck the group's collective judgment as long as those errors aren't systematically pointing in the same direction. One of the quickest ways to make people's judgments systematically biased is to make them dependent on each other for information. Second, independent individuals are more likely to have new information rather than the same old data everyone is already familiar with. The smartest groups, then, are made up of people with diverse perspectives who are able to stay independent of each other. Independence doesn't imply rationality or impartiality, though. You can be biased and irrational, but as long as you're independent, you won't make the group any dumber. (p. 41)

To use positive interdependence as a motivational strategy, it is important for school leaders to structure and embed the eight basic elements of collegiality into and throughout all daily staff activities. It is especially important that leaders develop, practice, and evaluate their use of skills of collaboration (e.g., interpersonal, communication, decision making, problem solving, team building, conflict management, and group processes). To build positive interdependence, leaders must build relationships, collective understandings, and a shared sense of urgency, commitment, and obligation so that everyone agrees, contributes, and shares the responsibility and accountability for accomplishing the school's morally compelling mission. There must, however, be a balance between structuring positive interdependence to achieve the collective school goals while maintaining the autonomy of individual members. It is vital that school communities consider *all* viewpoints when key decisions are being made by the group, such as: What data should we use to set goals? What are our priorities? What do we need to learn to achieve our SMART goals? How will we gain the necessary knowledge and/or skills? What strategies should we use to help all of our students successfully achieve our goals?

Although many administrators rely on site councils and school data teams to make these important decisions, we contend that the most effective school accountability plans and action plans are those that have input from all members of the school community through the use of a consensus decision-making process for determining what the actual goals, strategies, and indicators of success will be. This process creates that vested interest, ownership, buy-in, agreement, and support from all stakeholders. It also helps to build positive interdependence and a collegial learning community.

When school leaders understand positive interdependence, and how to structure cooperative small and whole group work, all staff members can participate. Whether leaders work with ten teachers or one hundred, using the eight basic elements of collegiality, they can structure groups effectively and efficiently so that everyone's voice is heard, and everyone is a vital part of the planning, implementation, and evaluation of the group's effectiveness toward achieving the desired goals.

Even when decisions are made by a representative group of people (e.g., site council, school-improvement team, curriculum committee), the perception from those left out of the group process is still that of top-down decisions being imposed upon them. Unless everyone's voice is heard, and all stakeholders are a part of the decision-making process, no matter the innovation, those left out will feel as if, "This is just one more thing we are being told to do." Many administrators—with the best of intentions—use committees, councils, or school-improvement teams to make collaborative decisions for the school. But unless positive interdependence is structured into the group process, relationships are developed, decision making is shared, and time is devoted to creating a collegial learning community that encompasses the entire school staff, the only difference perceived by staff will be that the top-down agenda is being imposed by group dictatorship rather than a single autocratic administrator. It becomes a process of "them" and "us" (win-lose, lose-win) instead of "all of us—we are in this together" (win-win).

## QUESTIONS FOR DISCUSSION

1. In the case study at the beginning of this chapter, it is obvious that the Blue House teachers are being forced to collaborate. In addition, Holcomb Middle School has isolated itself by creating four separate houses, using a school-within-a-school model. Before you read the rest of the chapter, decide what essential conditions for interdependence are missing, and what assistant principal, Michael Tomassetti, has the ability to do or change.

2. If you were Michael, how would you create a collegial learning community at Holcomb Middle School? How can he work with the principal, Dr. Bill Evans, to ensure all students, especially those in the at-risk cells, will be proficient and make AYP gains?

## ESSENTIAL CONDITIONS

There are several essential conditions that are not being met in the case study at the beginning of the chapter. Read along and see if you agree.

1. **Quality of life.** As we have said throughout this chapter, quality of life provides the foundation for building and sustaining a collegial learning community. Until the basic needs of all staff members are met, the administrators will not be able to build reciprocal relationships or structure positive interdependence and skills of cooperation. It is evident from the case study that the teachers do not feel supported by the administration. They do not feel appreciated, recognized, or rewarded for the work they are doing. Although it is unclear whether teachers have the resources they need, it is clear that the students come to class without the necessary materials to learn. Teachers have all but given up and have externalized their locus of control, blaming everything but themselves for why their students can't learn. They have no sense of efficacy when it comes to working with their students. The teachers do not perceive that this is a supportive environment. If it were, they would, for example, be involved in professional learning to help better manage their classrooms, differentiate the learning for individual students, and/or use the time they have to collaborate and work together as a team. In addition, there are no supportive structures in place to provide assistance to the struggling special education and ELL students within the regular classroom. It is obvious that even though the Blue House teachers have been divided into a team, there is still a norm of isolation rather than a culture of collaboration, sharing, mutual respect, and trust. Teachers do not share the responsibility for helping students learn. They are territorial and think of students as "mine" and "yours." It is clear that Michael and his principal, Dr. Evans, do not respect the teachers of the Blue House. It is also evident that Dr. Evans and Michael are not working together as an administrative team. After all, rather than talking with the teachers in each house together, Michael got stuck talking to the two houses that his principal didn't want to deal with.

2. **Mission.** Even if there were a clearly defined mission, vision, and goals, it is not shared by the Blue House teachers. The Blue House teachers do not have a clear understanding about the important work they do, nor do they have a vested interest in helping the school to achieve its mission and goals.

3. **Autonomy.** Even though the Blue House is a part of the school, it remains disconnected from the other three houses. Likewise, the teachers within the Blue House are disconnected from each other and segregated from the rest of the school. Although, on the surface, it may appear they are autonomous, we disagree. What they have is a separate existence from each other that does not fit our criteria for autonomy. We contend that autonomy does not mean that teachers (or schools-within-a-school) are simply allowed to shut their doors and do what they want. For teachers (or a school-within-a-school) to be autonomous, all faculty members "set personal goals and are self-directing, self-monitoring, and self-modifying" (Costa & Garmston, 1994, p. 129). At the same time, all faculty members must be committed to the mission. There must be a culture that is conducive to collaboration and

shared responsibility. Because the teachers in the Blue House think of what they do as a "job" rather than the important "work" they do (mission), it is clear that they do not perceive themselves as belonging to a "network of relationships" or as being "integrated" with "goals, values, thoughts, and actions" that are "in harmony." In addition, they do not "accept a place within a system of mutual responsibilities and shared meaning" (Gardner, Csikszentmihalyi, & Damon, 2001, p. 243). Costa and Garmston describe this state as "holonomy" (p. 4), with effective teachers being able to differentiate as well as integrate to their fullest extent. Teachers need to be able to "self-regulate and be regulated by the norms, values, and concerns of the larger system" (Costa & Garmsten, p. 4), and clearly that is not happening at Holcomb Middle School.

4. **Empowerment.** For teachers to feel empowered to do their work, they must have been delegated the responsibility and granted the authority to work. Teachers must have the autonomy (freedom and latitude) to work within clearly established boundaries to achieve their mission. Holcomb teachers have taken the freedom, but without responsibility for achieving the school's mission and goals. *"We are all here to teach. But when they don't want to learn, just get them out of my classroom,"* demonstrates that the responsibility may have been delegated by the administration, but teachers have not accepted it.

5. **Accountability.** For the reasons stated above, teachers have not taken responsibility, nor are they holding themselves accountable for accomplishing the school's goals and mission. They are merely covering the material without holding themselves accountable for student learning.

6. **Competence and capacity.** If teachers were using their common planning time to discuss March Madness, there is obviously not a shared norm for collaboration, professional learning, and building capacity as a team (or school) to help their students learn. Although March Madness could be seen as a form of bonding and team building, the fact that the teachers were not prepared to discuss anything else, especially student data, leads us to believe that this is a situation of congeniality and forced collaboration. The teachers are spending more than a few minutes at the beginning of the meeting "checking-in" with each other (group maintenance and inclusion) and are definitely off-task. The leadership has not been distributed, the mission is not shared, and there does not appear to be a willingness on the part of the teachers to use the allotted time to learn and work together. In fact, the teachers wait until they are "forced" to explore the data to identify student needs.

7. **Opportunities to actualize results.** The administration has created the structure for teachers to have a weekly common planning time for their house, and they should be commended for doing so. Unfortunately, they have neither provided the teachers with the skills to use student data to drive instruction, nor have they created the motivation to do so through a shared, morally compelling mission. In addition, the teachers have externalized their locus of control and have no sense of efficacy about their role in helping all students learn. It is clear that the administration has not helped the teachers make the connection between what they are doing to help their students learn and their student achievement results.

8. **Stages of group development.** The Blue House is clearly at the beginning (inclusion phase), working *congenially* with each other. They most likely have not reached the influence phase (storming) that will allow them to get to the stage of performing as a collegial learning community. Even though the teachers do not appear to have a shared set of group agreements, the norms of how the group operates are fully operational. For example, they do not use their common planning time to engage in discourse over student learning, no one brought the data to the meeting to discuss, and they work in isolation behind their own classroom doors rather than as a team. As we mentioned above, although the March Madness discussion could be seen as a team-building activity, the fact that this is the middle of the school year, and the group is not prepared to do anything else, leads us to believe that this is a situation of forced collaboration.

9. **Communication.** Although communication is congenial among the Blue House teachers, it is clear that there is a lack of open, honest, reciprocal dialogue between the teachers and between the administration and the teachers about student learning. It also appears that the administrators have not communicated their expectations (both long-term and short-term) for the common planning time. For example, did the administrators tell teachers they had prepared a list of students at-risk of not meeting AYP that teachers should be using during their meeting time to plan final student interventions before the statewide assessments? Finally, we would venture to say there is a lack of trust and respect between the teachers and administration as well as between houses.

10. **Reciprocal relationships.** For teachers to be able to work collegially as well as interdependently in a positive goal structure, there must be a strong, mutual relationship among all members. Teachers must care about each other and be willing to help and support each other through mutual respect, trust, and a shared set of values. In addition, they must share a vested interest (purpose) in achieving the shared goals and mission of the group. We view the Blue House teachers as being congenial toward each other. It is unclear how the teachers in the Blue House relate to the teachers in the other three houses.

11. **Social interdependence.** All groups operate in one of three goal structures: positive interdependence, negative interdependence, or no interdependence. For a group to be most effective, the members need to operate under a goal structure of positive interdependence, even when operating in isolation or competition. At Holcomb, the teachers are working in isolation (no interdependence) within the Blue House. Most likely, they are also working in isolation (no interdependence) from the other three houses at Holcomb. It is also highly likely that there is a sense of competition (negative interdependence) between houses because everyone knows that the Blue House is at the bottom.

12. **Skills of collaboration.** Although it is not explicit from the case study at the beginning of this chapter, we doubt that the teachers have developed or are using the skills of collaboration (e.g., interpersonal, shared decision making, effective communication, conflict management, professional learning, leadership).

13. **Basic elements of collegiality.** It appears that the administration has not established a clear purpose for the common planning time or structured the eight basic elements of collegiality into the group process (i.e., quality of life, positive interdependence, individual accountability, skills of collaboration, group processing, face-to-face promotive interaction, equal participation and responsibility, and simultaneous interaction) to build positive interdependence and collegiality.

## WHAT WOULD YOU DO?

1. After reading the above discussion about the essential conditions that need to be in place, do you agree?

2. Before you read the rest of the story, look back at what you said you would do if you were Michael Tomassetti. Is there anything else you would add to your list?

Read on to compare your list with what Michael decides to do.

## AND NOW FOR THE REST OF THE STORY

*"They are pathetic!" Michael was clearly upset as he walked into Dr. Bill Evan's office and plopped himself down in a chair on the other side of the principal's desk.*

*"You mean you couldn't get them to listen to you?" Dr. Evans laughed, clearly amused at his assistant principal's frustration.*

*"I mean, all they care about right now is March Madness. If they only cared as much about their students as they care about the Blue Devils and the Huskies." Michael took a deep breath and then let it out. "I don't know what to do. This is not what I signed up for when I left the Red House to be your assistant principal last summer."*

*"Welcome to the club!" laughed Bill, having baited Michael and now slowly waiting for the kill. "Now you know why you are the assistant, and I get paid the big bucks," he smiled smugly.*

*"Yeah, but the buck stops with you," Michael thought to himself, not having the courage to say it.*

*Instead, he looked Bill in the eyes and said, "If we don't do something, you and I both know that our school is going to be on 'the list.' I have never lost a fight, and I don't intend to lose this one. It must be that Taurus bull in me coming out," he thought, as he realized his fortieth birthday was quickly approaching. "I am not sure what the other three houses are doing, or even what we did in the Red House that is so different from what the Blue House is doing, but I intend to find out," Michael said, as he picked up his notes, "or I will die trying!" With that, he marched out of the office.*

*Michael went back to his office. He called all four of the guidance counselors, one by one, and asked them to meet with him at 1:00 P.M. for lunch. He said he would have the pizza and soda, all they needed to bring was a printout of the end of the term grades for each of their students. He intended to get to the bottom of this issue.*

*As soon as all four of the guidance counselors had grabbed their pizza and drinks, Michael asked the question that was weighing heavy on his mind. "Why is it that the Red House outperforms all the other houses? And, why does the Blue House have so many students who are failing? When the four of you assign students, do you stack the deck?"*

"Of course not," laughed Ray Bradley, the Blue House counselor. "How absurd! You know we would never get away with that. We divide the students as evenly as possible."

"Then what are the other three houses doing that the Blue House isn't?" Michael asked.

"Do you even have to wonder?" asked Judy Williams, the Red House counselor. "After all, it wasn't that long ago that you were one of us! Think about it. What's different?" she asked probingly.

"Well, for one thing, we used our planning time to talk about our students and the progress they were or weren't making," Michael said, quickly thinking out loud.

"Well, duh!" laughed Larry Freeman, the guidance counselor from the Green House. "What a novel idea!"

"And, we worked together to make sure that all of our students got the help and support they needed to be successful—no matter what the issue."

"And, probably more than anything, we all believed that what we were doing was making a difference. We knew we were helping our students to be successful," added Judy thoughtfully. Then she looked at Ray and said, "Do the Blue House teachers work together to make sure all of their students are passing their classes? How do you use your planning time, Ray?"

Ray wished he were anywhere but in that room. He looked sheepishly at each of them and then said, "Well, to tell you the truth," he hesitated, "Very little time is spent talking about students or what teachers are teaching. I really don't know what we talk about—nothing really, I suppose. We all get along, but I don't think that any of us really knows what the other person is doing, including how we are working with the kids on this list," he added, holding up the data that Michael had passed out at the meeting earlier that morning.

"Maybe that is one of the reasons we aren't helping all of our students learn," Michael said, thinking out loud. "Even when I was on the Red House team, I didn't know what the resource teachers were doing with their students. Special ed and ELL teachers have their own objectives, so I didn't worry about their kids." Then he looked down at the list thoughtfully and said, "But I bet a lot of the kids we are talking about, across the entire school, not just the Blue House, are those kids." He stopped and then said, "Check it out. How many of the kids on your house lists are special education or ELL?" Michael asked.

"All of our kids are either in special education or ELL," said Judy quickly, because the Red House only had a few kids on their list.

"All but seven of mine are special ed or ELL," said Larry, talking about the Yellow House.

"We have five students who are not special education or ELL," said Cynthia Milton, from the Green House.

Ray didn't want to share, but he finally looked up and said, "Forty-five. We have forty-five students who are on the list besides the twenty-five resource room and ELL kids."

"Wow!" Judy said, even though the others showed just as much surprise by the looks on their faces. "Why?" she asked. "That is over half of your total student load."

"The question of the day," Michael said with emphasis. "No small wonder our school is going to be on the list."

"This is amazing. I had no idea that we, as a school, had so many of our students substantially deficient. If you figure that we have," Larry paused, calculating, "roughly 500 students . . . with about 43 percent Hispanic. Wow!"

"And we have how many students altogether on this list?" Cynthia asked.

"There are 179 students who are really in trouble—meaning they are flunking more than one subject. But 287 of our students, over half, show up as having trouble in one of their subjects. Look at your lists," Michael said pointing to his list. "And, when we are talking about NCLB, it doesn't matter how many of our kids are special ed, ELL, or free or reduced lunch. In fact, it hurts us even more when those kids, all the kids on your list," he said, holding up the list once again, "don't make AYP gains."

*(Continued)*

(Continued)

*The four guidance counselors were stunned. Over half of the students in the school were failing in at least one area. "You know," Michael said softly, finally realizing the magnitude of the problem, "this is no longer a Blue House or a Yellow House problem. This is our problem. Our school's problem. This is Holcomb—all of us, together. Even if the Red House appears to be doing okay, it's not."*

*Judy looked up, surprised at what Michael was saying. "Do you realize," he continued, "all four Houses, all of us together, show up as Holcomb School on 'the list' when our students don't make AYP gains."*

*"You're right," Judy Williams said, realizing for the first time that her house was in just as much trouble as the Blue House, even though up until this point, she and the Red House teachers had never thought of themselves as being held responsible for what any of the other houses did or didn't do. They were always just so pleased they had the students with the highest test scores.*

*"So, now what do we do?" Judy asked, with the sobering reality of sinking with the rest of the ship.*

*"I don't know," sighed Michael, but we can't do this by ourselves. He picked up the phone and called Dr. Evans and asked him to join them in his conference room. The group quickly filled him in on their conversation. Dr. Evans was clearly amazed at what he had heard from the group.*

*When they had finished describing the situation to him, all eyes looked up at Dr. Evans, waiting for his response. He thought for a moment and then said, "I guess we have created a monster."*

*They all looked at him like he was crazy. "What are you talking about?" Michael heard himself ask.*

*"Think about March Madness. You said yourself, Michael, that the Blue House can't wait for the final four match-up to begin. Well, it has already begun at Holcomb. We have created our own madness, right here, with Blue versus Red, Yellow versus Green. We have our own final four line-up, and it isn't pretty." He paused and gave them time to picture it in their minds.*

*"Problem is," Dr. Evans continued, "that only one team wins the NCAA Championship, and the other three final four teams lose. That's sports. That works for teams from one college who are playing against teams from another college. But by dividing our school into four different houses and creating school-within-a-school teams, we are competing against each other, and we all stand to lose. Because," he paused, "no matter how we slice and dice it, we are still one school, which makes what we all do collectively important—not what we do alone. One of us can't win at the expense of the others. The only way we win is when we all win!"*

*"You mean we sink or swim together?" Larry asked.*

*"That's exactly what I mean," Dr. Evans said emphatically. Then he looked at Michael and said, "Thank you, for pulling this group together. You have given us all a lot to think about."*

*Michael smiled. "But it is only the beginning. We have a lot of work to do if we are going to stay off the list. We have only begun the conversation about what to do to help our students."*

*"Yes, and it is a very important first step. You're right, Michael, we have a lot of work to do. And it means that we all need to pull together to make it happen. Today after school, we have a faculty meeting. I would like to ask each of you to talk about what you realized during this meeting—just like you did when you filled me in on what you had been discussing. Then, I am going to divide each of the houses up into core-subject teams, and I would like each one of you to become the team leader for one of the groups. Will you do it?" Dr. Evans asked.*

*"Sure," they all agreed.*

*"We can start by having each group talk about what they are doing to help all of their students achieve academic success in their classes and as a house, and what they could be doing better. I am thinking out loud," Dr. Evans said, "but we could record the information on a T-chart and then have*

*groups share. This can start the conversations. We need to hear what all the teams are doing that is working and build on those successes. Likewise, we need to hear what the teachers need to help their students achieve mastery levels."*

*They all nodded.*

*"I will call down to the central office and see if we can get substitutes so that we can continue these conversations in cross-house subject-area groups. That way, teachers can take all of the students who are struggling, no matter what team, and work together to develop strategies that target each individual student's needs whether they are regular ed, special ed, or ELL. All of the teachers working with each student must be focused on the precise, personalized goals that will help each child meet the AYP benchmarks. Then we," and Dr. Evans stopped and looked at the other five people in the room, "that's we, all of us, will put our heads together and figure out how we can get the teachers the resources they need and do whatever we have to do to help them target their instruction and work successfully with all of the students. I don't know what it will mean, but I need each of you to be the eyes and ears for me, since I can't be in each of the groups. For example, we may need to bring in consultants to help them gain more content knowledge and learn new strategies. Or we may need to help them develop skills to work together as a schoolwide team. Heck, most of these teachers never even talk to teachers in any of the other houses, so we probably need to spend some time getting to know each other."*

*Dr. Evans stopped, before going on, "But whatever it takes, we are all in this together. We need to make sure that everyone steps up in this game and takes responsibility for making the goals. If we are going to win, we also have to make the assists."*

*"You're right, coach," Larry said, laughing. "If we are going to finish this game on top, we have to make some fourth quarter adjustments."*

*"That's right. You have all caught my attention, and now we have to make sure that we get everyone on the same court, focusing on the strategies and plays that will help us win," Bill said. Then added, "We need to take back our school. All of us, together, need to work together so we can win this game like the champions I know we can be!"*

*"Let's get in there, look at our stats, and come out in the remaining minutes showing the rest of them how good we really are!" Michael said, getting caught up in the spirit of the moment.*

*"Thanks again, all of you," Dr. Evans said sincerely, "for taking the time to meet about this crucial issue, for helping me realize what the real problem is, and how to focus on bringing us back together as a school. Most important, thank you all for agreeing to do what you can to help us develop a game plan, so that we can begin to function as a schoolwide team rather than to play the game like the final four."*

*They all got up and began to clear up their mess. As Michael bent over to pick up the leftover pizza, Bill looked at him and said, "Way to go, Michael! We may not be ready to cut down the nets quite yet, and we may not score all the points we need to stay off the list this year. But I am confident that it is not too late to regroup and come back next year as the winners I know we can be. You've got what it takes, kid. I'm glad you're on my team! Thanks."*

*"Anytime," Michael said.*

*"See you in a few minutes, when the real work begins," Bill said, as he left Michael's conference room smiling, this time because he finally realized, and appreciated, the fact that he was working with a "pretty darn good team!"*

## CHAPTER SUMMARY

We define *positive interdependence* as *the relationship that connects members of a group in such a way that everyone's contribution is vital to the success of the group, and the work that is done mutually benefits everyone.*

To successfully build interdependence, school leaders must schedule time within the school day for people to meet; build upon the relationships of team, group, and school members; structure elements of positive interdependence and individual accountability into the daily tasks and routines; and provide opportunities for all staff members to increase their skills of collaboration as well as frequent opportunities to debrief the tasks and working relationships. We believe that for groups to work effectively together, school leaders must use the eight basic elements of collegiality to organize group work. The more these elements are embedded into the group work, the more likely the group will successfully achieve its goals and work together as a collegial learning community.

Just because you are a group doesn't mean you are a team or that you can work together effectively or successfully. All groups are somewhere on the continuum ranging from congeniality, to cooperation, to forced collaboration, to collaboration, to a collegial learning community. Some groups progress faster than others through the stages of group development based on the way their groups are structured and their ability to use the skills of collaboration. For groups to work together as a collegial learning community, they must be able to move effectively and seamlessly through the different phases (inclusion, influence, and community) and stages (i.e., forming, norming, storming, conforming, and performing) of group development. School leaders must have a keen awareness of group development as well as the knowledge, understanding, and skills to lead and facilitate group processes. They must build a repertoire of tools they can use to lead groups through each of the stages until the group is able to perform as a community. A collegial learning community exists when a quality of life is present and members of the group have developed a mutual trust and respect for each other (reciprocal relationships), a vested interest in the outcome (mission), a voice in the decision making (communication, autonomy, and empowerment), competence and capacity for accomplishing the work, and a shared sense of responsibly for themselves and each other (accountability) for working together (positive interdependence) to achieve the desired results.

We define *collegiality* as *a group of professional educators who have a vested interest and take responsibility for achieving their shared goals, purpose, and/or school mission.* Taking this one step further, we define a *collegial learning community* as *one in which a group of professional educators within a department, school, or district hold themselves and each other accountable for working together to achieve their shared goals, purpose, or school's mission through positive interdependence, reciprocal relationships, shared decision making, professional development, and mutual responsibility.*

To structure and use positive interdependence as a motivational strategy, school leaders must communicate and apply strategies that help everyone to realize that "We are all in this together" and that "No one is as smart as all of us." Leaders who believe this, and work toward this end, understand that there is no better slogan for positive interdependence and a collegial learning community than, "Together, we can!"

## NEXT STEPS

1. Think about positive interdependence in your own school. What does it look like, sound like, and feel like in your current situation? What else would you like it to look like, sound like, and feel like? Make a list. Put a star by those things that are already in place in your school or system. Put a check by those things that you would like to implement or explore further.

2. If possible, discuss with others what you found interesting about this discussion on positive interdependence and what you found challenging.

3. Select one or two ideas that you checked above. List several strategies or changes that you can make to improve the positive interdependence within your own school.

4. Think about the barriers that may get in your way, and list choices that you can make to help you alleviate or decrease those barriers.

5. Decide on one or two things that you are going to implement at your own school or in your work because of this chapter. List them along with any notes to help you remember what you want to do.

# 12

# Results

*Achieving the School's Morally Compelling Mission and Goals*

## ■ PICTURE THIS

*Janice Robbins was clearly upset as she drove into the parking lot of Bartlett Primary School. Her head was spinning and her stomach felt nauseous from the realization that she and her kindergarten teachers had a lot of work to do. Janice had an inkling that her students were struggling last week when her literacy teacher, Cheryl Hamel, showed her the kindergarten students' mid-year Developmental Reading Assessment (DRA) scores. But until this morning, she had no idea how low her kindergarten DRA results really were.*

*The morning had begun just like any other day. Janice met with the climate committee before school to discuss a baby shower for one of the first-grade teachers. The group also discussed their upcoming plans for Read Across America Day, the best part being Dr. Seuss's birthday party during lunch. The students always looked forward to this celebration. Just as in previous years, teachers on the committee had volunteered to coordinate individual parts of the day. Janice was glad that she had such a young, enthusiastic staff with so many creative ideas. She never knew exactly what to expect, but each year they had celebrated Dr. Seuss's birthday, everyone did their part. Janice felt as if this year was no exception after listening to the teachers report on the activities and guests who would be reading to students.*

*(Continued)*

(Continued)

*Just after the first bell rang, Janice made the usual morning announcements. She handed out several birthday pins and pencils to the three students who were celebrating their birthdays. Mrs. Robbins also spent a few minutes in one of the kindergarten classrooms. She had promised to observe one of the boys who was having a difficult time paying attention in class. Anton's parents were coming in for a response to intervention (RTI) parent-teacher conference after lunch. His teacher, Rene Baldwin, had asked to have this conference because she didn't know how to help Anton. His birthday was December 12, and he had just turned five two months ago. Anton wasn't interested in learning to read. He, like many of the other kindergarten boys, just wanted to play. In fact, this year there were twice as many boys as girls. The eight kindergarten teachers had a standing joke about the water people were drinking five years ago because so many of the children, especially the boys, had late birthdays.*

*All kidding aside, Rene was worried about Anton because the more she pushed him to read, the angrier and more frustrated he became. Recently, he had started having temper tantrums and hitting other students for no apparent reason. Rene felt she was to blame because she was pushing him too hard. But she didn't feel like she had a choice, since the district had expected all of the students to be reading at a level 2 by now, and he was still at a level 1. Rene had talked with Cheryl Hamel, the literacy teacher, about getting Anton extra help with his reading and to Lee Hausser, the school psychologist, about putting him on a behavior plan and perhaps even doing some behavior rating scales to see if he had hyperactive tendencies. Janice had agreed to sit in on the meeting with his parents that afternoon. That meeting had been set up even before Janice realized how bad the kindergarten reading scores were.*

*The elementary principal's meeting at the central office that morning was cordial, as always. They got through several of the agenda items rather quickly, and in fact, Ned Taylor, one of the principals sitting next to Janice, had even remarked about how quickly the meeting was progressing.*

*Janice replied, "Yeah, maybe we will finish early and actually get something accomplished back at school today," knowing that rarely did they get out of their elementary principal's meetings before noon. In fact, on numerous occasions, the director of instruction would sneak out of the meeting and order pizza for everyone if the meeting dragged on too long. Since she had, until recently, been one of them, she knew when the meetings ran late, most of the principals wouldn't get lunch. "It was a nice touch, but leaving early would be even better!" Janice thought to herself, just before being caught off-guard.*

*The director of instruction had barely finished passing out the district DRA midterm report for all twelve elementary schools. Of course, all the principals scanned it quickly to see how they stacked up. Bartlett Primary School was usually right on top. But not this time, as Janice quickly realized. In fact, it was as if a bolt of lightening struck her and brought her back to the reality of just how low her kindergarten scores were.*

*But it wasn't until the assistant superintendent blurted out, "Look at this! Even Willowbrook's kindergarten DRA scores are better than Bartlett's!" It was probably what everyone was thinking, but nobody dared to say, except her.*

*The bomb dropped! As soon as the words left the assistant superintendent's mouth, the room got so quiet that you could hear the copy machine churning out the board packets three doors down.*

*All eyes were now fixed on Janice. She felt her face turn twenty shades of red, as everyone stared at her in disbelief. They all knew that the students at Bartlett came from the most affluent area in the town, with the most supportive parents, and that Willowbrook was made up of migrant workers' kids and a lot of low income housing project students. This was the first year the district had begun to pilot a full-day kindergarten program for the Willowbrook students. The superintendent and assistant superintendent were waiting for just such data, so they could go back to the school board and the city's finance board and say, "We told you so!" This was great news for central office, but Janice felt as if she had been run over by a train.*

*After the meeting, Mr. Norton, the superintendent, stopped Janice just before she left the room. He looked at her and said, "What happened to your kindergarten DRA scores? I expected your students to do much better than this."*

*"So did I," Janice said. "I'm not sure why we are so low. We are doing everything we have done in previous years." She stopped, thinking, then added, "We knew that our scores were lower. I just didn't expect them to be this low."*

*"Nor did I," replied Mr. Norton. "To think that Willowbrook had more students reach the district benchmark than Bartlett. I never thought I would see the day!" He stopped, looked at her in disbelief, and then said assertively, "You and your teachers have a lot of work to do before the May DRAs. You need to figure out what you want to do, then let me know your plan. I have some money, not much, but if you need money to do something that will help you get those scores up, let me know," he said, patting her on the shoulder and making her feel as if she had just been scolded by her father for backing the family car into the neighbor's mailbox.*

*"We'll put our heads together and figure something out," Janice said. "After all, our kindergarten kids are at the very bottom. They have nowhere to go but up!" Wishing this were all a dream, she pinched herself, but it hurt! In more ways than one.*

## ■ WHAT ARE RESULTS?

At no other time in the history of American education and school reform efforts has the demand to achieve results based on performance been so great, nor have the stakes been so high. No matter which side of the fence you sit on—right, wrong, or indifferent, good or bad—the accountability movement is changing the way schools operate and the way in which the outside world defines academic success.

None of us can argue with the worthy intentions of the NCLB legislation or with the admirable goal of closing the achievement gap. The intellectual debate instead rages over what and how to assess student learning, what and how to evaluate educator and school performance, and what and how to determine quality schools and programs. The difficulty lies with identifying the indicators of success that realistically, reliably, fairly, and consistently determine whether students are making adequate yearly progress or whether their schools have established quality learning environments with programs and practices that transform the school from good to great.

For results to be used as a powerful motivational strategy, however, the paradigm must change from that of sanctions and punishment when schools or students fail to make significant progress to one of celebrations and support. As we have explained earlier in this book, "the fear factor" doesn't work. In fact, if school communities are going to achieve deep learning, attain the desired results, and sustain these results over time, we must "reduce the fear factor" (Fullan, 2005, p. 22). Fear and distrust "undermine organizational performance and, specifically, the ability to turn knowledge into action" (Pfeffer & Sutton, 2000, p. 110) and, we would add, actions into desired results.

We define *results* as *the achievement of the school's morally compelling mission and goals, as defined by a predetermined set of indicators of success and desired outcomes, stemming from the decisions, behaviors, actions, and accomplishments of a collegial learning community.*

Results can be based on long-term or short-term SMART goals. The results can show long-term growth over time or small, short-term incremental gains. Results can be either positive or negative, depending on how well the collegial learning community is able to achieve the predetermined indicators of success or desired outcomes. But no matter the results, educators must analyze the data to gain information about student achievement and teacher performance. Depending on the summative results, school leaders are responsible for making sure that the school community recognizes and celebrates their successes, no matter how large or small, and facilitates the decision-making processes that refine school goals; indicators of success; and/or actions, behaviors, or strategies. This requires following the school improvement cycle as defined in Chapter 7 on accountability.

In order to monitor progress, there must be multiple forms of evaluation methodologies in place so that data are triangulated. Success for students, teachers, and/or schools must never be determined from the results of a single, isolated assessment. For reliability and validity purposes, the indicators of success must be measurable, using either qualitative and/or quantitative evaluation and assessment tools. In addition, educators will want to collect and use anecdotal evidence to support the data and provide additional insights and give further meaning to their results. So that educators are not caught by surprise, there must be multiple formative assessments along the way, or what Stiggins (2004) calls "assessments for learning" to measure daily and weekly progress. The data must be transparent (Fullan, 2008) so that the system and teachers then use this information to gain knowledge and wisdom that informs daily instruction. In addition, teachers must have the time to engage in self-reflection and self-evaluation, both alone and with colleagues, through analysis of student work and/or dialogue about pedagogy.

For results to be a powerful motivational strategy, educators must do more than simply collect and analyze the data. Educators must give the data meaning so that it informs instruction. Davenport and Prusak (2000) write that information is "data that makes a difference" (p. 3) and list five ways that educators can transform data to information by giving it meaning and adding value:

- *Contextualized.* We know for what purpose the data was gathered.
- *Categorized.* We know the units of analysis or key components of the data.
- *Calculated.* The data may have been analyzed mathematically or statistically.
- *Corrected.* Errors have been removed from the data.
- *Condensed.* The data have been summarized in a more concise form (p. 4).

If teachers are going to learn from the data and use the information as knowledge that informs instruction, they must have the time to process what they know and apply it contextually to their own unique situations. Davenport and Prusak state that "knowledge derives from minds at work" (p. 5) and they provide the following working definition of knowledge:

Knowledge is a fluid mix of framed experience, values, contextual information, and expert's insight that provides a framework for evaluating and incorporating new experiences and information. It originates and is applied in the minds of knowers. In organizations, it often becomes embedded not only in documents or repositories, but also in organizational routines, processes, practices, and norms. (p. 5)

Educators must take the information and transform it into knowledge. Davenport and Prusak state that "Knowledge-creating activities take place within and between humans. While we find data in records or transactions, and information in messages, we obtain knowledge from individuals or groups of knowers, or sometimes in organizational records" (p. 6). They list four ways that educators transform information into knowledge:

- *Comparison.* How does information about this situation compare to other situations we have known?
- *Consequences.* What implications does the information have for decisions and actions?
- *Connections.* How does this bit of information relate to others?
- *Conversation.* What do people think about this information? (p. 6)

Ahmed, Kok, and Loh (2002) describe the knowledge-creation process as one in which "knowledge is embedded in people, and knowledge creation occurs in the process of social interactions" (p. 26). They suggest that the "process of knowledge creation is a spiral, moving from tacit knowledge to explicit knowledge and back to tacit" (p. 26).

We agree that knowledge-creation is a powerful form of management, innovation, and professional learning. The power of collaboration comes from teachers sharing their knowledge, skills, and experiences with each other, through reciprocal relationships, a desire to achieve a shared and compelling mission, and the interdependent structures that afford teachers with the ability to work together in collegial learning communities. It is the exchange of tacit and explicit knowledge that leads to the wisdom that can be used to improve and enhance the teaching and learning process. We believe that by using a knowledge-creation model, educators can turn their *knowledge of results* into *wisdom* that is used in the classroom with students to inform instruction, achieve even greater results, and increase teacher satisfaction and motivation.

We also believe that educators using the knowledge-creation process to build upon their current results will be able to *break through* the "prescription trap" (Fullan, Hill, & Crévola, 2006, p. 2). In their book, *Breakthrough*, Fullan, Hill, and Crévola (2006) state that *breakthrough* "involves the educational community as a whole, establishing a system of expert data-driven instruction that will result in daily continuous improvement for all students in all classrooms" (p. 2).

To provide the setting for teachers to transform knowledge into wisdom, schools must become collegial learning communities. As such, teachers must be given the time, during the regular school day, to learn and work collaboratively with each other to gain knowledge from the results of the data and use their collective wisdom to achieve their school's mission. Teachers must have the time to engage in meaningful conversations about their own teaching in relation to student learning and assessment results. Together through collaboration, they can use the knowledge and insights they have gained by analyzing the results from the data and synthesizing these results within their own contexts, past experiences, observations, values, and beliefs. In addition, this may provide the impetus for just-in-time, job-embedded inquiry, as they seek to find additional strategies and techniques to help students who are struggling with a particular concept. Often teachers can brainstorm among themselves and draw from their collective knowledge, skills, and experiences. Just as important, however, the group needs to continue to look outside their own circles, networking with others across schools and districts, to learn about additional strategies and techniques.

If, in fact, teachers are going to use the knowledge they have gleaned from their results to break through and help their children achieve even higher standards and expectations, they will want to engage in the following three strategies as suggested by Fullan, Hill, and Crévola (2006): personalization, precision, and professional learning. To Fullan, Hill, and Crévola's strategies, we have added several questions that teachers need to ask themselves to transform their knowledge of results into the wisdom they can use to inform their instruction and take the action to help all students achieve even greater results.

## Personalization

- What do my (our) students know?
- What skills have they mastered?
- What additional knowledge or skills do they need to know, or be able to do, to achieve higher gains?
- What are the unique, individual strengths and needs of each student?
- What is expected growth? Did the students achieve it?

## Precision

- How can I best deliver instruction to meet the needs and learning styles of each individual child?
- What is the exact content (knowledge and skills) that I need to provide for each child to successfully achieve the learning goals?
- How can I differentiate student learning?

## Professional Learning

- What else do I (we) need to know to make sure all of my (our) students are able to achieve the learning goals?
- What has the data (results) told us about how/what our students are learning?
- What additional information do we need?
- How can we use this information to best inform our practices?

To generate the wisdom from the knowledge of results about student learning and use it to inform instruction and take appropriate action, we suggest that teams of teachers (collegial learning communities) use the "knowledge-wisdom-action (KWA) Helix," as illustrated in Figure 12.1.

**Figure 12.1**   The Knowledge-Wisdom-Action (KWA) Helix

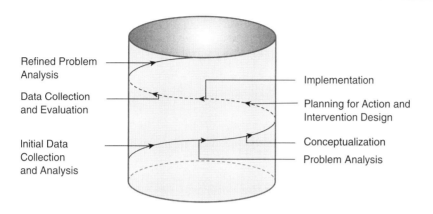

*Initial data collection and analysis.* School leaders determine who the right people (Collins, 2001, p. 13) are to do the work. The collegial team (e.g., department, grade level, vertical team, school-improvement team) works together to determine what data are important and what the data mean.

*Problem analysis.* The collegial team identifies where students are in relation to the goal(s) they are trying to achieve (target) and what it will take to achieve the goal(s). If it hasn't already been done, the collegial team will need to identify the indicators of success and how these will be measured.

*Conceptualization.* The collegial team identifies the right work (Marzano, Waters, & McNulty, 2005, p. 76) and the course of action. This stage may require outside consultation, professional learning, and/or a study of the research and best practices.

*Planning for action and intervention design.* The collegial team identifies the strategies (actions) that will be implemented to achieve the desired results. A timeline, resources, people responsible, assessment/evaluation tools, and indicators of success are identified and mapped out. It is important that the collegial team determine "the right stuff" and the school leaders make sure they have it to do their work.

*Implementation.* The action plan is put into place. The timeline is followed, with the collegial team meeting at regular intervals to monitor the process and progress. During the implementation phase, teams may decide to refine their work, using assessments for learning (Stiggins, 2004) to help them determine areas to refine.

*Data collection and evaluation.* Evaluations can be formative or summative at this point, depending on the length of the intervention and/or the goal(s) themselves. Assessments and/or evaluation tools are used to collect information about student learning and/or program effectiveness. Data are collected and analyzed by the collegial team.

*Refined problem analysis.* The collegial team identifies where students are in relation to the goal(s) they are trying to achieve (target) and what it will take to achieve the goal(s). The team takes time to celebrate their successes and makes refinements to their goal(s) as appropriate. For example, they may simply continue the actions they have already implemented, revise their goal(s) or strategies, or determine that their work is finished and establish new goals that build on the complexity of the students and/or more rigorous standards. If new goals are created, the collegial team will need to identify the indicators of success and how these will be measured.

NOTE: Collegial teams continue to cycle through the helix, moving from one level of complexity to the next. Some phases of the cycle may not be necessary to repeat, or may need less time, during subsequent cycles.

Simply put, teachers must use the knowledge they have gained from the data to determine what students know and can do. They work collegially together to balance what students know and can do against the indicators of success, to determine precisely what each student or groups of students need to accomplish to achieve the learning goals. In addition, they work collaboratively to develop and deliver quality instruction that helps students attain the learning goals. At regularly scheduled intervals, teachers must take time to individually and collectively reflect upon and evaluate their own performance in relation to new results (data-information-knowledge-wisdom-results) about student achievement. They then use this new knowledge of results to measure their progress toward accomplishing the school's mission and goals and to plan for further action. Educators must take time, however, at the end of each spiral to celebrate their successes and refine their efforts before working toward achieving even higher expectations and standards as they progress to the next cycle.

All too often, educators see results as the end point. Instead educators need to begin to visualize their results as a transition point between what they have been doing and what they hope to achieve. Until educators learn how to take the results and turn them into actions, akin to taking theory and turning it into practice, we will not be able to actualize the quantum breakthrough for public education that Fullan, Hill, and Crévola (2006) posit.

Collegial learning communities are among one of the most powerful and valuable forms for building competence and capacity for teachers. As teachers share in helping their students accomplish the school goals, and the results they have predetermined are actualized, teachers become even more motivated and passionate about the teaching and learning process. When a teacher is asked what the greatest benefit is of teaching, most often it is not the money or even the fact that they have time off in the summer. Most often, teachers garner their greatest satisfaction from teaching when, as they would say, "it's that 'ah, ha' moment, when for the student, the light bulb goes on, and I know they've got it!"

That is what results are all about!

## ■ NEEDS MET THROUGH RESULTS

Basic needs that are met with this motivational strategy include Maslow's (1998) esteem and self-actualization needs; Herzberg's set of motivators (as cited in Heller, 1998); Glasser's (1998a) control theory, especially fun; Sagor's (2003) competence, usefulness, and optimism; and Covey's (2004) spirit. (See Appendix A.)

## ■ WHAT RESULTS ARE AND ARE NOT

Figures 12.2 and 12.3 will help to clarify results. Figure 12.2 explains what it looks like for educators to focus on results. Figure 12.3 on pages 266–267 compares the differences between a results-supportive environment and a results-deficient environment.

**Figure 12.2**   Results Defined

| Educators Focused on Results | Educators Not Focused on Results |
|---|---|
| Clear understanding of what works, what doesn't work, and why. | Lack of understanding of what works, what doesn't work, and why. |
| Clear understanding and agreement of goals, indicators of success, and strategies that will help the school community achieve its mission. | Unclear understanding and lack of agreement for indicators of success, and strategies that will help the school community achieve its mission. |
| The school's mission is based on SMART goals. The vision (target) is clearly defined. | The mission and target are vague. Goals are either too easy, unrealistic, or lack clarity. |
| Educators have the necessary resources and support to successfully accomplish the goals. | There is a lack of resources and support to successfully complete the work and/or goals. |
| Teaching and learning activities are aligned with standards and focused on student learning goals. | Teachers design lessons independently, based on interests and wants, rather than teaching a defined curriculum. |
| Teacher behavior, student learning activities, and assessments are congruent. There is a strong focus on learning. | Curriculum, standards, student assessments, and/or student learning activities are not aligned with instruction. |
| Educators share a strong sense of efficacy and internal locus of control. | Educators share little sense of efficacy and externalized locus of control. |
| Educators feel empowered and intrinsically motivated to perform at optimal levels. | Educators lack authority, motivation, and simply spend time "on the job." |
| Educators receive ongoing, immediate, specific, and accurate feedback about the important work they are doing. | Educators lack feedback and knowledge about their performance and/or the work they are doing. |
| Educators hold themselves and each other accountable for accomplishing shared goals and the school mission. | Educators blame others when things don't go as planned and feel lucky when they achieve their goals. They do not take responsibility for, or hold themselves accountable for, their work. |
| Celebrations of success are frequent. Educators feel recognized and appreciated for their work. | Celebrations of success rarely occur. Educators do not feel recognized or appreciated. |
| Educators take time to analyze the data and refine their strategies and goals using a continuous improvement cycle model. | Educators take little time to analyze the data and refine their strategies and goals using a continuous improvement cycle model. |
| Educators are engaged in ongoing, quality, job-embedded professional learning activities. | Educators receive limited staff development, usually one-size-fits-all events. |
| Educators work in teams as colleagues to design creative and innovative lessons and activities that provide quality instruction based on personalized and precise student needs. | Educators work in isolation, doing many of the same activities year to year, because they and their students enjoy them—not because they know whether or not they are effective. |
| Every minute counts. Teachers align lessons with standards, learning goals, and assessments. | Teachers go through the motions, covering the material, often following a script/pacing guide. |

*(Continued)*

**Figure 12.2** (Continued)

| Educators Focused on Results | Educators Not Focused on Results |
|---|---|
| Teachers conduct ongoing formative (assessments for learning) as well as summative (assessments of learning) assessments. Data is used to inform instruction. | Teachers often conduct assessments that may not be aligned. Often there is data paralysis because there is too much data and not enough time to use it to inform instruction before the next assessments. |
| Administrators "stay-the-course." | Administrators' target (vision) keeps moving. |
| Concern for excellence and high standards. | Lack of concern for excellence and standards. |

**Figure 12.3**    Structuring a Results-Supportive Environment

| Results-Supportive Environment | Results-Deficient Environment |
|---|---|
| Quality of life exists, with all members of the school community having their basic needs, including resources, met. | Quality of life, the way we defined it in Chapter 3, is limited or nonexistent. Basic needs, including resources, are not being met. |
| All educators within the school understand and share an agreed upon and morally compelling mission, vision, and goals. | All members of the school community do not share or understand a clearly defined mission, vision, and goals. |
| All educators within the school accept responsibility and hold themselves and each other accountable for achieving the morally compelling mission, vision, and goals. | Educators blame external factors when results are not actualized. They do not take responsibility for achieving the mission, vision, and goals. |
| Hope and optimism. | Hopelessness and pessimism. |
| There is a strong culture that supports collaboration and positive interdependence. Educators have established reciprocal relationships with each other that allow flexible teams to work effectively together. | There is a culture of negative interdependence or no- interdependence. Educators work in isolation, often competing against each other for resources and support. |
| Within clear boundaries, educators are empowered to make informed, autonomous decisions and held accountable for results. | Teachers are told what to teach, often with scripts and strict pacing guides—taking little ownership, pride, or sense of responsibility. |
| The school's mission is aligned with the district's mission. There is alignment with curriculum, instruction, and assessments at the school, district, and state level that everyone supports and uses. | The school's mission holds little or no alignment with the district's mission. Likewise, there is little or no alignment between the curriculum, instruction, and assessment at the school, district, and state level. |
| Teachers work together to align their own behavior, student learning, and the goals of the district. | Teachers independently make their own decisions based on what they think/feel is best. |
| Frequent celebrations. Teachers share in the recognition and celebrations of their successes. | Few celebrations. Individuals are recognized. Single efforts/results are rewarded. |
| Communication is honest, open, and reciprocal. Information is shared with all stakeholders in a timely manner. | Communication is limited, unclear, and often conflicting. People do not feel listened to. Information is withheld—need-to-know. |

| Results-Supportive Environment | Results-Deficient Environment |
|---|---|
| Teachers are willing to share and dialogue in meaningful ways. There is mutual respect among staff members for ideas and beliefs. | Teachers are unwilling to share or communicate in meaningful ways. Teachers withhold information and work independently. |
| There is a sense of efficacy and internal locus of control. Teachers feel they can and do make a difference. | There is a lack of efficacy and external locus of control. Teachers feel that it doesn't matter what they do. |
| Educators move through the continuous improvement cycle when planning, implementing, and evaluating innovations. | Educators jump on the latest bandwagons, hoping that something works. Innovations are hit-and-miss. |
| Data is analyzed and information is shared. Knowledge is used to make informed decisions. | Data is collected with little or no effort to use it to inform decisions. |
| There is continuous feedback and support to all members of the school community, based on data analysis and results. | There is limited if any information shared or communicated to members of the school community based on data analysis and results. |

## ■ WHY ARE RESULTS IMPORTANT?

Results are important because they help educators determine where they are in relation to accomplishing their school's compelling mission. Without knowledge of results about student learning and feedback about their own performance, educators have no idea whether what they are doing is effective, meaningful, or making a difference.

Results are also important for accountability purposes. As the book by the title, *Results* (Neilson & Pasternack, 2005) states on its cover, results help organizations "Keep what's good, fix what's wrong, and unlock great performance." Fullan (2008) makes the case for how "transparency and the use of data on performance and practice can serve as powerful tools for improvement" (p. 102). The only way schools are going to move from good to great is by building upon what is working and refining those programs and services that aren't helping all students achieve their learning goals. In fact, Fullan argues that "We can say that transparency rules when it is combined with deep learning in context. Transparency and learning in context flourish when capacity building trumps judgmentalism, when peer interaction fosters coherence, and when employees and customers [students] are valued" (p. 102–104).

Mihaly Csikszentmihalyi (1997) says that the more our work "resembles a flow activity, the more involved we become, and the more positive the experience" (p. 38). He explains how "clear goals, unambiguous feedback, a sense of control, challenges that match the worker's skills, and a few distractions" (p. 38) provoke similar feelings as "what one experiences in a sport or an artistic performance" (p. 38). Clearly defined goals and results that provide specific, accurate, and immediate feedback are two characteristics that help educators work in a state of flow, or what we have defined as optimal performance. The more educators are working at optimal performance, the happier, more motivated, and productive they become.

Abraham Maslow (1998) describes self-actualization as the highest level on his pyramid structure. According to Maslow, a person achieves self-actualization when he or she finds that the activity or work they are engaged in provides its own satisfaction. It brings self-fulfillment and its own sense of self-achievement. The work becomes its own reward. When teachers see that what they are doing is making a difference (self-efficacy) and that their students are able to successfully achieve their learning goals (achieve results), teachers share in that success, and thus the work becomes its own reward.

Covey (2004) writes, "Effectiveness is the balance between production of desired results and production capability . . . the essence of effectiveness is achieving the results you want in a way that enables you to get even more of these results in the future" (p. 242). He says, "People play differently when they are keeping score" (p. 284). Covey believes that it is crucial to make the results visible and accessible, so that teams can stay focused on key priorities. He states that there is a "tremendous motivating power" that comes from seeing one's scores on a scoreboard. Because the scores are an "inescapable picture of reality," strategic decisions and plans depend on the knowledge that comes from results. "Unless you can see the score," Covey writes, "your strategies and plans are simply abstractions" (p. 284).

We agree that people play differently when they keep score. We would also suggest that people play differently, and are more likely to keep trying, when they have knowledge and feedback about their performance. If you have ever played "pin the tail on the donkey," broken a piñata, or played darts blindfolded, you know what we are talking about. Because you can't see the target, it becomes crucial that someone provides you with feedback. When you receive information about how close you are to the target and what you can do to improve, you are more likely to persevere and eventually achieve your goal.

Positive, verbal feedback that is specific, immediate, and accurate can be a powerful intrinsic motivator because it affirms a person's competence. The Northwest Regional Laboratory (Jarrett-Weeks, 2001, p. 19) lists several research studies that indicate when school leaders provide teachers with meaningful, constructive feedback (knowledge of their performance), student academic achievement improves along with teacher satisfaction and teacher motivation. Likewise, when educators collect data and monitor student learning over time, they are able to see the results of their own and their students' work. Often, as we stated above, the results are their own reward.

Educators feel good about their work when they get specific, positive feedback about their performance, or when they collect student assessment data that shows significant gains in achievement. In addition, educators gain self-efficacy as well as gain confidence in their ability to perform effectively. This builds self-esteem not only in teachers, but when teachers communicate the positive results to their students, this knowledge of results builds student confidence and self-esteem as well.

In her book, *Confidence,* Rosabeth Moss Kanter (2004) explains how important a culture of success and achieving results is to creating a high performing team. In order to create a "cycle of success" (p. 20), leaders need to instill confidence among their followers. She says, "confidence is not an artificial mental construct, solely dependent on what people decide to believe; it reflects reasonable reactions to circumstances. People are caught in cycles, and they interpret events based on what they see happening, on how they are treated by others around them" (p. 24).

Like a basketball team that is losing, when student scores are low, Kanter (p. 28–29) writes that teams need to "relax under pressure" and focus on the next steps. During this time, school leaders need to encourage and support their teachers and help them focus on what they are doing well, and build on those strengths. It is important to build on "your wins" or what you are doing well because winning produces confidence.

Kanter also says that there are four levels of confidence, and at each level "confidence both feeds winning and feeds off of it. Momentum builds because each success in a sequence of successes makes it easier to generate self-confidence, confidence in colleagues, confidence in the system, and investor confidence" (p. 29–30). The four levels she lists are:

*Self-confidence: an emotional climate of high expectations.* Winning feels good, and good moods are contagious. . . . It is easier to find the energy to work hard because it looks as if the hard work will pay off.

*Confidence in one another: positive, supportive, team-oriented behavior.* Winning makes people feel more engaged with their tasks and with one another . . . people share information, take responsibility, and admit mistakes, pull together, and find solutions.

*Confidence in the system: organizational structures and routines, reinforcing accountability, collaboration, and innovation.* Winning makes it likely to turn informal tendencies into formal traditions, by building winners' habits or responsibility, teamwork, and initiative into routines, processes, and practices that encourage and perpetuate them.

*External confidence: A network to provide resources.* Winning makes it easier to attract financial backers, loyal customers, enthusiastic fans, talented recruits, media attention, opinion leader support, and political goodwill. (p. 29–30)

"The best pep talks," Kanter writes, "include evidence" (p. 40). The results that demonstrate how a school community is performing and what they have accomplished toward achieving the school's mission and goals are the kinds of evidence that school leaders should use when they are giving their students or staff members "pep talks." To achieve results, or to win, requires that all staff members believe they have the ability to win. School leaders need to help all staff members move from "praying to win, to hoping to win, to knowing they can win, to expecting to win" (p. 32). Ultimately, it is the "high expectations of self and others that make it possible for people to rise to the highest standards" (p. 33).

Winning, or actualizing the results that help you achieve your school goals, is fun! It is fun to see the results in student progress and to know that what you did helped your students learn. It is even more fun to collaborate with colleagues—analyzing, creating, implementing, and evaluating your work, and together learning that the strategies you put into place to help students achieve academic success worked. Working collegially with others to achieve your goals is not only fun, but creates a sense of belonging and interdependence.

Finally, there is an intense passion that builds among all staff members when they understand the mission and what it takes to accomplish the school's goals. Like a whirlwind that gains momentum as it churns up dust across the prairie, collegial learning communities gain momentum and synergy as the important work they do bears the fruits of their labor. When leaders are able to communicate the mission, providing a clear focus and purpose for the important work all staff members do, they empower their faculty and staff to take appropriate actions. The more information teachers have access to about what and how their students are learning, the more likely they will be to take responsibility and ownership for creating and engaging their students in personalized and precise learning activities that are focused on helping the students achieve. When leaders empower teachers to take responsibility for their work and grant them the authority to make informed, autonomous decisions about how best to help their students achieve the goals, watch out!

When working with teachers on action research projects, we have found that when teachers believe a strategy or program will work, it usually does. When teachers are given the responsibility, take the ownership for their decisions, and are held accountable for the results, they make it work. If the results are less than what they expected or predicted, teachers will tweak what they are doing until they get it right. We have seen action research projects where teachers weren't always successful to begin with and needed to refine what they were doing; but we have never seen an action research project in which the teachers failed, gave up, and walked away when they had resources, support, and ownership of the project.

Positive results beget positive results. It's contagious! Like marathon runners who cross the finish line, teachers achieve their own personal best when their students meet or exceed their high standards and expectations. The endorphins kick in, and teachers feel that "teacher high." There is nothing like it!

Ask a teacher!

## ■ STRUCTURING FOR RESULTS

In this chapter, we have primarily discussed positive results. But results can also be negative. In fact, even when we work hard and put forth our best effort, all educators will, at some point in their careers, face disappointing and even discouraging results. Fullan (2008) cautions that:

> The world has become so complex that no one individual or group can grasp or predict what might happen, because the number or interdependent factors at work and their ramifications are impossible to predict. . . . Perhaps the failure to do this is related to the emphasis on systems *thinking* rather than systems *doing*. (p. 110)

No matter how hard we try, however, we are still dealing with the "human factor." When dealing with people, there are many variables, which may cause a student to perform well or not well on any given day, on any given assessment. It could be as simple as "she just didn't feel like trying" to a difficult social or emotional issue (e.g., her father was arrested last night, his grandmother was taken to the hospital, his parents are getting a divorce, she is hungry, or her dog was hit by a car). The list of social and emotional issues can go on and on, illustrating why it is so important to triangulate the data and never rely on a single, solitary assessment to make high-stakes decisions.

All too often, when test scores are low, and students are not meeting or exceeding the established benchmarks and performance standards, the easy solution is for leaders to tell teachers and students to work harder, faster, and longer. We take away recess and electives, filling the void for students with more of the same—whether it be reading, writing, or mathematics, to the detriment of educating the whole child. Instead of working smarter, we work harder, faster, and longer, spiraling out of control, but going nowhere fast. We frustrate ourselves and our students, because we haven't transformed the results of the data into the knowledge and wisdom that informs instruction to create meaningful learning experiences for teachers and students.

In order to use results as a motivational strategy, school leaders and administrators need to get smarter about the data we collect. That is, only meaningful, usable data should be collected—data that is deemed essential for making informed decisions about teaching and learning. Otherwise educators will be buried in data, with rigor mortis setting in from a lethal case of analysis paralysis.

It is imperative that educators have time during the regularly scheduled day to collaborate and use formative and summative data (student results) to create meaningful and purposeful instruction that is personalized and precise. Many schools have actually established and are using data teams for the purpose of analyzing student data. Unfortunately many of these data teams spend so much time analyzing the data and creating beautiful charts and graphs for data walls and data fair exhibits for patrons that they run out of time before they get to use the data to plan and personalize instructional activities. After all, 24/7 is still a finite amount of time; we need to learn how to use it wisely.

Administrators need to realize that analyzing data is only the first step in using it to inform instruction. The beautiful pie, bar, and line graphs, that many schools now display on prominent bulletin boards, stop short of changing teacher behaviors or improving student learning in the classroom. In fact, all too often, the creation of these beautiful charts and graphs takes away from the valuable time that teachers could be using to plan and improve daily instruction. Given that there is a finite amount of teacher planning time each day, it makes sense that we let a central office secretary, teacher aide, or graduate school intern create the well-intentioned, beautiful charts for the data walls—or accept the hand-drawn scribbles as a working piece of art that uncover the secrets, the power, and potential to illuminate and transform student learning. Then educators can spend their time having quality conversations around the design, teaching, instruction, and student results derived from purposeful and well-crafted units, lessons, and learning activities.

We are hopeful that someday we will be able to take full advantage of technology to assess students accurately and generate reports quickly so that teachers are able to use data to inform instruction. This accurate and timely information will allow teachers to spend their time designing lessons and units that make a difference in student learning. This is akin to how doctors use lab and X-ray reports. Doctors do not draw the blood, run the tests, generate reports, and then treat the patient. Instead, they decide what tests need to be administered, send the patient off to get the tests, and then wait for the reports, which are usually turned around as quickly as possible so the doctor can determine the best treatment for the patient. Now that we are in the mode of "teach-test-teach-test," the field of education needs to develop and use a similar model. In this way, teachers, like doctors, will be free to spend their time working with their students (the patients), rather than administering, scoring, analyzing, and recording (including charting and graphing) the assessment data. Far too often, teachers burn out before they get to the important work of determining the treatment (intervention) to provide personalized and precise learning experiences for each student.

As we said, we are hopeful that someday teachers will be emancipated—able to spend their time turning the results from assessments into knowledge, and through dialogue and professional learning with colleagues, transform that knowledge into wisdom that helps close the gap and enables all students to achieve high standards. This is already beginning to happen. For example, The Northwest Evaluation Association (NWEA), a not-for-profit educational organization with over thirty years of experience measuring academic progress for millions of children, is already doing this for many schools and districts across America. Groups of students in grades K–12 sit at their computer for approximately one hour for each Measures of Academic Progress (MAP) Assessment (K–2 assessments are approximately twenty minutes each). The MAP computerized-adaptive leveled assessments are state-aligned. They provide accurate, useful information about student achievement and growth in the core subject areas of math, reading, language, and science. What is even more germane to us is that as soon as the student finishes the assessment, the student and teacher have a Rauch Unit, an equal-interval scale, or RIT, score. Within forty-eight hours, often sooner, the teacher has a class report. As soon as the testing window is closed, school administrators and teachers have access to a wide variety of reports, with data already disaggregated for them to use to inform instruction. The student scores are based on a RIT continuum. Like a ruler, comprised of equal units, the RIT scores measure student growth over time. They are not based on student age or grade level, so a third-grade student's RIT score of 201 has the same meaning as a fifth-grade student's score of 201. Teachers can then match student levels with the DesCartes continuum of learning (again aligned to state standards) to scaffold and personalize the instruction to precisely meet each student's needs. (For more information see www.nwea.org.)

NWEA's MAP Assessment is an example of a tool that is able to provide that breakthrough (using precision, personalization, and professional learning) that Fullan, Hill, and Crévola (2006) have suggested we need if we are going to be able to reform and improve education. Once teachers receive the results of the student assessments, they can spend their time working collegially as a learning community to use the results (data) along with the DesCartes learning continuum to plan instruction. Because the RIT scores are based on growth along the RIT continuum, collegial learning communities can begin to work together horizontally at the same grade level or subject area or vertically across grade levels or subjects, to plan, teach, and evaluate student academic performance. Most important, teachers are freed from scoring, analyzing, and identifying targeted needs of individuals or groups because the software has generated it for them in a timely manner. As we said, we are hopeful that in this age of accountability and high-stakes testing, this type of assessment may become the norm, not the exception. When this happens, teachers and students will have specific, immediate, and accurate information to guide their learning. This use of knowledge of results is a very powerful motivator!

To structure the use of results as a motivational strategy that teachers will use to improve the teaching and learning process and help the school to achieve its mission, school leaders must begin by making sure that the other nine motivational strategies, which also serve as essential conditions, are established and firmly in place. We believe that the more these strategies are embedded within the school culture, the more likely the school community will be working at levels of optimal performance, and the more likely that collegial learning communities will be able to achieve their desired results.

To begin school administrators must create the quality of life within the school setting that ensures that all members of the school community have their basic needs met, along with creating a risk-taking culture that supports teacher collaboration. School leaders must create a shared, morally compelling mission, which includes the vision and goals and takes into account beliefs, values, and assumptions. Most important, school leaders must clearly articulate the shared mission, making sure that all members within the school community understand the mission, agree with the goals, and are willing to share the responsibility for accomplishing the mission. Communication must be honest, open, and reciprocal, with information transparent so that everyone can make informed, professional decisions that impact their daily work. Everyone within the school community must feel as if his or her ideas are listened to and valued. School leaders must work to help build the relationships and interdependence that will support collegial learning communities. Administrators must empower their faculty and staff and afford them the latitude to make autonomous decisions within well-crafted boundaries and frameworks, and then get out of their way and allow the faculty and staff to do their work. School leaders must hold themselves and their collegial learning community accountable for achieving the school's goals and accomplishing the school's mission.

We are not going to go into great detail here about how to structure each of the essential conditions mentioned above. These are each well defined and developed within this book. We would, however, stress that school leaders pay close attention to the continuous improvement cycle in Chapter 7 and the knowledge-wisdom-action (KWA) helix in this chapter. Most schools move through the phases of a school improvement cycle as part of their overall district accountability and school/district improvement process. We encourage school leaders to make sure that their process uses all of the phases of the continuous improvement cycle we presented as they move through the goal-setting phase, to the implementation phases, to the evaluation phases, and begin again. Even though it appears to have a cyclical order, it is normal to be in several phases at once, often moving backwards or skipping forward, rather than traveling through the cycle in a set order. We would also encourage collegial learning communities to use the KWA helix during meetings to study data and transform the information into knowledge and wisdom that can be used to determine precisely what all students need to know and be able to do. Teachers can then work together to design personalized instruction that helps close the gap and ensures all students successfully achieve high standards. What is important about both processes is that they complement each other and are cyclical—meaning that they are not one-time events. Instead, these two cycles (the continuous improvement cycle and the KWA helix) must be an integral part of your school's morally compelling mission—that is, the important work you do.

As we have said before, "The mission is the work, and the work is the mission." To be successful, you have to live it. The same is true of results. You can't look at them and put them away. School leaders need to keep the results in front of their faculty and staff, making sure that the teaching and learning taking place each day, in all classrooms and for all students, is intentionally crafted and designed to ensure all students achieve high expectations and standards.

All schools have results, whether or not they purposefully collect the data or recognize the value of the data that is available to them. This data ranges from student record data (e.g., attendance, discipline, grades, health, drop-out rates) to student assessment data (e.g., formative assessments, summative assessments, statewide assessments, common assessments). Likewise, administrators have access to teacher record data (e.g., attendance, salary schedule, university transcripts and professional development units) and to teacher classroom data (e.g, observation reports, evaluations, student data).

The most difficult responsibility of a school leader is deciding what data are important to collect, when to share the data, with whom they need to share the data, and most important, what actions they need to take to use the data to help them accomplish their mission.

In his book, *Good to Great*, Jim Collins (2001) writes:

> First Who . . . Then What. We expect that good-to-great leaders would begin by setting a new vision and strategy. We found instead that they first got the right people on the bus, the wrong people off the bus, and the right people in the right seats—and then they figured out where to drive it. The old adage "People are your most important asset" turns out to be wrong. People are not your most important asset. The *right* people are. (p. 13)

Once school leaders have determined whom the *right people* are to do the work, they need to determine what the *right work* is. As Marzano, Waters, and McNulty (2005) write:

> The downfall of low-performing schools is not their lack of effort and motivation; rather, it is poor decisions regarding what to work on. So the problem in low-performing schools is not getting people to work, it is getting people to do the "right work." (p. 76)

The way that school leaders help their collegial learning community decide on the right work is by analyzing the data to determine where you are and where you want to go, and then figuring out what the right work is (the actions) that are necessary to close that gap. This process becomes the KWA helix, which helps collegial teams (the right people) to determine their actions (the right work).

Once the *right people* are on board, doing the *right work*, it is up to the school leader to make sure that the people doing the right work have the *right stuff*. We define the *right stuff* as the quality of life. That is, access to all of the resources (e.g., time, including job embedded collaboration time; professional learning; access to information and data; technology; money); materials (e.g., curriculum frameworks, programs, books, software); and support (e.g., administration, outside consultations, central office support, volunteers or teacher assistants). It isn't enough to get the *right people* in place and decide upon the *right work*. Educators need to have the resources, materials, and support they need to do the *stuff right*.

In his book, *Good To Great*, Collins (2001) also writes about the importance of a "culture of discipline." He says:

> When you have disciplined people, you don't need a hierarchy. When you have disciplined thought, you don't need a bureaucracy. When you have disciplined action, you don't need excessive controls. When you combine a culture of discipline with an ethic of entrepreneurship, you get the magical alchemy of great performance. (p. 13)

When school leaders have implemented the essential conditions that enable collegial learning communities to work at levels of optimal performance, totally committed to the school's mission, and focused on achieving their goals, we contend that the faculty and staff will be working in a "culture of discipline."

There are two other strategies that will help school leaders take the positive results that their school community is actualizing and build upon those results to achieve greater gains. They are appreciative inquiry and amplifying positive deviants. Briefly we will explain each. For further information, see the resource list in Appendix B.

## ■ APPRECIATIVE INQUIRY

Most often, when leaders and managers embark on the change process, they begin by identifying the problem (what's wrong), decide on a solution, and implement it. The emphasis is on what is wrong—the problems—rather than what is right and working.

Appreciative inquiry is a process that was coined and developed in the mid-eighties by David Cooperrider and his associates at Case Western Reserve University (as cited in Hammond, 1998, p. 6). Instead of looking at what is wrong, appreciative inquiry begins by looking at what is working well for the organization and finds ways to capitalize on the organization's strengths. When members of an organization (or school community) focus on the positive results and what they are doing to achieve them, there is a sense of commitment, affirmation, confidence, and synergy that emerges from the group. Hammond writes, "It is the energy that distinguishes the generative process that results from Appreciative Inquiry. There is no end, because it is a living process. Because the statements generated by the participants are grounded in real experience and history, people know how to repeat their success" (p. 7–8).

Using appreciative inquiry provides school communities with hope and optimism, because it builds on what they are already doing successfully, and helps the school community envision what they can do in the future to achieve even greater gains and successes. It gives people the ability to dream about future possibilities rather than focusing on the problems, the causes, and the solutions.

Appreciative inquiry is a course of system self-study, with the most critical step being what topic to select to study (Hammond, 1998, p. 32). Once the topic is selected, appreciative inquiry uses a "4-D" cycle to approach the course of study: "Discovery—Appreciate what is; Dream—Imagine what might be; Design—Determine what should be; and Destiny—Create what will be" (Whitney & Trosten-Bloom, 2003, p. 6).

After deciding on the topic, members of the study group or team generate questions to explore the topic. For example, if a collegial learning community wanted to know why 95 percent of their students were able to solve word problems, while only 45 percent were able to estimate solutions to word problems, they might ask the teachers in their school questions like: How much time do your students spend solving word problems? What strategies do you teach your students to use when they solve word problems? What strategies do you use to teach your students to estimate word problems?

Once the group identifies the questions they will ask, and whom they are going to ask, they begin interviewing those people and recording their answers. The information is collected and shared among the group. The group uses the information to determine themes (e.g., strategies that teachers are using, or not using, to help students solve and estimate word problems; amount of time spent on each). By sharing the responses, the group will be able to identify common threads of success. This may happen based on successful strategies that teachers share or from a form of analysis, such as comparing and contrasting the difference between the amount of time spent on solving problems versus estimating. Teachers may find, for example, that few of them have students estimate the word problems (make a predication as to what the answer will be) before they solve the problem. Once the group creates a list of what teachers are doing to help students get better at estimating word problems, they create a "provocative proposition," which Hammond (1998) says, "describes an ideal state of circumstances that will foster the climate that creates the possibilities to do more of what works" (p. 39). In this, case it would be to help students estimate more accurately before they solve word problems.

---

To write a provocative proposition, the group needs to:

1. Find examples of the best (from the interviews).

2. Determine what circumstances made the best possible (in detail).

3. Take the stories and envision what might be.

4. Write an affirmative statement (a provocative proposition) that describes the idealized future as if it were already happening.

The next step is to write a provocative statement. A provocative statement is one in which the group takes something they know and describes what it could be. A provocative proposition for the math example we are using might be: (a) *We always have our students estimate their answers before they solve word problems, or (b) Students evaluate how closely they were able to estimate the correct answer.* Teachers then use the provocative statement and the strategies they uncovered as an intervention strategy to inform instruction.

This process is great for building synergy and commitment. But the only way that this happens is when the entire group responsible for doing the work shares in the appreciative inquiry process. Thus, it takes time for the group to do this work. Hammond writes, "I find that once people become excited about the process through the questions, they make the time to have the group discussion. . . . Appreciative inquiry touches something important and positive and people respond" (p. 47).

## ■ AMPLIFYING POSITIVE DEVIANTS

The positive deviant model for professional development is based on the work by Jerry Sternin (as cited in Sparks, 2004). "Positive Deviants are people whose behavior and practices produce solutions to problems that others in the group who have access to exactly the same resources have not been able to solve" (p. 46–51). Sternin believes that it is important to identify these people because "they provide demonstrable evidence that solutions to the problem already exist within the community" (as cited in Sparks, 2005a, p. 186).

The basic premise of this model is that people learn best when they discover the solutions that help them solve their problems by themselves rather than by being told what to do from an outside source. When teachers have the opportunities to dialogue with each other about instructional strategies, observe each other teaching lessons, or analyze student work, they learn with and from each other. That is what makes this such a positive and powerful professional learning model.

In all schools, there are teachers who are able to help students achieve greater gains than their colleagues next door. Using the six steps of the positive deviants model, teachers will be able to find solutions to helping their students achieve even better results from within the system. Teachers will also be more receptive to the ideas of change and less likely to sabotage or resist any new change efforts. The six steps of the process are: define, determine, discover, design, discern, and disseminate (Sparks, 2005a, p. 186). Sternin explains the model this way:

> The group begins its work by defining the problem and describing what success would look like—which is the inverse of the problem statement. . . . Next the group determines if there are individuals who have already achieved success. If there are such people, they are the positive deviants. Next the group discovers the uncommon but demonstrably successful behaviors and practices used by the positive deviants to solve the problem. And finally, the group designs an intervention, which enables its members to practice

those demonstrably successful but uncommonly applied practices. The process is beautifully simple because its strength lies in the solutions that are discovered and owned by the people in the community. (p. 49)

Once the intervention is in place, the teachers involved will discern the effectiveness of the strategy or innovation. Once they have determined that it works effectively and produces the desired results, they can disseminate it to others.

"Positive Deviance inquires into what's working and how it can be built upon to solve very difficult problems," Sternin says (as cited in Sparks, 2004, p. 51). "It requires that experts relinquish their power and believe that solutions already reside within the system. Our role is to help people discover their answers" (p. 51).

When collegial learning communities invest time and effort in working together to achieve results, there is a great deal they can learn from each other. These key learnings can be as simple as a graphic organizer that one teacher is using to help his students organize their thoughts before they write an expository essay. When other teachers see that students are able to organize their writing because of this graphic organizer, they, too, will want to use the graphic organizer with their students to help them improve their writing.

The positive deviant model doesn't have to be an extraordinary feat. In fact, when given the time to observe each other's teaching, engage in quality conversations about teaching and learning, analyze student work together, and design interventions to help their students achieve even greater results, we contend that most teachers will be able to share in the reciprocity of a positive deviant relationship. They will be able to serve as both a giver and receiver of knowledge and skills that work within their own school context and unique situations.

## QUESTIONS FOR DISCUSSION

1. In the case study at the beginning of this chapter, it is obvious that Janice Robbins and her teachers have a great deal of work to do if they are going to be able to get their kindergarten DRA results back to the levels they have been in previous years. What essential conditions are present in the case study that will be able to help the teachers achieve results? What essential conditions may be missing?

2. If you were Janice, how might you help the teachers use the information they have about their unique school culture and context to design an intervention that will help all kindergarten students achieve the district DRA benchmarks?

## ESSENTIAL CONDITIONS

There are several essential conditions that are not being met in the above situation. Read along and see if you agree.

1. **Quality of life.** The fact that Janice begins her day at a climate committee meeting, in which teachers are empowered to share the responsibility for making decisions about a baby shower and Read Across America Day, suggests that, at the very least, there is a conscious effort from Janice to create the quality of life we describe. We saw no evidence to suggest otherwise.

2. **Communication.** Janice appears to listen to her teachers' ideas and concerns. She appears to be open to suggestions from them. The fact that she tells the superintendent that "We'll put our heads together to figure something out," means that she respects her teachers and is willing to share information with them so that they can help her make decisions and design an intervention.

3. **Mission.** It appears that the kindergarten, literacy, and special education teachers are working together to achieve the district benchmark goals. In fact, a meeting has been set with Anton's parents, the kindergarten teacher, principal, school psychologist, and literacy teacher to discuss what they can do to help Anton with his reading. Everyone appears to be working on the same page.

4. **Relationships and interdependence.** Although it is not explicitly stated, the teachers appear to be working together in several different capacities: committees such as climate, grade-level teams, and ad hoc response to intervention (RTI). There appears to be some positive interdependence because the teachers are willing to meet and work together.

5. **Empowerment and autonomy.** Janice clearly appreciates her young staff's creative ideas and suggestions. She appears to be willing to grant them the responsibility and authority to make autonomous decisions about the work they are doing.

6. **Accountability.** There appears to be a strong accountability system in place, not only at a school level, but also at a district level. The accountability system is data-driven, with test scores being analyzed and teachers and administrators being held accountable for results. Because DRA scores were collected in February and will be collected again in May, there appears to be a detailed plan and timeline in place for collecting formative and summative student assessment data.

7. **Feedback and knowledge of results.** Although not what she wanted to know or hear, Janice did, in fact, receive specific, immediate, and accurate feedback as well as gain the knowledge about how her kindergarten students scored compared to other students across her district. In addition, the feedback and results were timely, providing Janice and her staff with the opportunity to take action before the next round of DRA assessments begin.

8. **Competence.** Because the students are not making gains, it would appear that teachers may need to learn additional strategies to help their students achieve the district benchmarks. The fact that this is the first time their students have scored this low may mean that other factors are contributing to student performance, and teachers may need additional knowledge and skills to be able solve the situation. Or they may simply

need time to collaborate with each other to discover what they can do to personalize instruction, targeting specific and precise interventions for each child in order to achieve the desired results. In addition teachers may need time to study what is working and not working in order to build upon their current results.

9. **Rituals and celebrations.** It is difficult to say if teachers are recognized, appreciated, and their results are celebrated because in this case study the results are negative.

10. **Clear focus, concern for excellence, and high expectations.** Even before the news about how well the students would score against others in the district, there was a clear focus on how to help the students achieve the district benchmarks. It simply became heightened with the news that the percentage of students meeting or exceeding the district benchmark was lower than at any other school in the district.

11. **Hope and confidence.** It appears that the teachers and even the principal are beginning to blame the low scores on the fact that they have more young boys than they have had in previous years. It is unclear, but also highly likely, that they are losing confidence in their ability to achieve the high standards and benchmarks that they have achieved in the past.

## WHAT WOULD YOU DO?

1. After reading the above discussion about the essential conditions that need to be in place to help teachers recognize, celebrate, and refine their results, do you agree? Is there anything else that you would add?

2. Before you read the rest of the story, look back at what you said you would do if you were Janice Robbins. Is there anything else you would add to your list?

Read on to compare your list with what Janice actually chose to do.

## AND NOW FOR THE REST OF THE STORY

*"Stop biting your fingernails!" Janice could hear her mother's voice as she stared out her office window, watching as Cheryl Hamel, her literacy teacher, got out of her car after attending the weekly literacy teacher meeting. Janice knew that this was the meeting when all the literacy teachers would deliver their May DRA scores to central office. She couldn't wait to hear how her kindergarten students compared with the district. The stakes were high!*

*Janice couldn't tell from the way Cheryl was walking how Bartlett's kindergarten DRA scores had stacked up against the rest of the schools in the district, especially Willowbrook. But if their scores weren't good, it wouldn't be because the teachers at Bartlett didn't try. Janice knew that her entire kindergarten grade-level team, along with her literacy teacher, intern, special ed teachers, and the students' parents, had all done everything they could to help the kindergarten students learn to read.*

*As Janice waited for Cheryl to walk across the parking lot, she saw the last several months of the school year quickly flash before her eyes. Janice would never forget how devastated the entire kindergarten grade-level team had been to realize that the percentage of students who met the district benchmark at Bartlett was lower than at Willowbrook—not to mention every other school in the city. The teachers had all been clearly upset, with the school's reputation on the line, as well as their own.*

*Janice remembered the weekly afterschool, grade-level team meeting, when all eight kindergarten teachers and the special ed teachers met in the conference room with Cheryl, the literacy intern, and Janice to talk about the student scores and what they could do to help all of the students reach the district benchmark by May.*

*The meeting had begun with Janice sharing what happened at the elementary principal's meeting. She had tried to soften it, but the entire teaching team was devastated. At first the teachers had talked about the fact that they all knew that the students were lower than other groups of students they had taught in previous years. They all realized that the group, as a whole, was younger, because of all the late birthdays. They also realized that there were twice as many boys as there were girls in the kindergarten this year. And, even though all of these factors shouldn't make a difference, the reality is that they did.*

*"But," Janice had been quick to remind the teachers, "every other school has extenuating circumstances, too. Just ask them. We can sit around and blame our low scores on 'the boys' or 'their birthdays' or 'their parents' or 'the fact that they have blue eyes instead of brown eyes.' None of that matters," she remembered saying, and she meant it.*

*"What matters is that the district has set a bar that until now we have not had trouble helping our students get over. This year shouldn't be any different, but it is." Janice looked at them, and she could see that her young staff members were blaming themselves.*

*"You can't take this personally, and you can't blame yourselves," she had said. "I have been in your classes, I have heard your conversations, and I know that you are all doing everything you can, every single day, to help these children. Like they were your own!" She said with emphasis, then stopped and smiled. "No matter what, I want you to know how much I appreciate everything you have done to help your kids. I know their parents feel the same way, too."*

*"That is, until they realize that Willowbrook kids scored better than their own children did on the DRA," Rene Baldwin had said. She always seemed to take things more personally than the other kindergarten teachers.*

*"Yeah, but remember, Willowbrook kids are getting a full day of kindergarten. Our kids are getting a half day," Cheryl said.*

*"That is true, and there isn't anything we can do about that either," Janice reminded them. "Mr. Norton pulled me aside after the elementary principal's meeting. He said he had some money, not a lot of money, but some. If we came up with a plan that we felt would really make a difference for our students to help them learn how to read and reach the benchmarks, he would give us the money to carry out our plan," she said. Janice looked at their glazed-over faces and knew how hard they were already working.*

*"What more can we do?" asked Pam Conroy. "Our day is so short already, and we have so much that we have to teach."*

*"You're right," Janice said. "I don't know how we can pack any more into the kindergarten day and the curriculum than we already have. The kids are on overload already," she said, then added, "and that may be part of the problem, especially with some of the younger ones. But our students in previous years have done better than this. I don't know what the difference is, and we can't spend a lot of time on that. It doesn't matter, so let's not play 'the blame game.' What we need to figure out is—what can we do to get the most bang for our buck?" Janice asked the group.*

*"The more children read, the better readers they become," Carla Senger said, remembering what she had learned in one of her undergraduate courses.*

*(Continued)*

(Continued)

"So, how can we help our students read more?" asked Belinda Carlson. "We already have the schoolwide reader's club, where minutes count."

"That may be part of the problem," Rene said. "Many of our parents are not reading to our kids or listening to them read. If they are, they aren't logging the minutes and sending them to school so we know."

"So, what we need to do is get our parents more involved," suggested Carla.

"But how?" asked Belinda.

"We could do a literacy night and talk with the parents about what we need them to do," suggested Pam.

"Last time we only got fifteen parents to come back to our school for the first-grade literacy night in the fall. Our parents just never come back at night," said Cheryl, remembering how frustrated the first-grade teachers always were each fall when they tried to get parents to come and learn about what first-grade students needed to know and be able to do by the end of the year.

"What can we do to get the parents to attend a literacy night? Because, you're right," Janice heard herself saying. "If we could just get parents to listen to their children read an extra twenty–thirty minutes each night, think of the difference that would make."

"I agree, but how do we get them to come back to school so we can talk with them about helping their child be a better reader?" Cheryl asked. "We don't have a very good track record for getting parents to attend literacy nights."

"Well, we have a lot of our parents who are involved with the PTA and with other activities at our school. What is it that is different? Why do they attend some activities and not our literacy nights?" Janice had asked.

"Because they are fun," Pam said.

"Because they can bring their kids," Rene added.

"Bingo!" Janice said.

"Bingo?" They all had asked at once.

"They come to play Bingo. Why? Because it is fun. Because there are prizes. And, because they can bring their kids. It is a family night out!" laughed Janice.

"So, what are you thinking?" asked Cheryl. "That we play Bingo?"

"No," laughed Janice. "But what if we did a literacy night, where parents bring their kids . . ."

"Yes, kind of like a family math night," Carla sparked, remembering how she had attended such a night at her own children's school and learned how to play games that helped her children practice math skills.

"Yes, and we could make it fun, with games, and prizes . . ." laughed Pam.

"And, we could make it into a 'make-and-take' type night, where parents and kids make games that they can play at home. Then everyone gets a prize to take with them," suggested Rene.

"And, we could even model for parents how to help their children retell stories and how to ask comprehension questions when they are listening to them read," suggested Megan Thompson, the literacy intern, who was getting excited, along with everyone else, about the possibilities.

"What if we gave the parents homework assignments and held them accountable for listening to their child read for twenty minutes every day?" asked Belinda.

"Then we could begin each session by asking parents what worked, and what they needed more help with," suggested Pam.

Janice had remembered being so excited listening to the teachers talk about how they would design the kindergarten family literacy nights. Their tone of being failures had quickly changed to one of hope. By the time they left that grade-level team meeting, they had decided to hold the literacy nights every Wednesday in March, from 6:30 P.M. to 7:30 P.M. They had all agreed to be responsible for several games, strategies, or management pieces. For example, Pam had volunteered to work with the PTA hospitality coordinator to provide snacks. Carla, Belinda, and Megan had volunteered to put together at least one reading game for each of the four weeks that parents could "make-and-take" *to play at home. Cheryl and several teachers used Lexile scores and DRA levels to identify and personalize a reading list that was specifically targeted for each child. Each week, the parents would get a bag with several books they could use to practice the reading strategies that teachers would model for parents during the family literacy nights.*

*Janice had volunteered to plan reading activities for the kindergarten children that she and the special education teachers would play with the children in the gym while the kindergarten teachers talked with parents and answered questions during the first twenty minutes of each session.*

*Janice remembered how skeptical Mr. Norton, the superintendent, had been when she told him about her plan. She told him that they didn't need the money because they had some grant funds they could use. Janice remembered Mr. Norton saying something like, "I thought the schools have done literacy nights before. What makes you think this will work?"*

*Janice tried to sound confident as she explained to him that, "We are making it fun, and we are having the parents bring their children to the sessions. We are giving them homework, and we hope the extra practice pays off. We believe that parents are their children's best teachers, and we want to capitalize on that," she remembered saying, sounding more confident than she really felt—truth be told.*

*"We'll see about that."*

*Janice would never forget Mr. Norton's comment. The only thing that was keeping her sane at that moment, as she waited for Cheryl's report from the literacy teacher's meeting, was that Janice knew how much the parents and kindergarten children had loved each of those weekly sessions in March. Janice, along with all of her kindergarten teachers, had attended each session. At the end of every night, Janice left feeling exhausted—like Arnold Schwarzenegger in* Kindergarten Cop.

*But Janice had only to remember watching as the parents and students made games to take home. Or think about the comments during the weeks following the sessions from the children and especially the parents. They had talked about what they were learning and how much fun they were having listening to their children read. It made it all worthwhile!*

*Now, they were at the day of reckoning! Just then, Cheryl walked into the office. Janice turned around and tried to read the expression on her face. Was it good news or bad? "How did it go?" Janice asked Cheryl.*

*"It was okay," Cheryl said, careful not to reveal anything.*

*"Well, did you analyze the DRA scores, like you usually do?" Janice asked.*

*"Yeah, it was a typical work session. All of the literacy teachers had their data, and Brenda gave us highlighters. We went through and color-coded each group."*

*"How did we do?" Janice asked, trying desperately to draw the information out of Cheryl, but it was like squeezing juice out of a raisin.*

*"The good news is," she stopped.*

*"Yes? Tell me," Janice asked, crossing her fingers.*

*"Out of all 156 students, we don't have anybody in the substantially deficient group. All of our students were reading at a level 4 or above!" Cheryl was clearly excited by this news, as was Janice as soon as she heard it.*

*"That is—wow! Who would have guessed?" Janice said, then quickly added, "But how did we do next to the other schools? Did you get to see?" Janice asked.*

*"Not officially," Cheryl said.*

*Janice's demeanor began to shrink back to normal. "What do you mean?" she asked.*

*"I just sat there, doing my own color-coding and not really talking to anybody. I was afraid to, because I didn't want to hear what they had to say once I told them we didn't have anyone below a level 4. So, I just kept quiet and listened," Cheryl said.*

*"And . . . ?" Janice asked.*

*"They all started bragging about how many students had met the district benchmarks. I started keeping track in my head. Nobody asked me, but. . . ."*

*(Continued)*

(Continued)

*"Tell me," Janice was almost shouting.*

*"We," Cheryl said, then stopped, "did it! Our students are number one!"*

*With that, Cheryl and Janice started dancing around the office, hugging each other, laughing and shouting together, "We did it! We did it!"*

*"But you knew we had to," Cheryl said, "when none of our Kindergarten students were substantially deficient." Then she sobered, stopped dancing, and looked Janice in the eye. "What if they don't believe us? What if they think we made this up?"*

*"Then let them come test our kids," Janice said. "There is not a doubt in my mind. I know how hard you all were working before. I know how hard you worked after we learned that we were at the bottom of the heap. I have talked to the parents and I know how much they enjoyed the March family literacy nights, and I have listened to our kindergarten kids read to me when I visit the classrooms." Janice stopped. "Bring them on," she said confidently. "This is the best news I have heard in a long time!" she said, as she smiled at Cheryl.*

*"You have to tell the kindergarten teachers!" Janice said. "They are going to want to know. They all feel so badly, and they have all worked so hard to make up for the fact that the children were so far behind. I keep telling them it wasn't their fault, but they just wouldn't listen. They have taken it so personally. We have to tell them. How should we do it?" Janice asked, then added, "I know, let's go get a cake. We can take it down to their classrooms right after school."*

*"Got it covered," Cheryl laughed. "It's in my car. If you go get the plates and a knife, I will get the cake. Meet you in the kindergarten wing," Cheryl said.*

*Cheryl hugged Janice. "Thanks for your support," Cheryl said.*

*"What do you mean, I owe everything we accomplished to all of you," Janice said, then stepped back, looked Cheryl in the eye, and said, "Thanks for everything!" and then added, "Let's eat cake!"*

## CHAPTER SUMMARY

We define *results* as *the achievement of the school's morally compelling mission and goals, as defined by a predetermined set of indicators of success and desired outcomes, stemming from the decisions, behaviors, actions, and accomplishments of a collegial learning community.*

In order to help their school community build upon the results that the school has already achieved, we suggested that school leaders use a continuous improvement cycle. Analysis of data (results) is only the first step. Creating beautiful charts and graphs may look nice, but doesn't change teacher behavior or student learning. Given the finite amount of time, school administrators would be better served by having others create data walls and allow teachers the time to work together to use the data to inform instruction.

If we are to achieve the breakthrough in education that allows us to close the gap and help all students successfully achieve the clearly defined expectations and standards, teachers must: *personalize instruction* for all students; become more *precise*, by using data that provides a laser-like focus to target individual student needs; and engage in *professional learning* opportunities to build complexity and capacity (Fullan, Hill, & Crévola, 2006). This professional learning must be customized, just-in-time, job-embedded, and everyday.

To do this, we suggest that collegial learning communities use the knowledge-wisdom-action (KWA) helix. The process begins with school leaders who must coordinate the effort by bringing together *the right people* to do the *right work* and then provide them with the *right stuff.*

These collegial learning communities would then use the KWA helix to transform data from information to knowledge and wisdom and then determine precisely what individual or groups of students need to accomplish to achieve their precise, personalized learning goals. In addition, teachers work together to design and deliver quality instruction that helps students attain the learning goals. At regularly scheduled intervals, teachers must take time to individually and collectively reflect upon and evaluate their own performance in relation to the new results (data-information-knowledge-wisdom-results) about student achievement. They then use this new knowledge of results to measure their progress toward accomplishing the school's mission and goals and to plan for further action. At the end of each spiral, teachers must pause to celebrate their successes. Once this is done, the collegial learning community reflects upon and refines their actions before working toward achieving even higher expectations and standards as they progress through the next spiral of the helix.

So often in education, we tend to focus on the negative numbers, looking for solutions to our failures in remediation rather than focusing on the positive results and finding answers from our strengths. We described two methods that school leaders can use to help teachers build upon their positive results—appreciative inquiry and amplifying positive deviants.

It is up to school leaders to help teachers build their confidence and self-efficacy. Leaders can do this by helping teachers focus on their successes, finding ways to expand and replicate what works well within their own unique context and situation.

"Winning begets winning" (Kanter, 2004, p. 29). All of us will try harder and persevere longer, even under pressure, if we believe we have the competence and capacity to achieve the goal and when we can see that what we are doing is making a difference. Collegial learning communities are more likely to achieve levels of optimal performance and accomplish their morally compelling missions when the focus is on results.

## NEXT STEPS

1. Now that you have had a chance to read the chapter on results, take a few minutes to think about what results look like, sound like, and feel like in your own school. Make a list. Put a star by those things that are already in place in your school or system. Put a check by those things that you would like to implement or explore further.

2. If possible, discuss with others what you found interesting about this discussion on results and what you found challenging.

3. Select one or two ideas that you checked above. Using the chart below, list several strategies or changes that you can make to improve the targeted use of results within your current situation.

4. Think about the barriers that may get in your way and list choices you can make to help alleviate or decrease those barriers in the chart above.

5. Decide on one or two ideas that you would like to try in your current situation. List them along with any notes to help you remember what you want to do.

# 13

# A Call for Action

*What if . . . the classroom, school, or district where you work was the one place you couldn't wait to get to each morning and the hardest place to leave at the end of the day?*

We began this book describing the reasons that teachers and school administrators find it difficult to wake up each morning and drag themselves off to work. It is depressing, frustrating, and difficult for us to go back and read. Yet, in far too many schools, it is a reality—one we hope to change!

As we noted at the beginning of this book, the "fear factor" doesn't work. Instead, as we explained, school leaders need to create the conditions to lead, inspire, encourage, motivate, and support their staff members so they *want* to do the work and accomplish their shared mission. We described ten motivational strategies that, when embedded within a school culture, have the potential of creating collegial learning communities that perform at optimal levels. In each chapter, we also presented a case study with one solution that worked for that unique situation. There are, however, many other steps and activities that each principal could have chosen to implement in order to create the essential conditions that would also have inspired and intrinsically motivated his or her staff. Each school context is different, even for schools within the same district. What works in one school may or may not inspire and motivate a different school staff to work together to achieve their mission. That is why it is so important that school leaders understand their unique context and know the people with whom they work.

Csikszentmihalyi's (1997) *flow*, that "sense of effortless action" a person feels "in moments that stand out as the best in their lives," (p. 29) is similar to *self-actualization, peak performance, getting your groove, living in the zone, aesthetic rapture,* and *finding your voice.* In other words, these terms represent individuals enthralled in an activity in which they effortlessly actualize and perform to their highest potential to achieve desired results.

We define *optimal performance* as the state in which *individuals within the school community are enthralled in complex, job-embedded educational work and learning experiences that serve a greater purpose; have a clear and specific focus; provide knowledge and feedback about the results of educator effort; intrinsically captivate educator attention; are balanced between the challenge of the activity and the knowledge and skill of the individual; and clearly make a difference in helping all students achieve personalized and collective learning goals.* Optimal performance consists of a stream of flow-like experiences within a school setting that empower interdependent, high-performing collegial learning communities to collaboratively and successfully accomplish their shared, morally compelling mission (work).

As leaders, if we want the educators within our schools to achieve optimal performance, it makes sense that we discover ways to create the conditions that afford our teachers the ability to perform at their highest levels as frequently as possible. To do this, we, as leaders, must be explicit and direct about creating and implementing the conditions to energize, motivate, inspire, and lead others in this age of the knowledge worker.

The time has come to recognize, respect, and utilize the knowledge and skills of all educators. We must retire the industrial age carrot-and-stick management strategies used to control the work of our teachers and students. As school leaders, we must inspire and empower educators, as we tap into their creativity, talent, and expertise. Most important, we must create the conditions that allow us to recognize and release the potential of all educators and create high-performing collegial learning communities.

As we explained earlier in this book, motivation is tricky. What works one time, may not work the next. What works for one person or group of people, may not work for others. What one person needs or wants, such as freedom to make professional decisions (autonomy), may not be what another person wants or needs. One size fits no one! School leaders must build relationships with each staff member by getting to know them well enough that they can personalize activities that will inspire, energize, motivate, and support each individual.

School leaders must embed the essential conditions described for each motivational strategy if they are to successfully build and sustain a collegial learning community that accomplishes the school's mission and achieves optimal levels of performance. Although the essential conditions remain the same, school leaders will need to purposefully select from a variety of activities and techniques to successfully implement the essential conditions. The activities and techniques leaders use will be dependent upon the unique context and culture of their schools and the individual needs of each member of their school communities.

## ■ A CALL FOR ACTION

Learning means nothing until you do something with it. As we stated in the results chapter (Chapter 12), a common perception is that the result is the end of the process. We believe, however, that results are the bridge we need to cross that takes us from what is, or what we have accomplished, to what could be, or where we want to go. Results are not the end point, but the transition point that informs a change in behavior that transforms teaching and learning. We hope that as you read this final chapter, you take time to reflect upon your own school's unique culture, climate, and community, and subsequently discover what you have already accomplished. Then, we encourage you to use what you have learned about the ten motivational strategies, from reading this book and from the numerous conversations we hope you had with others, to build upon the elements that are already working well.

We end this book by asking you, the reader, to step up to the plate, and accept our *call for action*. For, clearly, there is a lot of work to do to improve the quality of life within school organizations, to inspire those we wish to lead by creating the conditions that will motivate *all* of the school community, certified and noncertified, to put forth their greatest effort and achieve optimal levels of performance. At no other time in the history of education have the stakes been so high, the diversity so great, or the gaps so wide.

In many schools, the work has already begun. School leaders are building professional learning communities. But as we have stated throughout this book, just because school leaders provide opportunities for teachers to collaborate doesn't mean that they are able to move from congeniality to collegiality or from the forming stage to the performing stages of group development. For *professional learning communities* to become *collegial learning communities,* we must create the conditions in which educators *hold themselves and each other accountable for working together to achieve their shared, morally compelling school's mission through positive interdependence, reciprocal relationships, shared decision making, professional learning, and mutual responsibility.* We must build the competence, confidence, and capacity that afford educators the ability to close the gap by collectively using their knowledge, skills, and talents to perform at optimal levels and successfully accomplish their mission.

We have a lot of work to do. None of us is as smart as all of us. But *together, we can!*

## ■ NEW BEGINNINGS

Throughout this book, we have asked you to consider what your classroom, school, or district could look like, sound like, or feel like, in relation to each of the ten motivational strategies of our optimal performance model. We hope that as you read this book, you made notes about the essential conditions that you already have in place in your classroom, school, or district, and those essential conditions and other ideas you have gleaned from this book that you would like to integrate into your current situation. We encourage you to go back and look at your notes and refresh your memory about what you said you want to keep in place, and those things you identified that you want to change in your current situation.

## Change Begins With You

As you look back through your notes, identify something that you said you wanted to change after reading the chapters. You may decide to tackle something like one of our principals from the case studies, or you might try something totally different. *Remember, you can't change other people unless they want to change. But you can change yourself.* That is why we suggest that you begin this process by changing something within yourself.

## Take Care of Yourself First

As we noted earlier, as a school leader, you must remember to take care of yourself first, so that you have the strength to lead others. As flight attendants remind passengers at the beginning of each flight, make sure the adults you work with "put their own oxygen masks on first" before they help their students. Maslow's (1998) hierarchy begins with satisfying a person's basic needs before they can move up the pyramid to self-actualization. If we want our teachers to be able to work at optimal levels of performance and achieve the morally compelling mission, we must provide them with the quality of life that ensures their basic needs are met.

## Think Big; Start Small

Attending cooperative learning workshops with David and Roger Johnson helped us realize how important it is to think *big*, and yet, start small. We said, at the beginning of this book, that we hoped that you were ready to jump in and create the conditions within your school that will inspire and motivate your teachers to perform at optimal levels. But even if you are ready to jump off the highest diving board, make sure you take time to get to know all of your staff members, analyze your current situation, and understand your unique context. You must make sure that the activities and ideas that you use to create the essential conditions meet the needs of individuals within your school community—before you dive head first. It is much easier to dive into the calm waters of Diamond Lake than it is to navigate the white-water rapids through the Snake River Canyon.

## Build Momentum

It is always difficult to get started, but once the ball starts rolling, and people begin to see the fruits of their labor and begin achieving their goals, school leaders can seize the moment and build the momentum by sharing and making the results visible for all to see.

Most educators did not enter the profession for the money. As we explained in the results chapter, there is the something else—that little light bulb, that "ah-ha" moment—that turns on, often when you least expect it. This desire to turn on the light for someone has kept more than one teacher up at night trying to find a way to break through and help the lonely, isolated, disconnected, or struggling student find his or her way through the maze.

Collins (2001) describes the flywheel as the vehicle that helps good organizations become great. Most of us want to be able to find the recipe, the panacea, the trim-tab, the tipping point, or that one thing that will make the difference. But as Collins writes:

> There was no single defining action, no grand program, no one killer innovation, no solitary lucky break, no miracle moment. Rather, the process resembled relentlessly pushing a giant heavy flywheel in one direction, turn upon turn, building momentum until a point of breakthrough, and beyond. (p. 14)

Moving your school community from good to great takes a lot of axle grease, true grit, and hard work—but it can be done! There is no easy solution. We wish there were. But the good news is that once you get to know your staff, really know them, and you find those "little things that mean a lot," that make a difference, you will find that they are more willing to move with you than against you. But it takes time, it takes focus, and it means staying the course.

## Build Capacity

The more you know, the less you know. The more you read, the more there is to read. It is like sitting in a meadow on a warm summer day, doing nothing more than watching the grass sway in the breeze and the bees collecting pollen as they buzz from flower to flower. But sitting still long enough, and watching hard enough, the sultry meadow eventually reveals all kinds of intricate organisms, one dependent on the next, interdependently connected to the ecosystem.

School communities are ecosystems, with some being more resilient and capable of adapting to changing conditions than others. For collegial learning communities to continue to grow and flourish, there must be time for reflection that allows individuals and the entire group to take deep breaths, collect their thoughts, reenergize themselves, and build the resilience that comes from renewal and strength of purpose. Collegial learning communities must also afford themselves the opportunity for all individuals to share and learn from each other as well as from outside experts. These learning opportunities must be just-in-time, job-embedded, within the structure of every school day! Until this happens, for every teacher (and school administrator), every day, little will change within our schools! Nor will we achieve the breakthrough that will close the achievement gap.

We hope that we have demonstrated in this book that, from our balcony (Linsky & Heifetz, 2002), all ten motivational strategies are essential for improving the quality of life within each school and for developing the capacity for collegial learning communities to work interdependently and perform at optimal levels to achieve their goals. Like the organisms in the meadow, all staff members must develop their own unique interests and talents, as well as work collectively to build the capacity and strength of the school. This is the only way that a school community will be able to gain the knowledge, skills, and experiences that will help the group accomplish their shared mission and successfully achieve their collective goals.

When the work is mundane, people get bored and lose interest. When the work is too difficult, people give up. There must be a differentiated structure within the school community that supports initial learning and growth, as well as takes the knowledge and skills that exist and builds the complexity that allows the group to move to higher levels of achievement, behaviors, and skilled performance.

Staff developers spent decades inservicing teachers and workshopping them to death. We have reached a plateau in education in which we need to stop, catch our breath, and let what we know catch up with what we do. The world needs to wake up to the fact that education is a profession. It is time to amplify the work of the positive deviants and allow teachers to learn from each other, just-in-time, rather than from outside forces deciding what teachers need to know—for their own good.

## Knowledge Creation

Educators are the knowledge-creators of the future. It is time to treat educators as professionals by empowering them to make the professional decisions to ensure that all students, in all classrooms, achieve high standards. School leaders must get *the right people,* doing *the right work,* with *the right stuff.* Then, as the results are actualized, through processes like the continuous improvement cycle and the knowledge-wisdom-action helix, school leaders must find ways to appreciate and celebrate those things that teachers and schools are doing right and build upon those strengths rather than tear schools apart, brick by brick, and watch educators wither and die from fear of failure.

Most important, we, as educators, must begin to advocate for ourselves by communicating our stories and tooting our horns, because if we don't, nobody else will. If you have a story, it is time to share it. As Covey (2004) would say, "Find your voice and inspire others to find theirs" (p. 4).

## Go the Distance

All too often, educators get excited about a new idea, program, or innovation. They get caught up in doing so much so fast that all of a sudden they discover they have burned out and have nothing left to give. We all need to learn to pace ourselves. There is not sufficient time to do all we need to do. What I (Rosie) have told my staff on numerous occasions is that "You can only do what you can do." Therefore, you have to prioritize your goals and do those things that have the biggest impact and make the biggest difference first.

In order to go the distance and close the achievement gap, we all must realize that the educational race we are running is a marathon, not a sprint. If we are going to win this race, and finish our educational careers proud of our accomplishments, we must pace ourselves as marathon runners, not sprinters.

You and your staff won't win the race by living only for today and giving it everything you've got. You will all burn out after a short distance, never seeing your journey to an end. Like a marathon runner, you must stay focused on the goals, monitor your progress, find ways to replenish your energy levels when you find yourself slowing down, and use the draft of others to pull you ahead. Always remember, change is a journey, not a single event!

## Hope

Working in the trenches every day, it is easy to get discouraged and lose hope. So many social and emotional factors chip away at the mortar and bricks of the schoolhouse that it is easy to get buried in the rubble.

If we are to be successful, school leaders must create the conditions that allow people to be hopeful and optimistic. Educators must have the mental models that allow them to believe that they, and their students, are achieving success. They need to have the confidence in their abilities that together they can and will accomplish their mission and achieve their shared goals. They need to know that the work they are doing does make a difference in the lives of the students they teach. School leaders must create the conditions that shift the paradigm plaguing our schools today from fear of failure to hope for the future. We must find ways to help teachers regain their voice, their passion, and their joy for teaching and learning.

It is hard to do the work educators are being asked to do in schools each day. Our intent is to provide you with ideas to create the conditions in your school to build a better quality of life and inspire those around you to make a difference.

This important work begins by changing yourself first. We hope that you will be able to take time for yourself to rejuvenate, reenergize, and build resilience for yourself and those you lead. Even though the work you do is hard, that's okay, because it's so worth it! We, as administrators and school leaders, must never lose hope. Each day we must strive to help all those we work with continue to be hopeful as well.

As the school leader, it is up to you to help those you work with find their way and make a difference. Consider this your *call to action*! We challenge you to motivate, inspire, lead, and thus transform your school into a collegial learning community that accomplishes your shared, morally compelling mission and achieves optimal levels of performance.

May all your hopes and dreams come true!

—Best Wishes, and Keep Smiling ☺

# Epilogue

*It was difficult to listen to that lunchtime conversation I had with Allison and several teachers as they discussed their frustrations about the current state of the teaching profession. As we completed this book, I thought back to the teacher I saw in Allison, that day several years ago, and then, at the teacher I see today.*

*A number of things have changed for Allison. First of all, the stress of passing her BEST Portfolio, a substantial requirement for licensure of all new teachers in the state of Connecticut, was behind her. She passed with flying colors! This past summer, she was married to the guy she had been dating for several years. Her personal life appears to be more stable, and she has adjusted to life in our community. Most of all, I am happy to report that Allison has completed her fourth year of teaching and received tenure from the Board of Education, a rite of passage (and huge hurdle) looked forward to by all new teachers.*

*The other day, I asked Allison if she remembered that conversation we had at lunch several years ago, when she said that she wouldn't survive five years as a teacher. She looked surprised. I am sure she was hoping I wouldn't have remembered, but she smiled and sheepishly replied, "Yes."*

*I asked her what had changed, if anything.*

*She thought for a moment, and then, almost animated, responded with, "A lot! I love the kids, the people I work with, especially my grade-level team. Together, we have been able to create some exciting lessons for our students. I love being able to see my students score even higher than I would have predicted on our common assessments—and even those dreadful statewide assessments. I think I am finally getting used to all of the changes."*

*Allison paused for a moment and then continued, "I guess I know how to pace myself better. And, I have learned, as you have often said, that you can only do what you can do. There are some things I just don't have time to do. I hate it, but I guess I have just gotten used to it."*

*Again, she paused, taking a deep breath, and then added, "You know, there are so many things that have changed. But I have to tell you, I love working at this school. Some days I don't know where the time goes. It just flies! I feel as if we are a family. You have helped us to find time to meet on a regular basis to plan and reflect upon the lessons we teach as a grade-level team. You have empowered us to take what we know and use it to help our students learn. Even though you challenge us to make sure we know that all of our students are making the grade, and that we are doing everything we said we would be doing in our action plan, we still know that when we need something, whether it's more textbooks or time to meet with our grade-level teams, or . . . even just your ear—we know you are there, and we can count on you to help us. Like yesterday, when I was having a difficult time with Jasmine's mother."*

*"All I did was listen," I said, jumping in.*

*"But that meant so much to me. You help all of us in so many ways." She paused again, just for moment, before she finished, "You know, the one thing I love more than anything else about our school is how, no matter what, I know that I can go to anyone on the staff, and I can count on them*

*(Continued)*

(Continued)

*to help me. I know that no matter what, we are all working together. And what keeps me coming back is that I know that each day, I am making a difference. I love it when the light bulb goes on, and I hear one of my students say, 'I've got it!' Then I know I am really making a difference."*

*I asked Allison if she was glad she was a teacher. She didn't hesitate for a second. I immediately saw the twinkle in her eye as the lines of her lips formed a huge, gigantic smile. "I can't think of anything I would rather be doing!"*

*"Me, either," I replied.*

*We hugged, and I smiled, too.*

# Appendix A

## *Satisfying Basic Needs*

**Satisfying Basic Needs**

| Model | Stages, Factors, or Principles | Needs | Additional Educator Needs | Optimal Performance Strategy |
|---|---|---|---|---|
| Maslow's (1998) Hierarchy of Needs | Physiological needs. | Basic survival (e.g., food, shelter, clothing, money, water, and air). | Physical school environment (e.g., heating, light, furniture, solid roof) and resources (e.g., teaching supplies, curriculum materials, sufficient time to do work). | Quality of Life |
| | Security needs. | Safety and security in one's environment. | Safety and security in school environment (e.g., absence of weapons, violence, bullying). Job security, job stability, personal and professional identity, and trust in others in school environment. | Quality of Life |
| | Social needs. | Connection to others. Feeling recognized, supported, and appreciated. Friendships, feeling loved and a sense of belonging. | Sense of responsibility to others understanding that the work one is doing makes a difference. Collaboration with others. | Relationships<br><br>Interdependence<br><br>Mission<br><br>Communication |

*(Continued)*

(Continued)

| Model | Stages, Factors, or Principles | Needs | Additional Educator Needs | Optimal Performance Strategy |
|---|---|---|---|---|
| Maslow's (1998) Hierarchy of Needs | Esteem needs. | Personal and professional identity, satisfaction, and sense of accomplishment, which results from competence or mastery of a task. Attention and recognition that comes from others as well as self-respect for one's own achievement. | The "ah-ha" moments when an educator sees students learning. Realization that one can and does make a difference. Treatment, recognition, and appreciation as a professional. | Results Empowerment Autonomy Competence & Capacity Mission Communication Accountability |
| | Self-Actualization needs. | Work done for one's own self-fulfillment and self-achievement. The work is its own reward. | A love for learning everything that helps an educator accomplish his or her personal goals and help others. Skill level and challenge at optimal levels, meaningful work, and accomplishments that are one's own rewards. A sense of synergy that comes from collaborative efforts. | Competence & Capacity Mission Interdependence Autonomy Empowerment Results |

## Satisfying Basic Needs

| Model | Stages, Factors, or Principles | Needs | Additional Educator Needs | Optimal Performance Strategy |
|---|---|---|---|---|
| Herzberg's Motivation Theory (as cited in Heller, 1998, p. 10–11) | Hygiene. | Needs of workers that must be met if the workers are to be satisfied (i.e., salary and benefits, working conditions, company policy, status, job security, supervision and autonomy, interpersonal relationships, personal life outside of work). Note: Meeting these needs will not motivate workers. But when people perceive that these needs are not being met (low pay, not enough resources, job insecurity), morale will decline, people become dissatisfied, and disinterested in their work. | Same. | Quality of Life Autonomy Relationships |

| Model | Stages, Factors, or Principles | Needs | Additional Educator Needs | Optimal Performance Strategy |
|---|---|---|---|---|
| Herzberg's Motivation Theory (as cited in Heller, 1998, p. 10–11) | Set of motivators. | Achievement, recognition, job interest, responsibility, and advancement. | Same. | Empowerment Autonomy Accountability Results Communication |

## Satisfying Basic Needs

| Model | Stages, Factors, or Principles | Needs | Additional Educator Needs | Optimal Performance Strategy |
|---|---|---|---|---|
| 3 Inherent Psychological Needs from NWREL Report (Jarrett-Weeks, 2001; Deci, 1995, p. 9) | Autonomy. | An inherent sense of agency over one's own actions. Feeling in control of one's own behaviors and included in part of the decision-making process and given opportunities to make choices. | Same. | Autonomy Empowerment Communication |
| | Competence. | Feeling good at what one perceives to be important and at those things one wishes to accomplish. An ability to have the knowledge and skills that allow one to successfully complete the task. | Same. | Competence & Capacity Mission |
| | Relatedness. | Development of meaningful connections with others. Feeling that one is liked, wanted, and belongs. | Connecting and feeling like a part of the school community. | Relationships Interdependence |

**Satisfying Basic Needs**

| Model | Stages, Factors, or Principles | Needs | Additional Educator Needs | Optimal Performance Strategy |
|---|---|---|---|---|
| Glasser's (1998) Choice Theory | Survival. | Basic needs (e.g., water, clothing, money, and air). Essential elements that one needs to be able to survive. | Essential elements that a teacher needs to do his or her job (e.g., time, curriculum materials and supplies, a safe and secure school environment). | Quality of Life |
| | Love. | Being accepted by others, feeling a part of the group, and feeling like one belongs. | Same. | Relationships Interdependence |
| | Power. | Having a voice, being heard and understood, and being a part of the decision-making process when decisions directly impact the person. | Same. | Communication Autonomy Empowerment |
| | Freedom. | Making choices and decisions. | Recognition and appreciation for an educator's professional knowledge and skills. Choices in teaching and learning (e.g., menu of options, use of instructional strategies, models of teaching, supplemental materials). | Competence & Capacity Empowerment Autonomy |
| | Fun. | Enjoying what one is doing, and finding meaning and purpose in the work one does. | Same. | Quality of Life Mission Results Relationships Empowerment Competence & Capacity |

**Satisfying Basic Needs**

| Model | Stages, Factors, or Principles | Needs | Additional Educator Needs | Optimal Performance Strategy |
|---|---|---|---|---|
| Sagor's (2003) Basic Needs | Competence. | Being good at something. The more one perceives his or her work to be of value and importance to others, the more satisfied one is with one's accomplishments. | Understanding that what one is doing makes a difference. An educator needs to know that he or she is helping students achieve. | Competence & Capacity<br><br>Mission<br><br>Accountability<br><br>Results |
| | Belonging. | Feeling comfortable in one's environment and feeling accepted by the group. Feel like one belongs. | Same. | Relationships<br><br>Interdependence |
| | Usefulness. | Feeling that one is wanted and needed by others. Self-esteem increases when the work one does is valuable and helps others. | Same. | Mission<br><br>Relationships<br><br>Accountability<br><br>Results |
| | Potency. | Feeling that one has a voice and is able to influence and control one's ultimate success. | Feeling that what one is doing is useful and purposeful. An educator needs to feel in control and able to influence how he or she teaches and helps students learn. | Empowerment<br><br>Autonomy<br><br>Mission<br><br>Communication |
| | Optimism. | Feeling hopeful and seeing a bright future. | Connection to the other four factors (i.e., how competent one is, how well one fits into the school community, how well one helps students learn, and how much power and control one has on decisions that impact teaching and learning). | Connected to All Motivational Strategies |

**Satisfying Basic Needs**

| Model | Principles | Needs | Additional Educator Needs | Optimal Performance Strategy |
|---|---|---|---|---|
| Fish! Philosophy (Lundin, Christensen, & Paul, 2000) | "Be Present." | Having others pay attention to oneself and one's need to pay attention to small details. | Same. | Communication Relationships |
| | "Choose your attitude." | Make it a good day and staying optimistic and positive. | Same. | Quality of Life |
| | "Make their day." | Doing nice things and helping others. | Same. | Relationships |
| | "Have fun." | Finding enjoyment from the work one does by turning work into "play." | Same. | Quality of Life |

**Satisfying Basic Needs**

| Covey's Whole Person Model | 4 Needs | 4 Intelligences Capacities | Additional Educator Needs | Optimal Performance Strategy |
|---|---|---|---|---|
| Body | To live—survival. | Physical intelligence (PQ). | Basic needs, (e.g., food, water, clothing, money, and air). The essential elements that one needs to be able to survive. The essential elements that a teacher needs to do his or her job (e.g., time, curriculum materials and supplies, a safe and secure school environment). | Quality of Life |
| Mind | To love—relationships. | Mental intelligence (IQ). | Being accepted by others, feeling a part of the group, and feeling like one belongs. | Relationships Interdependence |
| Heart | To learn—growth and development. | Emotional intelligence (EQ). | Seeing that what one is doing makes a difference. Knowing that one is helping students achieve. | Competence & Capacity |
| Spirit | To leave a legacy—meaning and contribution. | Spiritual intelligence (SQ). | Feeling that what one is doing is useful and purposeful. Feeling as if one has control and is able to influence one's own teaching and help students learn. | Mission Results |

SOURCE: Adapted from Covey's "4 Universal Dimensions of Life Model" (Covey, 2004, p. 22).

# Appendix B

## *Further Reading*

## ■ INTRODUCTION

Fullan, M. (2005). *Leadership sustainability: System thinkers in action.* Thousand Oaks, CA: Corwin.

Lashway, L. (2001). *The new standards and accountability: Will rewards and sanctions motivate America's schools to peak performance?* Eugene, OR: ERIC Clearinghouse on Educational Management.

Pfeffer, J., & Sutton, R. I. (2000). *The knowing-doing gap: How smart companies turn knowledge into action.* Boston: Harvard Business School Press.

## ■ CHAPTER 1: UNDERSTANDING MOTIVATION

Csikszentmihalyi, M. (2003). *Good business: Leadership, flow, and the making of meaning.* New York: Viking.

Deci, E. L. (1995). *Why we do what we do: Understanding self-motivation.* New York: Penguin Books.

## ■ CHAPTER 2: LEADERSHIP WITHIN

Glasser, W. (1998a). *Choice theory: A new psychology of personal freedom.* New York: HarperCollins.

Loehr, J., & Schwartz, T. (2003). *The power of full engagement: Managing energy, not time, is the key to high performance and personal renewal.* New York: Free Press.

Milstein, M. M., & Henry, D. A. (2000). *Spreading resiliency: Making it happen for schools and communities.* Thousand Oaks, CA: Corwin.

## ■ CHAPTER 3: QUALITY OF LIFE

Fullan, M. (2005). *Leadership sustainability: System thinkers in action.* Thousand Oaks, CA: Corwin.

Gladwell, M. (2000). *The tipping point: How little things can make a big difference.* New York: Little, Brown, and Company.

Loehr, J., & Schwartz, T. (2003). *The power of full engagement: Managing energy, not time, is the key to high performance and personal renewal.* New York: Free Press.

# ■ CHAPTER 4: MISSION

Fullan, M. (2003b). *The moral imperative of school leadership*. Thousand Oaks, CA: Corwin.

Schmuck, R., & Runkel, P. J. (1994). *The handbook of organization development in schools and colleges*. Prospect Heights, IL: Waveland Press.

Secretan, L. (2004). *Inspire! What great leaders do*. Hoboken, NJ: Wiley & Sons.


# ■ CHAPTER 5: COMMUNICATION

Baldoni, J. (2003). *Great communication secrets of great leaders*. New York: McGraw-Hill.

Koppett, K. (2001). *Training to imagine: Practical improvisational theatre techniques to enhance creativity, teamwork, leadership, and learning*. Sterling, VA: Stylus Publishing.

Perkins, D. (2003). *King Arthur's roundtable: How collaborative conversations create smart organizations*. New York: Wiley & Sons.

Schmuck, R., & Runkel, P. J. (1994). *The handbook of organization development in schools and colleges*. Prospect Heights, IL: Waveland Press.

Sparks, D. (2005). *Leading for results: Transforming teaching, learning, and relationships in schools*. Thousand Oaks, CA: Corwin, National Staff Development Council, and National Association of Secondary School Principals.


# ■ CHAPTER 6: RELATIONSHIPS

Glacel, B. P., & Roberts, E. A., Jr. (1996). *Light bulbs for leaders: A guide book for team learning*. New York: Wiley & Sons.

Goleman, D. (1998). *Working with emotional intelligence*. New York: Bantam Books.

Robbins, H., & Finley, M. (1995). *Why teams don't work: What went wrong and how to make it right*. Princeton, NJ: Peterson's/Pacesetter Books.


# ■ CHAPTER 7: ACCOUNTABILITY

DuFour, R., Eaker, R. E., & DuFour, R. (Eds.). (2005). *On common ground: The power of professional learning communities*. Bloomington, IN: National Education Service.

Marzano, R. J., Waters, T., & McNulty, B. A. (2005). *School leadership that works: From research to results*. Alexandria, VA: Association for Supervision and Curriculum Development.

Reeves, D. B. (2000). *Accountability in action: A blueprint for learning organizations*. Denver, CO: Center for Performance Assessment.

Reeves, D. B. (2002). *Holistic accountability: Serving students, schools, and community*. Thousand Oaks, CA: Corwin.

Schmoker, M. (2001). *The results fieldbook: Practical strategies from dramatically improved schools*. Alexandria, VA: Association for Supervision and Curriculum Development.

Schmoker, M. (2006). *Results NOW: How we can achieve unprecedented improvements in teaching and learning*. Alexandria, VA: Association for Supervision and Curriculum Development.

Stiggins, R. (2004). *Assessment for learning:* New York: Prentice Hall.

# ■ CHAPTER 8: COMPETENCE AND CAPACITY

Hall, G., & Hord, S. M. (2001). *Implementing change: Patterns, principles, and potholes.* Boston: Allyn and Bacon.

Hord, S. M., & Sommers, W. (2008). *Leading professional learning communities: Voices from research and practice.* Thousand Oaks, CA: Corwin.

Knowles, M. S., Holton, E. F. III, & Swanson, R. A. (1998). *The adult learner: The definitive classic in adult education and human resource development.* Woburn, MA: Buttersworth-Heinemann.

National Staff Development Council (NSDC). (2001a). *The National Staff Development Council standards for staff development (Revised ed.).* Oxford, OH: The National Staff Development Council.

Schlechty, P. (1993). On the frontier of school reform with trailblazers, pioneers, and settlers. *Journal of Staff Development, 14*(4), 46–50.

# ■ CHAPTER 9: AUTONOMY

Ahmed, P. K., Kok, L. K., & Loh, A. Y. E. (2002). *Learning through knowledge management.* Boston: Butterworth-Heinemann.

Deci, E. L. (1995). *Why we do what we do: Understanding self-motivation.* New York: Penguin Books.

Sparks, D. (2005). *Leading for results: Transforming teaching, learning, and relationships in schools.* Thousand Oaks, CA: Corwin, National Staff Development Council, and National Association of Secondary School Principals.

# ■ CHAPTER 10: EMPOWERMENT

Blanchard, K., Carlos, J. P., & Randolph, A. (2001a). *Empowerment takes more than a minute.* San Francisco: Berrett-Koehler Publishers.

Blanchard, K., Carlos, J. P., & Randolph, A. (2001b). *The three keys to empowerment.* San Francisco: Berrett-Koehler Publishers.

Csikszentmihalyi, M. (2003). *Good business: Leadership, flow, and the making of meaning.* New York: Viking.

Covey, S. R. (2004). *The 8th habit: From effectiveness to greatness.* New York: Free Press.

Lombardi, V. J. (2001). *What it takes to be #1.* New York: McGraw-Hill.

Seifter, H., & Economy, P. (2001). *Leadership ensemble: Lessons in collaborative management from the world's only conductorless orchestra.* New York: Henry Holt.

# ■ CHAPTER 11: POSITIVE INTERDEPENDENCE

Johnson, D. W., & Johnson, R. T. (1989). *Cooperation and competition: Theory and research.* Edina, MN: Interaction Book Company.

*The Journal of Staff Development.* (JSD). (Summer 2008). *29*(3). [Note: The entire issue is full of information about Professional Learning Communities]

Kagan, S., & Kagan, M. (2009). *Kagan cooperative learning.* San Juan Capistrano, CA: Kagan Publishing.

Schmuck, R., & Runkel, P. J. (1994). *The handbook of organization development in schools and colleges.* Prospect Heights, IL: Waveland Press.

Surowiecki, J. (2004). *The wisdom of crowds: Why the many are smarter than the few and how collective wisdom shapes business, economies, societies, and nations.* New York: Doubleday.

## ■ CHAPTER 12: RESULTS

Fullan, M., Hill, P., & Crévola, C. (2006). *Breakthrough.* Thousand Oaks, CA: Corwin.

Hammond, S. A. (1998). *The thin book of appreciative inquiry.* Plano, TX: The Thin Book Publishing Company.

Kanter, R. M. (2004). *Confidence: How winning streaks & losing streaks begin & end.* New York: Crown Business.

Sparks, D. (2005a). *Leading for results: Transforming teaching, learning, and relationships in schools.* Thousand Oaks, CA: Corwin, National Staff Development Council, and National Association of Secondary School Principals.

Whitney, D., & Trosten-Bloom, A. (2003). *The power of appreciative inquiry: A practical guide to positive change.* San Francisco: Berrett-Koehler Publishers.

# References

Ahmed, P. K., Kok, L. K., & Loh, A. Y. E. (2002). *Learning through knowledge management*. Boston: Butterworth-Heinemann.

American Heritage Dictionary of the English Language (4th ed., p. 19, Adaptation). (2006). Boston: Houghton Mifflin.

_____. (4th ed., p. 362, Collegiality). (2006). Boston: Houghton Mifflin.

_____. (4th ed., p. 1161, Mutual). (2006). Boston: Houghton Mifflin.

_____. (4th ed., p. 1739, Support). (2006). Boston: Houghton Mifflin.

Baldoni, J. (2003). *Great communication secrets of great leaders*. New York: McGraw-Hill.

Bell, J. (Producer). (2007, February 20). *The today show*. [Television broadcast]. New York: National Broadcast Company.

Bennis, W. (2003). *On becoming a leader: The leadership classic*. New York: Basic Books.

Bennis, W., & Goldsmith, J. (2003). *Learning to lead: A workbook on becoming a leader*. New York: Basic Books.

Blanchard, K., Bowles, S., Carew, D., & Parisi-Carew, E. (2001). *High five! None of us is as smart as all of us*. New York: HarperCollins.

Blanchard, K., Carlos, J. P., & Randolph, A. (2001a). *Empowerment takes more than a minute*. San Francisco: Berrett-Koehler Publishers.

Blanchard, K., Carlos, J. P., & Randolph, A. (2001b). *The 3 keys to empowerment*. San Francisco: Berrett-Koehler Publishers.

Brill, P. (2004). *The winner's way: A proven method for achieving your personal best in any situation*. New York: McGraw-Hill.

Childre, D., & Cryer, B. (1999). *From chaos to coherence: Advancing emotional and organizational intelligence through inner quality management*. Boston: Butterworth-Heinemann.

Collins, J. (2001). *Good to great: Why some companies make the leap . . . and others don't*. New York: HarperCollins.

Connors, R., Smith, T., & Hickman, C. (2004). *The OZ principle: Getting results through individual and organizational accountability*. New York: Penguin.

Conzemius, A., & O'Neill, J. (2006). *The power of SMART goals: Using goals to improve student learning*. Bloomington, IN: Solution Tree.

Costa, A. L., & Garmston, R. (1994). *Cognitive coaching: A foundation for renaissance schools*. Norwood, MA: Christopher-Gordon Publishers.

Covey, S. R. (2004). *The 8th habit: From effectiveness to greatness*. New York: Free Press.

Covey, S. R., Merrill, R. A., & Merrill, R. R. (1996). *First things first: To live, to love, to learn, to leave a legacy*. New York: Free Press.

Crow, T. (2008). Declaration of interdependence. *Journal of Staff Development. 29*(3), 53–56.

Csikszentmihalyi, M. (1997). *Finding flow: The psychology of engagement with everyday life*. New York: Basic Books.

Csikszentmihalyi, M. (2003). *Good business: Leadership, flow, and the making of meaning*. New York: Viking.

Davenport, T. H., & Prusak, L. (2000). *Working knowledge: How organizations manage what they know*. Boston: Harvard Business School Press.

Deci, E. L. (1995). *Why we do what we do: Understanding self-motivation.* New York: Penguin Books.

Dorsch, N. G. (1998). *Community, collaboration and collegiality in school reform: An odyssey toward connection.* New York: State University of New York Press.

Dreher, D., & Tzu, L. (1996). *The tao of personal leadership.* New York: HarperCollins.

DuFour, R. (2005). *What is a professional learning community?* Bloomington, IN: National Education Service.

DuFour, R., & Eaker, R. E. (1998). *Professional learning communities at work: Best practices for enhancing student achievement.* Bloomington, IN: National Education Service.

DuFour, R., Eaker, R. E., & DuFour, R. (Eds.). (2005). *On common ground: The power of professional learning communities.* Bloomington, IN: National Education Service.

Evans, R. (1996). *The human side of school change.* San Francisco: Jossey-Bass.

Farson, R., & Keyes, R. (2002). *Whoever makes the most mistakes wins.* New York: Free Press.

Fullan, M. (1993). *Change forces: Probing the depths of educational reform.* New York: Falmer Press.

Fullan, M. (2001). *Leading in a culture of change.* San Francisco: Jossey-Bass.

Fullan, M. (2003a). *Change forces: With a vengeance.* London: Falmer Press.

Fullan, M. (2003b). *The moral imperative of school leadership.* Thousand Oaks, CA: Corwin.

Fullan, M. (2004). *Leading in a culture of change: Personal action guide and workbook.* San Francisco: Jossey-Bass.

Fullan, M. (2005). *Leadership sustainability: System thinkers in action.* Thousand Oaks, CA: Corwin.

Fullan, M. (2008). *The six secrets of change: What the best leaders do to help their organizations survive and thrive.* San Francisco: Jossey-Bass.

Fullan, M., Hill, P., & Crévola, C. (2006). *Breakthrough.* Thousand Oaks, CA: Corwin.

Gardner, H. (2000). *Intelligence reframed: Multiple intelligences for the 21st century.* New York: Basic Books.

Gardner, H., Csikszentmihalyi, M., & Damon, W. (2001). *Good work: When excellence and ethics meet.* New York: Basic Books.

Gibbs, J. (2001). *Tribes: A new way of learning and being together.* Windsor, CA: Centersource Systems.

Glacel, B. P., & Roberts, E. A., Jr. (1996). *Light bulbs for leaders: A guide book for team learning.* New York: Wiley & Sons.

Gladwell, M. (2000). *The tipping point: How little things can make a big difference.* New York: Little, Brown, and Company.

Glasser, W. (1998a). *Choice theory: A new psychology of personal freedom.* New York: HarperCollins.

Glasser, W. (1998b). *The quality school: Managing students without coercion.* New York: HarperPerennial.

Goleman, D. (1998). *Working with emotional intelligence.* New York: Bantam Books.

Guskey, T. (1999). *Evaluating professional development.* Thousand Oaks, CA: Corwin.

Hall, G., & Hord, S. M. (2001). *Implementing change: Patterns, principles, and potholes.* Boston: Allyn and Bacon.

Hammond, S. A. (1998). *The thin book of appreciative inquiry.* Plano, TX: The Thin Book Publishing Company.

Hargreaves, A. (Ed.). (1993). Individualism and individuality: Reinterpreting the teacher culture. In J. W. Little & M. W. McLaughlin. (Eds.), *Teachers' work.* New York: Teachers College Press.

Hargreaves, A., Earl, L. M., & Ryan, J. (1996). *Schooling for change: Reinventing education for early adolescents.* Bristol, PA: Falmer Press.

Hargreaves, A., & Fink, D. (2006). *Sustaining leadership.* San Francisco: Jossey-Bass.

Heller, R. (1998). *Motivating people.* New York: DK Publishing.

Honore, C. (2004). *In praise of slowness.* New York: HarperCollins.

Hord, S. M. (1997). *Professional learning communities: Communities of continuous inquiry and improvement.* Austin, TX: Southwest Educational Development Lab.

Hord, S. M., & Sommers, W. (2008). *Leading professional learning communities: Voices from research and practice.* Thousand Oaks, CA: Corwin.

Hudson, D. A. (Producer). (January 30, 2004). *The Oprah Winfrey show* [Television broadcast]. Chicago: Harpo.

Hunter, M. (1967). *Motivation theory for teachers.* Thousand Oaks, CA: Corwin.

Hunter, M. (1982). *Mastery teaching: Increasing instructional effectiveness in elementary, secondary schools, colleges and universities.* Thousand Oaks, CA: Corwin.

Jarrett-Weeks, D., (Ed.). (2001). Understanding motivation & supporting teacher renewal. *Quality Teaching and Learning, 40.*

JetBlue Airways. (2007a, February 20). *JetBlue's Customer Bill of Rights.* Retrieved August 15, 2008, http://www.jetblue.com/about/ourcompany/promise/index.html

JetBlue Airways. (2007b, February). Winter Storm February 2007. *JetBlue Press Room.* Retrieved February 15—24, 2008, from http://investor.jetblue.com/phoenix.zhtml?c=131045&p=irol-news&nyo=1

Johnson, D. W., & Johnson, R. T. (1987a). *Joining together: Group theory and group skills.* Englewood Cliffs, NJ: Prentice-Hall.

Johnson, D. W., & Johnson, R. T. (1987b). *Learning together & alone: Cooperative, competitive, & individualistic learning.* Englewood Cliffs, NJ: Prentice-Hall.

Johnson, D. W., & Johnson, R. T. (1989). *Cooperation and competition: Theory and research.* Edina, MN: Interaction Book Company.

Johnson, D. W., Johnson, R. T., & Holubec, E. J. (1994). *Cooperative learning in the classroom.* Alexandria, VA: Association for Supervision and Curriculum Development.

Kagan, S., & Kagan, M. (2009). *Kagan cooperative learning.* San Juan Capistrano, CA: Kagan Publishing.

Kahane, A. (2004). *Solving tough problems: An open way of talking, listening, and creating new realities.* San Francisco: Berrett-Koehler Publishers.

Kanter, R. M. (2004). *Confidence: How winning streaks & losing streaks begin & end.* New York: Crown Business.

Klatt, B., Murphy, S., & Irvine, D. (2003). *Accountability: Getting a grip on results.* Toronto, Canada: Stoddart Publishing Co.

Knowles, M. S., Holton, E. F. III, & Swanson, R. A. (1998). *The adult learner: The definitive classic in adult education and human resource development.* Woburn, MA: Buttersworth-Heinemann.

Kohn, A. (1993). *Punished by rewards: The trouble with gold stars, incentive plans, A's, praise, and other bribes.* New York: Houghton Mifflin.

Koppett, K. (2001). *Training to imagine: Practical improvisational theatre techniques to enhance creativity, teamwork, leadership, and learning.* Sterling, VA: Stylus Publishing.

Lashway, L. (2001). *The new standards and accountability: Will rewards and sanctions motivate America's schools to peak performance?* Eugene, OR: ERIC Clearinghouse on Educational Management.

Leyden-Rubenstein, L. A. (1998). *The stress management book: Strategies for health and inner peace.* New Canaan, CT: Keats Publishing.

Linsky, M., & Heifetz, R. A. (2002). *Leadership on the line: Staying alive through the dangers of leading.* Boston: Harvard Business School Press.

Little, J. W. (1990). Teachers as colleagues. In A. Lieberman (Ed.), *Schools as collaborative cultures: Creating the future now* (pp. 165-167). Bristol, PA: Falmer Press.

Loehr, J., & Schwartz, T. (2003). *The power of full engagement: Managing energy, not time, is the key to high performance and personal renewal.* New York: Free Press.

Logan, D., King, J., & Fischer-Wright, H. (2008). *Tribal leadership: Leveraging natural groups to build a thriving organization.* New York: HarperCollins.

Lombardi, V. J. (2001). *What it takes to be #1.* New York: McGraw-Hill.

Louisiana Lightning: LSU shocks Duke to reach Elite Eight. (2006, March 23). *ESPNU Basketball.* Retrieved August 16, 2008, from http://sports.espn.go.com/ncb/recap?gameId=264000053.

Lundin, S., Christensen, J., & Paul, H. (2000). *Fish! A remarkable way to boost morale and improve results.* New York: Hyperion.

Marzano, R. J. (2003). *What works in schools: Translating research into action.* Alexandria, VA: Association for Supervision and Curriculum Development.

Marzano, R. J., Waters, T., & McNulty, B. A. (2005). *School leadership that works: From research to results.* Alexandria, VA: Association for Supervision and Curriculum Development.

Maslow, A. H. (1998). *Maslow on management.* New York: John Wiley & Sons.

Maxwell, J. C. (1998). *The 21 irrefutable laws of leadership: Follow them and people will follow you.* Nashville, TN: Thomas Nelson Publishers.

Maxwell, J. C. (2004). *Be a people person: Effective leadership through effective relationships.* Colorado Springs, CO: Nexgen.

McGehee, T. (2001). *Whoosh: Business in the fast lane.* New York: Basic Books.

McMillan, T. (1997). *How Stella got her groove back.* New York: Signet.

Mitchell, M. (1936). *Gone with the wind.* New York: Scribner.

National Staff Development Council. (NSDC). (2001). *The National Staff Development Council standards for staff development (revised).* Oxford, OH: The National Staff Development Council.

National Staff Development Council (NSDC). (2008). *NSCD standards: Learning.* Retrieved March 5, 2007, from http://www.nsdc.org/standards/learning.cfm.

Neilson, G. L., & Pasternack, B. A. (2005). *Results.* New York: Crown Business.

Newmann, F. M. (1996). *Center on Organization and Restructuring of Schools: Activities and accomplishments, 1990–1996. Final report.* Madison, WI: Center on Organization and Restructuring of Schools.

Olson, L. (October 19, 2005). Purpose of testing needs to shift, experts say. *Education Week,* 7.

Ouchi, W., & Segal, L. (2003). *Making schools work: A revolutionary plan to get your children the education they need.* New York: Simon & Schuster.

Perkins, D. (2003). *King Arthur's roundtable: How collaborative conversations create smart organizations.* New York: Wiley & Sons.

Pfeffer, J., & Sutton, R. I. (2000). *The knowing-doing gap: How smart companies turn knowledge into action.* Boston: Harvard Business School Press.

Reeves, D. B., (2000). *Accountability in action: A blueprint for learning organizations.* Denver, CO: Center for Performance Assessment.

Reeves, D. B. (2002). *Holistic accountability: Serving students, schools, and community.* Thousand Oaks, CA: Corwin.

Reivich, K., & Shatte, A. (2002). *The resilience factor: 7 essential skills for overcoming life's inevitable obstacles.* New York: Random House.

Robbins, H., & Finley, M. (1995). *Why teams don't work: What went wrong and how to make it right.* Princeton, NJ: Peterson's/Pacesetter Books.

Robbins, P., & Alvy, H. (2004). *The new principal's fieldbook: Strategies for success.* Alexandria, VA: Association for Supervision and Curriculum Development.

Sagor, R. (2003). *Motivating students and teachers in an era of standards.* Alexandria, VA: Association for Supervision and Curriculum Development.

Samuel, M. (2001). *The accountability revolution: Achieve breakthrough results in half the time.* Tempe, AZ: Facts on Demand Press.

Schlechty, P. C. (1993). On the frontier of school reform with trailblazers, pioneers, and settlers. *Journal of Staff Development, 14*(4), 46–50.

Schlechty, P. C. (2005). *Creating great schools: Six critical systems at the heart of educational innovation.* San Francisco: Jossey-Bass.

Schmoker, M. (1999). *Results: The key to continuous school improvement.* Alexandria, VA: Association for Supervision and Curriculum Development.

Schmoker, M. (2001). *The results fieldbook: Practical strategies from dramatically improved schools.* Alexandria, VA: Association for Supervision and Curriculum Development.

Schmoker, M. (2006). *Results NOW: How we can achieve unprecedented improvements in teaching and learning.* Alexandria, VA: Association for Supervision and Curriculum Development.

Schmuck, R., & Runkel, P. J. (1994). *The handbook of organization development in schools and colleges.* Prospect Heights, IL: Waveland Press.

Sears, B. (1985). *The zone: A dietary road map to lose weight permanently : Reset your genetic code: Prevent disease: Achieve maximum physical performance.* New York: HarperCollins.

Secretan, L. (2004). *Inspire! What great leaders do.* Hoboken, NJ: Wiley & Sons.

Seifter, H., & Economy, P. (2001). *Leadership ensemble: Lessons in collaborative management from the world's only conductorless orchestra.* New York: Henry Holt.

Senge, P. (1990). *The fifth discipline.* New York: Doubleday.

Senge, P., McCabe, N. H. C., Lucas, T., & Kleiner, A. (2000). *Schools that learn: A fifth discipline fieldbook for educators, parents, and everyone who cares about education.* New York: Doubleday.

Shakespeare, W. (1984). *Romeo and Juliet (The New Cambridge Shakespeare).* G. Blakemore Evans (Ed.). New York: Cambridge University Press.

Sparks, D. (2004). From hunger aid to school reform: An interview with Jerry Sternin. *Journal of Staff Development, 25*(1), 46–51.

Sparks, D. (2005a). *Leading for results: Transforming teaching, learning, and relationships in schools.* Thousand Oaks, CA: Corwin, National Staff Development Council, and National Association of Secondary School Principals.

Sparks, D. (2005b). Leading for transformation in teaching, learning, and relationships. In R. E. DuFour, R. Eaker, & R. DuFour (Eds.), *On common ground: The power of professional learning communities* (pp. 155–176). Bloomington, IN: Solution Tree.

Stiggins, R. (2004). *Assessment for learning.* New York: Prentice Hall.

Surowiecki, J. (2004). *The wisdom of crowds: Why the many are smarter than the few and how collective wisdom shapes business, economies, societies, and nations.* New York: Doubleday.

Tichy, N. M., & Cardwell, N. (2002). *The cycle of leadership: How great leaders teach their companies to win.* New York: HarperCollins.

Vojtek, R. O. (1993, June). *Integrating staff development and organization development.* A Dissertation presented to the University of Oregon Division of Teacher Education and the Graduate School. Eugene, OR.

Whitney, D., & Trosten-Bloom, A. (2003). *The power of appreciative inquiry: A practical guide to positive change.* San Francisco: Berrett-Koehler Publishers.

# Index

## CORWIN
A SAGE Company

The Corwin logo—a raven striding across an open book—represents the union of courage and learning. Corwin is committed to improving education for all learners by publishing books and other professional development resources for those serving the field of PreK–12 education. By providing practical, hands-on materials, Corwin continues to carry out the promise of its motto: **"Helping Educators Do Their Work Better."**